Civil War Suits in the
U.S. Court of Claims

Civil War Suits in the U.S. Court of Claims

Cases Involving Compensation to Northerners and Southerners for Wartime Losses

GREG H. WILLIAMS

McFarland & Company, Inc., Publishers
Jefferson, North Carolina, and London

LIBRARY OF CONGRESS CATALOGUING-IN-PUBLICATION DATA

Williams, Greg H.
Civil War suits in the U.S. Court of Claims : cases involving compensation
to northerners and southerners for wartime losses / Greg H. Williams.
p.   cm.
Includes index.

ISBN 0-7864-2430-3 (softcover : 50# alkaline paper)

1. United States—History—Civil War, 1861–1865—Claims.
2.   United States—Claims.   I. Title
KF5914.W55   2006   973.7'1—dc22   2006011866

British Library cataloguing data are available

On the cover: Trial of Captain Wirz, Andersonville jailer, in the
Court of Claims, Washington, D.C. (sketched by Jos Hanshew)

Manufactured in the United States of America

*McFarland & Company, Inc., Publishers
Box 611, Jefferson, North Carolina 28640
www.mcfarlandpub.com*

Table of Contents

Preface

This book is a comprehensive collection of all the detailed, reported claims that were brought against the United States from the War Between the States as reported in *Cases Decided in the Court of Claims of the United States* (from Volume 2, published after the 1866 term, through Volume 57, published after the 1921–1922 term). The claims were filed initially in U.S. district courts, petitioned directly to the Court of Claims in Washington, D.C., or referred to the Court of Claims for fact finding through private acts of Congress. Appeals were made to the Supreme Court.

There were many hundreds of claims presented for seized cotton and thousands of claims involving various aspects of military pay but only a fraction of these were reported in detail in *Cases Decided....* If the claim presented no question of law, it was not reported in detail and is not included in this book. All of the reports that include the complete circumstances of the incident leading to the lawsuit are presented here. Appeals to the Supreme Court are mentioned only if the lower court's decision was reversed.

Additional background information from a wide variety of sources is included when necessary to set the stage and round out the story. Military details were found in *The War of the Rebellion: A Compilation of the Official Records of the Union and Confederate Armies* and *The War of the Rebellion: A Compilation of the Official Records of the Union and Confederate Navies.*

The claims include the following subjects:

- Disputed contracts to build fortifications, construct warships, requisition merchant vessels, or furnish weapons, forage, livestock, firewood, stores, and ice.
- Personnel pay disputes involving travel, servants, disability, resignations to join the Confederacy, enlistment bonuses and bounty pay, services of secret agents, and charges of desertion.
- Commodities and property seized from Northern residents and businesses, Southerners professing loyalty, slaves or former slaves, free blacks, and foreigners.
- Compensation for the use of buildings or property, or property lost, destroyed or damaged during military engagements or operations.
- Northern states suing to recover the cost of organizing and equipping volunteers.
- Quartermaster, paymaster, or commissary of subsistence money stolen, captured, or lost.
- Discontinued postal service contracts.

The cases are presented alphabetically by claimant surname. Companies and partnerships are entered by company name if the lawsuit was brought by the company, otherwise by the name of the partner bringing the suit.

Cases involving ships and boats with one owner are under the owner's name. Cases involving vessels with two or more owners are under the vessel's name. The names of vessels are listed in strict alphabetical order, as the name would appear on the vessel itself, so the *Kathleen R. Williams* will be found in the "K" section.

In essentially duplicate cases where the material facts are the same or very similar the later plaintiffs are added to the text of the first, fully detailed case.

Statutes, acts of Congress, Presidential proclamations, government departmental directives, and military general orders often cited by the courts are reproduced or summarized in Appendix II and Appendix III.

All geographic names, titles, spellings, abbreviations, company names, and language in original documents are preserved when quoted. Some quotes contain errors, such as one witness's reference to the Nashville & Memphis Railroad as the "Memphis and Nashville." In another case a communication addressed to General Edward Hincks was spelled "Hinks." In these cases, the error is left in the text and the correct form appears in the index.

Then there is the difficult matter of Pittsburgh, Pennsylvania. The original April 22, 1794, charter for the City of Pittsburgh spells the city's name with an "h" on the end, but throughout the 1800s the names of Pittsburgh and other communities ending in "burgh" were spelled either "burg" or "burgh" as the writer wished. This inconsistency created headaches for federal cartographers in the rapidly expanding Union, so in 1890 Congress created the U.S. Board on Geographic Names to standardize all geographic and place names on federal maps. Flexing its newly acquired muscle, the board ordered all towns and cities whose names ended in "burgh" to drop the "h." This was a sensitive issue in Pennsylvania, so Pittsburghers went on the warpath, and the original spelling was officially returned in July 1911.

In the 1860s and later the custom was to capitalize the proper names of streets, rivers, parishes, and such but to use the lower case for the "street" or "river," as in "Chowan river." Other spellings of the day include "inclosed" in contrast with our present day "enclosed."

Thanks to Simon Thompson of the University of Oregon law library; Virginia Gerace Benoist of Natchez, Mississippi; Georgia Meadows of Dale City, Virginia; Naomi Horner of the Senator John Heinz Pittsburgh Regional History Center; Roger L. Payne of the U.S. Board on Geographic Names; and Keri Shellenbarger of the Historical Society of Western Pennsylvania.

Some Legal Aspects of the War

Fort Sumpter was attacked at 4:30 A.M. on Friday, April 12, 1861. General Robert E. Lee surrendered his Army of Northern Virginia on Sunday, April 9, 1865, at the courthouse in Appomattox, Virginia. General Joseph E. Johnston surrendered his forces in North Carolina on April 26. The last skirmish of the war was fought at Palmetto Ranch, Texas, on May 11–13. On May 10 President Andrew Johnson proclaimed, "Armed resistance to the authority of this government in the said insurrectionary states may be regarded as virtually at an end." General Edmund Kirby Smith, commander of Confederate forces west of the Mississippi, formally surrendered on Friday, May 26, 1865. President Johnson issued a proclamation on August 2, 1866, declaring the war over in the secessionist states except Texas, because that state had no formal government. He proclaimed the war officially over on August 20, 1866, although Texas was still under military rule and would be until 1869.

For legal purposes, the Supreme Court considered the War for Southern Independence a foreign, or international, war that began with President Lincoln's proclamation of April 15, 1861, ordering the blockading of Southern ports and ended with President Johnson's proclamation of August 20, 1866. The war was declared over in various insurrectionary districts by proclamation as the military advanced, and these dates were sometimes used to decide the merits of claims and the actions of claimants.

Congress was not in session when South Carolina started the shooting war but convened on July 4 in response to President Lincoln's proclamation of April 15. The early measures Lincoln took were controversial and considered illegal by some, as exceeding the authority of the President, such as seizing private property, ordering officers to suspend the writ of habeas corpus, establishing martial law, and using the military to jail persons simply suspected of inciting or aiding rebellion. Some of these actions brought him in sharp conflict with the Supreme Court, which itself was divided. Justice John A. Campbell was not in favor of secession but he resigned and went home to Alabama anyway.

On July 10 the first session of the 37th Congress authorized the Secretary of the Treasury to reimburse the states for any money paid in duties to import arms used to suppress the rebellion between May 1, 1861, and January 1, 1862. On July 13 payment for militias and volunteers was authorized, and the President was authorized to close ports, seize vessels and cargoes, declare citizens in insurrection against the government, and use the Navy to enforce revenue laws. Other acts allowed the collection of duties in any port or place outside the established ports of entry, and prohibited commerce between loyal and insurrectionary states. On July 17 the position of paymaster was created in the Navy and the Secretary of the Treasury was authorized to borrow $250 million and issue 20-year coupon, registered, and Treasury bonds bearing interest not to exceed 7 percent per annum in amounts apportioned as he saw fit.

All the property of those within insurrectionary districts became liable to seizure and confiscation 60 days after President Lincoln's proclamation of July 25, 1862. International law prohibited the seizing of private property belonging to noncombatants, but one early goal was to remove from the South everything belonging to disloyal citizens that could be used to aid the rebellion, either as a commodity in and of itself or as something that could be sold or traded to acquire funds, which the Confederacy always lacked. The Confiscation Act of August 6, 1861, and the blockades were direct measures to legally seize property.

International law guided foraging — what soldiers on the march could lawfully take — and governed the seizing, condemning, and selling of enemy vessels, blockade runners, and cargoes on the high seas or property seized on land by naval forces as prize of war.

Cotton and other commodities became extraordinarily valuable, testing the morals and ethics of those charged with their safekeeping. Neutrality laws were tested, particularly in the interests of British textile mills. Since the high ideals expressed in law often failed, the Act of March 12, 1863, was passed to soften the harsh effects the Confiscation Act had on loyal citizens living within insurrectionary districts, although serious and flagrant abuses still occurred. The Act created the unique legal theory of "abandoned or captured property" and set up a special fund within the Treasury — the money itself remaining vested in the owner — and allowed citizens able to prove their loyalty to recover the net proceeds. It also relieved military commanders of the considerable amount of time and effort expended in dealing with large amounts of

private property. Deputy Treasury agents were appointed to contract with plantation owners within insurrectionary states or districts so that their products could be legally bought and sold and moved safely across military lines. The owner's alternative was to continue to expose the property to the unpredictable behavior of rebel or Union soldiers and sailors or loss through military engagements or deterioration in the weather. Processed farm products — ginned cotton, molasses, sugar, turpentine, or tobacco — were invariably hidden to keep them from being stolen or destroyed by combatants or outlaws from either side. Cotton was sold by the pound, and the more a bale was moved about, the less it would weigh, losing both volume and quality to wear and tear and weather damage. A typical bale of cotton weighed about 500 pounds and was not easily or quickly moved or protected.

The Act allowed the bypassing of the cumbersome condemnation and sale process. Normally this process would take place in a U.S. district court, but some courts located in Southern districts no longer existed. The property was reduced to net proceeds and the Court of Claims in Washington, D.C., became the prize court. Owners could produce their proofs of ownership and loyalty and recover the proceeds so long as they applied within two years after the end of the war.

One major complication affected the amount recovered. If property was seized by land forces it was sold at auction and the net proceeds deposited into the abandoned and captured property fund, but property seized by naval forces came under the various prize laws and entitled the sailors to a share in the net proceeds. In either case, owners or their heirs could recover only money proven to have been deposited into the Treasury, never the goods themselves, and only the net deposit after port fees, transportation, storage, prize awards, and other charges were deducted. Naval forces seized over 600 vessels, all types of cargo, and over $1.4 million dollars was distributed to sailors from the sale of cotton alone. Other valuable cargoes seized in quantity included tobacco, wool, corn, whisky, brandy, wine, rosin, turpentine, and livestock.

In Klein v. the United States in December 1871 (13 Wall. 128) Chief Justice Salmon P. Chase divided all property within the insurrectionary districts into four classes:

(1.) That which belonged to the hostile organizations or was employed in actual hostilities on land. (2.) That which at sea became lawful subject of capture and prize. (3.) That which became subject of confiscation. (4.) A peculiar description, known only in the recent war, called captured and abandoned property.

The first of these descriptions of property, like property of other like kind in ordinary international wars, became, wherever taken, *ipso facto,* the property of the United States.

The second of these descriptions comprehends ships and vessels with their cargoes belonging to the insurgents or employed in aid of them; but property in these was not changed by capture alone but by regular judicial proceedings and sentence.

Almost all the property of the people in the insurgent States was included in the third description.... But it is to be observed that tribunals and proceedings were provided, by which alone such property could be condemned, and without which it remained unaffected in the possession of the proprietors.

The Government recognized to the fullest extent the humane maxims of the modern law of nations, which exempt private property of non-combatant enemies from capture as booty of war. Even the law of confiscation was sparingly applied. The cases were few, indeed, in which the property of any not engaged in actual hostilities was subjected to seizure and sale.

As to property in the fourth category, the Chief Justice stated:

We have called the property taken into the custody of public officers under that act a peculiar species, and it was so. There is, so far as we are aware, no similar legislation in history.

The act directs the officers of the Treasury Department to take into their possession and make sale of all property abandoned by its owners or captured by the national forces, and to pay the proceeds into the national Treasury.

That it was not the intention of Congress that the title to these proceeds should be divested absolutely out of the original owners of the property seems clear upon a comparison of different parts of the act ... and it is reasonable to infer that it was the purpose of Congress that the proceeds of the property for which special provision of the act was made should go into the Treasury without change of ownership. Certainly such was the intention in respect to the property of loyal men.

Every person residing, remaining in, or conducting business within insurrectionary districts was considered disloyal until proven otherwise, except slaves, who were held to have a vested interest in the suppression of the rebellion. Free blacks had to prove their loyalty and were held to the same standards of conduct as all others. Citizens actively engaged in aiding and abetting the rebellion were considered traitors but were given conditional amnesty and pardon for acts of treason in five different presidential proclamations until President Johnson's sixth and final unconditional pardon of December 25, 1868.

Suits brought to recover the proceeds of property were brought in the Court of Claims, originally a three-member fact-finding tribunal set up in 1855 to advise Congress on whether or not a plaintiff was legally entitled to recover money in federal pension cases. If advised in the affirmative then Congress had to pass an act for the relief of the claimant that authorized the Secretary of the Treasury to pay out the money. In 1863 the court was enlarged to five members and given the authority to render monetary judgements in order to relieve Congress from the duty of dealing with the large volume of claims resulting from the war. This presented certain problems since the court and its duties were created by Congress.

In the aftermath of the war, President Lincoln, in his humanity, and President Johnson, in his sympathy for the South, wanted a just and amicable return to peaceful relations. Unfortunately, radical Republicans under an old Vermont sourpuss named Thaddeus Stevens wanted retribution and their views prevailed. In the General Appropriation Act of July 12, 1870, which funded the Court of Claims, Congress instructed the court and the Supreme Court to disregard the various amnesty proclamations, including President Johnson's unconditional pardon, and use loyalty as the sole condition for recovery (16 Stat. L. 235). The Supreme Court held this to be unconstitutional, as the legislature had no power to issue rules for decisions, and said in part:

> It is the intention of the Constitution that each of the great co-ordinate departments of the government — the Legislative, the Executive, and the Judicial — shall be, in its sphere, independent of the others. To the executive alone is intrusted the power of pardon; and it is granted without limit. Pardon includes amnesty. It blots out the offence pardoned and removes all its penal consequences. It may be granted on conditions. In these pardons, that no doubt might exist as to their character, restoration of property was expressly pledged, and the pardon was granted on condition that the person who availed himself of it should take and keep a prescribed oath.
>
> Now it is clear that the legislature cannot change the effect of such a pardon any more than the executive can change a law. Yet this is attempted by the provision under consideration.

The Supreme Court disregarded the Congressional injunction in John A. Klein's

case. The Court of Claims held that their jurisdiction extended only to the determination of loyalty as a provision for making awards under the Act of March 12, 1863, and could not consider pardons, but the Supreme Court decided that the conditional amnesty proclamations, if the provisions were adhered to and the claim was filed within two years, forgave acts of treason, restored civil and property rights and allowed the recovery of money from the special Treasury fund. President Johnson's unconditional pardon of December 25, 1868, ended all discussion of amnesty.

Foreign nationals could recover their losses under the Act only if proved loyal and if their country allowed reciprocal privileges for U.S. citizens.

Since the Supreme Court decided the war ended with President Johnson's proclamation of August 20, 1866, claimants had until August 19, 1868, to file claims under the Act. The first claim was filed on March 8, 1864. All told, 1,578 claims were presented in the Court of Claims; 512 cases were decided for the claimants, 1,066 in favor of the United States. The last claim filed under the Act was decided on May 28, 1883, while one other case was still pending. Reasons for delays included waiting for or finding War or Treasury Department records, locating witnesses, or acts of Congress waiving the two-year filing period. Many original plaintiffs never lived to see their money.

A total of $31,722,466.20 in gross sales was realized with $6,551,000 going toward transportation, storage, sales expenses, and commissions. The total amount of money applied for in claims was $77,785,962.10. Of this, $9,833,423.16 was paid out to claimants, $243,000 was transferred to the Freedmen's Bureau, and $1,406,000 was deposited as internal revenue taxes and commercial intercourse fees.

As one court stated, the Act of March 12, 1863, was passed "at the time when the success of the Union arms was at its lowest ebb. Two objects were intended—first, to reward those among the rebel population who had been true to the government, and also to induce the timid and neutral to withhold all voluntary aid from the usurpation then holding sway over them. To these parties Congress held out the inducement that if their property should be captured *jure belli* [military decision during war], the proceeds of it should be placed in the treasury, and after the close of the war should be repaid to them upon establishing the necessary facts before the court" (3 Ct. of C 85).

Until 1883, the Act of March 12, 1863, was the only Act that had ever been signed by a President after the Congress that passed it had adjourned. President Lincoln did not have the required 10 days to approve it or send it back to the House, but this was never challenged as unconstitutional. The Act was passed by the Senate on March 2, by the House on March 3, and the next day the 37th Congress ceased to exist. President Lincoln signed it eight days later, writing in his own hand, "Approved March 12, 1863." Lincoln was in the habit of always dating his signature when required rather than trusting that detail to a clerk.

Cases from the war also involved ordinary contract law and the special area of military exigency. The law required the military to make every major purchase by advertising for bids, to qualify the bidders, and to accept the lowest bid. An exception was made for peacetime or wartime emergencies when a commander was permitted to purchase supplies on the open market in a manner that anyone else would do in the ordinary course of business. The Union, and the nation as a whole, was wholly un-prepared for war and in the early days of the conflict some of the attempts made to procure arms and supplies raised eyebrows. In particular, the dealings of General John C. Frémont and his chief quartermaster, Justus McKinstry, who was later dismissed from the service for fraud, caused the formation of the Davis-Holt-Campbell commission to examine all contracts.

Military pay disputes were guided by statutes and military regulations, which, like all laws, the court had to interpret when unique or unexpected situations arose that weren't specifically spelled out in detail. Other areas of law, like patent infringement, were dealt with essentially as they would have been had there been no war.

The war disrupted Northern commerce to the extent that the federal government's receipts from import fees were reduced by tens of millions of dollars. To make up for the shortfall, the Act of August 5, 1861, established an annual $20 million direct tax apportioned to each state according to the assessed value "of all lands and lots of ground, with their improvements and dwelling-houses." Provisions for collecting the direct tax within insurrectionary states were authorized by the Act of June 7, 1862. Failure to pay the tax resulted in the condemnation and sale of the property. The tax, interest, and penalties were paid by the purchaser and the residue of the sale was deposited in the Treasury. Property owners or their heirs could file a claim to recover the money in the Treasury. Those who chose not to pay the tax were generally recalcitrant owners or, more often, those who fled the approach of Union forces and never returned home. This situation was especially pronounced in South Carolina.

THE CASES

Acker, Francis. John W. Acker was a first sergeant in Company I, 52d Illinois Volunteer Infantry. He was commissioned first lieutenant by the governor of Illinois on October 24, 1864, was mustered in on December 17, and his pay as first lieutenant began on that date. He claimed pay of $55.40 from October 24 to December 17. The War and Treasury Departments denied it pursuant to the Act of March 3, 1863 and War Department regulations. When he was commissioned his command "was reduced below minimum strength by the casualties of war."

John's widow, of Lake County, Illinois, petitioned Congress. The Senate referred the claim to a federal court on May 22, 1908 and on July 20, 1909 she filed suit under the Act of February 24, 1897.

Her petition was dismissed on January 16, 1911 as barred by statute of limitations.

Adams, Charles H. On or about April 1, 1865, assistant quartermaster Captain William Currie at St. Louis gave Adams a parol order to purchase and deliver corn to Cairo, Illinois. The corn was at Manteno, Illinois but the Illinois Central Railroad refused to carry it, claiming it was private freight. Adams reported this to Currie and on the 15th Currie told Adams to sell the Army 18,000 bushels at $1.30 a bushel, minus the freight. Currie then wrote to William R. Arthur, superintendent of the Illinois Central at Chicago, that he had purchased 18,000 bushels of corn from Adams and wished it delivered to Cairo.

The corn was carried at government rates and considered government property by the railroad. It arrived two or three days later and was rejected upon inspection. When Adams saw the corn it was "shoved down on one side of the side tracks of the railroad."

General Allen, Chief Quartermaster of the Grand Division of the Mississippi, ordered all the corn that might be immediately usable sent to St. Louis. From 3,000 to 6,000 bushels were shipped but only 1,600 was usable. Adams was given a voucher for 1,600 bushels but refused to accept it.

Adams sued for $23,400 but recovered only $2,080 on the 1,600 bushels on the ground that there was no military emergency that would allow Currie to purchase the corn without a bid so the unsigned contract was void.

Adams, Theodore. General John C. Frémont wanted 38 "mortar boats" and eight tugboats for his Western Military Department. The boats, or rafts, would mount guns, be moved around by the tugs, and double as pontoons and gun platforms.

General Justus McKinstry was quartermaster for the Department. Army Regulations for 1861, Article 47, § 1375 stated, "the Ordnance Department furnishes all ordnance and ordnance stores for the military service" and Article 42, § 1064 said "the Quartermaster's Department provides the quarters and transportation of the army" but neither offered specifics for military exigencies during wartime.

Congress appropriated $1,100,000 for the Western Rivers gunboats and on June 17, 1861 the War Department advertised for bids, said that specifications would be provided, and that "plans submitted by builders will be taken into consideration."

James A. Eads, of St. Louis, submitted a proposal which was accepted and he was awarded a contract for seven mortar boats. This took up the bulk of the appropriated money and contracting for additional boats was deemed inexpedient.

In July, Theodore Adams responded to the ad with a detailed proposal showing a type of boat nothing like what Eads was building. The plans were reviewed by Quartermaster General Meigs's office, the Navy, and General Frémont.

Meigs didn't want them but he deferred to Frémont as the general was to command military operations on the Mississippi and said he could take up the matter with the War Department.

On July 16 Congress decided that, "the western gunboat fleet, constructed by the War Department for operations on the western rivers, shall be transferred to the Navy Department."

On July 31 the War Department forwarded an order to Knapp, Rudd & Company at Pittsburgh to have sixteen 9-inch guns built for the Navy to be shipped immediately to Frémont in St. Louis and that thirty 13-inch mortars be manufactured as soon as possible and that shells for both guns be sent to St. Louis.

Adams then contacted Frémont's office to directly submit his proposal for mortar boats. He offered to build iron-sided mortar boats, which Frémont himself had suggested, for $8,250 each or for $5,250 without iron sides. Frémont was impressed and a contract was signed on August 24. Adams was told to begin construction of 38 iron-sided boats "with all possible despatch," reserving the right to increase or decrease the order. Meigs was instructed to draw up a formal contract and he turned the job over to Captain Turnley.

On September 3 Frémont got a letter from "Blair"—possibly Francis P. Blair, Jr.:

Meigs begged me this afternoon to get you to order 15-inch guns from Pittsburg for your gunboats. He says that the boats can empty any battery the enemy can make, with such guns. He advises that you contract for them directly yourself, telling the contractor you will direct your ordnance officer to pay for them.

On September 10 Frémont contracted with Adams for four steam tugs at $2,500 each, payable on delivery after inspection. The boats were to be completed within 30 days with a penalty of $50 for each day of delay. On September 21 Frémont ordered four more tugs on the same conditions, drew up an additional contract, and also contracted with Adams to build cabins, a pilot house with steering wheels, a towing windlass, do all the necessary painting, and get all eight tugs ready in all respects to sail for a sum of $800 per boat. The cabins were to be completed as soon as the engine work was done but no more than five days afterward. All the work was done, inspected, and accepted by the Quartermaster General's office and by Frémont.

On October 25 President Lincoln dishonorably dismissed McKinstry because of irregular-

ities in his dealings and directed Secretary of War Simon Cameron to form a board of commissioners to examine the claims and bills of all contractors on contracts signed prior to October 14, 1861. At that time, a contractor's only recourse was to petition Congress or the Court of Claims in Washington, but that court had no power to render a decision against the government. Congress had much to deal with during the war and on March 3, 1863 the court was given the power to render judgements to relieve Congress of the burden. The board met in St. Louis and consisted of David Davis, Joseph Holt, and Hugh Campbell.

Adams built the 38 boats and four steam tugs and on November 20 Captain Turnley requested Admiral Andrew H. Foote to have the mortar boats inspected and to report back with recommendations for the payment of Adams. The boats were inspected and Meigs was advised of a particular problem but ordered Major Allen to have them sent down the river to have their guns installed.

On December 5 Meigs wrote to Cameron:

Sir: I respectfully call your attention to the propriety of early provision to meet the expense of constructing the armed flotilla on the western rivers.

Under the appropriations, amounting to $1,100,000, for gunboats on the western rivers, made by Congress at its last session, I was directed to contract for seven gunboats. The plans of these vessels had been prepared by a naval constructor, specially assigned to that duty by the Navy Department. Proposals were invited by advertisement, and it was concluded that the building, equipment, and maintenance of seven of these boats, with payment for three other gunboats, then in service, would exhaust the appropriation.

The general commanding the department of the west ordered, at St. Louis, the construction of a fleet of mortar-boats, and of several tug-boats to be used with them, and the purchase and alteration into gunboats of two river steamers, the *New Era*, and the *Submarine*. All these were ordered by him in addition to those provided for by the quartermaster's department.

Under his orders, some money remitted to the quartermaster at St. Louis for other purposes has been paid upon contracts for this flotilla.

The officers of the quartermaster's department who have expended this money were bound by the orders of the general commanding in the department, and should be protected from pecuniary liability incurred in the execution of those orders.

While I am not called upon to express an

opinion as to the necessity for the construction of so large a flotilla, I have no doubt that the government is bound to pay the contractors their reasonable expenditures; and I have no doubt that if armed and equipped, and well manned, the vessels will add to the strength of the army in the west, and conduce to the success of the expedition intended to open the Mississippi.

In the annual estimate from this office, is an item of $1,000,000 for gunboats on the western rivers. Its early appropriation would enable the department to complete and pay for the boats under construction, some of which are in danger of being delayed at St. Louis until the interruption of navigation by ice.

It would relieve those who, in good faith, expended their labor and money upon these boats from heavy pecuniary liabilities.

On December 10 Secretary Cameron submitted the quartermaster general's report to the Speaker of the House about the "necessity of an early provision to meet the expense of constructing the armed flotilla on the western rivers..." and the same day Adams voluntarily appeared before the Davis-Holt-Campbell board to present his claim. Adams submitted a statement showing $313,500 owed on the 38 mortar boats. He had already been paid $130,000 for a balance of $183,500. Adams was allowed $75,959.24. The balance allowed on the four tugboat hulls, cabins, and additional work was $20,196 on a balance owed of $25,400, minus a payment of $9,000. Vouchers were made out for these amounts pending Adams's signature. Adams refused the amounts as too low but signed under protest.

On March 11, 1863 Congress passed a joint resolution to pay all military claims. Adams was included and he was paid the sum of the vouchers but claimed he was still owed $107,544 for the mortar boats and $5,204 for the tugboat work and went to court to collect, claiming duress by the board.

The government argued Adams had signed away his right to sue by accepting the vouchers and denied General Frémont's authority to enter into a contract on behalf of the government or to enter into a contract for boats technically belonging to the Navy, and said there was no military emergency at the time. Adams's counsel quoted Alexander Hamilton:

"It rests upon two axioms, simple as they are universal: the means ought to be proportional to the end; the persons from whose agency the attainment of the end is expected, ought to possess the means by which it to be attained."

The court held the commissioners who issued the vouchers were not authorized to bind a contractor to any specific terms, found the value of the boats and tugs to be $274,408.80, and awarded Adams $112,748.76 in 1866.

The government appealed to the Supreme Court where the judgement was reversed on the ground that Adams voluntarily appeared before the board, dismissing all other arguments from both sides as irrelevant. Frémont was an agent of the Secretary of War and the Secretary was responsible for all contracts and had the duty to supervise and affect remedies. The Davis-Holt-Campbell board was established as a favor to contractors, saving them the time, delay, and effort of going to Washington and by voluntarily appearing Adams relinquished his right to further action since the jurisdiction of the board was equal to the jurisdiction of the original Court of Claims.

The boats and tugs were used effectively throughout the war to move troops across rivers and bombard fortified positions.

Adler, Moses. Major Nathaniel Banks lead the Bayou Teche, Louisiana expedition in the spring of 1863. Banks said anyone could bring goods and merchandise out of the territory and the government would purchase it at market value where it stood. Adler owned 77 bales of cotton and nine hogsheads of sugar that was captured on April 14 by Captain A. B. Long, 52d Massachusetts Volunteers, and assistant quartermaster Lieutenant L. C. Baily, 22d Maine Volunteers, from New Iberia. Adler was given receipts and his goods were shipped to Brashear City and then to New Orleans.

Adler went to New Iberia and was one of the first to take the oath of allegiance to the United States. He then applied to Major Banks in July 1864 for the settlement of his claim. Banks ordered the quartermaster to remit 18 cents a pound for the cotton and 5 cents a pound for the sugar. The quartermaster, Captain Mahler, promised to pay and then refused saying that, "General Banks had no right to give such an order" all the while knowing the cotton had already been sold. It was undetermined whether the cotton had been sold in New Orleans, Boston, or New York but $13,333.09 on 73 bales had been deposited into the Treasury.

Adler was unable to prove the taking and disposition of the sugar but he recovered $13,333.09.

Aiken, Thomas. A black resident of Charleston who worked for a man loyal to the rebellion. Aiken refused to take payment in Confederate currency and since the employer had no other means to pay him, he gave him three bales of cotton. The cotton was seized at Charleston and Aiken was awarded $393.60.

Aker, Benjamin F. In April 1863 Major General Blunt, commander of the District of the Frontier in the Department of the Missouri, required 300 mules for his headquarters at Fort Scott, Kansas. His quartermaster, Captain M. H. Insley, advertised for bids and Aker proposed $140 each, which was accepted. Aker posted the required $50,000 performance bond and contracted for 325 animals. The mules were delivered, inspected, and accepted and a voucher for payment issued.

On April 17 Blunt requested Insley to get 500 cavalry horses. Aker proposed the lowest bid, posted a $75,000 bond, and delivered 500 horses at $129.45 a head. All were delivered, inspected, and accepted and a voucher for payment issued.

On May 29 Blunt ordered Insley to get 400 horses as quickly as possible at the current contract price so he could outfit the new 2d Kansas Cavalry, a regiment not in his command. Insley contacted several dealers and found Aker was the only one who had horses available at the prices Blunt wanted. Insley then purchased 400 horses at $129.45 each and all were delivered, inspected, and accepted.

Quartermaster General Meigs wasn't happy with the transaction and he refused payment on Aker's vouchers. On May 8 he told the Department of Missouri chief quartermaster, Colonel Easton, to let Insley know the contract should have been written by the Q.G. but that since Insley had acted under orders of General Blunt the vouchers would be paid. This was 12 days before the voucher for the first mule contract was issued and three to seven weeks before the first cavalry horse voucher would be issued.

Aker had delivered only a few of the 400 horses when he was notified the vouchers would be paid. Had Meigs told him was going to change his mind, Aker could rightfully have cancelled the contract but he was left holding a $13,021 feed bag. Meigs paid $135 each for the mules and $117 each for the horses.

Alexandria, Loudoun & Hampshire Railroad. Thomas J. Power was a War Depart-
ment civil engineer from May 1, 1861 to March 17, 1862. He worked on bridges for the Northern Central Railway and then supervised employees of the Alexandria & Washington Railroad on the Long Bridge and Sixth Street bridges in Washington and on other projects where he routinely purchased supplies and materials. He next examined and repaired the Alexandria, Loudoun & Hampshire Railroad.

While working on this project he purchased $3,043.49 worth of oil, picks, lumber, spikes, frogs, chairs, ties, and other items for the repair and maintenance of the Orange & Alexandria Railroad, which was in the possession of the United States. He also sent an engine to a station belonging to the Alexandria, Loudoun & Hampshire road and took away one baggage car and three gondolas without the railroad's consent and never returned them.

The Alexandria, Loudoun & Hampshire filed a claim for the cars with the Secretary of War on March 15, 1862. The claim was referred to Quartermaster General Meigs. Meigs rejected the claim as property captured from a disloyal company and said the majority of the stockholders were supporting the rebellion and if the company president were to express his loyalty he would probably be removed by a vote of the shareholders. No one communicated this to the company.

On September 11, 1862 a new claim was submitted and on November 11 the company president was told the reason for rejecting the original claim and it was rejected again for the same reasons.

The real property of the Alexandria, Loudoun & Hampshire had been rented by the government but not the roadbed — the road itself was never seized — and the rent money was paid to the company president. The president of the company was known to be loyal and he readily consented to the rental of the property.

No documents relating to the claim were found in the War Department files until 1873.

On February 2, 1874 the company's president, Lewis McKenzie, withdrew the claim from the Quartermaster General and petitioned Congress for relief but he was rejected there as well. The company went into bankruptcy and on November 3, 1886 the receivers filed a claim with the Third Auditor. The Third Auditor requested information about the claim from the Quartermaster General but no information was returned nor was any communication received. On June

17, 1887 the Third Auditor rejected the claim and sent it to the Second Comptroller who rejected it. On July 5 the receivers appealed to the Third Auditor for a rehearing and on January 30, 1888 the decision was reaffirmed with a recommendation to sue in the federal Court of Claims but the time allowed to file a claim was six years from the date of the loss. The case was barred by statute of limitations and the petition was dismissed on May 18, 1891.

Alleman, Louise J. John Slidell owned a 20 × 100-foot lot in New Orleans on Custom-House Street between Charles and Levee Streets. The property was condemned by the U.S. Circuit Court for the Eastern District of Louisiana under the Confiscation Act of July 17, 1862 and sold by the U.S. marshal on June 14, 1865 for $5,050 to Joseph Brugere, a French citizen living in New Orleans.

When Slidell died on July 30, 1871 his heirs sued to recover the property and rent from the date of John's death as beneficiaries of a life estate. On May 13, 1872 the plaintiffs prevailed in a district court for Orleans Parish. The decision was affirmed by the Louisiana Supreme Court on January 20, 1873 and by the U.S. Supreme Court on January 19, 1874. Brugere was evicted and ordered to pay the Slidells $1,800 for every year of occupation.

Louise Alleman, of Orleans Parish, Louisiana, and Augustine Bibes, of Robertson, Texas, the daughters and only heirs of Brugere sued to recover the purchase price. Their petition was dismissed on January 6, 1908.

Allen, David C. General John C. Frémont was in command at Springfield, Missouri in the fall of 1861. The Confederate Missouri State Guard under General Sterling Price was encamped "not far off" at Jollification but their size, strength, and intentions were unknown so Frémont wanted someone to visit the camp and report back for a fee of $1,000. Frémont knew a beef contractor named Martin J. Hubble in whom he confided. Hubble ran into Allen on the street in Springfield in October and told him he should get the information. Allen and another man named West visited the camp, obtained the information, and reported back to Frémont. Frémont requested he return and this trip resulted in the capture of a spy—the wife of a Confederate officer. Frémont requested a third visit but while Allen was away Frémont was relieved by General Hunter, whose Army retreated from

Springfield, and when Allen returned he was captured by the rebels and imprisoned.

Allen was never paid and he waited until 1884 to petition Congress. His claim was sent to the Senate Committee on Claims. Frémont stated by letter that he did not remember Allen. Mary J. Leathers testified that Allen was at their home and her father told her Allen was a Union spy. The committee recommended not paying since he did not file a timely claim. On April 16, 1888 the House Committee on War Claims recommended a payment of $2,000 under the Bowman Act pending fact finding by a federal court. This was not possible as the Supreme Court had stated, in part:

"It may be stated as a general principle, that public policy forbids the maintenance of any suit in a court of justice, the trial of which would inevitably lead to the disclosure of matters which the law would regard as confidential, and respecting which it will not allow the confidence to be violated. On this principle, suits can not be maintained which would require a disclosure of the confidences of the confessional, or those between husband and wife, or of communications of a client to his counsel for professional advice, or of a patient to his physician for a similar purpose."

On January 4, 1892 the court advised the House of its findings.

Allen & Street. Eugene B. Allen and Alexander Street verbally contracted with Major L. C. Easton to deliver 160 to 273 wagons with five yoke of oxen and complete outfits for each at $146.25 for each wagon and outfit and $55 per yoke of oxen to Fort Leavenworth, Kansas.

On November 1, 1861 they delivered 273 wagons with outfits and 1,312½ yoke of oxen and were given vouchers for $112,113.75. The War Department withheld $17,727 because the cattle and wagons came from Russell, Majors & Waddell, a company that was heavily indebted to the United States, and the firm was under indictment for an alleged robbery of Indian trust bonds. The company had gone bankrupt and assigned certain property to Allen & Street.

Allen & Street sued but the court found that between the middle of July and the middle of December 1860, Godard Bailey, an Interior Department disbursing clerk, illegally gave Mr. Russell certain bonds held in trust by the government for the benefit of various Indian tribes amounting to approximately $870,000. The bonds were used by the company and never returned to the government, all of which was admitted by Russell. The amount converted and owed with interest from October 1, 1860 was never recovered by the government.

Allen & Street's suit was dismissed on the ground "that the United States was entitled to priority of payment out of the proceeds of the property assigned to claimants by Russell, Majors & Waddell under the trust deeds recited."

Alstaedt, C. Louis. Alstaedt entered the all-German 54th New York Volunteers as a 19-year-old private in Company F at Hudson City, New Jersey on September 17, 1861 for a term of three years. On July 1, 1863 he was a second lieutenant, Company B, at Gettysburg when he was captured and held at Libby Prison in Richmond until March 1, 1865 when he was exchanged at Wilmington. He was taken to Camp Parole at Annapolis, Maryland where he arrived on the 7th. While there he requested a discharge from the service but on the 22nd he was given 30 days' leave. He returned on April 22 and was ordered to report to the commandant of the second battalion of paroled prisoners for assignment of quarters and to await mustering out. He received his final discharge on April 26, which he received on the 29th, effective the 22nd. He was not paid after April 1 on the ground that he performed no military service. When he sued to recover the court noted:

"The original term of enlistment of the petitioner and of his regiment expired on September 17, 1864 and at that time his regiment was re-enlisted and became a veteran organization, but at that time he was a prisoner to the enemy and his election to re-enlist or be discharged could not be made or known. He continued, therefore, in the service under his original enlistment, and the statutes continuing his pay while a prisoner and while under parole and on 22nd April, when his election was made by his application to be discharged because of physical disability and the expiration of his original term, the department referred the discharge to March 22, 1865, as the term when his leave of absence began and his military service to the United States ceased.

"As to the petitioner's right to three months' pay proper on his being honorably discharged, the statute of March 3, 1865 gives that bounty to all officers of volunteers below the rank of brigadier general who shall remain in the service to the end of the war, and the statute

of July 13, 1866 extends the bounty to all such officers who shall be 'mustered out at their own request' &c., after April 9, 1865, and both of these statutes fix and specify a definite period of time, which in their administration cannot be disregarded, nor can this court or the department fix any other."

Alstaedt received three months' pay.

Amoskeag Manufacturing Co. The Army's Ordnance Bureau agreed to purchase all the Lindner carbines the company could make, up to 6,000 within six months from April 15, 1863, at $20 each. The company began making them but on April 23 the Army changed the specifications. This required considerable re-tooling and redesign of parts. The company was never told the guns would not be accepted if they weren't delivered within the six months and no new contract was negotiated.

On April 5, 1864 the company presented one of the new guns for inspection and said they were ready to resume manufacturing and could deliver the entire 6,000 as fast as they could be inspected but General Ripley refused to accept them on the ground the six months' time limit had passed.

Without alterations, the company could have delivered the carbines within six months. Amoskeag sued to recover and it was found the undelivered carbines in the company's possession were worth $3 each and had no market value. The company's petition was dismissed but they appealed to the Supreme Court where the decision was reversed.

Anderson, Nelson. Anderson was a free black drayman and cotton sampler who owned real estate in Charleston. He bought cotton in a loose and damaged condition from Daniel F. Fleming, took it to Dr. North's farm near the racecourse, and dried, assorted, and made 10 good bales. During and after September 1864 he purchased 30 bales of upland and 10 bales of sea-island cotton from Philip M. Doucin, which he kept at his home at No. 33 Ashley Street. Blockade runners tried to purchase his cotton but he refused to sell and on March 8, 1865 he reported the 40 bales to the Army as required. It was seized and sold in New York for $7,362. He recovered the full amount on February 22, 1869.

Armstrong, Charles H. In May and early June 1863 the residents of Pittsburgh, Pennsylvania became concerned when Confederate forces began moving into Pennsylvania,

West Virginia, and southern Ohio. Pittsburgh had a major military depot and arsenal at Allegheny. A committee was formed to call on Secretary of War Edwin M. Stanton and General Henry W. Halleck, General in Chief, to request Army engineers build fortifications around the city. They were told the War Department had no plan or money appropriated for that and all the work would have to be done by the citizens themselves at their own expense.

On June 8 Halleck wrote a letter to General John G. Barnard:

Brig. Gen. Barnard
Washington, D.C.
General: You will immediately proceed to Pittsburg, Pa., and advise Capt. Comstock, Corps of Engineers, in regard to the best means to be adopted for the defense of that place. It is not anticipated that any hostile demonstrations will be made against Pittsburg other than a mere raid, and as any projected works must be constructed by the voluntary labor of the citizens, the projected defenses should be of limited extent and of the most simple character — mere earth batteries and rifle pits.

Capt. Comstock is charged with laying out these works, and you will remain there only long enough to give him the benefit of your advice and experience, after which you will return to Washington, where your presence is deemed necessary at the present crisis.

Brig. Gen. Brooks has been appointed to the command of the Department of the Monongahela, of which Pittsburg is the headquarters. Should he arrive there in time, it will be proper for you to show him these orders.

I would also suggest the propriety of your calling on and consulting the mayor and municipal authorities.

It should be distinctly understood that there is no appropriation for fortifying Pittsburg, and no troops which can probably be spared for garrisoning that place. The sole object of your mission and that of Capt. Comstock, at the present time, is to give the citizens of Pittsburg such assistance and instruction as may be practicable in preparing themselves against a possible rebel raid.

The Department of the Monongahela was in Pennsylvania west of Johnstown and the Laurel Hill mountains; Hancock, Brooke, and Ohio Counties in Virginia; and Columbiana, Jefferson, and Belmont Counties in Ohio. A volunteer army of infantry, artillery, and cavalry was to be raised and designated the Army of the Monongahela "for the protection and defence of public property within that department."

Major General William T. H. Brooks as-

sumed command on June 11 and three days later he got a telegram when he reached Pittsburgh on the 14th:

United States Military Telegraph
War Department
Washington, D.C., June 14, 1863
Gen. W. T. H. Brooks, Pittsburg, Pa.:
Lee's army is in motion towards the Shenandoah Valley. Pittsburg and Wheeling should be put in defensible condition as rapidly as possible.
H. W. Halleck
General in Chief

Brooks also found a second telegram waiting for him:

War Department
Washington, D.C., June 10, 1863
Maj. Gen. W. T. H. Brooks, Pittsburg:
You will receive by mail an appointment of major-general. Gen. Couch goes to Harrisburg and has command of the Department of the Susquehanna. Intelligence received this evening of the enemy's design make it certain that you can not be too early or busily at work, as Pittsburg will certainly be the point aimed at by Stuart's raid, which may be daily expected. You should frankly inform the people of Pittsburg that they must be at work.
Edwin M. Stanton
Secretary of War

Brooks immediately contacted all the prominent businessmen and told them to meet him that Sunday evening at the Monongahela House. Thomas Bakewell acted as chairman, G. H. Thurston as secretary. Brooks told them they needed to have 2,000 men at work by 8 o'clock Monday morning, the 15th, to start work on fortifications. The businessmen agreed to suspend commerce and requested Brooks to "declare martial law forthwith." They agreed to furnish all their employees for the task at $1.25 a day. Brooks was requested to have the Pittsburg, Steubenville & Pennsylvania Railroad, and other railroads, send their employees and equipment for the work. The notice of the meeting was published in the morning papers.

The next morning everyone was placed under the direction of General Barnard and Captain Craighill, Army engineers, who were paid by the businessmen.

Brooks made a request to his quartermaster through the assistant adjutant general:

Headquarters Department of the Monongahela
Pittsburg, Pa., June 14, 1863
Lt. Co. O. Cross
Depty. Qr. Mr. Gen'l Pittsburgh, Pa:
Sir: Major Gen'l Brooks directs that the requisite transportation be furnished by you to supply

subsistence to the troops in the different camps and working parties employed on the fortification in this vicinity and to haul guns from the Allegheny arsenal to the forts as they may be designated; also whatever dirt carts that may be required in the construction of the defensive works around this city.

Very respectfully your obd't serv't,

T. Brent Swearinger

A. A. Gen'l

Teams, carts, and drivers were hired and sent to the job site. Brooks signed vouchers and the payments to vendors were made.

Brooks sent a report to the War Department when the work was finished on July 3:

In answer to my call for labor on defensive works and intrenchments the whole community has responded in the most gratifying manner. Mills, factories, and works of various kinds have been closed and the employés sent to the intrenchments. Stores, both wholesale and retail, were closed and represented on the works. Liquor dealers of various kinds were at work, as were miners, builders, etc.

The colored population were well represented and did their share. I know of no class of people or business that was unrepresented. I doubt not when the hour of danger comes the same hands that made the intrenchments will be there to defend them. Until the engineers have time to make a survey, that will be forwarded, I can only say that rifle pits have been made by miles and batteries and forts constructed sufficient to mount guns by the hundred.

Brooks endorsed numerous vouchers for payment. A typical one was made out to Brown & Company:

The United States to Brown & Co., Dr.

For amount of money disbursed for work on fortifications from June 16, 1863 to July 3, 1863, as per statement below:

193 men worked within these dates, June 16, 1863 to July 3, 1863, inclusive, equaling 2,060¾ days, at $1.25.................................... $2,575.95

19 men worked 28 days, at $2, as watchmen...................................... 56

2 men, with horses and carts, worked 7½ days, at $2.50........................... 18.75

5 boys worked 29 days, at $1.......................... 29.00

2 boys worked 7 days, at 8⅔ cents................... 5.85

2 boys worked 8 days, at 66⅔ cents.............. 5.35

7 boys worked 74 days, at 50 cents.............. 37.00

2,727.90

Brooks attached and signed a note to each voucher:

I hereby certify that I believe the above account is correct and just; that the labor was furnished on

an appeal from me to the citizens of Pittsburg to put the place in a state of defense when the State was being invaded, and that the labor was necessary for the public service.

Between April 17, 1866 and 1876 claims totaling $73,828.26 were repeatedly presented to the War and Treasury Departments on the ground that a contract existed between the workers and General Brooks.

Besides Armstrong, claimants included Jones & Laughlin; Hussey, Wells & Co.; Lloyd & Block; James Millingar; Robinson, Minnis & Co.; Smith, Parks & Co.; Pittsburg, Fort Wayne & Chicago Railway Co.; Singer, Nimmick & Co.; Lyon, Short & Co.; James Wood & Co.; and King & Pennock.

The last official action was taken by Second Comptroller C. C. Carpenter on July 27, 1876 when the claims were denied after review and denial by the Third Auditor. Carpenter said even if there was a contract with Brooks, the General had no authority and was "even expressly prohibited, to make any such contract, and that payment could not be authorized by the War Department."

In 1890 Secretary of the Treasury William Windom referred the claim to the Court of Claims. Armstrong and 158 other claimants filed suit but their petition was dismissed on March 5, 1894:

"If the disallowance of a claim by a Comptroller is not opened for fraud, mistake in calculation, or the filing of material new evidence, the decision is final, and it is not within the power of the Secretary to transmit the claim to this court; and if transmitted, the court will acquire no jurisdiction thereby."

Henry A. Laughlin, representing Jones & Laughlin, sued for $3,862.82 for 450 men for 350 man-days. The court certified his claim and referred it to Congress on February 1, 1909.

Armstrong, Hibernia. Owner of the Armstrong plantation in Conway County near Little Rock, Arkansas. Her husband Robert died in or around 1859. In the winter of 1863, 102 bales of her 120 bales of cotton were taken by U.S. forces to Lewisburg and used for fortifications around Little Rock. When the cotton was removed from these positions, only 60 bales of hers could be identified with her markings and these were sold into the Treasury for $26,500.92.

She had two sons in the rebel army and when U.S. forces approached Little Rock, she took 30 or 40 of her slaves and fled south to seek aid from rebel commanders in keeping them from being emancipated. Although the court could not prove that she ever aided the rebellion her petition was dismissed. She appealed to the Supreme Court where the decision was reversed on the ground that she was not given the benefit of President Johnson's unconditional pardon of December 25, 1868.

Armstrong, James. A cotton merchant who owned 54 bales of upland and one bale of sea-island cotton that was stored on his Fordham farm on the Wandoo River "by water 12 miles, direct six miles from the city, and outside the fortifications" of Charleston. In March 1865, in response to military orders, he went to Captain Sturdivant's office and reported the amount and whereabouts of all his cotton. Apparently he was exempt from this order as a resident outside the city limits. Armstrong hired a schooner to bring the cotton to the wharf at Charleston where, he believed, it would be released to him after inspection but Treasury agent Francis A. Mitchell seized it. There was some discrepancy in the exact number of upland bales and Armstrong was credited with 53 bales. He had receipts for the upland bales but none for the sea-island bale, which he had purchased from F. A. Sawyer, the local internal revenue tax collector. He had purchased 20 bales only a month prior to the surrender of Charleston and another 20 on February 16, 1865, which he bought from Philip M. Doucin only a day before the city was evacuated, but this was not held against him since the city had been under assault and bombardment for over two years.

Armstrong's loyalty was supported in court by Union prisoners who said he aided them at Charleston and in the city of Florence. Armstrong testified:

> I voluntarily went and furnished the Union prisoners at the jail, racetrack hospital, and the workhouse. I went to Captain Gayr for a pass for the purpose. He was the Confederate provost marshal here. Myself and my sons went and I, in the night often sent my servants with food, liquor, and other refreshments. I kept four Union prisoners in my house. Captain Boram of the ship *Arcole,* a man named Fitzgerald, another man, Webb, of Sherman's army, and another named Rich. There was also C. D. Duncan, who belonged to the steamer *Diotching,* and I used to take them to my house. They were confined in the building on King street near Line. There were several parties up-stairs. I passed the guard and went up to see them. They remained here several days after the

Union army came in. They voluntarily gave me a testimonial of my aid to them. It is signed by them. The paper marked exhibit E by the commissioner is that paper.

> There was a vessel captured here and they were selling her effects. Among them were three flags, one an English flag, one a Confederate flag, and one a United States flag. On starting the auction none would bid on the United States flag. He said they seemed to be unwilling to bid on that dirty rag. I was close to the door and said I would start the flag and offered $10. There was another man behind who nudged him and he drew down the flag. I hollered to him that was not fair. He said he would not dwell on such a rag as that.

Acting Ensign Charles D. Duncan; Acting Master's Mate A. F. Rich; Acting Master's Mate W. H. Fitzgerald; First Lieutenant Dwight Webb, Company F, 22d Ohio Voluntary Infantry, 17th Army Corps; and Theodore Boreham, former master of the *Arcole,* of New York, wrote a letter attesting to Armstrong's "unremitted kindness" to them and on June 14 Rear Admiral John T. Dahlgren granted Armstrong's request for passage to New York on the USS *Massachusetts.*

Armstrong was awarded $7,088.04.

Aubert, Helen. Helen, her husband Marcus Thomas Aubert, their daughters Delphine and Corinne, and sons Oscar, Aristide, and Felix lived in Mobile.

Under Alabama law, any property acquired by a married woman remained hers and upon her death, one half of the property went to her husband and the other half went to other heirs. Helen owned 142 bales of upland cotton.

In the fall of 1860 Marcus went to Europe to have an eye condition treated. He returned to New York in the spring of 1861 and remained there until after the capture of Mobile in April 1865 when Helen's cotton was seized. That same spring, Oscar left for France to pursue a medical education at the Preparatory School of Medicine at Nantes and was there throughout the war. Aristide and Felix joined the Confederate military service.

Helen died in August 1866 and Marcus became the administrator of her estate. The cotton had been sent to New York and sold at $188.24 a bale for $26,731. In court the government argued that since Aristide and Felix aided the rebellion all the heirs should be excluded. The court determined the rest of the family, including the now Delphine Lacroix, were loyal and the only question for the court was Helen's title to the property and her loyalty at the time of her death. This proved, Marcus was awarded $26,731.50 in 1867.

Austin, Florine A. Sterling T. Austin was born in South Carolina and when he was seven he moved with his parents to Georgia. He married and accumulated a large plantation, 160 slaves, and much personal property in Alabama. He was described as "a man of thrift, and great energy and enterprise in speculation and business matters." He supported the John Bell–Edward Everett Constitutional Union ticket in the presidential campaign of 1860 and reportedly opposed secession but did not express his views publicly.

In the autumn of 1860 he established residency in Carroll Parish, Louisiana. Excitement over the coming war was very great there and public meetings were held to induce enlistments and to aid the rebel cause.

By 1861 he and his wife had a son and two daughters and in February the family moved temporarily to New Orleans. In March, Sterling went alone to Carroll Parish where he purchased the Three Bayou place, a 2,380 acre plantation on the Mississippi River for which he agreed to pay $47,600. In April he moved his family and part of his slaves to Three Bayou. He brought the slaves over in three groups, the last group arriving in late 1861.

In May or June of 1861 Austin attended a meeting about 6 miles from his home where "violent and inflammatory speeches were made to induce enlistment" in the Confederate military but he apparently said nothing either way and was not bothered or questioned about his views.

In 1862 a dinner party was given at a residence near a landing on the Mississippi about 8 miles from his home for a Confederate rifle company on their way to the war. Austin and his family were meeting a boat at the landing and when they saw the party they went over and had dinner without incident.

In 1861 it became the policy in Carroll Parish "by which planters subscribed negroes to work for persons who were absent in the Confederate army; that policy became general throughout the State." In late 1861 Austin attended the first meeting, held near his home, to deal with this subject and to subscribe the services of slaves. There was no record to show Austin took part in any way but in March 1862 a captain in the militia accompanied by a Confederate soldier visited Three Bayou to see if he would release any of his slaves for the work program. Austin was then in the field with a group of slaves and he and the officer met briefly after which Austin "called to one of the negroes and turned him over to the possession of the captain." The slave was taken to the plantation of a man who was in the Confederate service and remained there several months.

In August 1862 Austin left Louisiana and moved his family to Texas and then to Georgia leaving his plantation in the care of a manager and overseer of the slaves.

In late 1862 a barbecue was held about 8 miles from Three Bayou for the purpose of inducing enlistments in the Confederate army and which he attended uneventfully.

In December of 1862 the Army was approaching Three Bayou near Ashton's Landing where his slaves lived. Confederate policy at that time obliged planters to destroy all their cotton or produce on the approach of federal forces and take their slaves and any other moveable property away from the river into the interior. At this particular time Austin was in Georgia. When his manager and overseer received word that U.S. gunboats were approaching the landing he moved the slaves about 18 miles inland. There were no rebel forces in the area at the time. When Austin arrived he went to where his slaves were being held and from there he was advised to take them to Monroe by someone not associated with the Confederate military or government.

When Austin left Georgia to attend to the slaves, he and his family went through U.S. military lines and then into Confederate lines.

Austin stayed with the slaves in Monroe for some time and then took them to Shreveport in the summer of 1863. At Shreveport there were numerous Confederate gunboats being built and undergoing repair and refit. Austin had 60 adult male slaves in addition to the women and children and a number of the men were put to work on the gunboats and in building fortifications around the city. While in Shreveport Austin bought and sold cotton and other goods. The slaves had charge of Austin's teams and wagons and he allowed them to hire themselves out to contractors hauling wood to the Confederate arsenal. The slaves drove the teams and Austin collected the salaries of the slaves and money for the teams.

During the winter of 1863 he took the slaves to the plantation of a relative in east Texas about

75 miles from Shreveport then returned to Shreveport where they engaged in the same work as before then they were moved to San Antonio where they remained until 1865. While there, they were hired out by Austin, the wages were paid to him, and he again bought and sold cotton and other goods. After General E. Kirby Smith surrendered his forces on May 25, 1865 — the last operational Confederate department — Austin told his slaves they were free and advised them to remain where they were.

The Army captured Three Bayou, about 250 bales of cotton, and another 110 bales of Austin's cotton in Texas. All were sold and $59,287 deposited into the Treasury.

In 1867 he went to Washington to present a $367,500 claim for the seizure of 1,950 bales of cotton. The court found he was disloyal and all claims for cotton seized outside of Three Bayou and Shreveport, and Rush County, Millican, and Galveston, Texas were dropped. Over 150 witnesses were called, many were questioned extensively, and a "sharp conflict of testimony" resulted.

Sterling died on July 9, 1879 in Carroll Parish and Florine Austin renewed the claims. On June 9, 1890 her petition was dismissed on the ground that Austin was disloyal throughout the war. Florine appealed to the Supreme Court where the decision was affirmed on December 17, 1894 for the same reasons.

Austrell, Alfred. A cashier at the Bank of Fulton in Atlanta. On June 6, 1863 Austrell, V. K. Stephenson, T. W. Evans, and E. W. Holland, all of Atlanta, entered into an agreement to run the blockade under Austrell, Evans & Co. and ship cotton from any Confederate port and "bringing in return cargoes of such articles as may suit the wants of our people." They obtained all the necessary Confederate permits and hired the wrong agent, a man named Beringer. Beringer thought it advisable to obtain permission from Washington before actually undertaking any blockade running but he was captured on the way and no blockade running was ever carried out.

On May 6, 1864 Austrell purchased 52 bales of upland cotton from Z. A. Rice for $18,320.40 — 26,172 pounds at 70 cents a pound. Rice purchased it from John Carleton of Palmetto, Georgia and stored it in Rice's barn. On September 14 Austrell reported the cotton to the Army and 20 wagons were sent to cart it away.

He thought it advisable to take the loyalty

oath in August 1865 and in court stated that in early 1861 the governor of Georgia applied to the Bank of Fulton for $100,000 in the bills of the bank, which were to be replaced with Georgia treasury notes. He complied but said he was bitterly opposed "and never ceased to condemn it."

He recovered $12,385.88 on 52 bales in 1871.

Ayers, Asher. Asher bought 209 bales of cotton directly from the planters around Macon and Montezuma, Georgia. It was shipped to Savannah for storage and captured. He was forced into the home guard at Macon and recovered $35,011.68.

Ayers, Treadwell S. Ayers purchased a 74 × 148-foot, iron front, four-story building in Memphis built in 1860 for $100,000. On January 6, 1863 Captain A. R. Eddy directed his clerk, Edward R. Hill, to occupy the upper floor as office space for the pay department for an indefinite period under a verbal agreement with Ayers for a "fair and reasonable rent." The space was used until February 1865. When Ayers presented a $7,815 bill, the Quartermaster General refused to pay on the ground that Memphis was a "hostile city" and the building was seized as enemy property and the owner presumed to be disloyal. In court the government argued the city was under siege and martial law and no landlord-tenant agreement existed. Ayers's case was dismissed as an appropriation by the Army under the Act of July 4, 1864.

Backer, Abraham. Owner of 150 bales of upland and 89 bales of sea-island cotton seized at Savannah. Treasury records credited him with 229 bales — 122 upland and 107 sea-island. Backer took an amnesty oath on July 15, 1865 under President Johnson's proclamation of May 29, 1865.

Backer had a problem in court over his identity. The government showed there were two Abraham Backers in Savannah with the same occupation but only one was listed in the amnesty records. The assistant attorney general could not prove he was not the one who took the oath so Backer was awarded $40,150.57 on the 229 bales but the judgement was suspended pending the determination of Backer's true identity regarding amnesty.

Baird, Matthew. Matthew Baird was a partner with locomotive builder M. W. Baldwin in Philadelphia. Due to urgent military railroad needs in Tennessee, Colonel D. C. McCallum, general superintendent of military railroads, visited every major locomotive builder and made them an offer: They could either build the locomotives to government specifications at government prices or their works would be taken over by government officers.

McCallum contacted M. W. Baldwin & Co. and on March 17, 1864 signed a contract to build 15 locomotives as quickly as possible. At this time the company was under contract to build 98 engines for private operators and it would require at least eight months to complete them. This was pointed out and also the fact that materials were getting harder to come by, prices were constantly rising, and the company had not built engines at fixed prices since early November 1863.

McCallum ordered the engines built and assured Baldwin and Baird they would be compensated for any contractual losses. To find the kind he wanted, he looked through the company's order books and found a type of engine used in Kentucky with the same track gauge used in Tennessee. The company already had all the material needed for the new engines, bought for the existing contracts, and it was agreed to the base price of each locomotive at $18,947.72, a November 9, 1863 price. The first engine was delivered and the contractual computation of an advance on materials added $7,086 making a total of $26,034.19. McCallum sent the bill to Washington where a disbursing officer refused to pay the extra $7,086. This was partially reversed to increase the unit cost to $25,000.

Baldwin died on September 7, 1866 and Baird sued for $141,875 to cover all losses. The court decided the company was entitled to $1,250 on 15 engines and $5,000 in settlement costs with the Galena & Chicago Union Railroad for a total of $23,750.

Barnes, William A. Barnes was chaplain with the 5th New York Volunteer Infantry, dismissed from duty September 10, 1862, but continued to perform his duties. He was reinstated December 4 but not paid. He recovered $311.32.

Barnwell, James L. Owned property in Beaufort, South Carolina described by the U.S. Direct Tax Commission as lot B, block 61 that was assessed $7.98 in direct taxes. This was not paid and a penalty of $12 was added along with $1.80 in costs, and $2.22 in interest. The property was sold at auction to the United States for

$100. On November 1, 1866 the government sold it to Barnwell for $2,600 and he sued under the Act of March 2, 1891 to recover the difference between the $24 tax and the amount he paid to get his property back. On March 20, 1895 the court stated:

"The purpose of this act are beneficent; the intention of Congress was to repair as far as possible any injustice occasioned by the operation of the direct tax laws, which, in South Carolina, fell with peculiar hardship upon the inhabitants of two parishes, and to accomplish this result it divided the sufferers into several classes: First those whose lands had been sold for a sum in excess of the tax, and to these it gives the excess, over the tax, of the value of the lands, at a certain prescribed rate; second, certain third parties who purchased at the sale, made part payment, and failing payment as to the balance due forfeited their rights. These receive the money actually paid by them on account."

Special provisions were made for those who purchased the land from the United States and Barnwell was awarded $2,576.

Barringer, Paul B. Paul claimed 106 bales of his upland cotton were seized in November and December 1862 at his plantation in Lafayette County, Mississippi. He said he moved to another plantation in Panola County, Mississippi later that year but left the cotton at his previous residence.

The cotton was found, seized, and sent to Stephen W. Wilkins, the military cotton agent at Memphis, and sold in February 1863 in a lot of 500 bales that was sold in lots of 50 bales taken from numerous other places. The sale netted $137,287.56 from the highest bidder, Wilson King. Another lot of 272 bales was sold on the 19th at 80½ cents pound, also to King.

Barringer's ownership was satisfactorily demonstrated to the court. Concerning his loyalty, the court stated:

"The claimant shows by the testimony of his neighbors, with most of whom he differed, that he voted to use his influence against the secession of the State of Mississippi and consistently adhered to his sentiments throughout the rebellion, expressing them on all proper occasions as far as it was prudent or safe for him to do so. So strong and open was he in expressing his Union sentiments that the witnesses say that but for his high social standing and character and his age he would have been subject to personal violence."

The average net proceeds of the cotton sold were $307.30 a bale. Barringer was awarded $38,573.30 on 106 bales.

Basch, Evan B. The Georgia Importing & Exporting Company was incorporated at Savannah under the laws of the State of Georgia to run the blockade and export goods to Europe. The company had large amounts of cotton stored in Georgia, Alabama, and Florida.

On June 19, 1865 Colonel William K. Kimball's 12th Maine Infantry entered Thomasville, Georgia where the company had cotton in a warehouse and took possession of all Confederate property. On August 9, Colonel Kimball was ordered to turn all the cotton in the warehouse over to special Treasury agent A. G. Browne, which he did on the 15th and he was given a receipt. The company's cotton was intermingled with cotton belonging to others and after the Treasury agents rebaled the cotton Kimball was given another receipt dated January 24, 1866 for 1,018 bales "claimed to be the property of the Importing & Exporting Company of the State of Georgia" and 484 bales "claimed to be the property of Gazaway B. Lamar or the Importing & Exporting Company of the State of Georgia." Other cotton was alleged to belong to the States of North Carolina and Georgia but Browne stated it was impossible to invoice the cotton under the original receipt of August 15 except in bulk as the owners' marks and weights had not been ascertained. The cotton was sold and the net proceeds deposited into the Treasury.

Gazaway B. Lamar was the president of the company. Lamar was born in Georgia in 1798 and had the famous steamer *John Randolph* prefabricated in England. She was launched on July 9, 1834 in Savannah and was the first commercially successful iron steamer in America. Lamar became president of the Bank of the Republic in New York City and before the war did much to aid the Confederacy. After the war started he moved back to Savannah and ran the Bank of Commerce where he dealt mainly in cotton. In December 1865 all his papers were seized and he was arrested and taken to the Old Capitol Prison is Washington. He was tried and convicted of attempted bribery by a military tribunal and sentenced to imprisonment and a fine but he was pardoned by President Johnson.

In 1867 he sued to recover the loss of cotton seized at Savannah and recovered over half a million dollars. He also unsuccessfully sued

Browne and Secretary of the Treasury Hugh McCulloch in the Superior Court of Georgia to recover the Thomasville cotton.

Lamar died in 1874, the company went bankrupt in 1881, and the Superior Court of Georgia appointed receivers of which Basch was the only one left when he filed suit under the Act of March 3, 1911. The court cited a Supreme Court decision:

> Corporations created by the legislature of a rebel State while the State was in armed rebellion against the Government of the United States have power, since the suppression of the rebellion, to sue in the Federal courts if the acts of incorporation had no relation to anything else than the domestic concerns of the State, and they were neither in their apparent purpose nor in their operation hostile to the Union or in conflict with the Constitution but were mere ordinary legislation, such as might have been had there been no war or no attempted secession and such as is of yearly occurrence in all the States [22 Wall. 99].

Other claimants, including A. Stow & Co., came forward and on January 29, 1917 the court remanded the claims to a special auditor to examine the various "ancient records."

Bates, Edwin. A wealthy Charleston clothing merchant who continued in business during the war. Bates claimed the proceeds of 83 bales of upland cotton. Bates assisted Federal prisoners and "guided national troops through the city to the arsenal with the view of protecting it against threatened destruction by the retiring rebel soldiery," but he had difficulty explaining his position as a clerk in the Confederate treasury department, placing a substitute in the Confederate army in his place, his purchase of blockade goods, $10,000 in blockade stock in the Atlantic Steamship Company, $4,000 in the Cobia Blockade Company, and $10,000 in the Palmetto Company. The court stated:

"He is proven to have been in opinion and sentiment loyal to the flag of his government, but to have done many things calculated to give aid and comfort to its enemies. How such an inconsistent life — by assuming the claimant's professed devotion to the Union to have been sincere — can be accounted for, is a little difficult to determine. It may be that the allurements of private speculation, for the time, extinguished his zeal for the safety of his government. But that patriotism which, in time of war, exalts the man and sinks the State, is not such patriotism as commends itself to this court."

His petition was dismissed.

Battelle & Evans. In early May 1862, General Frémont's Mountain Department needed to move quickly south from New Creek in northwest Virginia to head off the approach of General "Stonewall" Jackson at McDowell. There was limited transportation available to carry supplies so Frémont directed assistant commissary Captain J. M. Mackenzie to get beef cattle for the march. A commissary depot was established at Petersburg, cattle ordered, and on May 8 Mackenzie sent a telegram to New Creek:

To Battelle:
No cattle yet received on my order, except 37 head from Mr. Shock, brought by Moorfield. Forward 300 head to this post immediately. No time to lose. Answer what you can do and when.

This was received at New Creek by Battelle's agent. The same day adjutant-general Colonel Albert Tracy telegrammed Mackenzie:

Captain: The general commanding directs that you procure 500 head beef cattle on the most reasonable and proper terms but procure them. No time to be lost.

This was forwarded to Battelle's agent. The next day Mackenzie wired Battelle:

Why cannot I hear from you? We want 500 head cattle here as soon as you can get them, Not a moment to be lost. Send forward to the post 100, more or less, at a time. I have brought 50 head here which will only last through to-morrow. Send on immediately at any cost.
In haste, yours, &c.

Frémont marched the 50 miles south from Petersburg to McDowell, where a battle took place on the 8th, then moved his headquarters to Franklin for ten days. Battelle employees drove cattle along the march and slaughtered them as needed. Two hundred head were delivered at Franklin and kept in a fenced pasture along a river. The next morning it was discovered that nine were missing. The cattle were owned by Battelle until actually used and they were issued vouchers at that time.

On the 23rd Mackenzie got an order for another 200 per day until further ordered. Mackenzie contacted Battelle with the same instructions the next day.

Frémont left Franklin on the 25th to assist General Banks. He passed through Petersburg and Moorfield, crossed the mountains at Hunting Ridge, went through Wardensville and reached the crossroads at Winchester and Strasburgh on June 2. A battle took place near Winchester on the 25th. Battelle people drove cattle from New Creek to accompany the troops, escorted by cavalry. It was very difficult for the company to find employees willing to drive cattle as reported:

"The cattle were driven from New Creek to Franklin under unfavorable circumstances as there was great difficulty in getting men to drive the cattle through the country, which was infested with guerillas and food for the cattle was difficult to be procured and the march of General Frémont from Franklin to near Strasburgh was a forced march over bad and broken roads and, in part, through hostile and mountainous country. The army moved rapidly and the cattle were overdriven and lost weight. The fences and fields on the way had been destroyed and it was difficult to secure the cattle at night. Guerillas following the army on either flank and the guard of cavalry was often insufficient for the protection of the cattle and some were lost."

One night, when the troops were encamped between Moorfield and Wardensville, 57 cattle were "surreptitiously taken by the troops and slaughtered and used by them." No vouchers were given the company for these.

At an encampment near Wardensville the army butchers were awakened one night and ordered to slaughter 40 head for use the next morning but at dawn the troops left quickly and the beef was left on the ground and the company received no vouchers.

All of the hides, tallow, and byproducts belonged to the company and were worth about $13 a head. The company requested transportation for the byproducts but none could be furnished. On occasion, Frémont ordered transportation to New Creek from Franklin but none was delivered and at other times he ordered the byproducts burned.

Captain McKenzie established the depot at Petersburg in early 1862 but before that he was with General Kelley at Cumberland, Maryland. On February 1 he contracted with Battelle to deliver fresh beef to General Lander's division at Camp Kelley at 6½ cents a pound. Lander's troops were not under Kelley, who was under Frémont at that time. Lander was under General Banks but the company was to accompany the planned expedition with 100 head of cattle, ox-teams, wagons, horses, and anything else required. If any cattle were lost beyond the company's control, the Army would pay an agreed portion of the loss. They would also get a 1-cent per pound bonus when difficulties were encountered.

When Banks retreated from Harrisonburgh he was chased by rebels through Winchester on May 24, 1862 and through Martinburgh the next day to the Potomac, which was crossed on the 26th. There were 19 head of Battelle's cattle at Winchester for the use of the hospital and these, along with the Battelle employees, were captured by rebels. The company sent 65 head from New Creek by railroad to Martinsburg and to pastures near the depot. Those 65 were captured but when they retreated they left 48 more near Winchester where they were taken by General Cooper.

The company was given vouchers for 362,711 pounds of beef used by Frémont on which Mackenzie paid the agreed price of 7½ cents a pound. The cattle weighed an average of 700 pounds on the foot. The company appealed to a War Department board to resolve unsettled claims but no agreement was made. The company sued and the court found they were entitled to 10½ cents a pound on the march from Petersburg.

The court disallowed the hides and tallow since byproducts were the company's responsibility.

Frémont commented on procuring the beef without a contract:

"The troops were entirely without provisions, so much so in the camp at Franklin, that there was an attempt at mutiny in some regiments for want of provisions and under these circumstances supplies were furnished for my command wherever they could be procured and in the most expeditious way."

They sued unsuccessfully to recover $45,712.33 because there was no contract and the cattle belonged to the company.

Beall, Lloyd. Sued to recover the proceeds on 22 bales of cotton seized in Floyd County, Georgia on June 1, 1864 by Major McCurdy's 10th Ohio Cavalry. Beall later transferred his interest in the cotton to Samuel Noble. Beall sued on behalf of Noble and recovered $10,571.22 in 1873.

Beard, Elias L. General John C. Frémont was appointed commander of the Department of the West with broad, loosely defined powers to protect the west from invasion and to descend the Mississippi. His headquarters were at St. Louis and he ordered fortifications built around that city according to plans previously drawn up by General Lyon. Elias Beard was a California

public works contractor Frémont had known there and the General invited him out to bid on the job. A contract with General McKinstry was proposed on September 4, 1861 which stated:

"The undersigned proposes to build all the fortifications, redoubts, bastions, and all else required, of timber and earthwork, for the defence of the city of St. Louis, from fortification No. 6 at St. Malachi church, to the northern limit of the city — all to be done according to and under the direction of the engineer or engineers in charge of the work — binding myself to complete the work in five (5) days after the same is laid out, for the sum of $315,000."

War Department auditors disallowed $207,673.22 on his bills and Beard sued to recover $107,326.78. The government argued the contract was invalid and the costs were grossly excessive. Lumber was charged at $100 a board foot while Beard paid $12. A total of 715,058 board feet was used, which would have cost the government $71,505.80; its value at St. Louis was then $8,586.96. Excavation for 32,555½ cubic yards was contracted at for at 45 cents per cubic yard ($14,739.90) but witnesses put the reasonable cost at 20 cents per cubic yard, or $6,501.10. The contract price for a 36,602 cubic yard embankment was $20,133.85 while witnesses put that work at $7,320.40. Additional work of sodding, paving with cinders, cisterns, fascines, gabions, subcontracted work for drains and iron works, and five flag staffs amounted to $298,326.78 when the whole job could have done for $59,456.27 at current St. Louis prices.

Army Regulations Section 1053 required "rigid economy in the expenditure of public money." The government alleged fraud based on the principle that "such as no man in his senses and not under any delusion would make on the one hand, and no honest or fair man would accept on the other, and of such unconscionable bargains even the common law has taken action."

Beard's defense stated he was required to complete the work in five days and keep the workers going around the clock. That did not impress the court:

"The proofs in this case show that the prices agreed to be paid for this work are grossly exorbitant. The judgment of the court is that the petition be dismissed and that the defendants go thereof without delay."

Beard was literally thrown out of court verbally.

Beasley, George W. Owned a blacksmith shop in La Grange, Tennessee. Army troops were in La Grange when Confederate forces attacked Davis's Mills. In order to protect themselves the Army troops tore down George's shop, destroyed his tools in the process, and carried off 50 cords of wood to build defensive breastworks.

The Southern Claims Commission stated, "when buildings are torn down, if the materials are used to erect other buildings for the use of the Army, such materials become supplies, and their value as materials for the purpose for which they are used is paid to the owner."

George appealed to the House War Claims Committee and his claim was referred to the Court of Claims under the Bowman Act of March 3, 1883.

Section 3 of the Act stated:

"The jurisdiction of said court shall not extend to or include any claim against the United States growing out of the destruction or damage to property by the Army and Navy during the war for the suppression of the rebellion, or the use and occupation of real estate by any part of the military or naval forces during said war at the seat of war."

George's petition was dismissed on April 5, 1886 for lack of jurisdiction.

Beaumont, Imogene A. R. P. Walt and A. M. Boyd purchased a 28 × 140 foot lot on the east side of Water Street in Memphis in 1860. On June 25, 1864 the U.S. Direct Tax Commission sold the lot, designated No. 118, for nonpayment of taxes. The highest bidder was Renel Hough at $255 and he was given certificate No. 1076. Hough was buying a large number of lots for himself and others. The tax owed was $7 plus a $3 penalty, costs, $2, and interest of $1.39 leaving a surplus of $241.11 which was deposited into the Treasury.

A dispute arose and Boyd & Walt continued to hold the property.

On June 2, 1865 Boyd & Walt filed suit in the Shelby County Chancery Court against C. H. Adams, Renel Hough, Imogene De Loach, administratrix of Claiborne De Loach's estate, and Guila De Loach to recover their property. On April 1, 1870 the court held that the certificate was the property of Claiborne De Loach's estate.

On December 31, 1873 Effie, Deborah, Guila, and Thomas De Loach's guardian, Thomas H. Allen, sued William T. Avery, T.

Graves, Amos Woodruff, R. C. Daniel, and Andrew Tafft in the 2nd Circuit Court of Shelby County to recover possession of the lot.

On July 8, 1874 the Shelby County Chancery Court held the purchase certificate to be void and on April 23, 1875 the 2nd Circuit Court of Shelby County decided in favor of the defendants.

Imogene Beaumont then applied to the Secretary of the Treasury on October 8, 1882 for a refund of the purchase money paid by Renel Hough. Boyd & Walt also filed a claim on November 25. Imogene claimed Hough and his assigns had been evicted. Secretary of the Treasury Hugh McCulloch rejected her claim on June 6, 1884 on the ground that the owners had not been evicted in a federal court. Boyd & Walt's claim was not allowed since they could not show they lost the property through the sale since they retained possession of the property, which was not a formal rejection.

Imogene Beaumont and Boyd & Walt sued in federal court. The court stated:

"It is now nearly thirty years since the lot was sold, yet Boyd & Walt, during all this time, have not only retained the possession of it, but have twice vindicated their right so to do in the courts of Tennessee.

"We know of no law by which they can be permitted to hold both the land and the purchase money."

"They [Hough] paid the purchase money to the Government, and have since been to much trouble and expense in unsuccessful efforts to obtain possession of the land. They have, however, no legal claim against the defendants unless it has been conferred by statute."

Both petitions were dismissed on May 19, 1890.

Beckwith, Edward G. An acting chief commissary at headquarters near Catlett's Station, Virginia. He had a field desk, iron safe, books, vouchers, and $778 in cash on board a train. On August 23, 1862 the train was raided and all of Beckwith's money and supplies were taken. A witness stated that "all broke for the woods" when the rebels appeared. Beckwith was charged for the loss. He sued and recovered the amount in 1866.

Belle Peoria. Captain William H. Reid was part owner of the sidewheel steamer *Belle Peoria* that had been in military service during the war. On June 1, 1865 she was at St. Louis when assistant quartermaster Colonel L. S. Metcalf ordered Reid to take a cargo of army stores to Fort Berthold, 1,700 miles up the Missouri River. Reid refused to comply due to the "lateness of the season." Metcalf told him his boat would be seized and loaded with the supplies anyway at a charter rate of $272 a day. Reid took aboard the supplies, under formal protest to protect his insurance interests, and they departed on June 3. The trip was uneventful, they reached Fort Berthold on July 22, and departed for St. Louis on the 24th.

The weather turned nasty on the 26th after traveling about 250 miles and the boat was blown aground in gale force winds while trying to make a landing. A one-week effort to refloat the vessel was unsuccessful, the river level was falling, so her master decided to leave the boat until next spring. The crew left on the 31st except for one mate, an engineer, and three watchmen. The departing crew reached St. Louis on August 10. The remainder of the crew left on September 10th and reached St. Louis on the 30th. The commander of Fort Rice also detached a detail to stand guard over the vessel.

The cost to Reid for wages and expenses during the time the skeleton crew was aboard was $101 a day.

Reid sent a salvage crew from St. Louis on April 3, 1866. On or about the 15th a spring freshet loosened tons of ice that broke up. The steamer was struck, carried away, and she was totally destroyed. The salvage crew arrived at the spot the boat had been on the 18th and saw no sign of her. They returned to St. Louis on June 3. It took them 15 days to get to the scene and 45 days to get back.

The charter rate was paid and the Army paid $80 a day up to the date the boat was destroyed and $30,000 for the value of the boat and also the $172 charter rate up to August 10. From August 11 until September 30 the rate was lowered to $101 a day. Reid filed a claim for $80 a day demurrage from October 1, 1865 to April 15, 1866. This total, $15,760, was disallowed. Reid sued in federal court for the demurrage and also for $5,041.41 for the salvage party. His petition for demurrage was dismissed since the delay in getting back to St. Louis was caused by the weather and not by any terms of the charter party. The court found the charges made by the salvage crew excessive and unreasonable and awarded Reid $2,500 in December 1868.

Belt, S. Sprigg. Administrator of the estate of a property owner whose standing timber was taken to fortify Fort Kearny in 1864. Kearny wasn't really a fort then; it was merely a station. Sprigg filed a claim for 2,680 cords of wood. Quartermaster General Meigs allowed three-fourths of that to be charged to his department: 2,010 cords at $1 per cord and 38 cords of fencing at $3 a cord for another $114.60.

On April 23, 1873 the estate accepted $2,010 from the Third Auditor for the Quartermaster Department wood and the claim for the remaining one-fourth, 670 cords, was referred to the Chief of Engineers. The Chief refused the claim on June 20, 1878 on the ground that "there is no authority of law for the payment of this and similar claims for injuries committed or materials taken to be used in the construction of defenses during the late war."

On September 17 the Third Auditor allowed a payment of $670 at $1 a cord from the "contingencies of fortifications" fund, which Sprigg accepted, but he felt $3 a cord was owed and sued to recover. The petition was dismissed on May 28, 1888 since the estate accepted the payment without protest.

Benton, Warren M. Warren and Mary Benton lived in Lexington, Kentucky but raised cotton with a number of slaves on two plantations in Carroll Parish, Louisiana. Warren lived on the Woodstock plantation on the Mississippi River about six miles below Lake Providence during most of the war. The other farm was the Pin-Hook place on Bayou Mason, also seven or eight miles from the Mississippi west of Lake Providence. Mary apparently visited Warren only once during the war.

Rebels burned a number of bales at Woodstock in 1861 on General Beauregard's order and some of the 1862 crop was burned but 171 bales had been hidden in two lots in the woods in back of the property, 96 from Pin-Hook and 75 from Woodstock.

In February 1863 Union troops encamped at Lake Providence and on the 20th an order was issued to gather up all the cotton in the area. Benton's was "pointed out," seized, and shipped to Memphis.

He filed suit on April 24, 1868 for the 171 bales and was described as "an old man of sixty-seven years." The Benton's claimed the cotton was their jointly held property but before the trial, Mary's name was removed as a claimant.

As Warren had discouraged his relatives from joining the rebel forces and gave valuable information to the Army he was awarded $36,965.07.

Bernheimer Brothers. A New York firm who employed Joseph Lippman, "a wealthy and respectable merchant in the city of Savannah" to collect their debts in Georgia, North Carolina, Florida, and Alabama.

Lippman came to New York in February 1861 to make his annual spring buys and told Isaac Bernheimer the situation looked pretty gloomy in Savannah but hoped things would blow over by the time he got back. In case they did not, the Brothers gave Lippman the power to act in their best interests as circumstances allowed.

Bernheimer Brothers was owed $300,000 by debtors in the South when the war began. Debtors in Lippman's territory owed $101,283.94. He managed to collect about $30,000 in debts before a law was passed requiring all monies owed to northern firms be paid into the Confederate treasury.

Lippman bought 720 bales of cotton stored in Edward C. Wade's warehouse and 300 bales stored in William P. Yonge's Savannah warehouse. During the second night of the capture of Savannah a fire in Wade's warehouse destroyed 236 bales and 57 bales were stolen from Yonge's warehouse when it was broken into the night Sherman entered the city.

The Army seized 465 bales from Wade and 247 from Yonge and other lots stored elsewhere for a total of 936. The Bernheimers sued and recovered $220.66 a bale on 529 bales of sea-island and $167.52 a bale on 407 bales of upland cotton for a total of $184,909.78.

Bestor, George C. A Mound City, Illinois shipbuilder who signed a $186,000 contract on May 14, 1862 to build the 180-foot, Ericsson designed, single-turret river monitor *Ozark*. The contract specified, in part:

"That the party of the first part do hereby contract and agree ... to build equip, and fit the hull, steam machinery, and all appurtenances, coal bunkers, instruments and tools, awnings, boats, anchors, cables, hawsers, casks, furniture, cooking utensils, and all the equipments and outfits connected therewith, necessary for an iron-plated screw-propeller gunboat, the load-draught of water of which is not to exceed four feet nine inches from the bottom of the keel when ready, in all respects, for service, having on

board an armament consisting of two eleven-inch guns and all her equipments, a compliment of 120 souls and all their effects, provisions and stores for 20 days, for which convenient storage shall have been provided, and 100 tons of coal in bunker. The said iron-clad gunboat to be delivered at Cairo, Illinois, at the expense of the party of the first part.

"It is further agreed by the said parties of the first part, that the vessel, perfectly fitted with all the machinery, equipments, and outfits of every kind complete, which this contract covers and is intended to cover, shall be delivered to the Navy Department, ready for naval cruising, (excepting only the armament, stores, provisions, and fuel for steam machinery, not provided for in this contract,) on or before the period of 150 days from the date of this contract — that is, the 11th day of October, 1862.

"And it is further agreed and mutually understood, that if the vessel's draught of water exceed four feet nine inches the United States shall have the option of wholly rejecting it, recovering from the said parties of the first part the sums which may have been paid under this contract, as hereinafter provided. And in case the speed of the vessel falls below nine miles in still water the said party of the second part is entitled to wholly reject the vessel, recovering from the said parties of the first part the amount of money that may have been paid, as hereinafter stipulated, and in like manner for any other default.

"A successful and satisfactory operation of every part of the machinery and appurtenances during a trial of 72 consecutive hours, under steam of the maximum pressure that the boilers can be made to furnish, not exceeding 140 pounds per square inch above the atmosphere, during which time the lubrication is to be thorough and easy, the journals free from working or motion on their fastenings, and the whole performance of such a character as to demonstrate the satisfactory strength, reliability, and practical efficiency and durability of the entire machinery. The said trial trip to be made at the expense of the said party of the second part."

Construction was supervised by Commodore John B. Hull. On January 9, 1863 the Navy Department directed Hull to install the "Whittaker apparatus for submarine firing" on the monitor at a cost not to exceed $5,000. She was still on the ways when work began to prepare the hull by putting in heavier timbers. As the work progressed it became obvious to Bestor and Hull that the alterations would upset the trim of the vessel and impair its efficiency. On the 20th the Department ordered work stopped, on February 10 word was received to forego installing it altogether, and the next day Hull was ordered to complete the vessel as fast as possible according to the original plans.

The ship was launched on the 18th but during her trial run she experienced vibration. The Department ordered further strengthening which added 50 tons to her displacement but slowed her. This was overcome by adding two additional boilers to make up for the loss of speed.

Trials were conducted and the boat was accepted even though her maximum speed was only 2½ knots. Bestor was paid the $189,000 contract price along with an additional $20,053.85 for extra materials and labor. He claimed he spent $31,400 for extra work and was owed an additional $3,437.46 for alterations plus his costs for the use of the ways during an extra 34 days at $100 a day which came to $3,400. His filed claim for damages of $16,537.45, which the Navy Department disallowed.

The itemization of charges listed the following:

Two additional boilers and appurtenances	$7,000.00
Blower engine, blower and pipe	2,100.00
One clock	15.00
Two thermometers and slate	7.50
Tackle for hoisting ashes	59.63
Extra steam gauge and pipe	54.94
Syphon pumps	523.52
One steam signal whistle	35.00
Engineer's lockers and drawers	49.19
Bench for large vise	47.50
Two wrought-iron lead ladles	11.00
Rachet drill brace	35.00
Crab for drill brace	85.00
Sixteen drills	24.00
Five tap wrenches	25.00
Six extra gauge cocks	75.00
Four pairs gas tongs	20.00
Bleeders to heaters and steam gauge	278.73
Enlargement of escape pipe from 6½ to 8 inches	375.00
Extra feed-water heater	277.75
Extra wood for cog wheels	15.00
Turret awning	275.00
Putting in extra timbers under transverse keelson to support turret machinery, not on Captain Ericsson's plan	71.00
Stanchions and fore and aft pieces and keelsons to strengthen floor of ship under engine frame	284.50

Changing bulkheads on account of change in cabin plans	340.00
Putting in athwart-ship hog chains	670.00

He went to court and it was noted by Bestor's counsel that "this class of vessels at that time was a new institution in this country, and, in fact new to the world, it was found necessary, or at least advisable, to make, during its construction, certain changes and alterations."

The court awarded Bestor $6,000 for the two boilers and $2,000 for 20 days' delay on the ways.

The *Ozark* was commissioned on February 18, 1864, exactly one year after launching, under Acting Volunteer Lieutenant George W. Brown. From March 12 to May 22 she took part in the Red River expedition to Alexandria, Louisiana. She was decommissioned at Mound City on July 24, 1865 and sold for scrap.

Blakeley, Thomas M. A resident of Davis County, Missouri who obtained a permit from Major General Ulysses S. Grant on March 25, 1863 to purchase 71 bales of cotton picked, ginned, and baled on William R. Harris's Madison Parish, Louisiana plantation on whatever the terms the two chose. Blakeley was to pay for all the work necessary to ready the cotton for market and the two would split the total amount of cotton 50/50.

This was done but on July 2 the cotton was seized by Treasury agents and sold by William P. Mellen. Blakeley sued. The government argued that Grant had no authority to issue the permit and the purpose of Congress in passing the abandoned or captured property act was to remove the military from the problem and turn it over to the Treasury Department and that Blakeley never owned it by title.

Blakeley argued he had a contract with Harris, the cotton was not abandoned property, he was a loyal citizen, and the agents had no right to seize it as captured from a hostile citizen of an insurrectionary district.

Blakeley's petition was dismissed on the ground that Grant's permit was not valid under the Act of July 13, 1861.

Blewett, Thomas G. Sued to recover captured cotton but two bills of sale to the Confederate government with his signature were found in the Confederate archives. Blewett objected to the evidence as a "mere comparison." His petition was dismissed.

Bliss, Calvin C. Albert Pike and Thomas

W. Newton owned the Odd Fellows Hall and State Bank properties in Little Rock, Arkansas. Pike and Newton joined the Confederate service and their property was subsequently seized under the Confiscation Act of August 6, 1861, condemned in the U.S. District Court for Arkansas, and sold to Calvin Bliss. The Act of June 6, 1862 imposed a U.S. direct tax on the property, which Bliss claimed he was made unaware of due to bureaucratic error, and the tax went unpaid.

The Direct Tax Commission condemned the property for back taxes in 1865 and sold it on May 4 to Bliss. On August 23, 1866 Bliss conveyed his interest in the property by quitclaim deed to Charles K. Thayer.

In 1868, John Wassel filed suit in circuit court against Thayer claiming he had acquired an interest in the land through legal proceedings against Albert Pike. While the suit was pending Thayer transferred his title by quitclaim to Ellen C. Brown. In March 1871 she did the same and Andrews & Yenley became the owners.

In April 1871 all the parties involved in Wassel's suit, including Bliss, agreed to resolve the dispute in favor of Pike. Others involved were Washington L. Schenck, John Mills, and Gordon W. Peay.

Bliss sued the United States but his petition was dismissed on June 27, 1892 on the ground Bliss did not protect his claim in circuit court:

"The decree indicates a want of proper diligence upon the part of the claimant. While the courts had made a decision, which in effect, might invalidate the action of the commissioners in the levy of the tax, admissions are made in the decree, which in law invalidate it as a decree binding on the defendants."

Block, Joseph. A French citizen residing in Opelousas, Louisiana who came to the United States in 1854. He owned 153 bales of cotton, 27 large boxes of tobacco weighing 2,779 pounds, and 36 small boxes of tobacco weighing 580 pounds. The town constable, John Cochran, ordered all cotton moved out of town and onto nearby plantations to protect the town.

The lot was seized by the 133d New York Volunteers during General Banks's approach to Port Hudson in May 1863. The tobacco was seized by Major L. E. Carpenter on April 21 for issue to the troops. None of the tobacco was sold and the proceeds from only 119 bales of cotton were deposited into the Treasury. He was awarded $22,848 at $192 a bale.

Block, Joseph. A resident of New Orleans who applied to the Treasury Department for permission to remove 250 bales of cotton from the west bank of the Mississippi River in St. Landry Parish. He got the permit on September 16, 1864 and went to get his cotton but during the process it was seized by the Army. The officer disregarded his permit and it was sent to New Orleans. Block protested but the Treasury agent refused to act until December. On the 24th the agent demanded Block sell the cotton to him at ¾ the appraised market value according to Treasury Department regulations pursuant to the Act of July 2, 1864. Block sold it for $43,690.07. The agent then resold it back to Block for $58,253.42 and the difference of $14,563.35 was paid to the agent. Block was also required to pay a cotton tax of 2 cents a pound, which came to $1,596.86; a 4 cents a pound fee for the permit, $3,191.72; and $48.60 in incidental expenses. The total of $19,399.33 was paid into the Treasury.

Block sued claiming duress but his petition was dismissed.

Blount, Edward A. Blount was the administrator of the estate of Joseph T. Baker of New York who had a contract to carry mail between San Augustine and Marshall, Texas. Baker ceased carrying mail after Texas seceded on February 1, 1861 and was owed $965.43. He evaded military service until 1863 when he enlisted as a private in the Confederate army and in early 1864 he was killed in battle. Blount sued to recover the money.

The Confederate government took over postal services on June 1, 1861. A Confederate act of August 30, 1861 directed postmasters to collect "all monies due and not paid over" from U.S. postmasters. The money was put into a fund to pay the pro rata payments on claims for postal service performed by those who were owed money by the U.S. postal service. Claimants were given six months to file and another act passed on September 27, 1862 directed Postmaster General John H. Reagan to pay the claims of mail carriers loyal to the Confederacy. A total of $502,017.19 was paid out before September 30, 1863 but no records were available to the court to show who was paid.

Blount recovered the money on April 12, 1886.

Board of Field Officers of the Fourth Brigade of South Carolina Volunteer State Troops. The Board of Field Officers of the Fourth Brigade of South Carolina Militia was a perpetual corporation created by the State of South Carolina in 1809 to purchase and hold up to 300 acres in St. Philip and St. Michael's Parishes for the use of the militia. On May 25, 1835 the Board purchased land and buildings in Charleston on Citadel Green, known as the Picquet-Guard-House. On August 1, 1856 another parcel in Charleston with the Boylston House was purchased.

When the war began the corporation members "actively engaged in the rebellion" and the Confederate government occupied the land and buildings until the city was captured in February 1865.

The Army took possession then released the property to the Bureau of Refugees, Freedmen, and Abandoned Lands. In October the Bureau turned the property over to the City of Charleston and it was returned to the corporation.

On August 20, 1867 the Army again took possession of the property, holding the Picquet-Guard-House until November 1, 1874 and the Boylston House until April 1, 1879. The government rented the Boylston House from the City of Charleston for $92 a month and the Picquet-Guard-House for $50 a month up to July 1, 1868. The rates were reasonable but no lease was executed and no rent money was paid after that.

On June 8, 1877 the State created another corporation, the Board of Field Officers of the Fourth Brigade of South Carolina Volunteer State Troops, with "all the rights, franchises, and property" of the previous Board. The new Board sued for back rent on July 21, 1880. Rent owed prior to July 21, 1874 was forfeited by the statute of limitations. On January 12, 1885 the Board recovered $166.12 for 3 months and 10 days for the Picquet-Guard-House, and $5,181.67 for 4 years, 8 months, and 10 days' rent for the Boylston House.

Bogert, David A. On April 23, 1864 Bogert's New York agent, B. F. Small & Co., signed an agreement with Assistant Quartermaster Captain Francis J. Crilly to charter his schooner *Haxall*. The war risk insurance would be borne by the Army and the marine risk insurance by Bogert. The vessel was inspected a value of $14,000 was agreed on. The charter stated the vessel would be "employed in such service as the party of the second part may direct."

Another provision stated:

"Should she be retained so long in the service of the United States that the money paid and due on account of said charter (deducting therefrom the actual cost of running and keeping in repairs the said vessel during the said time, together with a net profit of 25 percent, per annum, on said appraised value) shall be equal to the said appraised value, then the said vessel shall become the property of the United States without further payment, except such sum as may be then due on account of the services of the said vessel rendered under said charter."

The government also had the right to purchase the ship at any time prior to the rental amount reaching $14,000.

The schooner was ordered to the James River at a point below Richmond, Virginia. On June 15 Major General Benjamin F. Butler, commander of the Department of the James, was ordered by Lieutenant General Grant, "commanding all the armies of the United States," to sink vessels at Trent's Reach to block the channel to enemy vessels. The Navy loaded six sailing vessels, including the *Haxall*, and eight canal boats with sand, coarse gravel, and stone and sank them in the channel. Lieutenant R. H. Lamson, Commander, Torpedo and Picket Division, reported to Rear-Admiral S. P. Lee, Commander, North Atlantic Blockading Squadron, that the *Haxall* was sunk by making six holes on her port side opposite the mainmast and one hole on the opposite side.

Bogert appealed to Stewart Van Vliet, quartermaster in New York, for compensation and an amount of $13,717.84 was agreed upon. Bogert then presented the charter-party agreement and certificate of destruction to the Third Auditor, and claimed $13,717.84 due on the charter up to the time of sinking but the Auditor allowed only $10,000. Bogert sued for $3,717.84 and stated in court:

"I came first with the accounts to General Van Vliet, quartermaster in this city. There the accounts were all made out and sent to the Third Auditor in Washington. I heard nothing of it for some time and then I went to Washington and saw the Auditor and asked about the matter. He sent me, I think, to the chief clerk who told me he could not attend to it as presented. I then corresponded with the Third Auditor who requested me to send papers and documents, which I did. He then sent me a draft for $10,000."

The government argued that the sum awarded by the Third Auditor, and accepted by the plaintiff, was a "judgment on record" and unreviewable.

The court responded:

"If this be so, then the government is not bound by the contract; and if the United States is not bound by the contract, neither is the claimant, and thus, notwithstanding, a plain and clear agreement as to the value, the whole matter is left open for inquiry upon both sides, and neither party is bound.

"Again, the Third Auditor is not a judicial officer of the government of the United States. His estimates of value, &c., are not judgments on record. Section I, article III, Constitution."

The court held the case was not a "taking" of private property for public use or an "appropriation" by the military, nor could Bogert collect on the war risk insurance. He had accepted the $10,000 and by so doing essentially "abandoned his contract" and could not then come into court and sue for compensation under any provision of the contract, although one judge believed it was a taking.

Bowen, Charles. Bowen was mustered into the Regular Army's Third Regiment on March 9, 1861 and was honorably discharged on March 9, 1864. During that time, $1.57 was deducted from his pay at the rate of 12½ cents per month for the Soldiers' Home in Washington, D.C. Volunteers could have the contribution deducted only with their consent. Those who contributed during their service were allowed admission without surrendering their pension but those who did not contribute could be admitted only by surrendering their pension to the Home.

On March 13, 1865 he was granted an invalid pension at $8 a month, Certificate No. 39050. The pension was increased to $15 a month on January 21, 1867 to begin June 6, 1866, and to $18 a month on July 8, 1876 to begin June 4, 1872.

Admission to the Home was in descending order: "every soldier who served 20 years; every soldier or discharged soldier, regular or volunteer, rendered incapacitated by disease or wounds while in the service; and invalid and disabled veterans of the War of 1812 or subsequent wars, excluding convicts and other unworthy persons."

On September 13, 1876 he was admitted to the Soldiers' Home. The total pension money paid to him was $264.60 but after admission his money was deposited in the Home's account. He

sued to recover the money. Bowen retained his pension on a split decision due to ambiguous language changes by Congress in the statutes.

Bowley, Joshua E. Bowley's steamer *George Shattuck* was chartered by the Navy on December 5, 1864 at $350 a day to haul supplies from Boston to Fortress Monroe. She left her berth at the Eastern Avenue wharf and proceeded to the Charlestown Navy Yard to load supplies and have a bilge pump installed. She left on the evening of the 7th for New York then to Philadelphia, Fortress Monroe, Norfolk, Virginia, Beaufort, North Carolina, Fort Fisher, then back to Fortress Monroe where she got enough coal to get to New York. She arrived at New York on Monday, January 2. She could not get coal until late Tuesday and loading after dark by lamplight. She left Wednesday morning for Boston but ran into heavy weather from the northeast in Long Island Sound. The steamer managed to make New Haven Harbor in heavy seas, snow, and gale force winds. Her anchors barely held but by morning the weather had moderated enough to continue. When she backed down to get her bow around, the propeller fell off. A tow arrived and she was run aground at high tide so work could be done at low tide. This was only possible for about an hour at a time but by Sunday night she was ready to sail. She left the next morning, arrived at Boston Tuesday afternoon, and was discharged from naval service on the afternoon of January 10, 1865.

Her total charter time was 37 days but Bowley was paid for 31 days on the ground that no delay in getting back to Boston was caused by "any person acting under the authority of the Navy Department" and that 31 days was enough time for a voyage from Boston to Fortress Monroe and back. The Navy also said that since the charter agreement wasn't signed until December 6 the payments should start on that date and besides that Bowley got a bilge pump out of the deal.

Bowley sued and was awarded $2,100 for six days' service.

Bowman, Joseph. Enlisted in the 12th Tennessee Volunteers on September 24, 1863 for three years and was mustered out with the regiment on September 5, 1865. On September 16, 1871 he sued to recover mustering out pay and $100 enlistment bonus under the Act of July 28, 1866. These were disallowed at the time on a charge of desertion.

On November 1, 1863 he left on a "verbal furlough" and according to the prosecutor, "remained at home about his own business, having a comfortable time among his friends during almost the his whole enlistment, doing no services for the Government." Soldiers served under contract and under the regulations he was required to report for duty every 30 days to have his leave extended or revoked so his petition was dismissed pursuant to Section 12 of the Act of July 28, 1866.

Boyd, Thomas B. Enrolled at a general rendezvous on October 15, 1861 as second lieutenant in Company A, 25th Regiment Kentucky Volunteer Infantry. He was not mustered in until November 13 and up to that date was paid $105.50 by the State of Kentucky. The State was reimbursed by the United States. Boyd was never paid by the United States and he subsequently filed a claim for the same amount. His suit for double pay was dismissed on May 21, 1906.

Brady, Samuel P. Brady furnished supplies ordered by General McKinstry and Captain W. G. Rankin for troops forming at St. Louis. Brady's bills were held up by the Holt-Davis-Campbell Commission and $14,200 was withheld from payment. Brady sued and recovered the full amount.

Bramhall, Moses B. Moses was a New York merchant who hired Hill Gowdy in 1858 to buy cotton for him in the South. If Gowdy had purchased cotton in Bramhall's name during the war it would have been seized by rebels. On December 27, 1864 Gowdy notified Bramhall that 72 bales were ready to ship when in fact they had been seized at Savannah by the Army on the 21st. Bramhall's petition to recover was dismissed on the ground that he was not the legal owner.

Brand, Anselm P. The city of Altona, New York issued bonds to pay enlistment bounties of volunteers in response to President Lincoln's July 1864 call for a quota of volunteers.

The city supervisor turned three blank bonds intended for George Brimble over to Isaac G. Bates, who was assisting with recruiting. Bates delivered the blank bonds to George Clendon, acting provost marshal for the 16th Congressional district at Plattsburg for delivery to Brimble as Brimble had already been sworn in. It was intended to deliver them to him when he returned but he never reported for duty, probably had no knowledge of the bonds, and was

subsequently declared a deserter. Some unauthorized person then filled out the amounts making two $100 and one $400 bond dated September 20, 1864, payable on March 1, 1865 to George Brimble or the bearer. These bonds were found by Clenden's successor, Andrew J. Cheritree, on January 11, 1865. Cheritree contacted the War Department for instructions and was told they were the property of a deserter and should be sold at auction and the proceeds turned over to Captain C. H. Corning. Anselm Brand bought the bonds for $373 and the money deposited into the Treasury to the credit of the deserter's fund.

Brand attempted to cash in the bonds but was told the bonds were never delivered to Brimble and were worthless and the government never held title to them. He sued and recovered on the ground that he bought them in good faith under the authority of the government.

Brandeis, Adolphus. On December 31, 1864 Brandeis and his partner, Crawford, merchants in St. Louis, offered to sell the Army 150,000 bushels of corn during January and February 1865 at Cairo, Illinois at $1.55 a bushel and 150,000 bushels along the lower Ohio River at $1.58 a bushel. The corn had been purchased from George M. Hord & Company of Chicago. The offer was accepted by Captain David O. De Wolf, assistant quartermaster at Louisville, on condition that "no purchases are to be made on the line of the Illinois Central Railroad, as an arrangement has been made with Colonel William Myers, chief quartermaster at St. Louis, that he shall have exclusive control of operations along said railroad line."

De Wolf had been informed that 140,000 bushels of the corn had been purchased adjacent to the Illinois Central and had arranged for its transportation. All of the Ohio River corn was delivered but only part of the Cairo-bound corn could be delivered owing to the Illinois Central being at capacity delivering military supplies and equipment under military control. De Wolf agreed to accept the corn along the lower Ohio at $1.55, three cents less per bushel than the agreed $1.58. De Wolf later denied that Brandeis made that offer and on April 11, 1865 he informed the merchants that no more corn would be accepted as of the 10th. On May 1, they were informed that 12 cars of corn could not be accepted at Cairo owing to capacity of storage.

The corn was stored along the lower Ohio

and repeated pleadings gained an acceptance of 17,000 bushels. A residue of 39,277 bushels were left undelivered and the partners were obliged to sell it at 80 cents a bushel less than the contract price.

The court determined the price of corn was 70 to 80 cents a bushel at the time so the partners were awarded $29,420.25 at 75 cents a bushel.

Brewington, Sarah E. The remarried

widow of Colonel Leonidas Metcalf, commander of the 7th Kentucky Cavalry. President Lincoln ordered the regiment mustered for service at Paris, Kentucky on August 16, 1862, the "commencement of first payment, by time" but Metcalf was never officially mustered, only "joined for service and enrolled."

On August 23 the regiment participated in the battle of Big Hill near Richmond, Kentucky in which the major of the regiment was killed and Metcalf and his lieutenant colonel were captured as prisoners of war.

On August 30 the governor of Kentucky relieved Metcalf of his command and the War Department refused to recognize him as a member of the U.S. military on the ground that "a legal vacancy for a colonel did not exist in the Seventh Kentucky Cavalry Volunteers on August 14, 1862, the date from which Leonidas Metcalf was to take rank under the terms of his commission as such, for the reason that the regiment had not been recruited to the minimum number required by law and the regulations of the War Department to entitle it to an officer of that grade and had not been assigned to active duty in the field."

Sarah sued to recover his pay from August 16 to August 30. On April 11, 1904 she was awarded $83.80.

Briggs, James A. Charles S. Morehead,

an ex-governor of Mississippi, owned two plantations in Washington County, Mississippi. He was practicing law in Louisville, Kentucky with Charles M. Briggs when the war started. Morehead was at his plantations in the late spring or early summer of 1861 and when the war began he left one of the plantations in charge of his son Craig and the other under another manager.

After he returned home, Morehead was arrested "because of his sympathy with the Confederate cause" and confined at Fort Warren. He was released in February 1862 after he took an oath of allegiance.

In April he wrote a note to Briggs:

For and in consideration of money loaned and advanced heretofore by Mr. C. M. Briggs, and further valuable consideration by way of suretyship for me by said Briggs, I hereby sell and transfer to said C. M. Briggs all of the cotton on my two plantations in Mississippi near Egg's Point and Greenville. Said cotton, so sold, embraces all that I have, baled and unbaled, gathered and ungathered. This is intended to cover all cotton that I have now or may have this year on said two plantations, supposed to be about 2,000 bales.

C. S. Morehead

April 18, 1862

When the note was written there was no cotton on the plantations. The cotton was marketed by his son who had sold the 1861 crop to the Confederate government, but Morehead apparently gave no specific directions to his son. The 1862 crop was also sold to the Confederate government and in December 1862 or January 1863, 455 bales were brought to Wilson's Barn, a storage site for cotton sold to the Confederate government. It was marked "C.S.A." to keep it from being burned by rebel soldiers.

The cotton was assigned to Briggs for the repayment of debts but the exact amount of money Morehead owed Briggs was unknown as he more or less continually borrowed money from Briggs. It was known that Briggs paid from $8,000 to $10,000 in bank debt for Morehead and that he had collected a $5,000 legal fee belonging to Briggs.

In March 1863, 380 bales of Morehead's cotton was seized by Captain E. D. Osband on orders of General Grant and taken to Worthington's Landing on the Mississippi River where it was added to seized lots of cotton from other plantations. A lot of 2,180 bales was shipped to Memphis on the steamer *Empress*. It was rebaled to 2,111 bales and sold by Captain G. L. Fort. The net proceeds of $422,125.70 were turned over to the Quartermaster's Department. Of this, $91,000 was the proceeds from Morehead's cotton.

The owner's of the other cotton were Sam Worthington, W. W. Worthington, Evelina M. Hammett, Nannette Sweitzer, and Robert M. and Stephen A. Douglas.

In the late 1880s the executor of Charles Briggs's estate, James A. Briggs, filed suit to recover the proceeds from the sale of the cotton. The question for the court was whether two citizens of Kentucky could make a contract with respect to personal property located in hostile territory. On February 3, 1890 the court decided Morehead had no title to the cotton after seizure by the United States, Briggs could not be assigned title, and the petition was dismissed:

"The transactions of Morehead & Briggs were not only prohibited by the non-intercourse act, but by reason of the peculiar character of the subject-matter of the contract —cotton— and its production and situation within enemy territory were illegal as against public policy, and in violation of the obligation of all citizens not to do any act through which the enemy may obtain power, assistance, or advantage.

"Had Morehead owned a manufacturing establishment in disloyal territory at the breakout of the war, he might have continued the manufacture of arms and ammunition, and have contracted for the sale of the future production with as much legality as to have raised cotton on his plantations in disloyal territory, where it was subject to taxation for continuing the war, as well as all the laws of the Confederacy, and was within the grasp of Confederate authority to take and use for hostile purposes."

Briggs appealed to the Supreme Court where the decision was reversed on the ground that the sale and transaction were valid in law.

Brooke, Francis J. A Philadelphia resident who sent his agent on February 9, 1863 to purchase five boxes of quinine, morphine, gum opium, and nitrate of silver for $2,272 including commissions and shipping from Washington, D.C. druggist Joseph W. Nairn. The goods were delivered to Brooke in Philadelphia and left on the pavement near his store. Brooke paid for them and took possession of them.

Brooke was then arrested on order of Colonel Baker, War Department provost marshal, and taken in custody to the central guard house in Washington and from there to Carroll Prison where he remained until May 13 when he was released on taking the oath of allegiance. His goods had been seized and turned over to Henry Johnson, the U.S. Medical Department purveyor, and their return to Brooke was refused.

Brooke sued and recovered $2,008.72, the sum of receipts he could furnish.

Brown, Albert. A resident of Kingston, New Hampshire who signed a contract with Major Morris S. Miller on July 1, 1861 at Portland, Maine for 106 mule wagons at $141 each, delivered to Perryville, Maryland. Forty were to be completed by July 31 and 60 on August 31. Brown completed and delivered 100 but the remaining wagons were refused.

All the wagons were to be inspected from time to time as the work progressed and no painting was to be done until after inspection. The wagons were inspected at the plant, approved and shipped, but a second inspection was done at Perryville which apparently found deficiencies.

He sued for $14,100 and recovered on the ground that no second inspection was required.

Brown, Elias. Elias and his brother were conscripted into Confederate service but bought their way out with substitutes and by bribing officials. They also aided others in avoiding and escaping service. They owned 52 bales of upland cotton worth $18,138.83 that was seized at Savannah in 1864 and they were awarded $190.47 per bale or $9,904.44.

The Secretary of the Treasury paid only $9,181.12 based on his own calculations and interpretation of the Act of March 12, 1863. The brothers went back to court and got the additional $723.32 in 1870.

Brown, Ferdinand. A subject of the Kingdom of Hanover who owned 12 bales of upland and one 110-pound pocket of sea-island cotton seized at Savannah on December 22, 1864. Recovered $2,219.86.

Brown, Maria V. The Turnpike Road Company owned a toll road in Virginia connecting the south end of Long Bridge, opposite Washington, with Alexandria. On May 21, 1861 the Army seized the city and county of Alexandria including the toll road. The tollgate was removed, the tollgate keeper sent home, and the road opened to free travel to anyone.

The company demanded the return of the road from the Secretary of War in 1862 and was refused. The Secretary wrote a note to President Lincoln:

This road is in a rebel State, and its use by the United States, which obtained possession of it only by force of arms and at the cost of the blood of loyal men, should not be controlled or interfered with by private interests or corporations; and that military possession of the road be retained, and that no tolls be paid for its use by the officers, soldiers, or teams of the United States.

On November 12, 1866 the road was returned to the company. Maria sought to recover the amount in tolls the company would have received had it not been seized. The petition was dismissed on May 28, 1894 as barred by the Bowman Act.

Bruning, John H. John was a subject of the King of Hanover living in Charleston. He exempted himself from Confederate service with protection from the Prussian embassy. He was reimbursed $1,968 for 15 bales of upland cotton.

Bryan, Oliver N. The tug *Keystone* and barge *Cookendorffer* left Washington with government cargo on January 10, 1862 for General Hooker's position on the Maryland side of the Potomac about 40 miles below Washington. Also on board were some private goods belonging to the officers and crewmen.

About 16 miles below Washington the barge was holed by ice and it began to sink. The tugboat pilot attempted to run the barge ashore but it sank in four or five feet about 80 yards from shore. The barge crew got aboard the tug and all returned to Washington to get assistance.

Oliver Bryan, a local farmer who lived nearby, supposed the barge and her cargo to be abandoned and preceded to unload the cargo into a scow with the help of his hired hands. The goods were stored in a large, unoccupied house on his property. Work lasted the entire day and as he continued the next day a government steamer arrived and her officers took charge of the barge. The rest of the cargo was put aboard the steamer and Bryan was ordered to bring back all the goods he had carried away. The barge was raised and repaired.

Bryan sued for salvage and the two parties' stories differed on only one point. The government said the barge's anchor was securely set so as to prevent it from drifting and to show it wasn't abandoned. Bryan maintained the barge was not secured at all.

The court ruled the barge was not abandoned and Bryan's petition was dismissed.

Bulkley, Henry S. Contracted on March 21, 1865 with Colonel J. A. Potter, quartermaster at Fort Leavenworth, Kansas to haul supplies. A board of survey examined all shipments upon arrival to examine the contents and condition of the goods. Bulkey received a voucher on which it was noted the money owed would be due on November 16, 1865. The amount was short $1,713.39 over a problem with goods delivered at Denver, Colorado and the Army's failure to examine the goods in a timely manner. Bulkley sued to recover but he waited until December 28, 1871 and was barred by the statute of limitations pursuant to the Act of March 12, 1863.

Bulwinkle, Herman. A loyal alien resident of Charleston who bought 29 bales of sea-

island and 14 bales of upland cotton seized on February 21, 1865. He became a citizen on January 20, 1868. The government argued he had no standing in court, bought the cotton from those aiding the rebellion, and took advantage of General Sherman's advance on the city to profit but he was awarded $7,408.96.

Burchiel, Abraham. A citizen of Humphrey County, Tennessee. Recovered $1,823.95 due on 3,608 railroad ties at 35 cents each; 1,425 ties at 25 cents; 831 ties at 30 cents; 45 picks, and 91 shovels for the construction of the Nashville & Northwestern Railroad in Tennessee.

Burge, Sarah M. Young Burge signed two contracts on April 24, 1858 to deliver mail: route No. 7407 between Brandon and Paulding, Mississippi commencing July 1 through June 30, 1862 for $1,779 a year, and route No. 7600 between Paulding and Trenton for $793 a year. Route 7407 was discontinued on March 31, 1861 and route 7600 on February 28, 1861. Burge was paid through September 30, 1860 by the United States. Young subsequently died and Sarah sued on March 30, 1882 to recover money owed under the Sundry Civil Appropriation Act of March 3, 1877 on the contract from September 30 to May 31, 1861.

It was established that Young never received any compensation from the Confederate government and the only question for the court under the Act was to determine the date Mississippi "engaged in war against the United States." The state voted to secede on January 9, 1861.

The courts held that Virginia was engaged in war under the Sundry Civil Appropriation Act as of April 17, 1861. Virginia voted to secede on the 16th. The governor of Virginia refused to supply troops from his state in response to President Lincoln's call for soldiers and ordered his military units to stand in readiness to oppose the laws of the United States by military force. The actual shooting had begun at Fort Sumpter in South Carolina on the 12th with President Lincoln's proclamation and call for troops. The Supreme Court cleared up the issue of dates in a case referred from the U.S. Circuit Court of the Southern District of Alabama:

"Acts of hostility by the insurgents occurred at periods so various and of such different degrees of importance, and in parts of the country so remote from each other, both at the commencement and close of the war, that it would be difficult, if not impossible, to say at what precise day it began or terminated. It is necessary, therefore, to refer to some public act of the political departments of the Government to fix the dates, and for obvious reasons those of the Executive Department, which may be, and in fact was, at the commencement of hostilities, obliged to act during the recess of Congress, must be taken.

"The proclamation of intended blockade may therefore be assumed as making the first of these dates, and the proclamation that the war had closed as making the second. But the war did not begin or close at the same time in all of the States. There were two proclamations of intended blockade; the first of the 19th of April, 1861, embracing the States of South Carolina, Georgia, Alabama, Florida, Mississippi, Louisiana, and Texas; the second, of the 27th of April, 1861, embracing the States of Virginia and North Carolina.

"In the absence of more certain criteria of equally general application, we must take the dates of these proclamations as the commencement and close of the war in the States mentioned in them" (12 Wall. 700).

On June 11, 1888 Sarah recovered $1,286 for mail service performed from October 1, 1861 to April 19.

Burns, William W. Major Henry H. Sibley patented the Sibley tent on April 22, 1856. On the 16th he had assigned one-half interest in any royalties to Major Burns. The Army adopted it as its regulation tent and contracted to pay a licensing fee of $5 per tent. Sibley joined the Confederacy and Burns supposed he was the sole owner of the rights. Burns applied to Quartermaster General Meigs who denied his assertion and on April 27, 1861 commenced paying him $2.50 per tent. This was paid till the end of the war. Burns sued for the additional $2.50 on 40,497 tents and recovered $101,242.50. The government argued the contract violated Army regulations.

Burnside, James O. P. By early 1864 there were several million bales of cotton inside Confederate military lines and the worldwide demand for cotton was so great the price was 10 to 15 times the cost of production. Great efforts were made to devise plans to purchase cotton within rebel lines and transport it to northern markets at enormous profit. On July 2, 1864 Congress passed an act authorizing the Secretary of the Treasury to "purchase for the United States any products of States declared in insurrection" not exceeding the market value at the place of delivery nor exceeding three-fourths of the market value in New York "at the latest quotation known to the agent purchasing."

Since the government had a monopoly, or exclusive right, in this regard, the agents who could bring the cotton out were promised three-fourths of what the market would pay. Prior to passage of this Act it was unlawful for a loyal citizen to trade with anyone within insurrectionary states.

On September 24, the Secretary published his rules and President Lincoln, by executive order, directed all members of the military to afford safe conduct to any duly appointed agent.

On December 5, James Burnside contracted with Superintending Special Agent Hanson A. Risley to sell Risley, and Risley to buy, 10,000 bales of cotton, 5,000 barrels of tar, 5,000 barrels of rosin, and 50,000 pounds of tobacco from Virginia and North Carolina. On the 7th, Burnside was issued all the papers and documents he would need to identify himself and obtain safe conduct. Burnside then sent a subcontractor to Elizabeth City, North Carolina to purchase 41 bales of upland cotton with "greenbacks and North Carolina bank notes" from behind rebel lines. The cotton was to be shipped from Elizabeth City on January 2, 1865 to Risley at Norfolk, Virginia but the U.S. transport *R. J. Lockwood* appeared on the scene and her commander seized the cotton on January 1. The commanding officer ignored the agent's papers and said he was acting under direction of Commodore William H. Macomb, commander of the gunboat *Shamrock,* who ordered all cotton at Elizabeth City seized. The agent was arrested and the cotton shipped to a Treasury agent named Heaton at Newbern as captured enemy property. Burnside and his agent, having no idea of where the cotton or Captain Macomb were, appealed to General Shepley at Norfolk for safe conduct. Shepley wrote immediately to Macomb but no reply was received. Burnside then learned that Macomb's ship was aground off Roanoke Island. Burnside went out to the ship, presented his papers, Macomb approved them, and Burnside was told the cotton was at Newbern. Burnside hurried to Newbern, talked to Heaton, and on orders from Risley, the cotton was released and sent immediately to New York.

Heaton charged $1,999.72 in fees against

the cotton while it was at Newbern and this was deducted from the sale price in New York.

Burnside sued and at trial Macomb said he never received the President's orders from Secretary of the Navy Gideon Welles until January 7, 1865, six days after the seizure was made. It would have taken no more than ten days to get the cotton to New York and since it should have been there on the 12th, it was worth, on that date, $1.10 a pound. Instead, the bulk of the cotton was sold on the 4th and 6th of February for 75½ cents a pound owing to "a heavy decline in the price."

Burnside recovered $1,499.79.

Burroughs, William P.

On September 27, 1861 Colonel William A. Barstow made a proposal to General John C. Frémont to raise, mount, and equip a regiment of cavalry within 60 days. Frémont OK'd it on the 30th and the Secretary of War assented on October 28 but ordered it done in 30 days. Quartermaster General Meigs wrote the assistant quartermaster at Chicago on the 29th:

> The prices of horses not to exceed $110 average. The horses will be inspected under the direction of the colonel at Janesville, Wisconsin, as provided in the endorsement of Major Allen, dated October 7, 1861 forthwith.

Allen's endorsement authorized Barstow to appoint a board of inspectors at Janesville.

On November 15 Barstow hired Burroughs at $5 a day to serve on a 3-member board to inspect horses, which he did for 124 days, and for which he received a $620 pay voucher from Barstow's quartermaster. Burroughs subsequently lost the voucher, no copy of Major Allen's authorization was produced, and the War Department refused to pay. Burroughs sued but the court held that Barstow had no authority to hire Burroughs and his petition was dismissed.

Burton, Jonathan P.

Burton sold 151 horses to an agent named Reeside in General Frémont's Western Department in the autumn of 1861 for $130 a head. The Davis-Holt-Campbell Commission reduced the amount by $20 a head. He recovered $3,020 in 1866.

Burwell, Pricilla W.

Armistead Burwell owned 135 hogsheads of sugar at 1,000 pounds each and 14 boxes of sugar at 400 pounds each at Vicksburg. He left Mississippi in the early summer of 1861 and did not return, if at all, until after the Army seized the goods for its own use.

Armistead died and Pricilla presented a claim to the Southern Claims Commission on June 12, 1884. The Commission allowed 8 cents a pound for the sugar and paid $11,248. Pricilla accepted the payment under protest to the Secretary of the Treasury as being too low. Her petition to a federal court was dismissed on February 7, 1887 as being barred by the Bowman Act.

Bynum, Oakley H.

Owned 23 bales of cotton seized near Courtland, Alabama in January 1865. The cotton was shipped to Nashville with two other bales of someone else's cotton and consigned to General Donaldson there. It was received by Acting Quartermaster S. P. Brown, who transferred it to Treasury Department Assistant Special Agent Charles A. Fuller. Fuller sent it to Treasury Department Supervising Agent W. P. Mullen at Cincinnati where it was sold at auction for $5,136.79.

The charges at Nashville were $245.50 and Cincinnati, $938.63, leaving $3,952.66 in net proceeds. Bynum challenged the fees at Cincinnati as unlawful, specifically $511.24 in customhouse fees and $255.62 for a 2 percent internal revenue tax. The legality of a customs house fee had never been authoritatively determined by any court.

Bynum sued under the Act of March 12, 1863. Section 3 specifically stated that the owner is entitled to the "residue" or net proceeds.

As the war progressed, the Treasury Department was deluged with property and had no money to deal with it. The Secretaries no doubt chose to make the property pay its own expenses and this resulted in the regulation of September 11, 1863, which said in part:

"Supervising special agents will pay or cause to be paid, out of the general fund arising from the sale of all property collected and received in their respective agencies, all expenses necessarily incurred in collecting, receiving, securing, and disposing of the same, including fees, taxes, freights, storages, charges, labor, and other necessary expenses, being careful to avoid all useless or indiscreet expenditures..."

All fees were examined and audited with the idea of protecting the captured and abandoned property trust fund from fraud and injustice. But, as the court stated:

"But this practice of the Treasury Department does not always do exact justice to claimants. Unlawful charges may be made and admitted at the Treasury, which, in a proper case, a court of justice would be bound to correct. But how, in a proceeding like the one now before us, can this be done? The claimant's suit is under the captured and abandoned property act, and his right of recovery is limited to the 'residue' of the proceeds of his property in the treasury. If unlawful charges have been made against the proceeds and such charges were paid to third persons before the 'residue' of the fund reached the Treasury, how can we now hold the Government responsible therefore? There is nothing in the Treasury, in such a case, to respond to a judgement rendered on such a hypothesis, and no power in this or any other court to hold the United States responsible for mistakes, unlawful acts, or misfeasances of its own officers or agents."

Bynum recovered $4,405.87 in 1873.

Byrnes, Roderick. Byrnes, an Irishman, was a British subject living in Charleston. When the war broke out he applied to his consulate for "protection papers." He remained strictly neutral but when the city was taken his 57 bales of upland cotton and 4 bales of sea-island cotton were seized. In court, Byrnes never claimed to have aided the Union or opposed the Confederacy. The British Vice-Consul, H. Pinckney Walker, testified on his behalf and he recovered $8,418.96.

Calhoun, John C. Andrew P. Calhoun owned a cotton plantation in Marengo County, Alabama from which 115 out of 170 bales of cotton were sold to Treasury agent C. W. Dustan in July 1865. Another 27 more were sold to agent E. D. Montague on August 26, 1865. Only 13 bales of Montague's cotton reached New York netting $1,528.89 for the Treasury. John Calhoun's lawsuit was dismissed.

Camp, Benjamin F. Ralph S. Hart was the assistant special Treasury agent authorized to purchase cotton in the Natchez District of Mississippi. On January 26, 1864 he wrote a note to Camp:

Office Ass't Special Agent Treasury Dep't
              Natchez, Miss., January 26, 1864
To any officer of any United States gunboat, or any of the U.S. land forces:
These are to authorize Benjamin F. Camp, of New York City, to collect & take possession of any abandoned cotton or C.S.A. cotton, or other abandoned products of the country, which he may find within the Natchez district of the 1st agency, and to transport the same to Natchez, but not elsewhere, and deliver the same into the posses-

sion of the undersigned, and also to request any gunboat officer, or any officer of the land service of the United States, to furnish him such incidental protection in the fulfillment of these objects as may be consistent with the service.
                                              R. S. Hart
                              Ass't Special Ag't Tr'y Dep'm't,
                                    Natchez Dist., 1st Agency

Hart's district extended from the mouth of the Big Black River to the mouth of the Red River on both sides of the Mississippi. On February 26 he authorized Camp to seize any vessel having on board Confederate or abandoned cotton.

John K. Elgee had about 2,200 bales stored on the bank of the Buffalo River in Adams County, Mississippi, which Hart knew about.

On March 15, 1864 Hart wrote a note to John Lockwood of Milwaukee, Wisconsin:

You are authorized and directed by me, in case any attempt shall be made by any one, whether he hold an authority from me to remove the lot of cotton on Old or Buffalo Rivers, or whether he do not hold an authority, to seize said cotton and bring it to Natchez, and revoke, in my name and by my authority, any such authority, and if necessary to cause the arrest of any such person or persons.

You are furthermore authorized to direct the operations and guide the movement of any military that may be in the service in the getting out of said cotton, and to seize and bring to Natchez any and all steamboats and persons attempting to carry the same, or any portion thereof, elsewhere.

On or about March 31, Camp identified himself as a Treasury agent and engaged the services of the transport *Venango,* escorted by the U.S. gunboat *Champion,* to go up Buffalo Bayou and seize 572 bales of Elgee's cotton. The cotton was brought to Natchez and seized by General Tuttle when Tuttle suspected Camp had taken the cotton by fraud. Camp was held in custody in the government yard then contacted Hart and William P. Mellen, Treasury Department supervising special agent at Natchez. Mellen sent the cotton to St. Louis where Elgee filed a claim in the Saint Louis County Circuit Court to recover it from O. S. Lovell, the Treasury agent there. The United States intervened and by stipulation the case was moved to the U.S. Circuit Court for the District of Missouri. On June 24 the cotton was ordered sold and the Supreme Court affirmed the decision.

Camp presented his claim to the Secretary of the Treasury. The Assistant Secretary directed the Commissioner of Customs to make a statement of the account and make a payment to him of $30,000, which he received on December 6, 1865.

On May 2, 1864 Elgee took the oath of amnesty under President Lincoln's proclamation of December 8, 1863 then appealed to the Secretary of the Treasury. The Assistant Secretary directed the Commissioner of Customs to make a statement of the account and make a payment to Elgee of $30,000. On March 7, 1866 a payment of $15,000 was made to William Prescott Smith through the same process since Smith had acquired an interest in the cotton.

Elgee died on August 20, 1868 and his heirs filed suit to recover the proceeds of the sale and Camp filed suit to recover the entire net proceeds.

The gross proceeds were $381,428.27. From that, freight and expenses totaled $45,349.12; legal fees, $16,000; payment to Camp, $30,000; payment to Smith, $15,000 for net proceeds of $275,079.15. Interest on bonds amounted to $91,091.68 for total proceeds paid into the Treasury of $366,170.83.

Camp's suit was dismissed in 1879 since he didn't present a claim during the Elgee trial and the court found Camp's authorization to seize the Elgee cotton had been revoked.

Campbell, William B. Campbell was building a steamboat on the Wabash River in Illinois. He brought the unfinished hull to Caledonia and on October 19, 1861 General Grant ordered the hull and all its contents moved to Cairo to prevent rebels who were crossing the river from seizing it. Some parts useful only for that particular hull were left on the riverbank, including three old engines, machinery, a donkey engine, and various hull fittings from the *Eaves.*

Campbell appeared before a War Department claim board at Cairo and submitted loss statements totaling $8,168.65, which apparently was paid. He later amended his claim to $22,043.65 and then $32,068.65 saying he didn't have time to get witnesses or documents to prove his total losses. He subsequently sued for superintending the building of the boat, $900, and another $125 for bringing the hull from his yard on the Wabash to Caledonia where it was seized, and increased valuations. His suit was dismissed.

Candy, Charles. Commissioned by the governor of Ohio on November 25, 1861 as colonel of the 66th Ohio Volunteer Infantry at Camp McArthur, near Urbana while the regiment was still organizing and not yet up to its full complement.

Candy sued under the Act of February 24, 1897 to recover his pay from November 25 to December 17, when the regiment was organized and mustered in to the service of the United States.

Candy's petition was dismissed on May 31, 1910 as barred by statute of limitations under the Act of April 10, 1910.

Carlisle, Hugh. Carlisle and his partner Henderson, railroad contractors, were subjects of the Queen of Great Britain. In December 1861 they began manufacturing saltpeter at Santa Cave in Jackson County, Alabama. They ceased operations in April 1862 when Union forces approached, returned in October when Union forces evacuated Huntsville, and continued for about two more months.

On March 28, 1862 they sold 2,480 pounds of saltpeter to the Confederate government and were paid on June 27.

They filed a claim on 65 bales of cotton captured in Marshall County, Alabama in 1864. The government introduced a November 30, 1862 receipt for the sale of 4,209 pounds of nitre marked "for manufacture of gunpowder." Their petition was dismissed but on appeal to the Supreme Court the decision was reversed on the ground the lower court failed to consider the unconditional proclamation of amnesty of December 25, 1868.

Carpenter, James H. Owned most of Dutch Island in Narragansett Bay off the coast of Rhode Island. The government owned five or six acres on the island. In 1863 Major Edward B. Hunt of the Engineer Corps was authorized to purchase the island for a fort to guard the entrance of the Bay, volunteer encampment, and training ground. A price of $21,000 was agreed upon, the government took possession on July 26, and Carpenter executed a deed on January 1, 1864.

After many legal items regarding the title were concluded, which delayed payment, Carpenter was finally paid on August 7, 1866. He sued to recover rent of $3,821.90 for the government's use of his property from July 26, 1863 to August 7, 1866 — 3 years and 12 days — but his petition was dismissed since he had executed a deed.

Carroll, Anna Ella. On November 30, 1861 Anna Ella Carroll wrote to Assistant Secretary of War Thomas A. Scott:

The civil and military authorities seem to be laboring under a great mistake in regard to the true key of the war in the Southwest. It is not the Mississippi, but the Tennessee River. All the military preparations made in the West indicate that the Mississippi River is the point to which the authorities are directing their attention. On that river many battles must be fought, and heavy risks incurred, before any impression can be made on the enemy, all of which could be avoided by using the Tennessee River. This river is navigable for medium-class boats to the foot of the Muscle Shoals, in Alabama, and is open to navigation all the year, while the distance is but two hundred and fifty miles by the river from Paducah, on the Ohio.

The Tennessee offers many advantages over the Mississippi. We should avoid the almost impregnable batteries of the enemy, which cannot be taken without great danger and great risk of life to our forces, from the fact that our boats, if crippled, would fall prey to the enemy by being swept by the current to him and away from the relief of our friends. But even should we succeed, still we will have only begun the war, for we shall then have to fight to the country from whence the enemy derives his supplies.

Now, an advance up the Tennessee River would avoid this danger; for if our boats were crippled, they would drop back with the current and escape capture.

But a still greater advantage would be its tendency to cut the enemy's line in two, by reaching the Memphis and the Charleston Railroad, threatening Memphis, which lies one hundred miles due west, and no defensible point between; also Nashville, only ninety miles northeast, and Florence and Tuscumbia, in North Alabama, forty miles east. A movement in this direction would do more to relieve our friends in Kentucky and inspire the loyal hearts in East Tennessee than the possession of the whole of the Mississippi River.

If well executed, it would cause the evacuation of all the formidable fortifications on which the rebels ground their hopes for success; and in the event of our fleet attacking Mobile, the presence of our troops in the northern part of Alabama would be material aid to the fleet.

Again, the aid our force would receive from the loyal men in Tennessee would enable them soon to crush the last traitor in that region, and the separation of the two extremes would do more than one hundred battles for the Union cause.

The Tennessee River is crossed by the Memphis and Louisville Railroad and the Memphis and Nashville Railroad. At Hamburg the river makes the big bend on the east, touching the northeast corner of Mississippi, entering the northwest corner of Alabama, forming an arc to the south, entering the State of Tennessee at the northeast cor-

ner of Alabama, and if it does not touch the northwest corner of Georgia, comes very near it. It is but eight miles from Hamburg to the Memphis and Charleston Railroad, which goes through Tuscumbia, only two miles above, intersecting with the Nashville and Chattanooga road at Stephenson.

The Tennessee River has never less than 3 feet to Hamburg on the "shoalest" bar, and during the fall, winter, and spring months there is always water for the largest boats that are used on the Mississippi River.

It follows from the above facts that in making the Mississippi the key to the war in the West, or rather in overlooking the Tennessee River, the subject is not understood by the superiors in command."

The letter was received and considered but no immediate action was taken to follow Carroll's advice.

Carroll was a spy working for Assistant Secretary of War Thomas A. Scott. She left Washington in the fall of 1861 and went to St. Louis to obtain information for use in the proposed plan to descend the Mississippi.

Carroll claimed she was the first one to conceive of the idea of using the Tennessee River. The government claimed the campaign was successfully carried out based on existing military plans. She petitioned Congress for relief and her claim was referred to a federal court. Carroll could not prove that her information was ever transmitted to Generals Halleck or Grant by President Lincoln or the Secretary of War or that orders given were ever derived specifically from her information.

In 1861 and '62 she wrote pamphlets for the War Department and for which she was paid $1,250 from the Secret-service fund. She claimed she was owed $5,000. The government accountants said the payment was for publishing expenses and not literary services and no further money was paid. Carroll claimed the $1,250 was a partial payment and she produced three certificates:

1861

Sept. 25. To circulating the Breckinridge reply	$1,250
Dec. 24. To writing, publishing, and circulating the "War Powers," &c	3,000
1862	
May — Writing, publishing, and circulating the Relations of the National Government to the Rebellious Citizens	2,000
	6,250
Credit, October 2, 1861:	
By cash	1,250
	5,000

Her claim was referred to a federal court by the House Committee on Military Affairs. The court believed the certificates were genuine but could not order an award based on them and none of the documents she presented constituted a binding contract. A note written by Assistant Secretary Scott was introduced:

> The pamphlets published by Miss Carroll were published upon a general understanding made by me with her, as Assistant Secretary of War, under no special authority in the premises, but under a general authority then exercised by me in the discharge of public duties as Assistant Secretary of War. I then thought them of value to the service, and I still believe they were of great value to the government. I brought the matter generally to the knowledge of General Cameron, then Secretary of War, without his having special knowledge of the whole matter; he made no objections thereto. No price was fixed, but it was understood that the government would treat her with sufficient liberality to compensate her for any service she might render, and I believe she acted upon the expectation that she would be paid by the government.
>
> Thomas A. Scott

Philadelphia, January 28, 1863

Charles O'Connor wrote a note from New York in support of her on October 10, 1862 and Reverdy Johnson did the same on September 10, 1862 from Washington.

The court could not render a decision based on the unauthenticated evidence presented and on June 1, 1885 the Committee was informed the court was unable to establish any findings of fact.

Carroll, James T. Carroll was a black resident of Charleston who had two bales of cotton seized. He testified:

"I was never in the rebel service. I never subscribed to confederate loans and never did anything to help the rebels because I had my opinions, which was that it was wrong to rebel against the United States. I had to hide from pursuit and never came out till I heard that the Union prisoners were captured and being brought down and saw them coming in and the cars stopped and I had a chance to look and see them. I got a couple of loaves of bread and had to throw it. The men guarding the trains were very ferocious and when I handed them some water they told me what would be the consequences and I had to clear out. The last thing I did was when the procession went up I had the honor to make my prayer to Almighty God for the sick, distressed, and dead, and I did so be-

cause I loved the United States and I had my belief they were going to make our race free."

James recovered $262.52 for two bales.

Carroll, Lucy H. George W. and Lucy Carroll owned a cotton plantation near Little Rock, Arkansas. George died in the fall of 1863 and 389 bales of cotton were seized the following summer. Lucy sued to recover $110,772. Lucy's son, Charles A. Carroll, a soldier in the Confederate army and a member of the Arkansas legislature, didn't help. He said he would have voted for Davis and Stevens if he hadn't been in the army and proudly testified about his "secesh" father:

"My father was as loyal to the Confederate government as any man who was not in the service."

Another witness stated:

"Mr. Carroll left his plantation the latter part of August 1863 for Texas, taking his family and the greater portion of his slaves with him to keep them from being freed by the Federal forces."

The court stated:

"The administratrix stands in the stead of the decedent, representing his rights and equities and nothing more. To prove the loyalty of all the distributees of an estate which, like this, may be insolvent, would be an inconvenience and impossibility, neither of which does the law exact."

Her petition was dismissed. She appealed to the Supreme Court where the lower court's ruling was reversed on the ground that the cotton was in Lucy's possession when it was seized and therefore only her loyalty should be considered. She was awarded $93,353.65 in 1871.

Carter, Alfred B. A resident of Fauquier County, Virginia who lived near Warrenton Junction. He claimed the Army removed 7,500 cords of wood from his property, valued at $30,000, throughout the fall of 1865. When he sued in the late 1880s under the Bowman Act of March 3, 1883 to recover the money, he claimed the wood was taken after the war was over and he was a loyal citizen. The court found that part of the wood had been taken prior to April 15, 1865 while Carter was "personally engaged in active hostilities against the Government of the United States as a soldier in the Confederate army" and the bulk of it had been removed after May 1865.

President Johnson's proclamation of April

2, 1866 declared the war began in the states east of the Mississippi, including Virginia, on April 19, 1861 and ended on April 2, 1866. Section 4 of the Bowman required a finding of loyalty. Carter's petition was dismissed on June 4, 1888.

Cartlidge, Charles W. A.
On September 16, 1864 Cartlidge received orders:

> III. C. W. A. Cartlidge, citizen of Hannibal, Mo., having passed the board as captain of colored troops, is authorized to collect colored recruits and present them to the assistant provost-marshal at that point for enlistment.
> By order of Brig. Gen. Thomas Ewing, jr.,
> H. Hannah
> Lieut. And A. A. A. General
> To Capt. C. W. A. Cartlidge,
> Hannibal, Mo.

On October 7 he received another letter when the Senate was in recess:

> Capt. Charles W. A. Cartlidge,
> Eighteenth Regiment United States Colored Infantry:
> Sir: You are hereby informed that the President of the United States has appointed you captain in the Eighteenth Regiment United States Colored Infantry, in the service of the United States, to rank as such from the 7th day of October, 1864.
> Immediately on receipt hereof please to communicate to the war Department, through the Adjutant-General's Office, at Washington, D.C., your acceptance or non-acceptance of said appointment; and with your letter of acceptance return to the Adjutant-General of the Army the oath herewith inclosed, properly filled up, subscribed, and attested, reporting at the same time your age, residence, when appointed, and the State in which you were born.
> Should you accept, you will at once report in person, for orders, to Brig. Gen. Thomas Ewing, jr., St. Louis, Mo.
> Given under my hand at Louisville, Ky., October 7, 1864, by authority of instructions from the Secretary of War.
> L. Thomas,
> Adjutant-General

Instead of reporting in person to Ewing, he ordered Cartlidge to continue with his recruiting duties at Hannibal where he was engaged in arming, equipping, and commanding a company of colored troops for police and guard duty at Hannibal under John F. Tyler, the assistant provost marshal. He also worked in company with, and under the direction of, Colonel J. T. K. Hayward of the enrolled Missouri militia in guarding the railroads from numerous guerila attacks. His company performed picket guard duty on the outskirts of town, patrolled day and night, guarded public properties, organized and mounted scouts to seek information on guerila movements and individuals suspected of disloyalty, and searched homes for Confederate mail and dispatches.

On November 25 he reported to St. Louis and was mustered in. His pay as captain began on that date instead of October 7. From October 7 until November 25 all ten companies of the Eighteenth Regiment had the minimum number of enlisted personnel required but only six captains, including Cartlidge. His pay from October 7 to November 25, after taxes, would have been $200.74. He sued in 1888 and recovered the money on February 11, 1889.

Cartwright, James N.
A resident of Alexandria, De Kalb County, Tennessee who bought cotton in Barstow County, Georgia on January 15, 1863. The cotton was stored where it was bought until it was seized in the fall of 1864 and taken in wagons to Cartersville, Georgia.

Alexandria was under Confederate control when the cotton was purchased and remained so until the battle at Stone's River from December 31, 1862 to January 2, 1863. Nearby Murfreesboro was captured and held on January 4 but the county east of there, including Alexandria, alternately changed hands until late '63 or early '64.

Ordinarily Cartwright would have been barred from recovering pursuant to proclamations and acts forbidding commercial activity between those living within insurrectionary districts and those under federal control. The proclamation of August 15, 1861 forbid commercial intercourse as "may be from time to time occupied and controlled by forces of the United States" but did not prohibit a resident of a district alternately occupied by both sides from holding valid title to goods within Confederate lines. Cartwright recovered $14,193 on 57 bales at $249 a bale in 1873.

Carver, Thomas J.
On August 14, 1865 President Johnson wrote a note to Major General Thomas at Nashville:

> I have been advised that innumerable frauds are being practiced by persons assuming to be Treasury agents in various portions of Alabama in the collecting of cotton, pretended to belong to the confederate government. I also understand that they are connected with the commander of post of Montgomery. I hope you will appoint some efficient officer under your command to proceed and examine and ascertain the facts, and if any

parties shall be found, whether connected with the Treasury or military, that you will deal with them in the most summary manner, and report the names of persons engaged in each transaction and each case.

T. C. A. Dexter was the supervising special agent for the ninth agency, the area in question. One of his special agents was Duff C. Green.

Thomas Carver was a resident of Mobile and on July 1, 1865 Green appointed Carver and Israel Pickens, also of Mobile, as sub-agents to collect cotton in Choctaw County.

The sub-agents contracted with planters to bring cotton to Tuscahoma and Tompkins Bluff on the Tombigbee River and a relative of Carver's named Myer went to Tuscahoma to receive cotton there.

Green, Carver, and Pickens were paying planters from $1.50 to $5 a bale with Treasury vouchers to prepare it for shipping and hauling it to the loading sites, but then they started paying $40 to $50 a bale out of their own pockets to appropriate the cotton for themselves. Carver paid about $25,000 to purchase cotton from Choctaw County residents W. J. Coleman, J. A. Mills, John J. Williams, John Curry, Colonel D. Hopkins, and B. G. Littlepage. They arranged for warehouse keeper A. Hill at Tompkins Bluff to erase the growers' marks from 306 bales. The cotton was in storage when Carver was arrested on September 23 at Mobile.

He was brought before a military tribunal and charged with being in possession of 935 bales of fraudulently acquired cotton with a market quality of good ordinary to low middling, average value 34 cents a pound. The cotton eventually sold for $124,296.96, less $30,053.21 for repacking, hauling to landing, flat boat fees, internal revenue tax, weighing, and wharfage. The net proceeds paid into the Treasury was $94,243.75.

Carver denied all eight charges and specifications. He was found guilty and fined $90,000 and one year at hard labor or until the fine was paid. He paid the fine on November 7 and the sentence of imprisonment was remitted.

Carver sued to recover the fine and his commission fees although $1,243.75 worth of the cotton was never recovered. Carver argued the military tribunal was illegal, had no authority over him, and the fine was paid under duress. The court stated in part:

"It is immaterial whether the proceedings under which the claimant's money was taken from him can or cannot be justified in law. It is clear that the money subsequently passed into the Treasury with his consent for the purpose of making good the losses which the government had suffered through his frauds. Having consented to that legal application of the money, it is of no consequence whether it was originally acquired legally or illegally, and he cannot now, in his suit to recover the fine, set up that the original act was illegal."

Carver's petition was dismissed.

Cattel, Robert. A black drayman from Charleston who owned three bales of upland cotton seized there. He recovered $404.10.

Chaplin, Mary S. Edgar and Eliza Fripp owned a 50-acre plantation on Ladies Island, South Carolina adjacent to the Fairfield plantation and Benjamin R. Bythewood's 460-acre White Hall plantation. The property was taxed by South Carolina as usually cultivated land. The Fripps also owned a lot in Beaufort. Edgar died in 1861 and left everything to Eliza. Eliza died sometime before March 1863. She left the property in a life estate to her son James Fripp with his sister Mary as the fee simple owner.

The U.S. Direct Tax Commission assessed taxes but James failed to pay and in March 1863 the 50 acres were condemned and sold to the United States for $6 in taxes, penalties, and costs. The Commission described the lot in town as Block 2 and assessed it at $9,600. It was sold for $244.24 to the United States to satisfy $122.33 in taxes, penalties, and costs.

James bought the properties back from the government in 1866. He died in 1880 leaving Mary as the owner. Mary recovered the $121.91 of surplus paid into the Treasury from the sale of Block 2 but sued to recover $4,799.76, which included one half the value of the lot and the 50 acres at $5 per acre as allowed by law. Her petition was dismissed on April 16, 1894 on the ground that she "has not suffered a diminution of her estate, and is therefore not entitled to compensation as alleged in her petition."

Child, Pratt & Fox. Major General Frémont believed St. Louis was in great peril in August and September 1861 since "all of Missouri, save the great rivers and railways, being in the possession of the enemy, and her chief city threatened by both revolt and invasion." He ordered his quartermaster, Colonel Justus McKinstry, to immediately procure supplies. Government officers could buy goods on the open market without contracts in emergencies but only "in the manner in which such articles are usually bought and sold between individuals." The quartermasters went shopping, all the way to Canada. Child, Pratt delivered $478,119 worth of goods but their bills were later reduced by the Davis-Holt-Campbell board. They accepted payment but then sued for a balance of $163,111.47.

McKinstry testified:

"The department here was without supplies of any kind and without a dollar of money. The first thing required was covering in the shape of tents. Transportation in the shape of mules, and wagons to carry them to camp. Camp kettles, mess-pans for cooking purposes, and clothing, shoes, stockings, drawers, shirts, pants, coats, and blankets.

"To show that exigency, I will state that on the 29th of July, 1861, I was ordered to have at command during the next fortnight, clothing, camp and garrison-equipage, for 23 regiments of infantry, three regiments of cavalry, and one regiment of artillery — about 28,000 men."

The court stated:

"The merchants of St. Louis were as a class afraid to trust their government. Among the exceptions was the house of Child, Pratt & Fox, which from the first stood with unwavering faith for the government and which alone of the great commercial houses of St. Louis dared to hang out the American flag."

In evaluating the company's claim, the court noted the highest item of profit:

"Sold, from September 1 to October 1, 411 frying pans at 50 cents each. September 21, an invoice of 57 dozen, cost in Pittsburgh 17½ cents each. Profit 188¼ percent.

"It is thus apparent that the alleged profit of 188¼ percent on 411 frying pans, delivered at various encampments around St. Louis, on the 1st October, is based on what 67 dozen cost in Pittsburgh on the 21st September, no allowance being made for the cash and credit nature of the two transactions, for the expenses of telegraphing and expressage, of cartage and storage, of re-packing and re-delivery, nor for the fact that the goods were bought with gold and sold for depreciated quartermaster vouchers.

"The only other item where the difference of cost and price exceeds 100 percent is that of $836.30 for 3,374 curry-combs. Here the 'cost-east' was 11 cents and the price charged 23¾

cents but the time of purchase and sale ranges from the 15th August to the 8th October and there is no telling how much the articles might have advanced in the eastern market during this period."

The public was suspicious and indignant since McKinstry had been dishonorably discharged for fraud against the government but the company was awarded $163,111. The government appealed to the Supreme Court where the judgement was reversed since the company voluntarily accepted payment on vouchers signed by the Davis-Holt-Campbell board, as in the case of Theodore Adams.

Chisolm, George. A lot in Beaufort, South Carolina owned by S. Prioleau Chisolm was designated as block 7 and assessed by the U.S. Direct Tax Commission at $6,000. The tax was not paid so the lot was sold to the United States to pay $76.45 in tax, penalties, and interest.

On November 1, 1866 the United States sold the lot to S. Prioleau's wife, Sarah P. Chisolm, for $300 through her trustee, John F. Porteous.

S. Prioleau died in 1880 without a will leaving Sarah and four children: William, George, Ellen L. Fripp, and S. Prioleau Chisolm, who were Sarah's stepchildren. Each child inherited one-fourth of their share of the estate under South Carolina law.

Sarah died in 1890 and left all the property to Porteous R. Payne. The Act of March 2, 1891 allowed the children two thirds of one half of the assessed value of the property since the elder S. Prioleau Chisolm, as the legal owner under South Carolina law, did not repurchase it. Porteous R. Payne was entitled only to one third of the repurchase amount less the tax. On June 9, 1896 the children each recovered $487.26 and Porteous R. Payne recovered $74.52.

Chollar, Justus. Contracted with Quartermaster E. C. Wilson on June 11, 1862 to deliver 300 horses to Perryville, Maryland on or before July 8. Wilson reserved the right to change the place of delivery to Washington, D.C. and pay an extra expense of $600. Wilson ordered the horses to Washington but failed to pay the additional cost. Chollar sued for $2,500 and recovered $600 in 1866.

Christian, James. Captain Christian was an acting commissary of subsistence and quartermaster at Paola, Kansas. Christian supposedly received $2,048.56 in proceeds from the sale of contraband goods but had no official safe storage place for it so he deposited it in an iron safe in the H. S. & L. Fillmore store in Lawrence. Lemuel Fillmore was one of the sureties on Christian's official bond. Christian was mentioned in a letter to the commander at Paola:

HEADQUARTERS DISTRICT OF KANSAS,
Fort Leavenworth, April 8, 1863

III. Captain James Christian, commissary of subsistence at Paola, will, on the arrival of Colonel Lynde at the latter place, turn over all commissary stores and other Government property in his hands to the quartermaster of the Ninth Kansas Volunteers; having done which, he will report in person to these headquarters.

By command of Major-General Blunt:
(signed)
H. G. Loring
Captain and A.A.A. General

On or about July 1, 1863 Christian left Paola for New Madrid, Missouri. During his absence, on August 21, Quantrill's Raiders attacked Lawrence. The store was sacked and burned, Fillmore was killed, and all the money was taken or destroyed.

Assistant Adjutant General Loring later reported that Christian was at Paola on March 31; Fort Leavenworth on April 30; Lawrence on May 31; Fort Scott on June 30; whereabouts unknown on July 31; and at Fort Leavenworth on August 31.

Christian was charged by Quartermaster General Meigs with the loss of $2,048.56. When Christian told his story to the Treasury Department to apply for credit he was told to take his case to court pursuant to the Act of May 9, 1866.

The court was unsympathetic. He had orders to turn everything over to the volunteers and he had no proof that the money in the safe ever existed, only that he was charged with $2,048.56 by the Quartermaster General's office. Christian's character was reported to be good but his only witness was dead and he, as the only possible witness in the case, was prohibited by the common law from testifying, so there was no trial.

Clara Dolsen. The 268 × 42-foot, 939 ton sidewheel steamer *Clara Dolsen* was built at Cincinnati, Ohio and was issued Enrollment No. 91 at that port on January 16, 1861: "and that she is a steamer, has a plain head, and a transom stern, with tuck; no gallery." She was owned by Captain William T. Dunning, the master, (⁹⁄₁₆), A. P. Stewart (⁵⁄₁₆), and Samuel S. Edwards (²⁄₁₆), all of St. Louis, Missouri.

The boat ran cargo between St. Louis and Memphis, Tennessee until the war began when she was laid up at Memphis on May 1. From there she was "forcibly taken by the Confederate authorities and put into their military service."

On February 26, 1862, A. P. Stewart sold his five-sixteenths interest in the vessel to George W. Cable at New Orleans for $17,187.50 cash. After this the vessel was registered at the Port of New Orleans and enrolled as No. 117, Confederate States of America, which stated in part, "... whereof W. T. Dunning is at present master, and, as he hath sworn, is a citizen of the Confederate States of America, and the said ship or vessel was built at Cincinnati, State of Ohio, in the year eighteen hundred and sixty-one, as per U.S. enrollment No. 91, issued at the port of Cincinnati, 16 Jan'y, 1861, now surrendered..."

On February 28 Cable bought a one-sixteenth interest in the boat from Captain Dunning on behalf of Edward Walsh of St. Louis. Cable took possession of the vessel and put Captain George Sparhawk on board as master. Dunning and Stewart thereafter had nothing to do with the vessel. The *Dolsen* left New Orleans under Confederate orders the same day. Sparhawk remained on board until the boat was returned to Cable just before Memphis was captured. Sparhawk was replaced by Captain Jones who was ordered by Cable to hide the boat somewhere until after Memphis was taken and then proceed upriver until the Army or Navy was encountered and then surrender the boat and leave it in their care until he came down to claim it. Memphis was taken on June 6.

The boat was found and seized on June 14 by gunboat *Mound City* and tug *Spitfire* on the White River during the St. Charles campaign. The boat was then used by the Navy.

On July 31 a libel was filed against the vessel in the District Court for the Southern District of Illinois on the ground that she was used to aid and abet the rebellion with the knowledge and consent of her owners. The required notice was published and Walsh, Edwards, and Dunning appeared in court as claimants. The boat was appraised and $45,000 in surety bonds delivered by the three. The vessel was condemned and purchased by the Navy for $45,000 from the prize court. She was regarded as "one of the finest, handsomest, and in every respect finest steamers on the river."

On September 18, 1863 Dunning sold eight-sixteenths of his interest to D. W. Carter.

In May 1864 the boat was seized by the U.S. marshal and delivered to Walsh, Edwards, and Dunning. On the 24th she was enrolled at the port of St. Louis with Edwards as master and Mary E. Bofinger of St. Louis as five-sixteenths owner, but this share was claimed by Walsh. Walsh then bought out Edwards and Dunning.

On January 19, 1865 the boat was declared forfeited by the court and judgement entered against the three and their bonds in the amount of $45,000. They filed an appeal on the 23rd claiming loyalty to the United States. They were able to convince the court their boat was taken by force and used beyond their control and the judgement was set aside. On July 26, 1865 Secretary of the Treasury Hugh McCulloch conveyed title to the vessel to the three and ordered the bonds canceled.

Walsh spent about $30,000 to recondition and repair the boat. In 1866 she was sold at public auction by Walsh's representatives. Neither Stewart nor Dunning made any claim for revenue or a share in the proceeds.

On March 3, 1875 Congress appropriated $22,050 to the owners of the *Clara Dolsen* as payment for the Navy's use of the boat. Mary Bofinger sued for her share of the money but was unable to convince the court that she had any interest in the vessel during the time it was requisitioned for government use. Walsh received $8,268.75; Dunning, $11,025; and Edwards, $2,756.25. Bofinger claimed she purchased five-sixteenths of the vessel from A. P. Stewart on September 26, 1863 for $1,000 in cash. The vessel was then in U.S. hands and registered only at the port of New Orleans. Bofinger bought her share with money from the sale of the steamer *John Walsh*, owned jointly by Cable and Walsh. The *John Walsh* was sold by Cable for Confederate money within Confederate territory. Edward Walsh was never in the South but the proceeds of the sale were turned over to him by Cable. Bofinger's interest was recorded at Cincinnati on October 2, 1863 when Stewart sold five-sixteenths to Bofinger for $12,500 when the vessel was in U. S possession.

After much investigation into the various enrollments and other documents, Mary Bofinger's petition was dismissed.

Clark, Dr. Finley Y. Clark owned 6½ bales and 12 pockets of sea-island cotton and 7 bales of upland cotton that was seized at Savannah in December 1864. Clark was known to have given valuable information to Captain Ammen, USN, on the placement of torpedoes and also furnished intelligence to the Army. He was awarded $2,014.04 for the sea-island cotton and $1,333.29 for the upland cotton.

Clark, James S. Clark and E. Fulton purchased 3,435 bales of cotton in East and West Feliciana Parishes in Louisiana with the consent of U.S. Treasury Special Supervising Agent George S. Denison at New Orleans under the Act of July 2, 1864. They advanced $123,200 but felt constrained for some reason and left the cotton "exposed to the depredations of guerillas."

They appealed to Secretary of the Treasury William P. Fessenden who gave them permission to move the cotton "provided they shall first present to the acting collector of customs at New Orleans the original authorities or permits under which they acted, or copies thereof, certified by the officer with whom they are filed, with proof to his satisfaction that the cotton was actually purchased in good faith..." and they were required to post a $250,000 surety bond.

On October 26, President Lincoln gave his consent and ordered free passage through any and all military and naval lines. On November 10 they delivered their bond to Agent Denison, who was also the acting collector of customs at New Orleans.

On December 13, Lieutenant Commander John J. Cornwell, commanding officer of the USS *Choctaw,* then off Bayou Sara, Louisiana, and commander of the Second and Third districts of the Mississippi River, notified all commands between Bayou Sara and New Orleans to allow the steamer *Scotia,* with 336 bales of cotton aboard, to pass without detention.

The steamer arrived at New Orleans where the vessel and cotton were promptly seized by the U.S. military police under Colonel Harai Robinson, acting provost marshal of the Department of the Gulf under General S. A. Hurlbut. Hurlbut's boss, General Edward R. Canby, commander of the Department of the Military Division west of the Mississippi, directed that a certain number of bales be released to Clark and the rest turned over to O. N. Cutler, the U.S. purchasing agent, and Clark and Fulton should post bonds for their appearance. Robinson then sent for Clark and Fulton and the two appeared before him but showed no papers to him as the disposition of their cotton was not his concern and the cotton remained under arrest.

On the evening of December 21 Clark and Fulton went to Robinson's home and showed him the papers dated October 26 signed by Fessenden and Lincoln. Robinson had no knowledge of the permits and Clark and Fulton asked him what he thought of it. Robinson replied it covered everything and couldn't understand how the ship and cotton could be seized and the partners put under bond. Clark and Fulton said they were told it had no value unless their permit was signed by the major general commanding the department. Robinson asked if they had seen General Hurlbut and they said they had but he refused to honor it. Robinson told them to go see General Canby and they replied, "You know that is useless by the very order which put us under bond. It states by order of the general commanding the Military Division west of the Mississippi." They suggested it was obvious their cotton would not be released without a payment of some sort and they offered $10,000 to have the permit endorsed. Robinson said to leave the permit and he would see what he could do about it. The next day Robinson took the permit to Hurbut and told him the partners wished to have it signed. Hurlbut said he had seen it and refused to sign it. Robinson said, "General, these men have offered a large amount of money to get this permit indorsed. There's money in it." Hurlbut replied, "You must take that to Mr. Denison and have him certify that the proper bonds have been filed by these parties, Clark and Fulton." Robinson took the permit to Denison, said he had been sent by Hurlbut, and Denison endorsed the permit. Robinson took the permit back to Hurlbut and he issued an order on December 23 to obey President Lincoln's executive order.

The next day, or on Christmas Day, Clark and Fulton went to Robinson's home and presented him with $5,600 but later that day he gave it back feeling uncomfortable with receiving it in that manner. Clark and Fulton asked how he would like it and he said through Denison. The next morning Denison gave Robinson an envelope with $5,000 in it. Robinson took $2–3,000 out for Hurlbut and put the rest in his office. Clark saw him later and said, "Now I have the permit indorsed, see if you can get my cotton released. See if General Hurlbut will give an order releasing or justifying the release of my cotton."

Robinson went to Hurlbut and an order was written:

> Pursuant to executive order of His Exc'y the President of the United States, J. S. Clark & E. Fulton

are permitted to bring the number of bales of cotton in said order mentioned from Ratcliff's Landing, on the Miss. River, 25 miles above Bayou Sara, on the steamer *Scotia*, provided the same is received under protection of a gunboat. The taking of any passengers of freight to be landed at any point, or the payment of anything but United States Treasury notes, will work forfeiture of steamer and cargo. The cotton returning on the boat will be reported & identified by Mr. O. N. Cutler & the prov. mar. gen'l.

Clark and Fulton then paid Robinson another $5,000. Sometime prior to February 13, 1865 they paid Robinson another $3,000 and Robinson gave Hurlbut $1,000 and the rest put away. Two other parties were also paid off. In all, General Hurlbut got $8,000 but he returned all of it to Robinson around April 4. Robinson then purchased gold coins which he deposited in the First National Bank of New Orleans in certificates of deposit amounting to $7,602.25.

In January 1865 a special commission was convened by Secretary of War Stanton and on February 13 Robinson was placed in solitary confinement and the CDs deposited in a special account in the Treasury. Another $8,000 was taken from Robinson along with $40 in interest.

Clark and Fulton sued to recover their $10,000 but their petition was dismissed in 1877.

Clark, Jared H. Clark and his partner, Carlos A. Smith, signed a contract with Major Du Barry on June 22, 1863 to furnish potatoes at 85 cents a bushel at Cincinnati between July 7 and August 1 as required but not to exceed 3,000 bushels a week. A small amount was received and then Du Barry refused further shipments leaving Clark with 8,908–43/60 bushels that were spoiled. Clark sued to recover $$7,487.41 and accused Du Barry of either fraudulently, or by mistake, omitting the quantity of potatoes from the contract that Clark signed "without the advice of counsel."

The contract signed called for "such quantities (not exceeding 3,000 bushels per week) as may be required." Previous correspondence led the two to believe they were contracting for 9,000 bushels. They recovered $2,550 on 3,000 bushels, the contracted amount.

Clark, Oliver H. On March 4, 1862 Clark chartered his steamer *Massasoit* to the Army at $150 a day to carry freight on the rivers of North Carolina. Her master was Captain J. L. Crane. During one trip the *Massasoit* hit stumps that damaged planking and timbers and she was sent to New Berne for temporary repairs.

On January 22, 1863 she was sent to Wilmington with a load of coal and two 32-pounders and while there she was hauled out of the water and further temporary repairs were made. This yard was not able to make permanent repairs but all work was done at government expense. Clark was not paid for charter service during the 20 days the steamer was on the ways but after protesting he was paid $50 a day.

One of the 32-pounders was installed on the boat at the shipyard over Captain Crane's strenuous objections that the vessel was not built as a gunboat and could not take the shock if it was fired. The cannon was repeatedly fired during subsequent duty causing damage and the vessel went aground again on stumps resulting in further injury.

On May 9th, 1863 Lieutenant Colonel Herman Biggs, chief quartermaster of the Eighteenth Army Corps at New Berne, sent a letter to Captain Crane while the vessel was at New Berne informing him that because of the length of time the ship had been in Army service the charter rate should be reduced to $100 a day. Biggs requested an answer to his proposal before the *Massasoit* left port. Captain Crane reported back to Biggs that Oliver Clark had consented to $125 a day if the government continued to provide the war risk insurance but Clark never saw the letter from Colonel Biggs and Crane had no authority to consent to any agreement with respect to the charter.

Clark was notified of this change by his attorney, Mr. Barstow, who also advised him to remove his ship from Army service. Barstow also communicated this to Captain Crane. Clark and Barstow also filed a formal complaint with Captain Stinson at the quartermaster's office in New York. Stinson informed Clark that he should have received notification by letter concerning the reduction in rates for all existing charter-party agreements pursuant to the Quartermaster General's order to either reduce rates or discharge vessels from service if the owners objected. Clark assented to the new policy.

The *Massasoit* was sent up to New York in August for permanent repairs totaling $3,500, which Clark paid for. After these repairs a new charter-party was executed on November 26. On December 23, 1863 Colonel R. E. Clary in the chief quartermaster's office in Washington wrote to Major Stewart Van Vliet, quartermaster at New York, that the charter rate for the *Massasoit* was reduced to $80 a day starting January 1, 1864.

On December 29, Clark's attorney replied to Colonel Clary that the vessel's tonnage after leaving the shipyard was now 211 and they accepted the new rate of 45 cents a ton. The boat was released from service on May 25, 1865.

Clark sued for the cost of the repair work done in New York as the result of the cannon being fired and to recover $125 a day for the 53 days lost during the repair work less the $50 a day already paid.

The government's assistant attorney general disputed the owner's claim:

"After being a year and a half in southern waters, the vessel 'had permission to come to New York to make the repairs.' There is no proof of any specific damage which rendered these repairs necessary. The damages proved had been repaired by the Government. Captain Crane swears that the repairs made in New York 'were rendered necessary by the damages sustained by the boat in the Government service.' Sueden, the ship-builder who made the repairs, testifies that 'the damage done to the boat at that time was caused by the general use of the boat and the business she was in the South.' Anthony, a ship-carpenter, testifies: 'I did not know what caused the damage; she looked to me as though she had been pretty well wrecked in some way or other. She had had hard usage. She looked as though she had been in a heavy sea-way or something.' The defendants were only liable as insurers, and as insurers they were not liable for anything but injuries resulting from extraordinary casualties. He quoted from a previous marine insurance case: 'There must be something fortuitous, accidental, and not necessarily arising from the ordinary course of the voyage, to make the underwriter liable.'"

The court found the damage caused by the stumps was a marine risk to be borne by the owners and regarding the cannon stated:

"As to the injuries sustained by the use of the cannon put on board of her by the United States: This vessel was chartered for freighting, to which she was adapted, and she was not adapted nor chartered for a gun-boat. The United States, therefore, were not authorized by the contract to put and use a cannon on board of her for firing on the enemy without the assent of her owner, and they were expressly notified of his dissent by the objection and protest of her master; and as the act of the United States was unauthorized, it was an abuse of the vessel, in violation of the contract, and they are liable for its consequences, and the injuries thus sustained were specified and proved in the evidence.

"In these expeditions the cannon was fired on the enemy; grounding on the stumps, injured the bottom of the *Massasoit* and started her planks and timbers and firing the cannon shook the boat in every part, started the oakum out of her seams, and shook down her joiner work, and she was caused to leak.

"On these grounds we adjudge that the petitioner was entitled to recover the cost of the vessel's repairs in New York, and the per-diem compensation of $125 per day, which she was then earning, for the 53 days lost from her service by her repairs in New York, less $50 per day for the cost of her running expenses saved during that time."

The final judgement was delivered in December 1873.

Claussen, Frederick W. Claussen was a

naturalized citizen who owned 75 bales of upland cotton and 53 bales of sea-island cotton at Charleston. The citizens of Charleston who were loyal knew each other and generally associated with each other. None of this group, with the exception of Nicholas Culliton, seemed to know Claussen and it was later determined that Claussen bought or held 11 or 12 bales for Culliton. Claussen testified:

"I was a foreigner and took no part in the rebellion as I came here simply to make money and not to bother myself in politics and I did not. I took no sides between the two."

He invested in Confederate bonds but denied having Confederate loans or being invested in any blockade running company and would not affirm loyalty to the United States.

William J. Middleton, president of the Commercial Trading Company, said he thought Claussen was a director of the company which "never transacted business but its object was to purchase steamers and import and export merchandise." As the court stated:

"The willingness of claimant to embark in such an association, the very purpose of which was to violate the blockade, shows an absence of neutrality and a desire to give aid and comfort to the rebellion."

Claussen's petition was dismissed.

Nicholas Culliton sued to recover the proceeds from 11 bales of his sea-island cotton seized at Charleston. For many years Culliton was a member of a South Carolina militia unit called the Irish Volunteers. This company went to Morris Island to participate in the attack on Fort Sumpter but he left the company within a few days after their arrival and was at Charleston when the firing began. Soon after, the company went into the Confederate army. Culliton left and apparently evaded military service for the rest of the war.

He recovered $1,963.28.

The attack on Fort Sumpter marked the beginning of the war for legal purposes. Courts held it was at that point when a citizen decided to be loyal or disloyal to the Union. Prior to that, many Northerners and Southerners believed a separation could be peacefully accomplished or the differences resolved despite the election of a President perceived as uncompromising. Whatever lay ahead in the form of compromise or Supreme Court decisions regarding slavery or States' rights was squashed by the sound of gunfire from South Carolina. The seizing, hostile occupation of, and firing on federal military property forced the hand of the President.

Clay, Thomas J. Clay went into the rebel

army as an officer, was captured at Fort Donelson, and was paroled at Louisville. While there on June 20, 1862 he assigned money due him to his brother in law. His debtor refused to pay, claiming Clay was disloyal. Clay sued and the U.S. Circuit Court for the Kentucky District held the assignment was valid.

Clyde, Thomas. Chartered his barge

William E. Hunt to the Army on February 26, 1862. The barge was loaded with hay at Aquia Creek and made up to the steam tug *Atlantic* for a trip to Baltimore. When a severe storm came up on January 21, 1863 the tug's pilot put in at Cornfield Harbor just inside Point Lookout in the St. Mary's River, Maryland, anchored the barge, then moved away a safe distance and anchored the tug. The storm increased that night and the barge broke loose around 9 P.M., unseen by the tug's crew, drifted across the bay, and went ashore at 3 A.M. at Smith's Point, Virginia. The crew on the barge made signals, fired guns, and waved lanterns to the tug but no one saw them except a group of rebels. They came down at daybreak, took everything off the barge, burned it, and took the master prisoner. The barge was worth about $5,000.

Clyde's claim for restitution from the War Department was refused as a marine risk. He sued and recovered $5,000 on the ground that the proximate cause of the loss was due to enemy action.

On November 16, 1862 Clyde chartered his steam ferryboat *Tallacca* at $115 a day during the "emergency caused by the removal of the army of the Potomac to Falmouth." He transported troops and supplies and the vessel remained in service until July 31, 1863 but the rate was reduced to $75 a day on May 13 retroactive to the date of the charter. Clyde refused to consent to the reduction but allowed his boat to remain in government service. On December 1, 1863 he was paid $6,675.

He sued to recover the balance and the court ruled the Quartermaster General had no power to arbitrarily reduce a fixed-rate charter amount but because Clyde allowed the vessel to remain in service he could recover only the difference at the reduced rate. The government appealed to the Supreme Court on the ground the claim was never presented to the War Department for appeal and because of that Clyde had no standing in court, by the court's own rules, and his petition should have been dismissed. The Supreme Court reversed the judgement of dismissal on the ground the lower court improperly required Clyde to obtain certain documents not required by law.

Clyde also sought to recover $6,650 for the unlawful reduction in the charter rate his steamers *Rebecca Clyde* and *Emilie* but his petition was dismissed.

Cobb, Francis. Owner of the steamer *Rockland* who signed a charter agreement on March 7, 1862 at $200 a day for no stipulated length of time. On April 30, 1863 the rate was lowered to $100 per day over Cobb's objection for 83 days until July 22 when the vessel was discharged from service. Cobb sued for $8,200 to recover the reduction in rate. The court stated a principle governing charter-parties:

"The inferior agents of the government, such as assistant quartermasters, have no right to retain a vessel in service at her original charter rate after the receipt of the Quartermaster General's order to reduce it, unless the owner assent to the reduction; and the owner, with knowledge of the Quartermaster General's order, cannot leave his vessel in the service except as subject to his terms. In such cases it is for the defendants to bring the knowledge of the Quartermaster General's order home to the claimant; and it for the claimant to show that he

sought to take his vessel out of the service and was refused a discharge. If he voluntarily left his vessel in the service after knowledge of the Quartermaster General's order, he left her subject to the Quartermaster General's restrictions."

Cobb's petition was dismissed.

Cobb, Oliver P. In August 1864, around the time Atlanta was captured, General William Sherman's and George Thomas's commands were seriously short of animal forage. By November a large number of troops and about 100,000 "public animals" under general Thomas were gathered at Nashville, including General James Wilson's 30,000 cavalry troops, preparing to march against General Hood.

On November 25, 1864 O. P. Cobb, Christy & Co. signed a contract to deliver 150,000 bushels of shelled corn at Cincinnati for $1.55 a bushel in resewed gunnies; 50,000 bushels of ear corn, to be furnished by the government, at $1.24 a bushel; and 100,000 bushels of oats in new burlap bags at different points between Maysville, Kentucky and Madison, Indiana. This contract was fulfilled.

On December 1, about two weeks before the fight at Nashville, a number of transports at Johnsonville, Tennessee were set on fire to keep them from a Confederate force under General Forrest. This set fire to nearly 2 million bushels of forage being acquired for General Thomas at Nashville. The stores of grain at Cairo, Illinois were nearly gone, water and rail transportation was compromised, and Congress had neglected to appropriate enough money to purchase sufficient stores of grain and a large army was gathering at Nashville. General Hood was advancing on Nashville and a heavy cavalry push south under General Wilson was being prepared. Wilson had about 100,000 cavalry, draft, and artillery horses to feed.

General Thomas met with his staff and quartermasters to find a solution. Thomas declared an emergency and ordered his quartermaster to get a supply of grain any way he could.

In response to this emergency the company entered into a verbal contract to immediately duplicate the previous contract. The company got busy but on April 10, 1865 they were notified that no more than what they had furnished to date would be needed. The company sued on the remaining 600,000 bushels of corn and oats for the campaign. They recovered $154,107.84 in 1871.

On December 23, 1864 the quartermaster at Cincinnati verbally contracted with Cobb, Blasdell & Co. for 600,000 bushels of corn and oats to be delivered at 150,000 bushels a month.

On January 5, 1865 a meeting was called at St. Louis where 17 suppliers of grain the Army had previously contracted with met with Captain William Currie and an agreement was reached to furnish oats at 98.2 cents a bushel. Cobb was at the meeting and said he could immediately furnish 100,000 bushels of oats and 50,000 bushels of corn at Cairo or St. Louis. He delivered the goods and was promptly paid.

Captain Currie was ordered "to procure such supplies during the continuance of such emergency, but no longer, in the most expeditious manner, and without advertisement."

The war ended before the contract was fulfilled. Cobb claimed that between October 1864 and May 1865 he purchased a total of 970,000 bushels of oats and of that 616,000 was accepted by the Army and paid for, but the remaining 354,000 were sold "at a great loss." Cobb sued for $219,628.

The government argued all he had left were 350,000 bushels that were lost at Dubuque when the Illinois Central Railroad refused to ship it on the ground it was private merchandise. Cobb argued he was told by Currie to continue purchasing oats until he was notified the emergency was over. The trial questioned the length of the emergency and Currie's authority to essentially hire the contractors to act as purchasing agents for the government. Cobb's petition was dismissed in 1883 since he couldn't furnish sales receipts to prove there was any loss.

Cole, Alexander.

Enlisted in the Navy as a landsman on July 25, 1864 for a term of three years. He was assigned to the USS *Metacomet* and served aboard the gunboat until August 15, 1865 when he was declared a deserter. The ship decommissioned at Philadelphia three days later on the 18th.

Cole was owed $38.85 in prize money and a $1.64 bounty for the destruction of an enemy vessel.

The *Metacomet* was commissioned on January 4, 1864 and assigned to the West Gulf Blockading Squadron. On June 6 she captured the blockade runner *Donegal* in Mobile Bay. On the 30th she participated in burning the Confederate steamer *Ivanhoe*. On August 5 she was part of a force that captured the Confederate

ram *Tennessee* and gunboat *Selma*. On November 28 she captured the blockade runner *Susanna* off Campechy Banks, Texas. The schooner *Sea Witch* was captured on December 31 and sloop *Lily* was captured off Galveston on January 6, 1865.

Cole attempted to claim his money without success. On January 27, 1892 Secretary of the Navy Benjamin F. Tracy dismissed the charge of desertion and granted Cole a certificate of discharge dated August 15, 1865. Cole's claim was still pending in the Treasury Department when Treasury Secretary Charles Foster referred his claim to a federal court. Cole filed suit on October 11, 1898.

The court had to determine the origin of prize money and bounty money and if either was considered "pay" according to the statutes. Bounty is a reward paid by a government for a particular service. In the United States, it is often given upon enlistment or reenlistment. Prize money is paid out of proceeds from the sale of captured enemy property, none of it coming from the U.S. Treasury.

Cole was awarded $40.49 on June 5, 1899 under the Act of August 14, 1899. The court stated:

"The purpose of the act of August 14, 1888, was to remove from many worthy soldiers the stigma of being deserters and give them all the rights and emoluments to which they would have been entitled had not the charge of desertion been made."

The Act further provided that any bounty or prize money due shall be paid to the serviceman or his heirs.

Collie, Alexander.

A British subject who bought 1,757 bales of sea-island and 3,696 bales of upland cotton in Confederate territory through Theodore Andræ and stored it at Savannah ready to ship to either New York or England. All was seized in Savannah in January 1865 and sold for net proceeds of $952,076.71. Collie was engaged in blockade running but no munitions were known to be involved so he recovered in the absence of proof that he aided the rebellion.

The government appealed to the Supreme Court where new evidence was presented. It was shown that he furnished four steamers for blockade running and made arrangements with Confederate government representative, Colin J. McRae, to furnish £150,000 worth of quartermaster stores and £50,000 of ordnance and medical stores over six months in exchange for cotton.

In March 1864 Collie presented the authorities at Wilmington, North Carolina one "Whitworth gun for field-service, with carriage, caisson, limbers, and all other customary appendages together with a large quantity of shot of the proper caliber for the gun." As he described it:

"I have shipped on board the *Edith* a new kind of gun which is reported to be particularly destructive, and I have to ask the authorities at Wilmington to accept it as a 'substitute' for some of our people, who, but for our business, would have been doing business in another capacity."

The gun was used at Wilmington for the defense of the port and also on steamers to repel Union gunboats chasing them. He delivered two more Whitworth guns and donated $30,000 "to aid the needy and suffering in the insurgent States, and more particularly those who had been made so through the war."

The decision was reversed in 1877.

Collins, John. Collins owned a large cotton plantation in Hale County, Alabama. In 1860 he raised somewhere between 1,000 and 1,200 bales of cotton but after the war began his production fell off dramatically. In November 1862 he sold 220 bales to the Confederate government at 15 cents a pound. The next month he sold another 219 bales at the same price. Collins was paid with 8 percent Confederate bonds. He was to store the cotton until the government's agent called for it but no one ever came to claim it.

In early August 1865 Collins had 432 bales shipped to a warehouse at Demopolis, Alabama. It was seized there on the 26th by special Treasury agent E. D. Montague who was under contract to seize all the cotton in Marengo County. Collins was given a receipt for the cotton and Montague was supposed to have marked each bale "J. Collins" before putting it in with several other lots he had seized.

Sometime later Montague sent 793 bales to Mobile aboard the steamer *Jackson's Flats*. Of this, 372 belonged to Collins. At Mobile, Montague was given 700 bales as payment out a lot of 1,362 bales he had seized altogether, mostly from the cotton belonging to John Collins. Montague's payment for seizing cotton was 1 bale out of every 4 he seized in excess of 100 bales and he was paid an additional 20 cents a mile for transporting it.

It was later discovered that 93 bales of cotton belonging to Collins did not have his mark on them and were held in reserve. It was also known there were still 60 bales of Collins's cotton at the warehouse in Demopolis. Montague went back to Demopolis and put these aboard the riverboat *Bridge's Flats* and from there no accounting was ever made and no money from their sale was ever deposited into the Treasury.

Out of the 1,362 bales, 28 were given away as payment to others. The 93 remaining unmarked Collins bales out of the original 793 were repacked into 80 bales. Eventually, 439 bales were shipped to New York in lots of 4 shipments and sold at auction for $18,192.36. None of John Collins's cotton was sent to New York and sold so no money from the sale of his cotton was ever deposited in the Treasury and his petition was dismissed.

John Collins died on June 22, 1867 after unsuccessfully appealing to President Andrew Johnson for restitution. Charles W. Collins and Francis S. Lyon were his executors. Charles Collins filed suit on April 12, 1912 to recover under the abandoned or captured property act of March 12, 1863 but before any action was taken they both died and in March 1920 Harry T. Collins was appointed administrator of the estate and he took the case back to federal court.

In October and December of 1920, Harry Collins requested the court to contact the Treasury Department in an effort to establish the ownership and disposition of the cotton. He believed that the Treasury Department had the records from the warehouse in Demopolis. The court had urged Charles Collins to procure this evidence but he never did. In their decision of December 13, 1920, the court dismissed the claim on the ground that even if the records showed ownership, none of the money from John Collins's cotton was ever deposited into the Treasury so none could be owed. Any money in the Treasury could be taken out only by an act of Congress so he was left to appeal to his representative.

Colman, Anna M. Captain Charles D. Colman was appointed provost marshal for the First Congressional District of Missouri at St. Louis on June 2, 1863. As provost marshal he was a member of the board of enrollment for military service.

The Act of March 2, 1863 to "commute liability under a specific draft," approved by the

Secretary of War on June 30, allowed a payment of $300 from those wishing to avoid the draft. The practice of using brokers arose since a substitute could take enlistment bounty money from a draftee and disappear if he was rejected for service. The substitute brokers in St. Louis requested Colman to keep money paid to them by draftees to pay their substitutes. Colman initially declined since it was not his duty but then agreed and, without authority from his superiors, began taking money from the brokers and draftees or their agents to give to the substitutes. If the substitute was not enrolled he was to return the money to the draftee. He was not required by law to deposit the money in any account. Colman paid every substitute accepted for service and more than $1 million passed through his office.

In early February 1865 Colman deposited a package with the Bank of St. Louis containing $30,049 including $20,000 in compound interest notes; $4,500 in 7.30 percent Treasury notes; and $5,449 in greenbacks. The package was seized on the 10th on order of Colonel J. H. Baker, Provost Marshal General of the Department of the Missouri, and on the 28th he informed Colman the money was in the custody of Captain Hamilton.

In May he was charged with fraud and attempting to procure substitutes for James K. Knight, John H. Rankin, Charles M. Elleard, C. B. Burnham, E. C. Cushman, John Whittaker, and seven others; embezzling $30,000 on February 6, 1865 belonging to substitutes, deserters, and conscripts, refusing to hand the money over; making false payroll entries; making false vouchers; and conduct unbecoming an officer and a gentleman, and he was court-martialed.

The court found $18,963 of the total had been embezzled from draftees. He was sentenced to dismissal from the service, turn over the $18,963, pay a $700 fine, and serve seven months in prison, or until the money was returned and the fine paid. He refused to turn the money over but the military already had the money and was used for government purposes. He remained in the Missouri State Penitentiary until April 28, 1866 when he was released on a writ of habeas corpus from the U.S. Circuit Court for the Eastern District of Missouri.

His widow, Anna sued to recover the balance of $11,086 and was awarded that on February 24, 1903.

Conard, E. J. Conard and 20 other claimants sued together in the "Loudoun County Claims" for the loss of livestock in northern Virginia.

In November 1864 General Philip H. Sheridan issued an order:

> Headquarters Middle Military Division
> November 27, 1864
> Bvt. Maj. Gen. Wesley Merritt.
> Commanding First Cavalry Division:
> General: You are hereby directed to proceed, tomorrow morning at 7 o'clock, with the two brigades of your division now in camp, to the east-side of the Blue Ridge, via Ashby's Gap, and operate against the guerillas in the district of country bounded on the south by the line of the Manassas Gap Railroad as far east as White Plains; on the east by the Bull Run range; on the west by the Shenandoah River; and on the north by the Potomac.
>
> This section has been the hot-bed of lawless bands, who have from time to time depredated upon small parties on the line of the Army communications, on safeguards left at houses, and on troops. Their real object is plunder and highway robbery.
>
> To clear the country of these parties, that are bringing destruction upon the innocent as well as their guilty supporters by their cowardly acts, you will consume and destroy all forage and subsistence, burn all barns and mills and their contents, and drive off all stock in the region the boundaries of which are above described. This order must be literally executed, bearing in mind, however, that no dwellings are to be burned and that no personal violence be offered the citizens.
>
> The ultimate results of the guerilla system of warfare is the total destruction of all private rights in the country occupied by such parties. This destruction may as well commence at once, and the responsibility of it must rest upon the authorities at Richmond, who have acknowledged the legitimacy of guerilla bands.
>
> The injury done to this army by them is very slight, the injury they have indirectly inflicted upon the people and upon the rebel army may be counted by millions.
>
> The Reserve Brigade of your division will move to Snickersville on the 29th. Snickersville should be your point of concentration and the point from which you should operate in destroying toward the Potomac.
>
> Four days' subsistence will be taken by your command. Forage can be gathered from the country through which you pass.
>
> You will return to your present camp, via Snickersville, on the fifth day.
> By command of Major-General P. H. Sheridan.
> James W. Forsyth
> Lieutenant Colonel and Chief of Staff

The livestock they encountered were grouped together and driven along on the march. Some were used for food during the expedition, others were later sold at auction and the proceeds deposited into the U.S. Treasury. Many residents of Loudoun County presented claims to the Southern Claims Commission but the Commission could not rule since "the large herds of horses, cattle, and sheep were driven off together" and there was no record of which animals were used by the Army for food and which were later sold. The Commission stated:

"We have therefore declined examining them, thinking Congress may make some special provision in regard to their examination and settlement."

In March 1872 the House Committee on War Claims recommended to the Senate the passage of an act for the relief of the Loudoun County claimants and this was done on January 23, 1873. Ten years later, without any action, the claims were referred to a federal court under the Bowman Act of March 3, 1883. On June 9, 1890 the court stated:

"Claims for destruction or damage to property during the late war are excluded from our jurisdiction and it becomes incumbent upon claimants to show whether their stock was killed and wasted upon the march when driven before troops supplied with rations, or whether they died by the way, or were afterwards, by proper direction applied to Army use, or whether they were sold and the proceeds of the sale turned into the Treasury. This has not been done; from the nature of the occurrence it can not be done."

Cones, William W. Cones went to St. Louis in October and November of 1862 to obtain permits from customs officials to buy and remove cotton from Tennessee and Mississippi "within the lines of the United States Army."

On December 11 Major General Grant declared that, "on and after Monday, December 15, 1862 trade and travel will be open to Oxford, Miss., which place will constitute the southern limit until further orders, and beyond which persons not connected with the army are prohibited from passing."

On the 18th Cones was at a plantation nine miles southeast of Oxford and five miles beyond the picket lines when he made three agreements to buy cotton. One was with Mrs. D. N. Porter to buy her entire crop of cotton, around 70 bales. The second was to buy the entire crop of the Price plantation, about 116 bales ready for market and about 20 bales in the seed. The third was with M. A. Oliver, around 59 bales and about 29 yet to bale. All agreements were at 25 cents a pound on delivery at Oxford.

Just at this time the Army sent out wagons to "seize the cotton of certain obnoxious rebels" and disloyal persons who were in the area. No specific orders or destinations were given and all the cotton bought by Cones was seized, put into a lot of around 1,600–1,800 bales, and taken to Oxford. Some of the cotton was released to its owners at Oxford and the rest sent on to Memphis.

Cones went to Memphis and appealed to Major General C. S. Hamilton. Hamilton investigated and released his cotton on February 3, 1863. There were 772 bales from Oxford at Memphis then and Hamilton decided that 500 of those would never be reclaimed and ordered them sold leaving 272 bales to satisfy any valid claims including Cones's.

On the same day Cones paid $8,000 to Porter, $17,125 to Price, and $6,375 to Oliver. Before Hamilton's order could be carried out General Grant arrived and ordered the quartermaster to sell all the cotton at Oxford and to reimburse all the claimants who could establish their rights at 25 cents a pound. Cones never received any money and the 272 bales were auctioned on the 19th. Cones's portion of the sale amounted to $92,598.40. The money was used by the quartermasters for their own purposes and wasn't deposited into the Treasury until May of 1865.

Cones sued and recovered $92,598.40 in 1872.

Conrad, Peter. Resident of St. Louis, Missouri who owned the barge *Equinox*, made from the hull of the 1852 steamer *Equinox*, which he bought for $2,500 in 1859.

In 1862 his barge was loaded with ice at Memphis, Tennessee. Conrad sold the ice to George W. Willard and loaned the barge to Willard for a period of 90 days provided he could sell the ice to the Army. After 90 days the Army was to return the barge to Memphis, but if that was not done the Army was to pay Conrad $3,500.

The barge was taken down the Mississippi River to Young's Point, Louisiana, 12 miles above Vicksburg, where the ice was sold on July 3 to Henry H. Elliot, acting quartermaster at Young's

Point, on approval of Brigadier General Thomas Williams, commander of the land forces in the Gulf area. The ice was greatly needed for the relief of many sick soldiers in the area. The barge was conveyed by receipt to the quartermaster with instructions to return it to Memphis within 90 days but the barge was never returned and Conrad was never paid.

Shortly after July 3 the Army and Navy moved out of Young's Point. The barge was towed by steamer to Helena, Arkansas and the steamer's operator notified the quartermaster there of the barge's arrival. The wooden roof of the barge was taken apart during the trip to Helena and the wood used to build coffins. The barge was tied to a riverbank at Helena and left unattended where it eventually sank.

Conrad appealed unsuccessfully to the Army for the loss of his barge so he sued. The court brought in an expert who declared the value of the barge to be $2,000 to $3,000. The court noted that vessels do not appreciate in value and a hull built in 1852 couldn't be worth much more than the lower estimate so Conrad was awarded $2,000.

Coogan, Patrick J.

Coogan and George L. Cunningham bought 126 bales of upland cotton in July 1863. One-third of the money was Cunningham's. They agreed the cotton would be sold after the war and that Patrick would retain control of it. Coogan fled from the Confederacy sometime in 1864 for some reason, and he turned the cotton over to Cunningham. Around January 1, 1865 the Confederate military authorities told Cunningham they knew the cotton belonged to Coogan. Cunningham then offered Major John S. Ryan, a Confederate commissary, 20 bales of the cotton if he would spare the rest from destruction or confiscation.

Cunningham reported all the cotton to another Confederate officer as his own, Ryan affirmed the statement, the cotton was not seized, and Cunningham delivered the 20 bales to Ryan. None of this was done with the knowledge or consent of Coogan and Coogan didn't find out about it until after the cotton was seized at Charleston.

Coogan sued to recover the whole lot as the rightful owner on the ground that his cotton and Ryan's cotton had all been seized together and Cunningham's actions were unlawful. Ryan claimed his 20 bales. The court held Cunningham's actions, as the sole owner, were valid in saving the lot from destruction. Ryan's petition was dismissed.

Cook, Frank.

On October 30, 1863 Captain William Budd's gunboat *Somerset* was off Apalachicola, Florida. Budd reported to Secretary of the Navy Gideon Welles on December 15, 1863 from his ship at West Pass, St. Georges Sound, Florida:

> Sir: I have the honor to report that on the 30th of October, while on a scouting expedition at the town of Apalachicola, I found 10 bales of cotton secreted in a warehouse, which I captured and brought off. A negro named Frank Cook claimed to be the owner and stated that he had kept them hid there for some months to prevent them from falling into rebel hands. Some of the rebels in town, however, knew that the cotton was there, and we did not. In my opinion the real owner did not make his appearance. I have sent the cotton to Key West by the USS *Henderson,* and respectfully forward the prize list of this vessel at the time of the capture. The USS *J. S. Chambers* was at anchor at West Pass, but not within signal distance when the cotton was captured.

The cotton was sold at auction as a maritime prize for $2,763.13 on order of the district court prize commissioner. The proceeds were deposited in the U.S. Treasury, half credited to the Naval Pension Fund and the other half to the crew of the *Somerset.* The crew's half was later paid out to them through the Navy Department.

Cook sued in federal court under the Act of March 12, 1863, the same Act the cotton was seized under. His position was that Captain Budd had a duty to turn the cotton over to a Treasury agent pursuant to Section 6 of the Act and since that didn't happen, the district court had no jurisdiction to adjudicate an illegal action.

The court found the district court could not have jurisdiction over an illegally disposed of "maritime prize." The problem was with the cotton's location. By being taken on land, it could not legally be classified as a prize for the benefit of the naval captors. The court cited the Act of July 17, 1862 titled "For the better government of the Navy:"

"That the proceeds of all ships and vessels, and the goods taken on board of them, which shall be adjudged good prize, shall, when of equal or superior force to the vessel or vessels making the capture, be the sole property of the captors; and when of inferior force, shall be divided equally between the United States and the officers and men making the capture."

The court awarded Cook $2,487.39 since the Act did not include property taken on land by naval forces.

Cooper, Charles and John.

In the summer of 1863 the Army established a huge cavalry depot at Giesboro Point, Maryland. On April 6, 1864 Cooper signed a contract to build a feed mill in Giesboro, near Washington, D.C. to cut hay, grind grain, mix, cook, and deliver food for 10,000 horses a day. The government was to pay $26,500 for the machinery, one half, or $13,250, when the parts were delivered at Giesboro and the other half when the mill was inspected and approved. The main drive belt was four-ply rubber 24 inches wide.

The machinery arrived on July 28 and the company received a voucher for $13,250. On October 8 they received a further $10,000, leaving $3,250 due on inspection and acceptance. The inspectors were happy and on November 8 the balance was paid and receipted.

The contract was later amended to provide stronger drive belts, bigger buckets, pulleys, extra cutter knives, tools, and gearing and on January 9 the company sent a bill for an additional $3,563.09. A board was appointed to review the bill but the members could not agree on the reasonable value of the additions. The Coopers sued and recovered $3,563.09 in 1871.

Corson, Richard R.

Enlisted as a volunteer private in August 1861, subsequently commissioned captain and assistant quartermaster, summarily dismissed from the service on March 27, 1865 by President Lincoln, fully restored on June 9, 1865 by President Johnson, and honorably mustered out on October 7. He sued for $328 in back pay and $210 for three months' separation pay and recovered $538 in 1880.

The government appealed to the Supreme Court where the decision was reversed in 1884:

"The judgment of the court below is reversed on the ground: (1) That an officer of the Army, dismissed from the service, during the recent civil war, by order of the President, could not be restored to his position merely by a subsequent revocation of that order. (2) The vacancy created could only be filled by a new appointment, by and with the advice and consent of the Senate, unless it occurred in the recess of that body, in which case the President could have granted a commission, to expire at the end of its next succeeding session."

Coté, Elie.

Coté owned 75 bales of upland cotton that was seized in February 1865 at Charleston. On May 6, 1865 he assigned the interest in the cotton to numerous creditors. When the creditors sued to recover, their petition was denied on the ground that seized property became the property of the captor after 24 hours of "undisturbed possession" pursuant to the Act of July 17, 1862 and "an assignment or transfer of a claim arising under the Captured and Abandoned Property Act executed before a judgment is recovered, is void under the act of 26th February, 1853."

Cramer, A. F.

The A. F. Cramer & Co., of Cumberland, Maryland, was composed of Lloyd Lowndes, A. M. C. Cramer, and A. F. Cramer and had a branch office in Martinsburg, Berkeley County, Virginia. During the war, Lowndes lived in Clarksburg, West Virginia and A. M. C. lived in Cumberland. A. F. lived in Martinsburg, West Virginia until the fall of 1862 when he sold out the business there and moved to Cumberland. A. F. purchased cotton with the proceeds through an agent, W. H. Morrison, who moved about the region and was at all times a supporter of the rebellion.

Cumberland and Clarksburg were always under U.S. control. The occupation of Martinsburg shifted until about October 1, 1862 when Union forces took control and their cotton was seized.

The court held the company violated the Non-Intercourse Act of July 13, 1861 and their petition was dismissed.

Crary, Humphrey H.

Owner of the steamer *J. A. Stevens* chartered on December 31, 1862 at $120 a day. On May 4, 1863 the rate was arbitrarily reduced to $60 a day. Crary sued for $8,680 and his petition was dismissed.

Craycroft, Thomas J.

Enrolled at Louisville, Kentucky on June 12, 1863 for three years and was mustered in as sergeant in Company B, 34th Kentucky Infantry on September 10.

On August 31, 1864 he apparently left his regiment and joined the 11th Tennessee Cavalry. On October 21 he was officially discharged from the service as of June 28, 1864 by Major General John M. Schofield so he could be commissioned a first lieutenant by the governor of Tennessee.

On November 7, 1864 he was tried before a general court martial and on April 4, 1865 he was dismissed from the service with loss of pay and allowances. He was reinstated to rank on

February 24, 1897 and sued to recover his back pay. His petition was dismissed on December 2, 1912.

Cromwell, William A. Owned a lot in Memphis, Tennessee the Direct Tax Commission designated No. 16, block 14, and assessed a tax of $10.50 which Cromwell did not pay. Tax, penalty, and interest accrued to $18.64 and on June 18, 1864 the lot was sold at auction to James Boynton for $360 and he was given tax-sale certificate No. 478. The surplus paid into the Treasury was $341.36.

The certificate was assigned and re-assigned and on January 12, 1866 it was given to J. B. Wetherill. On February 15, Cromwell sued Wetherill in a state court at Memphis but the case was moved to the U.S. Circuit Court for Western Tennessee. On February 11, 1873, while the case was still pending, Cromwell executed a warranty deed to William G. Wilkins for $3,500 and on July 22, 1873 Wetherill and his wife conveyed whatever title they might have in the property to Wilkins for $554.75 and the lawsuit was dropped. On March 25, 1884 Wilkins re-assigned the tax surplus money to Cromwell who submitted a claim to the Secretary of the Treasury, which was disallowed on April 19. Cromwell sued and recovered the $341.36 on May 14, 1888.

Crowell, De Witt Clinton. Resident of Norfolk, Virginia who signed a contract on May 16, 1864 at Butler's Landing, Bermuda Hundred, with Dr. Charles McCormick, medical director of Major General Butler's army in the field in Virginia and Kentucky, to furnish ice for hospitals at $30 a ton or 1½ cents a pound. McCormick's duties as outlined in Army regulations were "to see that the depots and ambulances are provided with the necessary apparatus, medicines, and stores." He was the medical purveyor in the district he was in and as such had the authority to execute contracts. There were 3,000 sick and wounded in hospitals with no ice owing to the failure of another contractor to deliver ice. A serious lack of ice lasted nearly six months.

Crowell delivered 1,003,447 pounds of ice from August 1 to November 7 to hospitals, hospital transports on the James and Appomattox Rivers, in the field where directed, and at Bermuda Hundred, Broadway Landing, and Point Rocks. He was paid $10,009.91 and received a $15,051.70 signed voucher from Dr. McCormick. The Surgeon General objected to the voucher based on the price charged and on his opinion that it should have been obtained at Fort Monroe and transported by the Quartermaster's Department.

Crowell sued and recovered the money in 1866.

Crussell, Thomas G. W. Owner of 73 bales of cotton seized at Atlanta, taken by wagon to the Western & Atlantic Railroad depot, and shipped to Cincinnati. Crussell's loyalty was well known and he was appointed foreman of the masonry department on the military railroad by General Sherman.

Asbury P. Bell testified:

"It was a public rumor on the street here that Mr. Crussell, in company with Ed Murphy and others, appropriated provisions collected by the Southern Relief Committee to the feeding of a train load of Union prisoners captured at the battle of Chickamauga and sent to this place. It was charged that this was done while the train stopped over here one night."

He recovered $26,275.62.

Cushing, William. The Confederate ironclad ram *Albemarle* was sunk at Plymouth, North Carolina at about 3 A.M. on October 28, 1864 by 15 Navy men from seven ships with a torpedo carried by a small steam launch commanded by Lieutenant William B. Cushing.

In October 1864 Lieutenant Cushing was detached from the *Monticello* to report to Rear Admiral David D. Porter, commander of the North Atlantic Squadron, and lead the expedition. Cushing took 14 sailors from various ships with him on *Picket Launch No. 1*. The picket boats had no assigned crews "on the books" and were part of Commander William H. Macomb's Division of the Sounds of North Carolina. A cutter from the *Shamrock* manned by Acting Gunner William Peterkin and Acting Master's Mate W. D. Burlingame was also brought along.

Cushing reported to Porter from Albemarle Sound on the 30th:

I have the honor to report that the rebel ironclad *Albemarle* is at the bottom of the Roanoke River. On the night of the 27th, having prepared my steam launch, I proceeded up toward Plymouth with 13 officers and men, partly volunteers from the squadron.

The distance from the mouth of the river to the ram was about 8 miles, the stream averaging in width some 200 yards, and lined with the enemy's pickets. A mile below the town was the wreck of the *Southfield*, surrounded by some schooners, and it was understood that a gun was mounted there to command the bend. I therefore took one of the *Shamrock's* cutters in tow, with orders to cast off and board at that point if we were hailed. Our boat succeeded in passing the pickets, and even the *Southfield,* within 20 yards, without discovery, and we were not hailed until by the lookouts on the ram. The cutter was then cast off and ordered below, while we made for our enemy under a full head of steam.

The rebels sprung their rattle, rang the bell, and commenced firing, at the same time repeating their hail and seeming much confused.

The light of a fire ashore showed me the ironclad made fast to the wharf, with a pen of logs around her about 30 feet from her side.

Passing closely, we made a complete circle so as to strike her fairly, and went into her bows on. By this time the enemy's fire was very severe, but a dose of canister at short range served to moderate their zeal and disturb their aim. Paymaster Swan, of the *Otsego,* was wounded near me, but how many more I know not. Three bullets struck my clothing, and the air around seemed full of them.

In a moment we had struck the logs, just abreast of the quarter port, breasting them in some feet, and our bows resting on them. The torpedo boom was then lowered and by a vigorous pull I succeeded in diving the torpedo under the overhang and exploding it at the same time that the *Albemarle's* gun was fired. A shot seemed to go crashing through my boat, and a dense mass of water rushed in from the torpedo, filling the launch and completely disabling her.

The enemy then continued his fire at 15 feet range, and demanded our surrender, which I twice refused, ordering the men to save themselves, and removing my own coat and shoes. Springing into the river, I swam, with others, into the middle of the stream, the rebels failing to hit us.

The most of our party were captured, some were drowned, and only one escaped besides myself, and he in another direction. Acting Master's Mate Woodman, of the *Commodore Hull,* I met in the water half a mile below the town, and assisted him as best I could, but failed to get him ashore.

Completely exhausted, I managed to reach the shore, but was too weak to crawl out of the water until just at daylight, when I managed to creep into the swamp, close to the fort. While hiding a few feet from the path, two of the *Albemarle's* officers passed, and I judged from their conversation that the ship was destroyed.

Some hours' traveling in the swamp served to bring me out well below the town, when I sent a negro in to gain information and found that the ram was truly sunk.

Proceeding through another swamp, I came to a creek and captured a skiff belonging to a picket

of the enemy, and with this, by 11 o'clock the next night, had made my way out to the *Valley City.*

Acting Master's Mate William L. Howorth, of the *Monticello,* showed, as usual, conspicuous bravery. He is the same officer who has been with me twice in Wilmington harbor. I trust he may be promoted, when exchanged, as well as Acting Third Assistant Engineer Stotesbury, who, being for the first time under fire, handled his engine promptly and with coolness. All the officers and men behaved in the most gallant manner. I will furnish their names to the Department as soon as they can be procured.

The cutter of the *Shamrock* boarded the *Southfield,* but found no gun. Four prisoners were taken there.

The ram is now completely submerged, and the enemy have sunk three schooners in the river to obstruct the passage of our ships.

I desire to call the attention of the admiral and Department to the spirit manifested by the sailors on the ships in these sounds. But few men were wanted, but all hands were eager to go into action, many offering their chosen shipmates a month's pay to resign in their favor.

The name of the man who escaped is William Hoftman, seaman, on the *Chicopee.* He did his duty well, and deserves a medal of honor.

Cushing misspelled Houghton's (Hoftman) and Howarth's (Howorth) names.

Cushing's purpose for taking the cutter in tow was to land at the wharf if they were not discovered and cut the *Albemarle* loose and set her adrift in the river. Cushing and Edward J. Houghton, an ordinary seamen, were the only ones to escape capture.

Acting Ensign Thomas S. Gay reported on his capture to Secretary of the Navy Gideon Welles on March 7, 1865 from his home in Plymouth, New Hampshire:

On turning around we were hailed from the ram. We made no answer. We were hailed again, making no answer, but still getting in a fair position.

The next call was not so pleasant, for we were discovered, and the grape and canister began to play on our small craft in rapid succession, which was returned by our 12-pounder. At the same time Lieutenant Cushing sang out with several others, 'Leave the ram, or I'll blow you to pieces!' Having backed our boat sufficiently to get headway enough on her to jump the log pen which encircled the ram, we succeeded in jumping the logs and lowering the torpedo boom, and by a vigorous pull Lieutenant Cushing succeeded in exploding the torpedo under the port bow of the ram. Everything now was in the greatest of excitement on account of the heavy musketry we were receiving from the ram. Having backed our boat off from the *Albemarle,* we came in contact with the logs which were encircled around her. Finding it impossible to extricate our boat, and being twice ordered to surrender, Lieutenant Cushing gave the order not to surrender, at the same time sang out, 'Men, save yourselves,' and immediately sprang overboard, several others following this example. I had not proceeded far from the boat when I fell in with Acting Ensign William L. Howarth on a log, unable to proceed farther without assistance. Having a life preserver with me, I gave it up to him and returned to the boat to procure another, not knowing how far I might have to swim, and at the same time I destroyed two boxes of ammunition and several carbines. I had not gone far the second time when I found myself chilled, and after a severe struggle I regained the circle of the logs, where I found several of the crew, with a boat from the ram in charge of Lieutenant Roberts. We were all taken on shore and marched to the prison, where we remained until our gunboats made their approach up the river. We were then marched to Tarboroa, N. C., a distance of 60 miles, at which place we arrived on the 2d of November, being very tired and feet badly swollen. On the 3d we were sent to Salisbury, where we arrived on the 5th. After marching about 2 miles we arrived at the stockade, where we were enclosed with some 10,000 prisoners. Here we suffered immensely for the want of shelter from the inclemency of the weather and also for provisions, as our fare was very poor, being one-half pint of meal per day, which was very inconvenient on account of having no cooking utensils. On the 13th we were sent to Danville, where we arrived on the 14th. Here we were placed in a brick building with about 500 army officers. This place we found to be more comfortable, as we were sheltered from the weather, but still not having a blanket or cover of any kind, which made it very severe for us. Our ration here was a piece of corn bread, 4 inches long, 2 wide, and 1½ half thick; this consisted of our day's ration. On the 11th of December we were sent to Richmond, Va., and confined in Libby prison. There we found the treatment much the same as at Danville. On the 21st of February, 1865, we were paroled, and arrived at Cox's Landing the same afternoon and repaired on board of the flag of truce steamer *New York,* where we received a bountiful supply of eatables.

Two sailors, John Woodman and Samuel Higgins, were reported drowned and their bodies were recovered.

The *Albemarle* was later salvaged and towed to Norfolk, Virginia by USS *Ceres* where they arrived on April 27, 1865. She was appraised by a board of naval officers at $79,944 and that amount was deposited into the Treasury. She was condemned as a lawful prize in the U.S. District Court for the District of Columbia and distribution of the prize money commenced.

The Prize Act of June 30, 1864 provided for the distribution of prize money in two ways. The first among the capturing vessels' crews or between the crews and the government. The second among fleet officers and individual captors. Allotments in the first category were decreed by a prize court, those in the second by the Treasury and Navy Departments.

On August 21, 1865 the prize court decreed that $77,298.70, less $2,645.30 for costs, be deposited into the Treasury for distribution among the captors and stated:

"Now, therefore, it is adjudged and decreed that the prize was of superior force to the vessel making the capture, and that the whole of the residue of said valuation be paid to the captors, as follows: One-twentieth of said residue to the officers commanding the North Atlantic Blockading Squadron at the time of said capture, one-hundredth part of the said residue to the fleet captain of said North Atlantic Blockading Squadron, and the remainder distributed to the other persons doing duty on board said torpedo launch in proportion to their respective rates of pay in the service."

Three of the crew were promoted before any money could be distributed: Cushing to lieutenant commander, Acting Master's Mate William L. Howarth to acting ensign, and Acting Master's Mate Thomas S. Gay to acting ensign.

The value of the *Albemarle* was disputed so Congress, with the approval of President Grant, sent the case back to court in June of 1872. An appraisal for the court was made by Post Captain Earl English, Commodore William E. Le Roy, and Commander Robert F. R. Lewis. They concluded her value at the time of capture in "hull, armor, engines, guns, stores, and equipments" was $282,856.90. The previous judgement was subtracted from the new judgement and $202,912.90, minus $7,076.51 for costs, was deposited in the Treasury, leaving $195,836.39.

Commander Macomb, Peterkin, and Burlingame also filed claims. The court awarded Macomb one-fiftieth, but held that Peterkin and Burlingame had no standing as their cutter was turned back prior to the actual attack on the ram and they took no part in the action.

After the officers were paid off, there remained $251,284.29 for the crew of *Picket*

Launch No. 1, accrued since the first judgement in 1865. A peculiar aspect of the Prize Act of 1864 decreed that the commander of a single ship making a capture was entitled to one-tenth of the prize money instead of an amount computed from his rate of pay even though his award might be less than his subordinates under this system.

Under the two decrees (pay rates in parentheses) Cushing ($1,875) was paid $56,056.27; William L. Howarth ($480), acting master's mate, $35,887.50; Francis H. Swan ($1,300), acting assistant paymaster, $31,102.50; Thomas S. Gay ($480), acting master's mate, $28,710.00; William Stotesbury and Charles L. Steever ($1,000), acting third assistant engineers, $23,925.00; John Woodman ($480), acting master's mate, $11,484.00; Samuel Higgins ($360), first-class fireman, $8,613.01; Richard Hamilton ($240), coal heaver, $5,742.01; Edward J. Houghton ($192), ordinary seaman, $4,593.60; Bernard Harley and William Smith (aka Daniel G. George), ordinary seamen ($192), $4,593.60; Robert H. King, Henry Wilkes, and Lorenzo Deming, landsmen ($168), $4,019.40.

These awards were disputed by Francis Swan and he was joined in a new lawsuit by Steever, Harley, Smith — going by his real name, Daniel G. George — Wilkes, Richard Hamilton's wife, Mary, and the heirs of six others, all claiming the awards were too low and that Lieutenant Cushing was overpaid under the one-tenth provision of the Prize Act. The case went back to court in 1883.

The crew and the heirs of deceased crewmembers, were represented by James Fullerton. William Stotesbury retained his own counsel, H. C. Cady. Cushing, Howarth, and Gay did not take part in the proceedings.

The government's defense centered around the idea that *Picket Boat No. 1* was not a "single ship" within the terms of the Prize Act and that the one-tenth amount given to the commander was intended for vessels "with its complement of sailors, gunners, stokers, engineers, and marines" and further:

"Claimant's counsel contends that the man whose brain conceived and whose nerve and courage executed this scheme should receive only $25,128.43, while to Paymaster Swan of the *Otsego* should be given $45,794.80, and to the third assistant engineers $35,226.77 each. Further, the crew had already accepted the Prize Court's and District Court's decree. Claimants

acquiesced in two distributions, well knowing that distribution meant exhaustion of the fund, and that if they received too little some one else was receiving too much, yet without protest or complaint they accepted the sums awarded. They knew or could have known the principles on which the first distribution was made. They acquiesced in it at the time, and through their silence the money now claimed by them was paid out."

The court cited the definition of a ship under the 32nd section of the Prize Act:

"That in the term, 'vessels of the Navy' shall be included, for the purposes of this act, all armed vessels officered and manned by the United States and under the control of the Department of the Navy."

The court held that the district court was not authorized to distribute prize money. That belonged to the Treasury and Navy Departments under the Prize Act. Another problem was found with the district court:

"But we have found as a fact, that none of the captors but Cushing was so represented [by counsel] in that court; and it is quite plain that he was directly and largely interested in having the decrees put into that shape."

The court concluded that Cushing was overpaid by $30,927.84; Howarth overpaid $18,979.02; and Gay overpaid $11,801.52 and the rightful balance of $61,078.38 should be redistributed to the remainder of the crew. The court lamented the one-tenth provision of the Act but said:

"We are free to say that we would avoid it in framing our judgement if we could. It is an accidental outcome of a capture such as might not happen again in all the wars that the world may know in all the future. That it occurred in this case was simply because a very valuable prize was captured by only fifteen men, to whom the whole of the prize money was awarded. The defect in the law, however, is one that we have no power to cure. We can only administer the statute as we find it written, not as we think it ought to have been; and under its terms we have seen no way to avoid a result which certainly does not commend itself to our sense of justice.

The new awards gave Cushing $25,128.43; Swan $45,793.80; Stotesbury and Steever $35,226.00; Howarth, Gay, and Woodman $16,908.48; Higgins $12,681.36; Hamilton $8,454.24; Houghton, Harley, and George $6,763.39; King, Wilkes, and Deming $5,919.62.

Cuthbert, Sarah B. Sarah was tenant for life on her rented property in Beaufort, South Carolina. On March 13, 1863 the property was sold to pay the direct tax, penalty, costs, and interest of $94.07, which she owed by law. The $425.93 surplus was deposited into the Treasury and she sued to recover. The owner of the property apparently was unavailable and the court recognized Sarah's interest in the surplus but could not recover it "in the absence of the other." Her petition was dismissed on February 16, 1885.

Cutner, Solomon. Apparently sued on behalf of Samuel Schiffer, the surviving partner of J. Schiffer & Co. of New York to recover the proceeds of 30 bales of cotton. Cutner was a naturalized citizen of Prussia who was a merchant in Blackshire, Georgia on the Atlantic & Gulf Railroad line.

Cutner bought 29 bales of sea-island and one bale of upland cotton and shipped it to 171 Congress Street in Savannah. The cotton was captured in December 1864, shipped to New York, and sold for $6,897.24. On March 6, 1865 he sold his interest in the cotton to J. Schiffer & Co. for $2,250. His suit was dismissed since he didn't own the cotton.

Danolds, Charles A. To buy horses, the Army normally called for dealers to bring animals to a particular place at a particular time, but it would often happen that orders would be received from Washington to stop buying and the quartermasters would have to refuse delivery of horses that had already passed inspection. Breeders then stopped bringing animals in altogether.

In the fall of 1863, Captain C. E. Fuller of the Cavalry Bureau was ordered by Quartermaster General Meigs to go to New York and buy as many horses as he could as quickly as possible to meet the "pressing exigencies of the public service." Fuller bought ads advising sellers to bring horses to government depots in the principle cities with a guarantee that every horse passing inspection would be bought.

On December 10, Danolds brought about 300 horses to Rochester unaware that Fuller had received orders the previous day to stop buying. Fuller felt bound to accept them but he was overruled by Captain Cram, the inspecting officer, who refused to inspect them. Danolds sent his agent to see General George Stoneman, Chief of the Cavalry Bureau. Stoneman told the agent,

"You go and tell Mr. Danolds to build corrals or barns for the horses, feed them well during the winter and take good care of them, and the government would accept them in the spring and pay for their keeping."

Danolds had stables constructed and kept the horses until May when inspectors arrived. Danolds said, "These are the same horses I sold Captain Fuller" although an informant said that 111 horses belonging to neighboring farmers had been added to the lot. Nevertheless, 193 horses were purchased at $135 each and 179 at $140 and paid for by Captain J. L. Trumbull.

Danolds spent $2,000 building corrals; grain, $12,393; hay, $10,120; and labor, $4,027 for the 274 of the original lot of 300. Eleven horses died and 15 were rejected.

He sued for $28,326.50 plus $1,430 for the 11 that died and $1,507.50 for the keep of those rejected. There was considerable disagreement over what was said and understood and the court found that orders from undisclosed sources clouded the issue but neither Captain Fuller nor General Stoneman executed a valid contract with Danolds and his petition was dismissed.

Dauphin, Dr. Maximilian A. A French citizen and physician in New Orleans. He lived in New Orleans until March 1863 when he obtained a military pass to accompany a patient, Mr. Caldwell, to Biloxi, Mississippi. Caldwell died shortly after arriving and Dr. Dauphin remained in Biloxi until January 1865 when he returned to New Orleans.

While in Biloxi he purchased 130 bales of upland cotton in several lots from brokers in Mobile. A number of other bales were bought and resold until 95 were left and captured in the N. W. Perry & Co. warehouse at Mobile on April 12, 1865.

A total of 3,221 bales of Mobile cotton were sold. Dauphin's netted $17,879.95, which he recovered in 1870.

Day, Nancy E. James L. Day, of Norwich, Connecticut, had a contract to carry mail on his steamer on route No. 8151 between Mobile and New Orleans from July 1, 1858 through June 30, 1862. On May 24, 1861 the Postmaster General discontinued the route and notified Day. He wrote to Washington on July 10:

To the Postmaster Gen'l.,
      P. O. Department, Washington:
   Dear Sir: I received on the 1st June, under date of the 24th May, official notice to discontinue the

service on route No. 8151, and that the contract was annulled. This course on the part of the Department (though doubtless rendered necessary through the present sate of the country) bares hard on us, who have invested a large amount of money in boats to enable us to carry out our contract, and, 1st, in view of the balance due us on the last quarter, which would have ended yesterday, are we not entitled by our contract to 30 days' pay additional after notice is given to annul the service by the Department, as a small compensation to the contractors for discontinuing the service? This, I hope, if correct, you will allow me at the proper time; and in view of the balance due me on quarter ending the 31st March, '61, I hope the Department will forward the amount as early as convenient, and oblige yours, very truly,

James L. Day

The Second Assistant Postmaster wrote back on the 19th to inform Day that no 30 days' pay would be allowed and stated, "In no instance has this been allowed in the order of discontinuance in the seceded states."

James Day died some time after that and the administratrix of his estate, Nancy Day, sued to recover $3,041.66 and was awarded that on April 12, 1886.

De Arnaud, Charles.

A lieutenant of engineers in the Russian army during the Crimean War who came to the United States in 1860. In August 1861 Major General John C. Frémont, commander of the Western Department of Missouri, hired him to spy on Confederate forces in Kentucky, Tennessee, and Missouri. De Arnaud furnished maps, information on troop movements, roads, outposts and stations and their condition, and as much as he could ascertain about future movements. He reported back to Frémont on August 12 at St. Louis. Frémont was pleased with the information he got and made arrangements for De Arnaud to continue and he left again that same day for Confederate territory. In early September he was returning to St. Louis to report on a plan to attack Paducah, Kentucky but when he got to Cairo, Illinois he felt constrained by time and telegraphed Frémont before reporting in person to General Grant with the same information. Grant mobilized his forces and headed immediately for Paducah. Confederate General Leonidis Polk took Columbus on the 3rd and Grant occupied Paducah ahead of him.

Frémont issued a voucher to De Arnaud:

Headquarters Western Department
Camp near Jefferson City, Oct. 6, 1861
Major Phinney, U.S.A., paymaster, etc., will pay to Charles De. Arnaud the sum of three hundred dollars ($300), for secret service.

J. C. Frémont
Major-General

De Arnaud was paid at Warsaw, Missouri on October 26. On the 23rd Frémont signed another voucher for $300 and he was again paid that amount. On January 6 Arnaud presented a bill for $3,600 to Quartermaster General Meigs and Meigs approved it on the 9th. On January 13 De Arnaud called on President Lincoln and gave him three letters:

Hon. A. Lincoln
President, U.S.A.:
The bearer, Charles de Arnaud, has to my knowledge rendered important services to the Government. He, at the risk of his life, gave information which led to our capture of Paducah, Ky., in advance of the rebels; thereby he saved the country thousands of lives and millions of dollars. I fully indorse his certificate of Maj. Gen. J. C. Frémont. He is entitled to the largest remuneration the Government pays for such services.
Respectfully, etc.,

A. H. Foote,
Flag Officer

Headquarters District Southern Missouri
Cairo, November 31, 1861
Chas. De Arnaud:
Sir: In reply to your request, and the note from Major-General Halleck presented me by yourself, I can state I took possession of Paducah, Ky., solely on information given by yourself, and to the affect that the rebels were marching upon that city with a large force. This information I afterwards had reason to believe was fully verified: First, because as we approached the city secession flags were flying and the citizens seemed much disappointed that Southern troops expected by them were not in advance of us. It was understood that they would arrive that day. I also understood afterwards that force of some four thousand Confederate troops were actually on their way for Paducah when taken possession of us by my order. A point through which many valuable supplies were obtained for the Southern army was cut off by this move, and a large quantity of provisions, leather, etc., supposed to be for the use of the Southern army, captured. For the value and use to which these were put I refer you to General Paine, whom I left in command. Only remaining in Paducah a few hours, and being busily engaged with other matters during that time, I can make no estimate of the cash value of the stores captured.
Yours, etc.,

U. S. Grant
Brig. Gen.

Astor House, New York, January 2, 1862
This is to certify that Mr. Charles de Arnaud was employed by me from about the first of August in traveling throughout the rebel parts of Tennessee and Kentucky, with the object of ascertaining the strength, condition, and probable movements of the rebel forces. He made under my direction many such journeys, reporting fully and in detail upon the force of the various encampments and the condition and strength of garrisons and various works in Tennessee and along the Mississippi River. He obtained this information at much personal risk and with singular intelligence, and performed the duties entrusted to him entirely to my satisfaction. He continued on this duty until the termination of my command in the Western Department. His services were valuable to the Government, and I consider him entitled to the largest consideration that the Government allows in such cases or to such agents.

J. C. Frémont
Maj. Gen., U.S.A

Lincoln folded the papers together and wrote a note on the back of General Grant's letter:

I have no time to investigate this claim; but I desire the accounting officers to investigate it, and if it be found just and equitable to pay it, notwithstanding any want of technical legality or form.

A. Lincoln
Jan. 13, 1862

The next day the Secretary of War wrote a note:

I have considered this claim, and can not bring my mind to the conclusion that the sum charged is not exorbitant. I am willing to allow $2,000 in full of the claim, and the dis. Clerk, War Dept., is authorized to pay Charles de Arnaud that sum.

Simon Cameron
Sec. War.

War Dept., Jan'y 14, 1862

De Arnaud was paid $2,000 by John Potts, War Department disbursing clerk, which he accepted under protest the same day. De Arnaud had suffered some sort of head trauma in the fall of 1861, while in government military service, "but the effects of his wounds in the head were beginning to affect him mentally, and he was in a condition of nervous apprehension and unnaturally desirous of securing his personal safety by getting out of the country, and he accepted the money paid by the War Department in order that he might do so."

In late 1861 De Arnaud became mentally incapacitated and did not recover until early 1886. On September 4, 1886 he presented a $50,000

claim to Secretary of the Treasury Daniel Manning citing the case of James W. Magoffin, one of General Frémont's Mexican War secret agents, who was paid that sum. The Act of July 17, 1861 appropriated $200,000 "for contingencies of the Army" and Second Auditor William A. Day recommended to the Second Comptroller that De Arnaud be paid his claim from that fund. On June 29, 1888 Second Comptroller Sigourney Butler rejected the claim "because payment in full seems to have been made and accepted years ago, and because this office has no means or jurisdiction to consider so plain a case of unliquidated damages."

Captain De Arnaud was informed of Butler's decision on July 10 when he was in Washington. On October 20, he petitioned Secretary of the Treasury Charles S. Fairchild to review the claim. Butler replied and told him his case could be resolved only in a federal court and the appropriate papers were transferred to the court.

On June 8, 1891 his petition was dismissed on the ground that payment was accepted and as barred by statute of limitations. Arnaud appealed to the Supreme Court where the lower court's decision was affirmed on July 29, 1894.

De Bébian, Louis. Louis was the administrator of his father's estate. The father, also Louis, was lost on the steamer *General Lyon* on March 31, 1865 along with all his books and receipts when the ship burned up off Cape Hatteras, North Carolina. Dad owned 211 bales of cotton seized at Wilmington in February 1865. The cotton was stored in his son's warehouse.

Junior claimed all the cotton but when the case went to trial Alexander Oldham claimed ownership of 70 bales. Louis conceded, leaving his father's estate with 141 bales. Cotton captured at Wilmington was not treated as cotton captured at Savannah or Charleston and as the court stated "with it much of the confusion, neglect, and anomalies that we have, unhappily, been taught to anticipate."

De Bébian's cotton was broken up and only 131 bales reached New York on July 21, 1865. On August 8, 1868 the Secretary of the Treasury reported that the 841 bales of Wilmington cotton netted an average of $133.74 per bale in currency.

The cotton arrived on three ships, the *Herschel, Raymond,* and *Enterpe.* The court found the earliest cotton sold in March 1865 brought the least price and the latest in August brought a price below the Treasury's reported price. De Bébian was awarded $100 per bale on 32 bales and $125.95 on 109 bales for $16,833.65 and gave De Bébian 20 days to appeal. Apparently he did not.

Deeson, Hattie L. William M. Deeson owned six bales of cotton captured in Carroll Parish, Louisiana but he died prior to his wife filing a claim. The law required an intestate's claimant to prove the decedent gave no aid to the rebellion. Hattie was unable to do that so her petition was dismissed.

De Give, Lawrence. A citizen of Belgium who sued to recover the proceeds on 11 bales of sea-island cotton seized at Savannah. All resident aliens and foreign owners had to prove that U.S. citizens could prosecute claims against their government before they could recover any losses in U.S. courts. Sometimes evidence was taken from the actual treaty or trade documents, other times expert witnesses were examined. In this case, Victor Frader, a resident of Staten Island, New York who practiced law in the Court of Appeals of Brussels, was questioned extensively about Belgian law. He affirmed the right of a U.S. citizen to sue in Belgium:

"In Belgium each village or city constitutes a commune, as each province. They are individually considered as persons and they can sue, be sued, and have execution enforced upon them as private persons. They are independent corporations under the general law of the government."

De Give was awarded $2,317.90 on ten bales.

Dent, Warren R. A resident of Jefferson County, Mississippi who owned the Holly Grove plantation on which 176 bales of cotton were captured in February 1864 by General Alfred Ellet's Marine Brigade. With Ellet was Treasury agent Sherard Clemens, hired by John A. McDowell, Treasury Department assistant special agent at Vicksburg, to bring out captured and abandoned property on a commission basis. McDowell filed a libel against the cotton as authorized by General Sherman in a letter dated January 30, 1864. Of the 176 bales, 101 reached Cincinnati where they were rebaled into 100 bales prior to sale. The lot brought $27,240.40 at auction. Transportation and sale expenses came to $4,142.91 leaving net sales of $23,097.49. From this Clemens was paid $5,173.59 on July 30, 1864 and the balance of $17,923.90 was paid into the Treasury.

In court, Dent's attorney argued vehemently against the right of McDowell to hire Clemens and said the whole thing was a scheme to create a maritime case in collusion with McDowell whereby they would establish McDowell's own private prize court and libel the goods so as to award Clemens a salvage fee.

The court questioned the Treasury Department's authority to pay Clemens for the service but had no means to reduce or enlarge the amount of money that was actually paid into the Treasury. Dent recovered the $17,923.90 in 1873.

Dereef, Joseph M. F. Dereef was a "free colored citizen in Charleston, of intelligence and respectability." Two months prior to the occupation of the city he purchased two bales of upland cotton that was seized. The court awarded him $262.40.

De Rothschild, James Mayer. A French citizen of the De Rothschild Brothers of Paris who owned 366 hogsheads of leaf tobacco purchased in the summer of 1860 and stored in Anderson's warehouse at Richmond, Virginia where it was captured in April 1865. A claim was presented in the civil courts at Richmond but was dismissed and the tobacco sold for $64,471.68, less $4,000 for cooperage and storage and $3,000 in commissions for a net sum of $56,800. He went to federal court in 1870 and recovered $56,800.

Desmare, Alphonse. A partner in the New Orleans firm of Laforest & Desmare. New Orleans was taken on April 27, 1862 and after that commercial activity was allowed. Desmare's whereabouts at that time were unknown but he had an office in Opelousas, St. Landry Parish, where he bought cotton with Confederate bonds and notes. This area was under Confederate control until April 1863. Between October 1, 1862 and April 1863, Desmare bought 268 bales of cotton, all seized and sold for $51,456. On March 3, 1863 he and another partner bought 84 bales and this was seized and sold for $16,128.

Desmare sued to recover under the abandoned or captured property act but he was held to be an agent for the Confederate government and in violation of the Non-Intercourse Act of July 13, 1861. His petition was dismissed.

Devlin, John. Devlin was arrested at his home at 128 Hudson Avenue, Brooklyn, New York in February 1865 for fraudulently enlisting in the Navy and other crimes. He was tried in

Washington on March 6 on orders from the War Department, found guilty, and sentenced on April 5 to ten years at hard labor and a $10,000 fine with imprisonment at Clinton State Prison at Dannemora, New York until the fine was paid, imprisonment not to exceed 15 years.

During the trial he was held at the Old Capitol Prison in Washington. On April 2, prison Superintendent W. P. Wood received six $1,000 7.30 U.S. bonds, with one coupon detached, a $500 U.S. certificate of indebtedness to Moran Crane & Co. at 6 percent interest, with one coupon detached, and $380 in cash, all told $6,880. On May 5 Wood received eight $1,000, 5 percent interest U.S. Treasury bonds amounting to $7,670. On May 31, 1865 Devlin was released from prison.

All the securities were sold for $14,956.25 by the Army and paid into the Treasury and on November 9 Devlin was given $4,956.25.

On July 28, 1866 he wrote to Samuel Brecht requesting a receipt for the payment of the $10,000 fine. Brecht had sent him copies of his release order.

Devlin got the receipt and then sued to recover the fine as illegally imposed. The court agreed and he was awarded $10,000 in 1877.

De Witt Clinton. William H. Fogg and

his partner Mosher chartered their steamer to the Army on January 10, 1863 for one voyage, or three months, at $3.50 per registered tons per month to carry a battery of artillery with horses and stores to New Orleans. She was unloaded by May 16 but the ship was not ballasted or made fit for service until June 18 when she was discharged at New Orleans as of May 16. The owners sued to recover $3,856.89 in wages due from May 16 to June 18 and recovered that amount.

Diekelman, Eugene. A citizen of the

Kingdom of Prussia and owner of the ship *Essex*.

President Lincoln proclaimed the port of New Orleans open to commerce on May 12, 1862. On June 19, 1862 the *Essex* left Liverpool, England and arrived at New Orleans on August 24. Major General Benjamin F. Butler had the city under martial law and was under strict orders not to let any vessel leave port with supplies that might be of use to the rebels and he had issued orders to that end.

The *Essex* completed loading under the supervision of a customs officer and on September 15 her master, Captain Klatt, applied to the collector of customs for clearance to sail. This was refused without any specific reason being given. Klatt went to the Prussian consul the next day and was given a note requesting the reason for the refusal. He took it personally to the collector the same day and was told the ship had contraband cargo on board that would have to be unloaded before clearance would be granted. This was listed as items 10 through 14 on the document:

> 10. Shipped by Robert Clark, silver ware, one package, valued at $3,000, and one valued at $500, consigned to George Green & Sons, Liverpool.
> 11. Shipped by Hoghton, Rankin & Co., three cases containing family plated ware and silver plate in use, valued at $8,000, consigned to Rankin, Gilmour & Co., Liverpool.
> 12. Shipped by T. B. Ehlers, two boxes old silver ware, valued at $6,000, sealed and consigned to Messrs. A. Duranty & Co., Liverpool, as British property.
> 13. Shipped by Francis Olroyd, two boxes containing bullion, valued at $4,305, consigned to James Harris, Sun Life Insurance Office, London, care Bahr, Behrend & Co., Liverpool.
> 14. Shipped by Cramer & Co., as Hamburg property, one box, said to contain, in gold, $4,745.50; in silver, $520, consigned to order."

General Butler informed the acting Prussian consul on the 19th that the ship could leave as soon as the specified items were unloaded and the next day the collector told the consul he was bound by the general's orders to refuse clearance.

A formal protest was presented on September 22. On October 4 a customs officer, a sergeant, and two soldiers went aboard the ship with a letter from Robert Clark, owner of item No. 10, requesting the master to deliver his goods to the customs officer. The visitors did not have the bills of lading for the goods so Klatt refused to hand over them over. There was another customs officer already on board with keys to the holds and the soldiers demanded he hand over the keys. The soldiers opened the hold and removed Clark's goods over protests from the master and supercargo.

Another request to sail was made at 9 A.M. on the morning of the 9th, which was again refused pending removal of the rest of the goods. Two hours later a customs official came aboard and told the captain General Butler said he could leave port as soon as he presented himself at the customs house. The paperwork was cleared up, Clark's goods reloaded, and the ship left New

Orleans with all the cargo, 31 cabin passengers, and four in steerage.

Diekelman appealed to the State Department claiming $500 a day in gold was owed for daily expenses during the detention. Much correspondence ensued between Prussia and the United States over the 20 days' detention. Congress passed a joint resolution for the owner's relief pending fact-finding by a federal court.

The 1785 treaty with Prussia was consulted and the difference of opinion between General Butler and Captain Klatt over who should remove the goods was examined. Klatt feared doing so without a show of force by the military would hold him liable under the bills of lading. The government's position was that martial law, in and of itself, was military force. The court held that Klatt had the option of "surrendering the goods or suffering the detention" but a judgement for an award for detention was recommended to Congress.

The government appealed to the Supreme Court where the decision was reversed on the ground that Diekelman had no claim against the United States under the treaty with the King of Prussia, "or by the general law of nations," and there was no provision in the treaty for compensation.

Dillon, Robert. A New York merchant who owned 195 shares of the Central Cotton Press in Savannah. Dillon had "an old and intimate friend" in Savannah named Octavus Cohen. Cohen was a commission merchant, an agent for the Black Star Line, a director of two railroads, a prominent member of the local Jewish community and, after the war started, an assistant quartermaster general in the military service of the state of Georgia

Dillon and Cohen concocted an elaborate scheme to keep Dillon's assets from Confederate control. No money was ever actually exchanged, all correspondence was sent through Liverpool, England, and entries in Cohen's books were made to look as if he had purchased Dillon's stock for $23,500 when in fact he had not. Cohen got Dillon's dividends from Central Cotton and after passage of laws forbidding commerce with the states in rebellion Cohen bought 153 bales of upland cotton weighing 75,295 pounds in his name with the money.

This worked well until Savannah was captured and the cotton was seized. Dillon sued but the court stated:

"During the entire war, the claimant, a resident of New York, was carrying on trade in Savannah in the name of an enemy, but for his own sole and direct benefit, and that in connection with the preparation of an article on which the hopes of the rebel confederacy for financial success were mainly founded. This trade in the name of Cohen was equally unlawful as if carried on in the claimant's own name. The mere cover of nominal ownership in Cohen did not change the nature of the transaction. From such illegal acts claimant can claim no benefit here."

Donahue, Thomas. Donahue was hired on September 6, 1861 by an assistant quartermaster to finish horseshoes and put them on horses. He worked for 12 days, finished 1,225 shoes, and shod the horses. The quartermaster who hired him died and Donahue was unable to obtain payment for his services. He had to go to court to get it and was awarded $306.25 in 1866.

Donnelly & Co. William Donnelly and Patrick Egan were partners in Donnelly & Company and they resided in various places throughout the South. When Wilmington was occupied on February 22, 1865 they owned 348 bales of cotton weighing 166,600 pounds and the location of the cotton was duly reported to General Joseph Hayes. Of the lot, 268 bales were shipped to New York on the schooner *Sir John Herschell* and the balance on the schooner *Charles J. Raymond*.

General Hayes testified:

"It was part of my duty to investigate the loyalty of parties whose property I seized. I spent a large part of my time in such investigations. I know what the general speech of people was in regard to claimants having given aid or comfort to the rebellion. The general information we had was that claimants were foreigners and had never given aid or comfort to the rebellion.

"I saw an order issued by the commander of the confederate forces to burn the cotton of all Union citizens and these claimants' names were on the list."

Donnelly testified:

"After the rebellion broke out I followed the army [Confederate] doing a general trading business.

"I had expressed my sentiments, so far as I could, always in the success of the North. My name was on the black list. That was a list of men of Union proclivities and Wade Hampton issued an order that the property of those who had Union proclivities should be destroyed and I had great trouble in saving our cotton. This order of Hampton's was issued some time in January 1865."

During the trial, criticism was raised over the partners conflicting reports of the others' whereabouts and activities during the war. They failed to convince the court of their loyalty and their petition was dismissed.

Dothage, Joseph. Claimed two bales of cotton captured at Charleston but could offer no proof of loyalty.

Douglas, Robert M. and Stephen A., Jr. Sons of Stephen A. Douglas of Chicago, Illinois. Their grandfather, Robert Martin, died when Robert and Stephen were minors in Chicago. The boys were the heirs-at-law of his estate in Lawrence County, Mississippi. The boys' father was the executor of the estate, which was managed by James Strickland.

On December 1, 1857 Douglas entered into a partnership with James A McHatton of Baton Rouge, Louisiana to run a cotton plantation in Washington County, Mississippi on 2,000 acres of land McHatton owned.

Douglas furnished 142 slaves who were removed from Martin's plantation along with mules, cattle, wagons, and other equipment. Profits were to be divided according to the amount of capital each contributed. The land was valued at $80,000; the 142 slaves, $113,300; 32 mules, $4,000; 20 head of cattle, $500, 4 wagons, $200, all told $118,000. McHatton and James Dodds ran the day-to-day operations. Dodds managed a next-door plantation belonging to C. G. McHatton, the brother of James McHatton, who was also appointed supervisor of their plantation in May 1860

On May 31, 1859 the partners executed a formal agreement naming the boys as heirs. Sections 3 and 5 of the agreement stated:

"3d. That the said slaves were to be, and it is hereby stipulated that they shall be, well fed, well clothed, humanely treated, and kindly and properly cared for according to the laws of the State and the customs and usages of the best regulated plantations, under the most kind and humane masters, during the entire period of said partnership; and to this end the following stipulation shall be inserted in the contract with every overseer and person having charge or control of said plantation, to wit:

"That he will supply himself with at least two copies of Thomas Appelby's Record and Account Book No. 3 for Cotton Plantations, and that he will keep his daily record of events for each day faithfully and truly, according to the forms and requirements of said book, noting the births and death of each slave, with their names; the number sick, with their names; the number absent, with their names and causes of their absence; that he will keep a quarterly inventory of the stock and implements; a daily record of the cotton packing; a record of clothing, tools, &c.; a detailed account and receipts for supplies, showing the dates, amounts, descriptions, and quantities of each kind, &c.; a record of physician's visits to the sick, &c.; record of the weight of each bale of cotton and the number of bales; record of sales and shipments of cotton and all other property leaving the plantation; annual list of the negroes; the general results of the season; and, in short, that he will keep a full and complete account in all respects according to said book..."

"5th. That the said partnership shall continue until Robert M. Douglas (the older of the two boys) shall become 21 years of age, which will be on the 28th day of January, 1870, and with his assent shall continue two years thereafter, when his brother Stephen will become of age."

The settlement of profits was made by Dodds.

In 1860, 400 bales of cotton were produced. Other amounts from '61 and a small amount of unbaled cotton from '62 were on the plantation.

Stephen Douglas remained in Chicago and he died on June 3, 1861.

In October 1862 McHatton had over 335 bales hidden in a shed to preserve it for his partner's sons. In December he moved 70 of the slaves—"the best of the force"—to Texas, and the rest were moved in May 1863. He abandoned the plantation, left the cotton hidden away, and raised two crops of cotton in Texas for himself.

Between March 24 and 26 all the cotton was seized, brought to a nearby landing, put aboard the steamer *Empress,* and taken to Memphis with many other bales of seized cotton. The lot of 2,209 bales was rebaled to 2,111 bales and sold into the Treasury for $429,663.39. The amount was subsequently reduced to $421,663.39 for additional expenses. The McHatton/Douglas cotton sold for $58,422.46.

The boys had no knowledge of the cotton until 1870. McHatton swore off all interest in the cotton and died in 1872.

From the $421,663.39, Amanda Worthington was awarded $165,673.42 on 814 bales on March 13, 1871 and William A. Worthington was awarded $45,177 on April 1, 1872. The residue of $210,212.97 representing 1,173 bales gave a net worth of $179.21 per bale. In 1878 the boys were awarded $58,419.20 on their cotton.

Dowdy, Lucy E. William P. Dowdy lived in Fayette County, Tennessee. At various times during the war the Army took $5,130 worth of items and goods from his farm. His claim was submitted to the Quartermaster General pursuant to Section 2 of the Act of July 4, 1864 and March 28, 1866, which extended the provisions of the Act to the loyal citizens of Tennessee.

The claim was reviewed and Dowdy was paid $500 for 4 mules; $165 for 330 bushels of corn at 50 cents a bushel; and $59.25 for 7,900 pounds of fodder at 75 cents per 100 pounds for a total of $724.25. He was not happy with the settlement and refused to sign a "full and final discharge' receipt. William died before Congress appropriated the money on March 11, 1878 and the executrix of his estate, Lucy Dowdy, received the money. Lucy protested the amount as insufficient and produced an accounting of the goods.

4,000 pounds of fodder (receipted)	$80
4 No. 1 mules (receipted)	$800
2 men's saddles and bridles (receipted)	$100
250 bushels corn (receipted)	$250
10,000 pounds fodder (receipted)	$200
12 loads corn and fodder (receipted)	$300
75 barrels of corn, at $5	$375
4 mules at $800; 1 horse, $200	$1,000
1 saddle and bridle	$75
2 mules and bridles	$605
1,500 pounds fodder (receipted)	$30
2 mules and bridles	$405
3,000 pounds fodder	$60
1 mule	$200
1 buggy and harness	$400
3½ bushels corn, 1,000 pounds fodder	$10
800 pounds bacon, $120; 4 head beef cattle, $120	$240

She petitioned the House Committee on War Claims. Her petition was referred to a federal court for fact finding but it was dismissed on February 6, 1888 as barred by statutes of limitations and the Bowman Act.

Dozier, John T. Owner of the steamboat *Isabella*. The boat was seized on April 25, 1864 at St. Louis, a new crew was put aboard, and she was sent up the Missouri River to carry goods between Forts Rice and Sully in the Dakota Territory for Brigadier General Sully's northwestern Indian expedition. Fort Rice was about 1,700 river miles from St. Louis. On July 24 the boat was underway downriver in ballast when she struck an underwater obstruction. Her bottom was holed but good damage control saved her and she arrived at St. Louis on August 17. She was hauled out and underwent repairs until September 6 at a cost of $3,972.84.

Dozier carried $25,000 of ordinary marine risk insurance on a valuation of $36,000. The boat was in government service from 6 P.M. April 25 to 6 P.M. August 18, 115 days, at $85 a day. Dozier was paid $9,775 minus the time for repair. His insurance paid $2,560.56 for the damage. Dozier sued for rent during the repair period and recovered $1,445 for 17 days.

Duncan, John. John and Archibald Duncan owned a machine shop in Charleston, South Carolina as Duncan & Son. On February 20, 1865 Captain Tower seized the works for blacksmithing, boiler making and repairing until August 9, 1865, a total of 169 days. On September 26 the two filed a claim with Brigadier General W. T. Bennett, commander at Charleston. They were eventually referred to the superior provost court at Charleston. The court adjudged the value of the use and occupation of their shops and materials to be $50 a day for a total of $8,450 but no money was ever paid.

Archibald died in 1880 and on September 2, 1893 John filed suit to recover but his petition was dismissed on November 11, 1895. He appealed to Congress who appropriated the money and referred the case to a federal court for fact finding. On November 10, 1913 the court held that the loyalty of the two was not convincing but they were entitled to the award and reported that to Congress.

Dunnington, Charles Allen. Charles W. C. Dunnington purchased lot No. 3, square No. 688, in Washington City on April 2, 1852 "with the improvements, buildings, rights, privileges, appurtenances, and hereditaments, containing 5,372 square feet."

On May 12, 1863 the United States filed a libel on the property under the Confiscation Act of July 17, 1862 in the Supreme Court of the District of Columbia on the ground that Dunnington was in rebellion against the United States. The lot was condemned as enemy property and purchased by A. R. Shepard on June 29.

In May 1872 the government sought to

acquire property to enlarge the grounds around the Capitol and lot No. 3 was included in these negotiations. On June 11, Secretary of the Interior Columbus Delano went to court and said he was unable to acquire title to the various properties through agreements with the owners. The court appointed a commissioner to appraise the properties. On October 16 the commissioner reported that lot No. 3 was worth $1.50 a square foot and the improvements $1,500, for a total value of $9,858. The owners refused to sell within 15 days and on March 15, 1873 the purchase price for the properties was deposited with the Supreme Court of the District of Columbia to the credit of the owners. The properties were seized on the 31st and lot No. 3 became included "in the ornamental grounds about the Capitol" known as the Capitol Grounds.

On April 3, 1873 the heir of the deceased owner, Martin King, petitioned the court for the money for lot No. 3 and they were paid the full amount as the rightful owners in succession of A. R. Shepard.

Charles W. C. Dunnington died in early 1887 and on August 14 Charles Allen Dunnington, his heir, filed suit under the Fifth Amendment to claim the property. On that date it was worth $2 a square foot, $11,114, plus the $1,500 improvements, for a total of $12,644. The court held the heirs of Charles W. C. Dunnington had no right to the property until his death, and the government, as last purchaser, was holding a life estate in trust for the heirs of the rebel and were obligated to compensate the rightful owners of property condemned for public use. Dunnington was awarded $9,858 on May 6, 1889.

The government appealed to the Supreme Court where the decision was reversed on December 8, 1892:

"The Supreme Court holds that by payment into court of the appraised value of the condemned property the United States were discharged from liability and not entitled to notice of the order distributing the money."

Dykes, Benjamin B.

Owned 873 acres near Anderson, Georgia. Sometime in 1862 the Confederate government appropriated all but 12 acres of his land to establish the Andersonville prison-pen. His house was occupied and several temporary structures were built for officers, guards, cooking, hospitals, and other purposes. The area was captured in May 1865. Dykes requested the return of his property through 1868

but in that year a 25-acre national cemetery was established in which 13,705 soldiers were interred. In 1869 Quartermaster General Meigs wrote to Secretary of War Rawlins to vehemently oppose "returning the property to its former owner as hallowed ground that should forever be denied those who caused so much horror." Judge Advocate General Holt concurred.

In the spring of 1875 the War Department purchased about 101 acres from Dykes to encompass the cemetery and adjacent land.

Dykes sued to recover $2,031.25, the reasonable rent on the land from September 29, 1869, six years prior to his lawsuit set by the statute of limitations in the Court of Claims. He died before any action could be taken and Jerre Aycock was appointed administrator by the ordinary of Sumpter County, Georgia on January 6, 1879. The petition was dismissed as there was no contract for rent and the court had no jurisdiction to prosecute a case of trespass, occupation, and use of real property by the government.

Judge Advocate General Holt stated:

"When a claim adverse to its occupation of the premises shall be urged, and the grounds on which it rests brought to light, then it will be time to consider and determine whether the nation can be brought to surrender soil consecrated by the martyrdom and as the resting place of its fallen heroes, to the keeping and desecration of the traitors through whose barbarities these graves have been filled."

Ealer, Henry A.

An Allentown, Pennsylvania native who was a riverboat pilot between New Orleans and St. Louis for over 25 years before the war. In 1858 he moved his family to New Orleans and worked on the *Clara Dolsen* until she was laid up after the blockade of New Orleans. In the fall of 1861 he worked on the *Alonzo Childs* and then the *National*. He was paid in Confederate money and on May 10, 1862 he went to see his brother Charles at Opelousas, Louisiana and asked him to buy cotton for him. Charles bought 115 bales, later captured in Louisiana.

On the 30th he went to Washington on Bayou Catobleau, hired a skiff with another man named Block, and went to Indian Village at the mouth of Bayou Plaquemine. From there they went by buggy to Plaquemine, about 110 river miles from New Orleans. They got another skiff and made their way to New Orleans, arriving there on June 3 when the town was under Union control. He went to work on federal vessels. He was given an honorable discharge by Captain James Alden, Jr. for piloting service on the USS *Richmond*.

He sued to recover the cotton and Vice Admiral Farragut testified:

"Mr. Ealer was much more willing and anxious to serve the government than any other pilot. In fact, he was the only one that I know of who did it with good grace."

Ealer recovered $20,736 on 108 bales.

Edmonds, Olivia S. Olivia was a schoolteacher in New York. In 1856 she was "induced to take charge of a public school in Charleston." She was compelled to remain in Charleston after the war started, having no means to return home. She was being paid in Confederate money but believed it would soon be worthless. She was a friend of Frederick A. Sawyer, the U.S. collector of internal revenue at Charleston, and he advised her to buy cotton. She agreed and he acted as her agent in purchasing eight bales of Charleston upland cotton. Around this time she also moved in with his family. The cotton was seized and she was awarded $1,049.60.

Elliott, Alfred H. Thomas R. S. Elliott owned property in Beaufort, South Carolina designated as block 91 by the U.S. Direct Tax Commission. In November 1861 he fled St. Helena Island and did not return until after the war. His lot was assessed at $10,000 and sold in two parcels on March 13, 1863. On November 1, 1866 he repurchased lot A for $200. Lot B was sold for $225 to Thomas M. S. Rhett.

After Elliott repurchased lot A it was seized and sold at a sheriff's sale.

Twenty-nine thirtieths of the property was willed to Elliot's minor children: Alfred, William, Phoebe, Ann C., James C., Arthur H., Isabella R., Seiguley C., Montrose, and Apsley H., who died in 1867. Thomas Elliott died in 1876 and the sheriff's sale purchaser subsequently turned over the value of his interest in the property to Mrs. Elliott.

The children sued and recovered $4,185.98 on May 8, 1893.

Elliott, Anne H. and Emily. Anne and Emily's father, William Elliott, owned three plantations in St. Helena Parish, Beaufort County, South Carolina known as Cedar Grove, 350 acres; Shell Point, 330 acres; and the Ellis place, 66 acres. William died on February 3,

1863. The Direct Tax Commission imposed a tax of $28 on Cedar Grove, $26.40 on Shell Point, and $5.28 on the Ellis place. The taxes were not paid and the property was sold to recover the total amount of $94.74, including penalty and interest charges. The surplus deposited into the Treasury was $1,011.87.

Cedar Grove was bought by Jane A. McCreary for $655; Shell Point by John and A. E. Conant for $305; and the Ellis place by the United States for $150.

William left a will:

"I will and direct that the rest and residue of my estate (excepting such portion as I have already devised or shall hereafter devise), whether consisting in houses, lands, slaves, bonds, notes, stocks, monies, boats, horses, mules, cattle, plantation stock, and chattels of every description, not already devised as aforesaid, shall be appraised on oath by seven impartial persons (each of my seven children interested therein having a voice) and distributed at such valuation among my then remaining children, Anne, Caroline, and Emily, share and share alike, to them and their heirs forever, until the share of each of the above-named Anne, Caroline, and Emily shall have reached the amount of $16,000 aforesaid. The balance accruing from the rest and residue of my estate to be distributed equally among my seven children hereafter named, to wit: Mary, Harriet, William, Ralph, Anne, Caroline, and Emily, or among each of them as may be living at the time of my death, or, being dead, shall have married previously thereto and left legal representatives to inherit their share."

Caroline died, without having married, while her father was still living. Much of the property was lost during the war and the estate seriously depreciated. The remaining children filed suit in the Court of Common Pleas for Beaufort County and a July 23, 1883 decision gave each child $654. Anne and Emily applied unsuccessfully to the Secretary of the Treasury to recover the surplus from the Direct Tax sale. The two sued and were awarded $505.93½ each on May 11, 1885 on the ground that the lien the children had on the property by virtue of their father's will was transferred by the sale of the property from the land to the proceeds of the sale.

Emery, Hosea B. Owner of the schooner *Montezuma* of Bangor, Maine who sought to recover $1,808.99 on a $1,090 a month charter agreement. The boat was seized at New Orleans for use in the Mobile campaign. Emery was paid $9,181.85 and recovered $540.

English, Lydia S. Surgeon General Finley applied to Quartermaster General Meigs to lease property belonging to Lydia in Georgetown, District of Columbia, known as the Female Seminary, for use as a hospital. She replied on June 24, 1861 with proposed rental terms of $300 a month. Rent at $300 was paid from July 1, 1861 to July 1, 1862 when it was reduced to $200 a month. Miss English protested but issued receipts for rent paid in full and then abandoned her claim in October 1864. On June 25, 1865 she was notified that occupation and rent on the building would cease that day. She claimed rent money for the whole month and was subsequently paid the balance of the month at $200 a month.

She sued for $3,600 but her petition was dismissed on the ground that she assented to the change in terms by giving receipts for $200 a month.

Ensley, Enoch. Owner of a plantation 10–12 miles south of Memphis. He moved to Memphis when it was occupied on June 6, 1862. In 1864 Ensley engaged Christian Dickmann, a subject of Denmark and resident of Memphis, to sell a number of his slaves who were at Mobile and to invest the proceeds in real estate, cotton, or anything else he liked. Dickmann was issued a U.S. military pass by the provost marshal and was able to travel freely but Mobile was still under Confederate control. The slaves were sold for about $200,000 in Confederate money and Dickmann purchased 77 bales of cotton and a quantity of rosin and turpentine. The cotton was subsequently seized at Mobile.

Ensley sued to recover but his petition was dismissed for violating commercial restrictions.

Erdman, Adolphus. Entered the 15th Missouri Veteran Infantry at St. Louis as a second lieutenant on August 14, 1862 for a term of three years. On May 19 he was advanced to first lieutenant and on December 5 became the regimental quartermaster. He tendered his resignation at New Orleans on October 3, 1865 "on account of physical disability" sustained in the line of duty. He was honorably discharged by Major General Sheridan "with condition that he shall receive no final payments until he has satisfied the Pay Department that he is not indebted to the Government."

His pay and commuted value of his rations were $4 a day and the distance to New Orleans was 1,230 miles "by the most direct mail route."

He sued to recover one day's pay and subsistence for every 20 miles traveled from the place of discharge to the place of enrollment and was awarded $246 in 1877.

Erwin, Robert. A partner in Erwin & Hardee who owned 283 bales of cotton captured at Savannah and sold into the Treasury for $49,618.30. On December 31, 1868 the firm filed for bankruptcy. Robert sued to recover the cotton but the court found it was assigned to the receivers and his petition was dismissed.

Fagan, William N. In 1860, lot No. 9, Mosby subdivision, fifth civil district, Memphis, Tennessee was entered in the assessor's records as belonging to W. F. Dyer. The Direct Tax Commission assessed $5.42 in tax, which was not paid. On June 24, 1864 the property was sold to Hugh Canley for $85. He was issued certificate No. 914 and the surplus of $79.58 was paid into the Treasury.

On June 28, 1883 Fagan applied to the Secretary of the Treasury for the surplus and was refused on April 12, 1884. Fagan sued and presented a deposition by J. C. McDavitt who testified that on May 27, 1859 a deed to the property was registered in Shelby County's book 39, part 1, page 463 to William N. Fagan, no record of conveyance was recorded prior to July 1, 1864, and Fagan was shown as the owner through 1864. McDavitt could not state who conveyed the deed to Fagan or on what date it was executed. Fagan's petition was dismissed on February 25, 1886 for failure to prove ownership.

Fain, John H. Fain sued for three bales of cotton weighing 1,227 pounds, purchased by his father-in-law Samuel Rhea, and seized at Atlanta. He recovered $8,360.

Faulkner, Asa. A resident of McMinnville, Tennessee who owned a cotton factory there. It was destroyed in the spring of 1862 on order of General William S. Rosecrans.

Faulkner hired Ira G. Wood, of Winchester, to buy cotton for him. It was stored at Point Rock, Jackson County, Alabama where it was seized by Colonel Platter of the 4th Indiana Cavalry in the fall of 1862. Ten bales of the lot were shipped to Cincinnati and netted $2,301.15. The military commander let him keep the rest of the cotton.

McMinnville and Nashville were both captured on February 25, 1862. A rebel attack on March 26 was unsuccessful but in the fall of 1863

Confederate forces retook the town and Faulkner moved his family from McMinnville to Nashville. Nashville remained under Army control.

Faulkner's residence in Nashville was under Army control but Point Rock, where the cotton was purchased, was under rebel control. Commercial transactions within rebel territory were illegal under the Act of July 31, 1861 but applying the law when lines shifted was impractical so the courts looked to the claimant's loyalty. Faulkner passed the test and was awarded $2,301.15.

Fawcett, Thomas. A resident of Pittsburgh, Pennsylvania who had extensive business interests in New Orleans.

On August 31, 1861 the Confederate government began judicial proceedings to confiscate the assets and businesses of citizens loyal to the Union. Thomas's assets, amounting to $55,006 in cash, promissory notes, and property were seized on October 4, sold, and paid into the Citizen's Bank of New Orleans to the credit of the Confederate government.

The city was captured by Major General Butler and on June 11, 1862 the accounts in the bank were seized and examined. Fawcett's money was sent to the U.S. Treasury on July 17 on his account as a part of $106,812 taken from the bank. No money was returned to him and on November 14, 1889 he demanded the money from the Secretary of the Treasury. The Secretary replied that the money was not available to him pursuant to the Act of June 30, 1868 when the money "was covered into the Treasury and that there is no law authorizing the Secretary of the Treasury to adjudicate and pay such claims."

Fawcett sued under the abandoned or captured property act but on March 3, 1890 the court found he had no case. He could appeal to Congress or he could amend his petition before May 1, 1890. He apparently never went back to court.

Fennerty, Peter A. Resident of Pine Bluff, Arkansas who owned 13 bales of cotton. During the Confederate advance on Little Rock, General Joseph R. West ordered all cotton bales from Pine Bluff seized for use in fortifications and his were taken. He was away in service to the Union at the time and when cotton belonging to loyalists was returned to them by the Army he was not present to identify and his. It was sold and he was awarded $1,458 at $243 a bale.

Fernandez, Anthony. Orrin Howes sold 118 bales of upland cotton to Fernandez, a British subject, on December 15, 1864 at Savannah with a down payment of $15,000 in Confederate money. The arrival of General Sherman's forces was imminent and Howes's intention was to get the cotton into the hands of a neutral who would be considered loyal to the Union. Cotton was selling for $1.25 a pound and that amount was worth about $68,000. Fernandez and Howes made a gentleman's agreement that Fernandez would make additional payments if the cotton survived the war but would owe nothing more if it were lost. It was seized within a few days and Fernandez recovered $20,688.94 in 1871 as the legal owner.

Fichera, Michele. A subject of the King of Italy whose five bales of cotton were captured at Savannah. He recovered $876.65 after the court determined that an American citizen could sue in an Italian court.

Field, Rachael A. Charles F. Field chartered his steamer *M. S. Allison* to the Army on May 4, 1863 for $110 a day. That rate was paid up to October 4, 1863 when it was lowered to $90 a day and on January 12, 1864 the New Berne, North Carolina harbormaster, Edward M. Lonan, delivered a note from Captain R. C. Webster, chief quartermaster, to the master of the *Allison* informing him the charter rate had been reduced to $80 a month from January 1 and requested he deliver his copy of the charter to his office "at once" to be endorsed. Lonan had been appointed by Colonel Herman Biggs by order of General Burnside and had control of all merchant shipping.

The captain refused to deliver the documents and on January 20 the vessel was ordered up the Chowan River in North Carolina with a government pilot to Colerain with troops, stores, equipment, and munitions. The vessel began taking on water into a lower hold while moored to a bank bow-on with another steamer and the stern eventually settled in 17 feet of water and mud. As a rebel attack was considered imminent, the commander ordered the boat hauled off and towed away. She was towed 30 miles downriver, across Albemarle Sound, and up the Roanoke River to Plymouth. None of the crew could explain how the leak started. No one felt any shock or explosion and there was no evidence of unsound wood or fasteners. The boat was temporarily repaired about six weeks later by divers who patched a hole in the hull. She was used for another 30 days when permanent repairs were made by the Army in 48 days. The vessel was out of service for a total of 117½ days. She was released from government service on July 15, 1865.

Charles subsequently died and his wife, Rachael, brought suit to recover $18,300 on the rate reductions and time out of service due to repairs occasioned by wartime service. Her petition was dismissed on the ground that the owner did not protest the rate reduction, the government pilot was in no way negligent, and no evidence of rebel activity could be found that would have caused the injury.

Filor, James. Asa F. Tift, a resident of Key West, Florida since 1838, had owned Tift's Wharf and warehouse for over 20 years. He was a member of the convention that passed the ordinance of Florida's secession from the Union and which he signed on January 9, 1861.

On May 10, President Lincoln declared Key West, the Tortugas, and Santa Cora excluded as insurrectionary districts.

On May 21 Tift gave his brother, Charles Tift, power of attorney to sell his real property while he headed for Albany, Georgia to aid in the rebellion.

James Filor, William Pinckney, and another partner named Curry were aware of this but purchased the property on December 28, 1861 for $18,000 on notes due only after the rebellion had been suppressed. Major B. H. Hill, commanding at Key West, had intended to seize the property from Tift for Army needs but changed his mind and sought an agreement with the new owners.

That December, Lieutenant James S. Gibbes, 1st Artillery acting quartermaster, desired to lease the property but the new owners refused and on January 13, 1862 Major Hill ordered the property seized. On the 24th, Filor and his partners leased the "wharf, houses, cisterns, offices, and wharf property of every kind" for $6,000 a year, payable in quarterly installments retroactive to January 1.

No money was ever paid on the lease, the excuse being the lack of money in the Key West quartermaster's department. The bills were regularly submitted to Quartermaster General Meigs, who never disapproved or cancelled the lease until February 8, 1866, but when Filor sued for $30,000 on rent due from January 1, 1862 to January 1, 1867, Meigs refused to return the property.

Filor argued that no money from the sale ever aided the rebellion. It was deposited in a bank in Havana for the express purpose of keeping it safe.

The court ruled the deed from Asa Tift to Filor was a "contract between enemies' and therefore void and that the officers at Key West knew the circumstances of the sale were invalid and had no authority to bind the United States to the agreement. As the court stated:

"If such deeds as that of Asa Tift were valid in law, then in the late rebellion every rebel preparing for that or engaged in it, could have sold his lands in the loyal States, and thus withdrawn them from the reach of our laws, and secured the proceeds for the aid of the confederacy."

Finn, John. Finn and William P. Milliken were in the livestock business as John Finn & Co.

The chief quartermaster at St. Louis for the Department of the Missouri was General William Myers. Robert Allen was assistant chief quartermaster, and Hiram G. Finch was the head horse inspector at the general depot. The policy of these three during 1862 and 1863 was to purchase as many horses and mules as possible in Missouri within rebel military lines for the purpose of depleting the enemy's supply. This policy created some personal and financial risk among the suppliers so some adjustment from the normal purchasing methods had to be made.

Hiram Finch contracted with individuals to go into the countryside and purchase animals on their own account and upon inspection and acceptance by a government officer they would be purchased. When a quantity of animals had been assembled at a given place an inspector would come out from St. Louis. If a horse or mule was accepted it may or may not have been branded depending on whether or not the inspector had a iron with him at the time since it wasn't always convenient to take one along. The animals were usually branded on arrival at St. Louis with a "U.S." on the left shoulder.

When the animals were accepted in the field by the Army the contractors paid off the sellers and subcontractors, if any, at which time the Army assumed all expense and risks for getting them to St. Louis. This was necessary "as contractors would not risk bringing stock across the country in Missouri, as the enemy was moving about there at that time." The quartermaster's office would issue payment vouchers to the contractors after the animals had arrived.

On October 1, 1863 Finn & Co. made an informal agreement with Allen's office to find horses and mules and bring them to Sedalia for a price of $153.70 each, very expensive but the Army was in great need of animals. On the 10th Allen's office was requested to send an inspector to Sedalia where 32 horses and 94 mules were accepted. The inspector had no government branding iron so he used a private iron to put a "P" on the neck of each animal so he could identify it later.

The subcontractors were paid off and the inspector and Finn & Co.'s agent began the 20-mile drive east to Tipton where they would board a Pacific Railroad of Missouri train to St. Louis but rebels captured the two men, 24 horses, and 78 mules prior to reaching Tipton. No money was ever paid to Finn & Co.

In late 1866 Finn bought out Milliken's interest in the business and he presented a $15,677.40 claim to the Quartermaster General on July 3, 1874. The case was presented to a federal court by the House Committee on War Claims under the Bowman Act where it was dismissed as barred by statute of limitations. The claim was then sent to the Third Auditor who also rejected it on July 14, 1879. The Second Comptroller concurred but reopened the claim on July 20, 1886 on new evidence. On August 13, 1886 the Secretary of the Treasury referred the case to a federal court by special act of Congress and on June 8, 1891 Finn was awarded $15,677.40 on the ground that the animals had been accepted by the government according to the practice at the time.

First National Bank of West Virginia.

On July 1, 1864 Major General David Hunter, Commander of the Department of West Virginia, had only 367 horses in depots. On July 7 he ordered his quartermaster to purchase up to 1,000 horses within seven days and on the 13th he ordered an additional 1,000 if they could be had immediately, the price not to exceed $165 each.

The horses were purchased but the quartermaster had no money so pay vouchers were issued to the sellers by the post quartermaster at Parkersburg for redemption by the Cavalry Bureau.

Some vouchers were sold to the First National Bank of West Virginia or the Northwest-ern Bank of Virginia at Parkersburg, Riggs & Co., Jay Cooke & Co., and others were sent directly to Quartermaster General Meigs.

When the banks presented the vouchers to Meigs he refused to honor them because of the irregularity of the purchase and because the prices paid were in excess of Cavalry Bureau standards. The Bureau was paying from $145 to $155 a head for horses at that time. In February 1865, Cavalry Bureau chief Colonel Ekin recommended paying the vouchers. Meigs ordered them paid at the rate of $150 a horse and in May First National received $131,850 leaving a balance of $13,185 on their original vouchers. Seven claimants filed suit and the court held that General Hunter had the authority to make the offer, the vouchers were valid, and all recovered.

Fisher, Daniel B. Fisher had a small farm near Americus, Georgia and owned eight bales of upland cotton seized at Savannah from the back of a store at 97 Bay Street on February 8, 1865. He was described as being in feeble health and spent his time wandering throughout the south to avoid conscription. He was reported in Manassas, Warrenton, Lynchburg, Savannah, Americus, and did some trading in Florida and Texas. His suit for $2,120.40 was dismissed since all of his relatives were shown to be disloyal and he couldn't prove he never gave aid or comfort to the rebellion.

Fletcher, Bird L. Fletcher enlisted in the "general mounted service of the Army" on December 27, 1859. On January 18, 1860 he was ordered to the First Cavalry, Troop I. He joined up on February 18 and the outfit subsequently became Troop 1 of the Fourth Cavalry. He was promoted to corporal on January 23, 1863 and on February 24 he was commissioned second lieutenant in the Fourth Regiment of Cavalry retroactive to February 19. He accepted the appointment on March 27 and on May 10 he was brevetted first lieutenant for gallant and meritorious service at Franklin, Tennessee and was officially promoted to the rank on October 12, 1864. On August 25, 1867 he made captain and on June 19, 1868 he was given a medical discharge as "the result of sickness and exposure incident to the service."

In the early 1870s Fletcher borrowed money to purchase the "stock and fixtures" of the Cumberland House in Paducah, Kentucky and on June 29, 1872 he was charged with conduct unbecoming an officer for failing to pay debts owed to

Strondsburg, Pennsylvania merchants: H. S. Wagner, $75; Joseph Wallace, $55.10; R. F. and H. D. Bush, $62.51; Simon Fried, $28; J. Ingraham Allender, proprietor of the Strondsburg House, $42 for board; and Edward Baker, 1st district internal revenue assessor at Paducah, Kentucky, $30.

He was charged with fraud and a court martial was convened at Philadelphia on July 10, 1872 at which he represented himself. He pled not guilty to all charges and specifications, was found guilty on all counts, and sentenced to be dismissed from the service. Results of the proceedings were forwarded to Secretary of War William Belknap. He endorsed the record on July 24, 1872 with a note to forward the documents to President Grant. An officer must either resign his commission or be dismissed by the President. Enlisted personnel serve under contract for specific periods of time.

It was later determined that Grant never saw the records of the trial or any documents related to it as required by law and on April 21, 1888 Acting Judge Advocate General G. Norman Lieber transmitted the documents to Secretary of War William C. Endicott. Endicott noted that Bird was still in the Army according to the law and the court was technically still awaiting the action of the President. Lieber officially approved the sentence on May 18 and Fletcher's dismissal from the service was approved by President Cleveland on July 5, 1888. Fletcher sued to recover back pay from the date of his dismissal and was awarded $9,654 on June 8, 1891.

The government appealed to the Supreme Court where the decision was reversed on March 6, 1893 saying, "if he acquiesces for a long time in the action of the Secretary of War dismissing him, it is an abandonment of the office equivalent to a resignation."

Floyd, Robert. Sometime in September 1864 General A. B. Eaton, commissary general of subsistence, directed Major Henry C. Symonds, commissary of subsistence at Louisville, Kentucky to study the prospect of buying packaged pork for the Army. Eaton stated, in part:

"The details of the business are left to your discretion. As it is an experiment that may not turn out to meet your and my anticipations, it is not desirable to arrange the matter for permanence, nor for a very heavy pack. I advise that you aim not to exceed, say, 20,000 hogs, until considerable progress shall demonstrate the entire feasibility and advisability of the measure."

Symonds reported to Eaton on October 13 and said the various meat packers had colluded to "extort very large prices from the government" but that he had begun negotiations with Robert Floyd and J. Smith Speed. He reported, in part:

"I can readily get 100,000 hogs in Kentucky, and by General Burbridge's order control the whole price and movement of them in Kentucky; whereas if I undertake only 20,000 or 30,000, I will be easily outstripped by the pork packers, who, by my present plan, will have little to do."

The next day he reported:

"For 100,000 hogs, the difference between the best of my first offers and the present one, there is about $175,000 in favor of the United States, and I do not believe I can do any better than this. I had no idea of the difficulties and complications, and as soon as these wealthy semi-loyal parties find that their occupation for this season is about gone, they will compass everything to break it up.

"They claim that reasonable packing profits are $1 per hog, at least. My arrangement gives no promise of over 40 cents, and the capital and risk are with that. I know I am about right in my measures."

On the 17th he reported again:

"I find that I have outgeneraled the packers, and they do not seem to feel that any wrong has been done to them, but attribute their misfortune to their own greed, and they seem to agree that I have done the best thing possible. So I think my fancied danger from that source is passed."

Eaton was happy and replied, in part:

"The whole subject of packing pork at Louisville is placed, subject to your direction, under the advice of Colonel Kilburn. It is a novel undertaking for the Subsistence department, but I expect from your zeal and devotion to the subject to realize satisfactory results."

Symonds again reported on October 19:

"If General Burbridge concurs in my wishes—and I do not doubt he will—I will, by the 25th of November, be able to forward to the front at least 2,000 barrels pork daily, and so I do not think we need make any provisions for this point beyond that date.

"I have made contracts for killing at least 100,000 hogs, and have made arrangements for cooperage. The parties are going to work to get their houses in order, and I think we will get at least 25,000,000 pounds meat, at not exceeding 15 cents per pound, in shipping order."

Symonds continued negotiations and reported again to Eaton. Eaton cautioned Symonds not to injure the business community in his enthusiasm:

"Our packing may interfere with the business of the regular packers; this, however, is not our object nor our wish. If it incidentally occurs, and we have conducted our business in a fair and unoppressive manner, reasonable people will not complain, and the government will sustain us."

Symonds concluded a contract with Floyd on October 25 "to slaughter, dress, cut, pack, and cure into pork or bacon, 50,000 hogs, as follows, or otherwise, as the commissary of subsistence shall direct." Payment was to be "in currency or its equivalent, the sum of 92½ cents per 100 pounds net of hog meat, the weight to be determined by weighing the hogs when cooled ready for cutting at the block."

On the 27th he signed an identical contract with J. Smith Speed, doing business as Speed & Davis, who subcontracted with Jarvis & Co.

The pork-packing season for the Louisville area was from about November 10 to Christmas Day. After Symonds had supplied Floyd with 16,107 hogs and Speed & Davis with 17,132, it became apparent to Symonds that he was creating a situation in the marketplace that was dooming his scheme. Hogs were getting scarce, the prices rose much faster than he anticipated, and the program was abandoned when the savings from curing and packing was no longer cost effective.

Speed & Davis felt they were owed $24,651 on 75 cents a pound for 32,868 undelivered hogs. Floyd claimed $59,628 on 33,823 undelivered hogs. The War Department was unresponsive so Floyd sued.

The government argued that the Commissary Department had no authority to contract for packing and curing pork and even if they entered into valid contracts, they weren't approved by the Commissary General; no bids were advertised, and no money had been appropriated to pay the vendors.

Symonds told Commissary General Eaton he thought the packers would make about 40 cents profit per hog. Several witnesses testified, on which the court commented:

"The opinions of these witnesses prove too much, if they are not mistaken. They would make the clear profits of Floyd's contract nearly 80 percent of the total sum to be received for the service. It shows how carefully testimony resting merely on the opinions of witnesses, however respectable and truthful they may be, should be weighed and considered, and how uncertain it is to amounts."

Floyd recovered $20,293.80 for 33,823 undelivered hogs at 60 cents per hog. Speed & Davis $19,720.80 for 32,868 undelivered hogs at 60 cents per hog.

Fluker, Isabella Ann. Isabella owned the Asphodel plantation in East Feliciana Parish, Louisiana on the east side of Thompson's Creek and another called the Alps plantation in West Feliciana Parish on the west side of Thompson's Creek.

In June 1863, troops under General Nathaniel Banks at Port Hudson took 296 bales of her cotton for fortification breastworks. After Port Hudson surrendered on July 8, Banks ordered all the waste cotton turned over to his quartermaster to sell and to use the proceeds to pay the expenses of organizing and equipping "a body of colored troops intended to be constituted as a part of the military forces of the United States, and to be known as the Corps d'Afrique."

A total of 1,207 bales of waste cotton were sold for $229,846.75. The money was used for his stated purpose and for the relief of freedmen and their new schools.

Isabella sued to recover and it was proved that 50 bales of her cotton reached New Orleans and net proceeds of $8,650 deposited into the Treasury. She was awarded that in 1878. She could recover only on proceeds in the Treasury.

The court noted the task General Banks had in dealing with former slaves:

"To provide and care for this numerous population, suddenly changed from slaves into freedmen, was one of the new questions presented to the commanding general of the Department of the Gulf, to be dealt with by him at his own will. They became, at the instant of the change, an important element in all his military plans and calculations, and necessarily in his military expenses. What should be done by them, with them, and for them, was to be, and necessarily had to be, determined by his will."

Flushing Ferry Co. The company chartered their steamer *Flushing* to the Army at $350 a day on March 5, 1862 to load as much cargo at New York as she could carry, leaving room only for the ship's cable, material, officers, and crew.

At Alexandria on the 27th, Captain Nimmo took on board the Second Regular Infantry and the next afternoon at 4 P.M. they reached Fortress Monroe. While the vessel was under control of a government pilot hired by Captain Nimmo she struck an underwater obstruction and sank. A marker buoy over the obstruction was displaced and was not replaced until the day after the accident. The ship was salvaged, brought to New York, and rebuilt at a cost of $37,791.63.

The company's petition for $160,997.63 total costs was dismissed as a marine risk and the fault of the company's officers.

Foley, Bartholomew. Foley was a naturalized citizen who had a clothing and shoe business in Charleston, which the war disrupted. In 1864 he began purchasing cotton "in the ordinary course of his business" to pay off creditors, mainly Taylor & Sons in Albany, New York. His two bales of sea-island cotton and 201 bales of upland cotton were captured at Charleston and sold in New York. He claimed $52,873.11.

Foley owned eight slaves, openly condemned the secession movement, and when the rebel authorities sent for two of his slaves to work on fortifications he freed them rather than let them contribute to the work. He never took out Confederate loans, never took the rebel oath, or supported the rebellion. He regularly contributed to the Sisters of Mercy's work with Union prisoners and donated clothing, money, and shoes to Generals Prentiss, Milroy, Corcoran, Major Dempsey, and others. Having proved his loyalty, he was awarded $26,846.49 — $237.64 a bale for the sea-island and $131.20 for the upland.

Foley, James. Claimed net proceeds on eight bales of upland cotton seized at Savannah on March 6, 1865. He recovered $1,402.64 in 1871.

Folsom, Henry C. Folsom paid $3,062 in import duties for goods shipped into occupied Memphis. He did not object at the time and thus could not recover.

Ford, William G. John G. Robinson was a subject of Great Britain who lived in New Orleans. He purchased 238 bales of cotton from Robert B. Hurt in Madison County, Tennessee at 70 cents a pound totaling $88,260 for 119,000 pounds, more or less. The cotton was shipped to Ponchatoula, Louisiana and on March 7, 1863 it was seized and sold in New Orleans.

Robinson died on August 25, 1869 at Biloxi, Mississippi leaving a will. Ford was administrator of the estate and on March 20, 1872 he filed a claim with the Mixed Commission on British and American Claims at Newport, Rhode Island pursuant to Section 12 of the treaty of May 8, 1871 claiming he was owed $66,195, the balance of the proceeds paid into the Treasury from the sale of the cotton. On September 24, 1873 the Commission awarded $29,638 in gold to Mary G. Barker, the only surviving legatee under Robinson's will. Ford got nothing so he petitioned Congress for relief and the Senate Committee on War Claims referred the case to the Court of Claims in 1883.

Section 3 of the Bowman Act of March 3, 1883 retracted the court's jurisdiction over "any claim against the United States which is now barred by virtue of the provisions of any law of the United States."

The abandoned or captured property act of March 12, 1863 gave the Court of Claims a jurisdictional period of two years after the suppression of the rebellion to hear claims presented under the Act. President Johnson proclaimed the war over on August 20, 1866 and the Supreme Court considered that date the legal end of the war.

In commenting on the Bowman Act the court stated:

"The manifest intention of that declaration is to prevent the first step in favor of a barred claim, and so to keep out of Congress old and stale demands. It is the duty of this court not to attempt to overstep the limit thus assigned to its powers.

"The Abandoned and captured property Act was a notice to every man whose property had been captured and sold, that he could follow its proceeds here, and, on making certain proofs, reclaim them. Is it not fairly presumable that if Congress intended to open this court again for such claims, they would give now as clear and broad and universal notice of the fact as was given in 1863? We think it would, and we therefore decline to assume that the Bowman Act was intended to open a side door into this court, into which would come only such claimants as should happen to hear of it, and be able to get their claims referred to this court by a committee.

"Any such legislation as that would be entirely alien in spirit to the act of March 12, 1863, which gave to all loyal men an equal right and an equal chance to come here. We have had before us claims of all sizes, from that of a poor negro for a single bale of cotton, to that of the rich man for thousands. If Congress should see fit to permit such claims to be again brought here, is it not reasonable to suppose that its legislation would be, at least, as unequivocal in terms and as enlarged in spirit as that of 1863?"

This was the first case under the Bowman Act. Ford's petition was dismissed in 1884 and a copy of the order sent to the Senate Committee on Claims.

Fordham, Edward.

A free black who lived on a farm just outside Charleston who owned 12 bales of upland cotton seized by the Army. He recovered $1,574.40.

Foster, Erastus S.

Erastus Foster was a native of Wyandotte, Kansas who went to Mobile, Alabama in December 1860 to sell horses in the widely held belief that "the political excitement would die away and there would be no attempt to destroy the Union." He was unable to sell the horses at the price he wanted prior to the start of the war so he opened a livery stable. He intended to go back to his family after selling the horses but said it was impossible to get out. In July or August 1863 he booked passage on a blockade runner but that vessel was captured and he was returned to Mobile.

He began buying cotton with Confederate money from the horse sale and by March 1864 he "was actively engaged in business" and owned 75 bales of upland cotton that was captured along with Mobile. He immediately returned to Kansas and died shortly thereafter.

His son, Erastus S. Foster, filed suit to recover the loss. The court declared his father loyal and awarded his estate $13,023.82 at $183.42 a bale.

Fowler, Mary J.

Mary and her husband, William J. Fowler, were residents of Monroe County, Tennessee when the Amy seized $3,200 worth of goods for its own use from their farm. In 1878 William presented a claim to the Quartermaster General for the return of property. After an investigation and the questioning of witnesses, his claim was rejected in August 1882 since his loyalty during the war was not proved. No claim was presented to the Southern Claims Commission and Mary's loyalty was never examined.

Mary petitioned the House Committee on War Claims for relief claiming the property was actually hers. Her claim was referred to a federal court under the Bowman Act and she filed suit on August 15, 1888. Her petition was dismissed on January 13, 1890 on the ground that her claim was separate from her husband's and hers was barred by statutes of limitations and the Bowman Act.

Freeman, Henry O.

Melancthon Freeman, Henry O. Suckley, and John H. Suckley were partners in the New York firm of M. M. Freeman & Company. On April 25, 1861 Henry signed a charter agreement with Colonel D. D. Tompkins for the steamboat *Cataline* for a term of not less than three months at $10,000 a month, payable monthly. The vessel was to be operated at the owners' expense and the government would have the option to purchase the boat. The owners carried the usual marine and fire risk insurance, the government the war risk insurance. If the boat was lost due to enemy action, the government was to pay $50,000 and all injuries in proportion.

Regular payments were made but on July 2, 1861 the vessel caught fire and burned. Freeman sued for a balance of $12,666.64 owed on the charter and was awarded that in 1867.

Friend, Robert C.

In July 1864 General Grant got a note:

> July 28, 1864
>
> Lieutenant-General Grant:
> Allow me to submit to your consideration a thought which has struck me. The rebels have fortified Howlett's house bluff with nineteen guns and a very strong work. Trent's Reach is so shallow that our iron-clads cannot get up without great labor in dredging the channels. Now, what hinders us from turning the Howlett house battery by taking the hint from that Dutchman and cut a canal at Dutch Gap? It is but 200 yards from 16-foot water to 16-foot water across the gap. The land is but 30 feet high as an average, and we should have for a 50-foot cut but about 35,000 cubic feet of excavation, or ten days' labor for 1,000 men. By that means our iron-clads could get out and Howlett would be useless. If you will look upon the map you will get my idea at once. I have made my examination by the Coast Survey map. I should not depend on the current to do any part of the cutting, as at Vicksburg, although it might help. The gun-boats cover the place.
> Respectfully,
>
> Benj. F. Butler
> Major-General, Commanding

The owner of the land Butler was talking about was Henry Cox, of Henrico County, Virginia. Trent's Reach was a meander on the James

River that nearly came back on itself. The project was across the narrowest part of the peninsula and it completely divided his land. The area excavated had always been a natural depression and it had been possible to haul small boats across it to save 5 or 6 miles going around the long bend of the Reach and the area opposite the mainland across the depression had always been called Farrar's Island.

The Dutch Gap Canal was open to navigation in 1864 by General Butler and when the war ended Cox filled in the upper end of the canal with an earthen causeway. In the spring of 1870 heavy rains washed it away and a huge flow of water went through the canal washing away a lot of Cox's land.

Army Corps of Engineers Major William P. Craighill recommended forming a commission composed of James B. Jones, Clay Drewry, Rich A. Willis, Dr. Cathorn Archer, and George D. Pleasant to study the situation and make a report. They met on March 6, 1871, went out to the site, and concluded that 800 acres of Cox's land was cut off, the damage amounted to $7,500, and the loss to him in building the Canal was $100 an acre. The City of Richmond paid Cox the money.

Cox died in 1888 and left the 670-acre Farrar's Island to his nephew, Robert Friend. He shipped produce and wool to market from various landings on the river that had existed before the Canal was built.

A plan was devised to improve navigation on the James River by widening and deepening the Canal and in 1889 Colonel Craighill began to fill in the bend of the river with mud, sand, gravel and other material opposite Friend's farm which eventually caused the water level at the landings he used to drop and become useless, which was anticipated by the Corps of Engineers. Friend sued in the federal Court of Claims and estimated his losses at $3,000. The government argued the State of Virginia owned the bed of the James River and controlled commerce in and on it. The court dismissed the petition on February 17, 1895 on the ground there was no taking of property for public use under the Fifth Amendment and for lack of jurisdiction.

Fripp, W. Washington. William Fripp owned property known as the Burlington and Fripp Point place on Saint Helena Island, South Carolina. William died on January 9, 1861 leaving W. William Fripp as executor but no instruc-

tions for disposing of the property. It was subsequently sold by the U.S. Direct Tax Commission and the surplus deposited into the Treasury. W. Washington sued to recover the surplus in 1884 but his petition was dismissed since he held no title to the property.

Furlong, James. James owned a wharfboat in Arkansas worth about $7,000. In 1864 the Army hired his boat for use at the mouth of the White River, promising to return it to him in the same condition minus normal wear and tear. When the Army was done with it they returned it in poor condition and James refused to accept it. The Army said they would keep it until they could fix it but it was carried downriver and lost. James waited until the late 1880s to petition Congress for restitution. His claim was referred to a federal court and dismissed on January 3, 1888 as barred by statutes of limitations and the Bowman Act.

Furman & Company. Francis Furman and George Searight were wholesale dry goods merchants in Nashville. In the fall of 1961 Confederate forces took over their business and prohibited them from collecting debts in Tennessee and Alabama to pay their creditors in New York, Philadelphia, and Baltimore.

Later that year, Searight moved his family from Nashville to Florence, Alabama where his wife had kin and set about collecting what debts he could locally and in southern Tennessee before he was conscripted into Confederate service. He paid a substitute named Ham to serve for him.

The notes and Confederate currency he collected were deposited with McAlister, Simpson & Co. of Florence. In February 1862 he asked McAlister to purchase 100 hogsheads of sugar through their connections in New Orleans for Furman & Co. This was done on March 6 and the sugar was stored at Wood's cotton press until it was seized, along with the cotton press, in July 1863. By then, shrinkage had reduced the total amount to 67 hogsheads and this was sold at auction by acting quartermaster Captain John W. McClure for $10,421.71 cash.

Furman & Co. sued and recovered $10,421.71.

Gaither, Varina B. Horace Gaither's wife, Varina, inherited the Amandlia cotton plantation in Concordia Parish, Louisiana. In July 1863 she was driven off her land and the place was occupied by Captain James T. Organ.

Organ used the slaves to gin 67 bales of cotton, which was sent to Natchez.

A friend and representative of Varina's, Joseph Winchester, produced another 50 bales before G. B. Fields, an abandoned land commissioner, leased the place to Ware & Williams Company to pick and gin the remaining cotton on shares, for which Organ paid about $224 a bale. The company apparently claimed Winchester's 50 bales as their work.

Horace died after the property was seized and she was the sole heir under Louisiana law. During the initial investigation of her claim there was some dispute over the number of bales seized owing to what the court described as Captain Organ's "nefarious" dealings.

Major General Henry W. Slocum testified: "I had command of the department of the Mississippi in the spring of 1864. In the discharge of my duties I visited Natchez several times. I was invited by Mr. Gaither to make my headquarters at the house of his mother, Mrs. Stanton, which I did. While there I conversed with Gaither more or less on matters connected with the war and read several speeches he had made in opposition to the secession movement. The impression made on me, from the conversation with the family and their treatment of the Union soldiers, was the family had been and were Union people. I knew Mrs. Gaither personally. They treated our folks very kindly."

Varina's mother, Huldah L. Stanton, related how Varina was in her carriage coming from Huldah's Ballina plantation, about 20 miles from Amandlia, when she came upon a U.S. soldier along a road through a wooded area within Confederate lines. He said he had escaped from the prison camp at Alexandria and was making his way to Vidalia. She put him in her carriage and took him the rest of the way. Generals Canby, Slocum, and Gresham made their headquarters at Ballina while Varina was staying with her mother there.

Nancy Davis, a 48-year-old freedwoman and Mrs. Gaither's waiting woman for 22 years, stated she had no knowledge of her employer ever giving aid to the rebellion. Captain Organ testified to her loyalty: "The claimant is a quiet, modest, unassuming lady and though she never said much I have no doubt of her loyalty to the government." She was awarded $58,422.98 on 262 bales.

Gallaudet, James. James had two sons-in-law named Irwin and Hardee. They gave him a gift of 32 bales of sea-island cotton. It was captured at Savannah and James recovered $7,417.28.

Garrison, Cornelius K. On September 1, 1861 Garrison signed a contract with the War Department to furnish 10,000 French Liege rifles at $27 each. On the 10th Major General Benjamin F. Butler was authorized by Secretary of War Simon Cameron to "raise, organize, and uniform and equip a volunteer force for the war, in the New England States, not exceeding six regiments of the maximum standard, of such arms, and in such proportion, and in such manner as he may judge expedient," provided "the cost of such recruitment, armament, and equipment did not exceed in the aggregate that of like troops now or hereafter raised for the service of the United States."

On October 7 Garrison signed a contract with Butler to furnish 6,000 "Minie rifles of the Liege pattern, with saber bayonets and all appendages complete and agrees to pay for each of said rifles, as shall pass inspection, the sum of $27, or such less sum as the Ordnance Department may have paid for guns like in quality or description, or contracted to pay for to said Garrison." Delivery was to be within 15 days but Garrison had never fulfilled his original War Department contract.

The New England Department chief of ordnance, Major Strong, suggested replacing the Lieges with Enfields. Butler agreed and he, but not Garrison, signed an amendment to the contract:

"It is agreed by the United States to accept from C. K. Garrison, the contractor, the long Enfield rifles, with bayonets of the triangular pattern in place of the saber bayonets, upon the value conditions as are herein specified."

The War Department had paid $20–23 for each Liege from other dealers. By November 9 Garrison had delivered 2,800 Enfields and he was paid $27 each. The remaining 3,200 were delivered by December 11 but the War Department paid only $20 each for these. No Liege guns were delivered.

Garrison sued to recover the $22,400 difference but his petition was dismissed on the ground that he had been overpaid on the contract. The court found he had delivered 2,800 Enfields at the Liege price of $27 each and 3,200 at $20 each for a total of $139,600, an overpayment of $1,600.

Garrison appealed to the Supreme Court where the decision was reversed. The court was troubled by the language of the amendment allowing the substitution of Enfields, which Garrison never signed, and held there was no contract to deliver Enfields at $20–23 each.

Gearing, Charles.

A shipbuilder and resident of Pittsburgh, Pennsylvania who built two shallow-draft riverboats in 1860 at a cost of $38,000, ostensibly for two Texas men who lived on the Trinity River, Colonel John D. Stell and John F. Carr.

Stell was born in Georgia in 1804 and moved his family to Texas in 1855, became a prosperous cotton planter, got involved in river transportation, and served in the Texas legislature from Leon County. When the war began he sold his property and moved to Smith County to work at the munitions factory in Tyler. He died at Tyler on October 28, 1862.

The *John F. Carr* was financed entirely by Gearing, the *Colonel Stelle* three-fourths by Gearing and one-fourth by James R. Richardson, of Pittsburgh. Gearing was in financial difficulty and sought additional funds from Richardson. The 138-foot sidewheel steamer *Colonel Stelle* was also known as *Colonel Stell* and *J. D. Stelle,* but appears in court records as "Stelle."

The *John F. Carr* was licensed and enrolled at Pittsburgh on October 19, 1860 and the *Stelle* on December 12

Gearing and his son Franklin delivered the boats to Galveston, Texas where they met Stell and Carr. The boats were delivered just prior to the war. Both men refused to pay for them, apparently fearing that war was imminent and that commerce would be disrupted or the boats would be confiscated, captured, or destroyed. Gearing then ran the boats himself on the Trinity River.

After the war started, the vessels were seized by the Texas Army's Marine Department as the property of northerners and were impounded for three weeks then returned to Gearing.

The *Carr* was chartered by Commander W. W. Hunter, CSN, at Galveston on September 29, 1861 and the *Stelle* was chartered the next day. Both boats had a draft of only 30-inches— very useful in Southern waters. The boats carried general freight, tents, horses, corn, hay, railroad iron, lumber, arms, troops, and performed towing duties in and around Bolivar Point, Buffalo Bayou, Pelican Spit, Harrisburg, Houston, and San Jacinto. They were held until they were captured by the United States.

Gearing bought the *Reindeer* for $10,000 in gold in 1862. He loaded her with 288 bales of cotton, obtained papers for Havana, Cuba, attempted to run the blockade, and was captured by U.S. naval forces. Franklin was aboard as supercargo. He ran his mouth off in his zeal and hope for the Confederacy's final victory and this was duly noted at the time.

Gearing and Richardson applied unsuccessfully to Washington for the return of their property. Treasury agents sold the *Stelle* for $2,200 and the *Carr* for $900, the money going into the abandoned or captured property fund. They sued to recover the value of their property under the Act of March 12, 1863 pursuant to President Lincoln's proclamation of July 1, 1862. The government contended Gearing aided and abetted the Confederacy, perhaps to protect his financial interests as he claimed, but he did so voluntarily and willingly and therefore violated the law.

Gearing claimed he was compelled by Major-General John B. "Prince John" Magruder to work for the rebellion. He said he refused pay and had no choice but to protect his property or go home and face financial ruin at the hands of ruthless creditors.

He said he made a dangerous 350-mile journey from Houston to Natchez in the fall of 1863 to warn General Walter Q. Gresham of a plan to ambush Generals Nathaniel Banks and William B. Franklin during the Bayou Teche campaign. His counsel stated:

"This journey was made overland through a section of country infested with robbers and guerillas, and manifestly the most dangerous of any within the theatre of war. He was environed by every peril and surrounded by every danger."

Gearing returned to Pittsburgh in 1864 and was met with charges of disloyalty. He was arrested by the local military commander, General Thomas A. Rowley, thrown into jail for five weeks, brought before Rowley's military tribunal and found innocent, "It being officially declared that the charges were the offspring of hatred, envy, and spite on the part of Millingar against Gearing."

James Millingar was the owner of the Monongahela Planing Mill and Gearing's brother-in-law.

The government argued that Gearing could have tried to find buyers for the boats in another market, but he and his son engaged in a regular business of carrying Confederate troops and passengers and chartered the boats to the Confederacy until they were seized by General Magruder.

Gearing testified:

"After these boats were thrown back on my hands I ran them on the Trinity River. I tried to sell them, but failed to do so on account of the excitement produced by the rebellion or the anticipation of it. I could not get the boats back and they were taken by the State of Texas in consequence of reports there that I was an abolitionist. The State of Texas returned the steamers to me after about three weeks' detention when these reports were denied by letters from Pittsburg and the boats were returned to me by the intervention of Masonic friends in Pittsburg. This was a short time before Fort Sumpter was fired upon. After this I was taken sick and went home to Pittsburg, this being the fall of 1861. My creditors thought these steamers, if left in Texas, would be confiscated if it was known I was in the north, and they insisted upon my returning south. After my return there, these steamers were taken from me by an order from General Magruder, a Confederate general. I did not consent to their being taken but protested against it. The vessels were appraised after they were taken. I in no way attempted or tried to obtain payment for the steamers from the Confederate government. I understood that other owners were paid for steamers taken in the same way by the Confederate government. They were taken by the Confederate government in 1862. The United States forces got possession of them at the time of the surrender of the rebel forces. I was involved at the time I built these boats about $18,000 outside of the insurance and hence under obligations to listen to the suggestions and requirements of creditors. During all this time I was loyal to the United States government. I could not talk much in Texas in favor of the United States as it would have caused my imprisonment. I never did aid, comfort, or encourage the rebellion against the United States. I never did act voluntarily in favor of the Confederate States. Being well known there as a mechanic, General Magruder called on me to superintend some of the cotton-clad boats and I tried to get out of it by recommending someone else whom I represented as more competent than

myself and I did all in my power to escape this service, but I was compelled by an order from General Magruder to do this work for which I received no compensation whatever. Nor did I receive any vouchers or sign any pay-rolls, though other men, who worked in the same way, did receive pay for their services.

"I returned to Pittsburg in May 1864 and immediately thereupon an excitement was raised about my disloyalty and I was arrested by an order of General Rowley, who, after an examination of three days, discharged me after an imprisonment of five weeks in the common jail. These reports were started and circulated by a Mr. Millingar and his friends. Mr. Millingar had a large amount of my money in his hands for which I had sued him and this was the cause of his persecution against me and they hoped thereby to compel me to run off."

Gearing's statement on cross-examination about the *Reindeer* was not to his advantage:

"Mr. Millingar was my brother-in-law, having married my sister, and the money in his hands was the proceeds of cotton sent by me from Texas and which I succeeded in getting through the blockade, shipped on board the *Reindeer,* owned by myself and with the usual customhouse papers issued by the Confederate authorities in Houston, Texas. I purchased the *Reindeer* in 1862 and for this voyage the papers were taken out for Havana or a market. She was commanded by a man named Stevens, who was unknown to me, except that he was recommended as a good navigator. I had owned no other vessel prior to this and she cost me $10,000 in gold. This was the only trip made by the *Reindeer* and she was captured by the United States naval forces in the Gulf on her way to Havana. Whether she was condemned in a prize court or not I cannot say, but I presume she was. I had 288 bales of cotton on the *Reindeer* at the time of her capture and the cotton found its way to New York but in what way I don't know. I had a confidential friend, Mr. B. O. Hamilton, of Galveston who was first mate on the vessel who was to act with the supercargo, my son Franklin, in getting the proceeds on to Pittsburg for distribution among my creditors. From January 1861 to the fall of 1862 I was in Texas except an absence therefrom of five or six months when I was home in Pittsburg, Pennsylvania. And I was speculating, after the seizure of my vessel, mainly in cotton, buying and selling in Texas. I was in Matamoras in July 1863 — but not at any other time — trying to get some cotton there for sale in order to raise funds by bills of exchange to remit to my family at Pittsburg. The draft purchased there was sent to New York. The Confederate government, by order of Kirby Smith, took my cotton [264 bales] along with all other cotton within their reach and that much, in that way, I lost. Beyond the voyage of the *Reindeer* I had never attempted to run the blockade and I confined my cotton operations to the States of Texas and Louisiana. In the spring of 1864 I had 800 bales of cotton, all of which was lost to me, some of it being jayhawked, and the rest burnt within the Confederate lines and by their authority near Alexandria, Louisiana. All these commercial transactions of mine in Louisiana and Texas were carried out within Confederate lines."

In December 1867 the court said:

"But unfortunately for this panegyric the claimant's testimony shows that he travelled with perfect ease and freedom through the scenes of his 'commercial transactions,' appearing one day at Alexandria, Louisiana, and another at Brownsville, in the furthest bounds of Texas, and that as late as July, 1863, he was in the Mexican town of Matamoras, from which he voluntarily a second time returned to place himself under the control of the rebel General Magruder. There have been one or two cases where citizens of the insurrectionary States have come into this court and had the hardihood to attempt to cover their disloyal acts by loud assurances of secret loyalty, but there has been no case where a northern man, owing allegiance to both State and country, has left his home to enter the rebel lines and work in rebel navy yards and transport rebel troops, and then had the brazen effrontery to come into this court and prefer a claim whose very foundation is the loyalty of the claimant.

"As to the valuable information which the claimant pretends he gave to General Gresham, the story is unsupported by proof or probability, and the tale, if it was told, was probably coined as an excuse to enter our lines after his blockade runner had been captured by our cruisers and the Confederate troops had burnt his cotton, for he says, 'I made no effort to return to Pittsburg till 1864, when everything I had had been lost to me.' The excuse for all this dishonor and iniquity was the poverty of the claimant and his laudable desire to save the remnant of his property for his creditors; but here again his self-convicting testimony shows that he had

money enough to buy 264 bales of cotton seized near Matamoras and the 800 bales burnt near Alexandria, and to invest $10,000 *in gold* in a vessel designed to break our blockade. Money appears to have been the only being to whom the claimant rendered 'true allegiance,' and it seems a most just retribution that he was so entirely forsaken by his deity."

Franklin Gearing also testified, loudly proclaiming his sympathy with the Southern cause, despite his insistence that "home" was Pittsburgh:

"During the winter of 1860 and 1861, the boats were running in their legitimate Trinity River trade. In March of 1861 we were preparing to run the boats to New Orleans and the rebel State authorities took possession of them. They held them for two or three weeks without employing them in any service. Then they were released and sent up Buffalo Bayou and laid up by my father. Then, in the fall of that year, father took them out and run them in the Galveston and Houston trade. They were run there until February or March 1862. Then they were laid up again until the Confederate government seized them. After that, they were run as Confederate government transports, and in other capacities. The *Stelle* was used as a headquarters boat. The *Carr* was sent down west among the western bays. After the *Stelle* was seized by the Confederate government, they retained the same pilots and a portion of the engineers. Father remained on the boats until about March 1862. The Confederate government seized them in the fall of 1862. General Magruder seized them. I did not remain on them after their seizures, in 1862, until May 1863. Until laid up, in March 1862, the boats were engaged in the regular business of carrying freight and passengers. During that time we carried Confederate troops or passengers. I do not remember to have carried any ammunition or military stores, except what the troops had with them. I don't know that we ever carried artillery. We once carried a couple of guns from Galveston up to Houston."

Their petition was dismissed.

The *Carr* was involved in General Magruder's campaign to retake Galveston on January 1, 1863 and from August 1863 she was a gunboat stationed at Saluria on the eastern end of Matagorda Island, Texas to protect the inland ports used by the Confederacy.

The *Stelle* sank on February 10, 1864 off Pelican Island in Galveston Bay. She was refloated and returned to service. In May 1864 she worked as a salvage vessel on the scuttled USS *Westfield* to remove the propeller shafts, which were converted to gun barrels. The *Carr* also got a 30-pound Parrott rifle from the *Westfield* in January 1864 complimenting her original armament of one 18-pounder and one 12-pound howitzer. The *Colonel Stell* was reported lost on December 21, 1867.

Geilfuss, Augustus. A native of the Kingdom of Hanover who became a citizen on October 28, 1853. He Claimed 14 bales of upland cotton and 117 barrels of turpentine seized at Charleston. He was credited $1,885.80 for the cotton and $2,425.40 on 60 barrels and ten gallons of turpentine.

Geilfuss, C. R. His wife purchased 10 bales of sea-island cotton from S. M. Elliot at $4 a pound and stored it at No. 6 Calhoun Street, Charleston where it was seized in the spring of 1865. He aided Union prisoners and was imprisoned for refusing rebel military service. He recovered $2,376.40.

Georgia, State of. The Direct Tax Act of August 5, 1861 apportioned $584,367.33 to Georgia to pay for the war. Georgia never officially assumed the debt and by September 30, 1885 the state still owed $548,811.91. On July 31, 1885 the Second Comptroller admitted the state was owed the $35,555.42. Warrant No. 7188 was issued on September 30, 1885 as a set-off against the unsettled balance due.

Gerstmann, Simon. A Savannah merchant who bought 45 bales of cotton at 10 P.M., two days before Savannah was captured, from a person known to be disloyal. The cotton was seized and sold. Expenses of $15.60 per bale were deducted making the average net per upland bale deposited into the Treasury at $190.47. The average net for sea-island was $215.97 in gold. He sued to recover and testified:

"I served five years in the regular army of the United States. I was discharged on the 8th day of February 1859 after a faithful service of five years. I was three years and a half in Florida, then was in the Kansas war, then went to Utah. I belonged to company E, second artillery. I was discharged at Fort Leavenworth. I commenced my residence here in 1859. As soon as I was discharged I went to New York and was there advised to come out here and came out as a clerk. I have been loyal to the United States and the

flag all the time. I never aided the rebellion in any way. During the war I organized a church of my faith with my own money in order to get appointed reader so to keep me out of the rebel service. Our church was organized with that motive. I suggested I would fix up a church, pay rent, gas, and other expenses, and they would elect me reader and that way I kept out of the service."

He recovered $27,335.58.

Gibbons, Francis A. A resident of Baltimore who contracted on November 16, 1863 to furnish 200,000 bushels of oats within 30 days: 100,000 bushels delivered to Baltimore at 98 cents a bushel, and 100,000 bushels to Fort Monroe at $1.01¾ cents a bushel.

The Army's storage facilities were small and continually full and his shipments were initially refused. The quartermasters began accepting his deliveries halfway into the contract but as before they were usually turned away for the same reasons. By December 16, only 29,759 bushels had been accepted at Baltimore and 25,317 at Fort Monroe. On December 30 Gibbons told the officers they were in breach of contract for not receiving his shipments. He was told to deliver the balance or they would purchase oats on the open market and charge the difference to him. He was already owed about $50,000 for oats delivered but not paid for. The balance was delivered and instead of receiving money Gibbons was given a "pink check" for $196,828.63. Cashing the voucher cost him $1,646.88 in discount fees to the Farmers and Merchants Bank of Baltimore.

Gibbons sued, claiming he should have been paid the market price of oats after December 16, which was about 10 cents above his contract price; he wasn't paid in money; and he should be reimbursed for his expenses for drayage, storage, and $333.35 in demurrage on the steamers *Townsend* and *Martin* in taking back the shipments that were refused; and on an overcharge for 7,000 bags. He was awarded $1,726.52 in 1866.

He also recovered $1,647.58 on a contract to dispose of cattle byproducts in North Carolina and Virginia for $11.40 a head.

Gilbert, Calvin L. Owned 24 bales of upland cotton captured at Savannah. Recovered $4,570.32.

Gilman, James D. A resident of Jefferson County, Kentucky. In September 1861 the governor of Kentucky authorized Curran Pope to recruit and organize a regiment of volunteers to be known as the 15th Kentucky Volunteers with the promise that Pope would be the colonel of the new regiment. Gilman entered into an agreement with Pope to recruit not less than 84 men to form a company over which he was promised the position of captain. For 60 days he traveled throughout Jefferson and adjoining counties with a wagon, driver, and three musicians he paid around $13 a day for a total of $780. He provided subsistence for the recruits he enlisted — an average of 30 were present on any given day — at a cost of 50 cents per day per man or a total of $1,350. The company of 47 recruits was camped at Louisville for three months at Gilman's expense before they were ordered to New Haven, Kentucky. At New Haven 21 of the recruits were taken from Captain Gilman over his objections and assigned to other companies to complete their complements.

He claimed $2,000 but no money was ever paid. On March 3, 1887 Congress appropriated the money and sent the claim to a federal court for fact finding.

The court found the reasonable value of Gilman's captaincy was $150 a month or $450 and the expenses he incurred to be $550. On April 28, 1913 the court held the agreement between Pope and Gilman was purely personal and incurred no liability on the part of the government.

Gilmore, Charles D. A colonel who was entitled to two servants or $32 a month for the pay, rations, and clothing of two servants beginning on May 1, 1864 to March 3, 1865. He never got the servants and received on $22 a month in lieu of them. He filed a claim for $101.

The rate of a servant's pay for officers was the pay of a private in the Army in 1812 and Congress never changed it. The pay fixed by the Act of July 6, 1812 was $5 a month. In December it went to $6; in 1838, $7; in 1854, $11; and in August 1861 it became $13 a month for regular and volunteer for three years. Officers who elected to take the pay instead of the servants were thus entitled to $13 a month.

In 1864 a private's pay increased to $16 a month. The Act of March 3, 1865 fixed the allowance for the pay of an officer's servant at a private's pay.

Gilmore was awarded $101 in 1866.

Lieutenant Colonel Bassett of the 2d Regiment Kansas Volunteers recovered $89 in 1866.

Gilmer, Susan C. Owned a plantation in Lowndes County, Mississippi where she had 63 bales of cotton in 1863. On May 2 she sold the cotton, weighing 28,382 pounds, at 25 cents a pound to the Confederate government for $7,095.50 in Confederate bonds. The cotton remained on her plantation until it was taken to Crawfordsville Station by Charles Baskervill, the local Confederate cotton agent.

On May 8, 1865 the Secretary of the Treasury appointed Harrison Johnston to collect and receive cotton "purchased by and held on account of the Confederate States Government" in Lowndes County and other counties in the state. Johnston collected 30,610 bales, including Susan's, on which net proceeds of $1,588,882.16 was paid into the Treasury.

She sued to recover but her petition was dismissed in 1878 when her bill of sale to the Confederate government was found in the Confederate archives. At the time she was "a very aged woman, living in a distant part of the country."

Glover, James S. In South Carolina a mortgage was considered a contract, not a conveyance. The seller of property (mortgagee) ceased to own the land, holding only a lien on the real property or money due from the buyer (mortgagor).

On January 5, 1860 Benjamin R. Bythewood executed a mortgage to buy the 460-acre White Hall plantation on Ladies Island, Beaufort Parish, for $10,000, and lots numbers 93, 94, 96, and 98 in Beaufort for $5,000 from Catharine B. Verdier, of Walterborough. The plantation was taxed by South Carolina as usually cultivated land. Its location on "Laders Island" was described as "bounded to the north and west on Beaufort River, to the east on the creek and marshes of Bedford, dividing it from the plantation of Mrs. Eustice, and to the south and southeast on lands belonging to Joseph Hazel, esq." A $5,000 payment or more was due June 1, 1861 and any amount left unpaid would accrue interest until the mortgage was satisfied.

In November 1861 Port Royal was occupied by the Army and the entire populations of Ladies, St. Helena, Parris, and other islands within St. Helena and Port Royal Sounds fled their homes. Bythewood never returned to White Hall.

Catharine Verdier died leaving all her property to her sister Elvira C. Glover.

On March 13, 1863 the U.S. Direct Tax Commission sold the lots, assessed at $7,000, to pay $89.20 in unpaid taxes, penalties, and fees, and 300 acres of the plantation was sold to pay $39.22 in taxes, penalties, and interest. A surplus of $145.82 on the subsequent resale of 155 acres at White Hall was paid to the Verdier family.

Elvira Glover died without a will in July 1865. Her heirs were a daughter, Catharine J. Stewart, a son James S. Glover, Margaret A. Glover, the widow of a deceased son, and her children, James B. Glover, Ann E. Glover, Katy Paul Glover, and Florence Spencer Glover.

James S. sued to recover $3,951.76 for one-half the assessed value of the lot, $5 an acre on 145 acres, totaling $725; less $127.42 in taxes and the $145.82 in recovered surplus.

South Carolina law prohibited mortgagees or their heirs from prosecuting a claim on mortgaged property, since they didn't own it, so Glover's petition was dismissed on April 23, 1894.

Gooch, Mary Ann and Nathaniel M.

This couple executed a pre-nuptial agreement on October 19, 1858 before a probate court judge in Madison County, Alabama whereby Mary Ann Selleck would retain all real and personal property acquired by her prior to and after her marriage to Nathaniel Gooch.

The happy couple moved to Mary Ann's plantation in Noxabee County, Mississippi where the agreement was recorded by the clerk of the chancery court on December 16.

Nathaniel took charge of the business and the slaves. On January 1, 1863, with the knowledge and consent of his wife, he sold 185 bales of cotton weighing 85,220 pounds to the Confederate government and received $12,783 in Confederate bonds. The bales were marked "N. M. Gooch" and stored on the plantation.

On May 8, 1865 Harrison Johnston was appointed a deputy Treasury agent to seize cotton held by the Confederate government in Noxabee and three other counties in Mississippi. Johnson seized the cotton, rebaled it to 182 bales, combined it with 11,655 other bales from Noxabee County, and added it to other bales from the other counties to make a lot totaling 30,610 bales. The lot was taken to Columbus, Mississippi where part of it was burned, some seized by the military, some sold by Johnson to cover his expenses, some given to the Mobile & Ohio Railroad Co., and other bales were burned or given away in Memphis and Mobile. A total of 16,334 bales reached Simeon Draper, the cotton agent in New York, where it was sold for net proceeds of $1,588,882.16 deposited into the Treasury.

The couple waited until 1873 to file a claim, too late to sue under the abandoned or captured property act. The court held the cotton was enemy property, lawfully seized from the enemy in wartime, and their petition was dismissed.

Goodman, Benjamin B.

Owned sea-island cotton in the seed equaling 18 bales raised on his Saint Helena Island plantation in 1861. After the war started he abandoned his farm and on May 5 joined the 20th Pennsylvania Volunteers until discharged on June 28, 1865.

On November 27 General Thomas W. Sherman received an order:

> Sir: The General-in-Chief desires you, through your quartermaster, to seize all cotton and other public property which may be used to our prejudice. The cotton, and such other articles as may not be required for the use of your command, will be shipped by return transports to the quartermaster in New York, there to be sold on public account. The services of negroes will be used in picking, collecting, and packing cotton, as well as in constructing defensive works, &c. Private property of individuals should not be interfered with, unless it of military utility under the circumstances you mention; and you will be justified in taking measures to prevent pillage or any outrage, so far as the exigencies of the service will permit, no matter what relations the persons or property may bear to the U.S. government."

In November 1861 the Treasury Department published its regulations for disposing of "the productions of the soil and of all other property found within the limits of States or parts of States declared to be in insurrection against the United States, and now occupied by the troops and authorities of the Union." Slaves were to be used, where found, and paid for their labor.

In December 1861 Goodman's cotton was seized by Treasury agents and put aboard the *May Flower* with other seized lots.

All the cotton from Port Royal, Hilton Head, and Beaufort, South Carolina was seized and shipped to New York and sold into the Treasury for net proceeds of $480,310.85. The average price per bale was $161.25 so Goodman's cotton sold for $2,902.50.

He recovered the money in 1878.

Gordon, Michael.

Owned one bale of upland cotton weighing 510 pounds, one bale weighing 515 pounds, and 2–3,000 pounds of loose cotton seized at Savannah. He sued for $1,059.36. In his defense, two soldiers wrote a note to Brigadier General John W. Geary:

> General: The bearer, Michael Gordon, a citizen of this city, at the risk of his life, as he was hiding from conscription, at the time concealed the undersigned, escaped Federal prisoners of war. He has some cotton which he wishes to obtain protection for. Hoping, general, that you will grant it and any other favor that he may request, we have the honor to be, very respectively, your humble obedient servants,
>
> Louis Nugent,
> First Sergeant Troop F, 12th New York Cavalry
> J. F. Williams,
> Company H, 95th New York Volunteers

Gordon recovered $1,051.98 on six bales in 1870.

Gowdy, Lorin.

A gin distiller in Enfield, Connecticut whose son, Edmund J. Gowdy, of Savannah, sold his father's goods in the South. In the fall of 1860 he sent his son 125 to 150 casks of gin that E. J. received around the first of the year. E. J. sold a portion of the gin and sent his father around $1,200 in March 1861. After the war began, he had no communication with his father and acted without instructions. E. J. sold the remainder of the gin in Savannah in the fall of 1863 and bought cotton on his father's account, sold that, and bought five more bales of cotton that he marked as belonging to "Ned Gowdy." These were stored in the store of Hill Gowdy, E. J.'s uncle for whom he was a clerk. E. J. reported its location with the capture of Savannah and claimed it as his own.

The seller of the cotton recalled E. J. saying "that he was indebted to his father for gin, which he had been selling on commission for his father, and that he purchased this cotton to reimburse the claimant after the war."

E. J. also volunteered in the rebel service as a soldier for 60 days in the Savannah Volunteer Guards. He was then conscripted and served in the quartermaster department for 16 months until the end of the war.

Dad sued to recover but the court stated:

"Where the debtor, at the time of the capture, has reported the captured property as his own, where he has previously treated it as such, and the ownership of the northern creditor has rested exclusively within the debtor's breast, so that his calling it another's might be a mere after-thought to defeat the lawful effects of the capture, there we have uniformly held the debtor

to be the owner, and the pretended transfer in fraud of the act."

Dad's petition was dismissed.

Grant, William S.

On March 5, 1860 Grant and his partner, T. W. Taliafero, offered Secretary of War John B. Floyd all the supplies the Army needed in the Arizona Territory south of 33°36'N and 106°35'W until March 26, 1862 at 12 percent less than they were paying their current contractor. Transportation would be estimated from the nearest established posts. The offer was accepted, a contract was signed on March 9, and a large order placed with Grant. No inspection of the supplies was required. The two got busy but soon afterward Taliafero sold his interest to Grant.

On July 9, the Secretary modified the order to limit the amount of supplies, which Grant protested. On September 9, Grant signed another contract with Lieutenant Horace Randall, acting assistant commissary of subsistence, to furnish all fresh beef, bacon sides, hams, flour, beans, candles, and soap. On September 18 Secretary Floyd further modified the agreement by requiring all merchandise purchased in eastern cities to be inspected but without specifying where. He also repudiated both contracts as not being consistent with the original understanding he had with Grant, and because they could not be subjected to the Act of June 23, 1860, which required advertising for bids.

Grant moved to Arizona to establish a depot and agency in Tucson. He purchased his supplies in New York and Boston for shipment to Port Lavacca, Texas. The first order was ready for shipment to Lavacca on September 24 but no inspection was made until December 6.

In order to get the supplies the 1,200 miles to the furthest posts in the Territory from Port Lavacca, Grant had to have a large number of wagons, teams, teamsters, and workers. They were in place on November 10 but the supplies didn't reached Lavacca until January 10, 1861, and by then the supply train couldn't move very far due to a shortage of forage and severe weather. They had to sit out the winter and got underway in spring. On April 20, when the supplies were 50 miles west of San Antonio and 950 miles from their destination, they were seized by armed rebels.

Unbeknownst to Grant, the Army had cancelled his contract on April 3rd. The cost of the merchandise, freight charges, teams, wagons, and other expenses was $84,370.14.

Grant sued to recover the $84,370.14 plus $200,000 in lost income from the contract under the Act of March 3, 1849: "An act to provide for the Payment of Horses and other Property lost or destroyed in the Military Service of the United States." Grant claimed that if the goods had been inspected in a timely manner all would have been delivered by April 20.

The court held that Grant delayed the process by having the goods inspected in Boston and New York to protect himself from shipping goods the Army wouldn't accept in Arizona, he selected an unusual route of travel, which presented greater hazards, and all troops left the Territory in 1861 so he would have lost money anyway. His petition was dismissed.

He had invested heavily in flour mills, storehouses, shops, corrals, and homes to fulfill his contracts. He had large stocks of flour, oats, wheat, corn, barley, beans, general, merchandise, furniture, and many other goods. Grant was also storing large quantities of supplies that had been sold to the government.

The local population was described as "lawless adventurers and intensely hostile to the Government of the United States" and "traitors of the deepest dye," according to Lieutenant Lord, commander of a company of dragoons, and that " they openly talked secession long before the war commenced, especially those in the vicinity of Tucson." Captain Chapin, commander of Fort Buchanan, said, "Tucson was full of gamblers and murderers. Large numbers of the white people were southerners in feeling and ready to take up arms for the southern cause. Exceptions to this were rare."

The Confederate flag was flown at Tucson and soon full-blown rebellion started. On July 10, 1861 Captain I. N. Moore, commander at Tucson, received information that Fort Breckenridge had been abandoned and burned, troops at Fort Buchanan were getting ready to leave, and Texas rebels had taken Fort Union and intended to storm the Territory and cut off the Army.

Captain Moore sent Lieutenant Lord, commanding troops en route to Tucson from Fort Breckenridge, written orders to destroy whatever government stores could not be taken out by train, along with any of Grant's property "that might be of value to the public enemy or to the disloyal people of Tucson" and Moore took a contingent of troops and headed for Fort Buchanan.

On July 15, Lord gave Grant a half an hour

to get his papers and then he set fire to his works and prepared to leave by train. When the property was fired, a large, armed mob assembled and Lord believed his train would be attacked.

Grant filed a claim for $61,418.44. Investigation showed that $11,280 worth of property survived along with 50,000 pounds of beans, $660; 35,000 feet of lumber, $1,448.44; and other credits for a total of $19,888.44. He was awarded $41,530 in 1863.

Green, Alexander L. P. A resident of Nashville who did business with Fite, Shepard & Co., a firm who employed his son. On February 16, 1862, when the capture of Nashville was imminent, he was requested by the company to take a large amount of Confederate money and Southern bank notes into the interior for the purpose of making investments with the soon-to-be-worthless tender and which could be used in future to pay northern creditors.

Green owned buildings in Nashville that he left in the care of an agent. On December 24, 1864 his buildings were seized as abandoned property. A U.S. Treasury agent leased the buildings through July 8, 1865 and collected $8,766.54 in rent. The rent money was transferred to Brigadier General Clinton B. Fisk, assistant commissioner of the Freedmen's Bureau.

Green sued to recover the rent but his petition was dismissed.

Green, Charles. A British subject who had "large business operations" in Savannah and owned 16 bales of upland and 659 bales of sea-island cotton seized there.

He sued to recover in 1872 and as a foreign national the question was whether or not President Johnson's December 25, 1868 unconditional pardon for crimes of treason included him. The Supreme Court held that violations of the abandoned or captured property act of March 12, 1863 applied to three groups: citizens, resident aliens, and foreigners. Johnson's General Amnesty Proclamation applied to citizens and resident aliens but no decision had been made regarding foreigners.

The only question the court addressed was whether a resident alien living in the insurrectionary states during the war could be guilty of treason. Since Green was never charged with any crime by the government or violation of the Act he was awarded $155,554.89 on all the cotton. The sea-island was $231.79 a bale.

Green, John W. James Green owned the Mansion House Hotel in Alexandria, Virginia — the city's finest hotel. He willingly rented the building for use as a 1,000-bed hospital to the Army by verbal agreement at $750 a month commencing November 11, 1861. It was well ventilated and near the railroad. Colonel Rufus Ingalls, 19th Infantry quartermaster at the Arlington, Virginia depot, turned the job over to 2d Lieutenant C. B. Ferguson, acting assistant quartermaster at Alexandria.

When Quartermaster General Meigs was notified he replied that he thought the rent was extravagant and wanted to know if the owner was loyal. When Green applied for the first months' rent he was asked to take the oath of allegiance, which he declined to do, so no payment was made as he was believed to be disloyal. Green asked his brother, Edwin Green, of Washington, D.C., to write to Meigs about the rent. Meigs wrote Edwin a note on March 24, 1864 saying the "alleged rent" was not paid because his brother refused to take the loyalty oath and was believed to be disloyal.

James took the oath on May 5, 1865. The Army occupied the building until June 30, 1865 when it was returned to him in a damaged condition but no rent was ever paid.

On May 3, 1872 Green wrote to Secretary of War William W. Belknap claiming he was owed $32,750 in rent and $5,000 for damages. Belknap turned it over to the Southern Claims Commission but they said they weren't authorized to settle claims for rent. Belknap then sent it to the Treasury Department. The accounting officers applied to the War Department for documentation but none could be found. Green then petitioned the Congressional Committee on War Claims for relief. On May 27, 1876 the Quartermaster General's office said no papers relating to the case could be found but in December 1877 a clerk found them on the fifth floor among a "mass of old documents."

James died and his executor, John W. Green, filed suit in 1880 to recover $32,000 in unpaid rent. The court held the claim was barred by the statute of limitations but on appeal two years later the heirs were awarded $32,000 on the ground that Green's original request for the rent money was made before the time had expired and prior to locating the lost records.

Greene, William H. William's wife, Estelle G. P. Greene, bought 47 bales of sea-island cotton with money given to her by her mother. The cotton belonged to William under South Carolina law when it was seized at Charleston. Estelle unsuccessfully attempted to recover under own name under the Act of March 12, 1863 but the only way to recover was for her husband to file suit. By the time he did, the two-year statute of limitation under the Act had expired. The court recognized that William had taken the loyalty oath on March 4, 1865 in the presence of First Lieutenant Myron Jarvis, 127th New York Volunteers, who was the assistant provost marshal, and recognized that Estelle's original suit had been brought within the time frame of the Act so William was awarded $10,885.67 in 1871.

Griffin, John and Sarah. Owned 26.67 acres within three miles of the courthouse in Louisville, Kentucky. Fruit trees had been planted, the outhouses were almost complete, and the Griffin House was under construction. In 1862 the house was seized by Major General J. T. Boyle and converted into a 140-bed smallpox hospital. On December 24, 1863 Sarah signed a receipt for $1,033.20 to cover rent and damage to the premises as a full settlement. They refused to renew the lease on November 22, 1865 so the Army seized and occupied the property until July 1, 1866. The Griffins subsequently moved to Greenville, Mississippi and sued to recover $15,125 for damage to the property. Their suit was dismissed on March 21, 1898 as barred by statute of limitations and the Bowman Act.

Grossmayer, Henry. Elias Einstein, of Macon, Georgia, owed money to Grossmayer who authorized Elias to invest it in cotton and hold it for him. In 1863 Einstein purchased 48 bales of cotton and had it shipped to Abraham Epstein at Savannah for storage in Abraham Backer's storehouse. The cotton was seized and in 1866 Einstein and Grossmayer settled leaving Grossmayer to recover. He was awarded $8,040.96 in 1868. The government appealed to the Supreme Court where the judgement was reversed on the ground that Grossmayer never owned the cotton.

Grover & Gardner. Recovered $2,790 on a claim for $3,785 loss of profits to furnish 50,000 bushels of grain at Baltimore.

Habersham, Eliza A. The wife of John Habersham, the slave of Robert Erwin, and a "sampler in the commission house of Erwin &

Hardie" at Savannah. Ten bales of John's upland cotton was kept at No. 3 and No. 6 Bay Street, the Jones Building, and four were on Reynolds Street when it was seized. John died and Eliza sued to recover.

Erwin testified about John:

"About ten years ago, to the best of my recollection, he sought me and asked me to purchase him. I told John to go to his master to ask him the lowest price that would buy him, make his own trade, come to me and I would give him a check. I bought him and put him in the office of Erwin & Hardie. He received, sampled, and weighed all of our cottons. While he was sampler with us I told John that all the sample cotton and pickings he should take and should have and, in addition to that, he must let me know from time to time what was the expense of his living and we should give him a salary accordingly. I know that John saved, from time to time, these samples which he had pulled and put in proper shape and at my suggestion all the money he had on hand he invested in cotton from time to time. A part of this cotton, I know, was stored with us. I gave him free storage for everything he had. We put it in bales for him. There were some few lots he bought from us. We kept a regular account and we credited him with services and we would sell him a lot at usual prices and let him retail it out for his own benefit, such small lots as two or three bales at a time. This may have been as often as three or four times. We would let him buy single bales and I would charge the money to his account. I advised him to invest in cotton and am somewhat responsible for his loss today. The cotton he had in our store was taken by the United States government. I do not remember the number of bales. John had the immediate charge of our warehouse. He carried the keys."

Eliza recovered $1,670 on 14 bales.

Hall, Warren.

Hall, Warren. Warren's mother was a free Indian woman who lived in Alexandria, Virginia when Warren was born. Warren was Indian and African and was taken and sold at Washington as a slave to Thomas Williams, brought to New Orleans, and sold to Mr. Roach in 1844. Roach owned the Bachelor's Bend plantation on the Mississippi River near Greenville, Mississippi. The elder Roach died in 1847 and the plantation was taken over by his son Benjamin. Warren continued to work as a field hand and stock minder.

On April 17, 1863 Lieutenant William H. Barlow, acting quartermaster of the 31st Missouri Infantry, seized 74 bales of cotton hidden in a cane thicket on Roach's plantation. It was hauled to the river, put aboard a government transport, and taken to Milliken's Bend. Warren and Roach's overseer, McDowell, followed the cotton. Warren claimed it as his; McDowell said it belonged to the Roaches. Warren later admitted to McDowell the cotton did not belong to him and later swore out an oath to that effect.

Warren decided to sue anyway. In court, with Mary (possibly Margaret) Roach, the deceased Benjamin's wife, he claimed to be a free man employed by the Roaches and had acquired the cotton as payment for his raising and selling livestock prior to the Emancipation Proclamation. The question for the court was Warren's status. Under Mississippi law, Warren could have asserted his right to freedom if he believed he was being held illegally. He never did, no one else had the right to do it for him, and it was illegal for him to conduct business if he was a slave. The Revised Code of Mississippi 1857 stated:

Section 1, page 235: "all negro and mulatto slaves, in all courts of judicature in this State, shall be held, taken, and adjudged to be personal property."

Section 3, Chapter 33, page 236: "It shall not be lawful for any person, either by will, deed, or other conveyance, directly or in trust, either express, or secret, or otherwise, to make any disposition of any slave or slaves, for the purpose or with the intent to emancipate such slave or slaves within the State, or to provide that any such slaves shall be removed to be emancipated elsewhere, or by any evasion or indirection so as to provide that the Colonization Society, or any donee or grantee, can accomplish the act, intent, or purpose designed to be prohibited by this article."

Section 8, Article 32, provided for a $50 fine to any master or employer of a slave who gave license to a slave to trade in the marketplace as a freeman.

The $8,911.83 net proceeds of the cotton was awarded to Mary Roach on the ground that Hall was barred by Mississippi law from any business ventures. A dissenting opinion held that Hall was born free, kidnapped, and sold illegally into the slave trade and was therefore never a slave and should recover a portion of the cotton as agreed between him and Mary Roach.

Hamilton, John F. Owned 92 bales of cotton and invested in a Savannah blockade runner that ran cotton to Nassau. He took a loyalty oath on March 26 and July 3, 1865 and recovered $16,293.79 for 85 bales of upland and six bales of sea-island cotton under President Johnson's amnesty proclamation of December 25, 1868.

Hamner, J. C. George M. Hamner owned 126 bales of upland cotton at Prairie Bluff, Arkansas seized in April 1865. Only 67 bales reached New York and $5,020.98 at $74.95 a bale net proceeds ended up in the Treasury. George died June 1868 in Wilcox County, Alabama leaving nine children. George's son J. C. filed suit in 1868 claiming ownership of the cotton but had trouble with the title.

On January 9, 1873, George W., J. C., and the others filed an amended petition showing their father as the owner of the cotton and that no one has been appointed administrator of the estate. In 1875 J. C. was appointed but by then the statutue of limitations had run under the Act of March 12, 1863 and their petition was dismissed.

Hancock, Enoch T. Between March and July, 1863 Hancock purchased 33 bales of upland cotton from Lewis D. Lowry, C. O. Martindale, and Lee Howard in Charleston and 32 bales were later seized. Hancock claimed an aggregate value of $10,293.40. He described his efforts to stay out of the rebel army:

"I worked as hard as I could to keep out of the rebel army. In March 1862 they had a general conscription and there was a considerable fuss about what should exempt people. It was rather easy to get off. There was no money to be paid, my hand is deformed, and a board of physicians exempted me when the war had been going on about one year. In September 1863 they had another conscription, coming in with a new broom and that cleaned me out. They decided I would have to go in. They gave me one week to get ready and I secreted myself in Cumming street and kept myself so from October 1, 1863, the day I was to report, and I stayed there till very nearly Christmas. We had supposed every day the Union men would open up the batteries. Just the day before Christmas they did open them and in the latter part of January I had given up the idea of our taking the city. I went to Wilmington, North Carolina, having a friend in a blockade-running house there, thinking I could get through the blockade or with a little

money buy off a surgeon who was there examining conscripts.

"I was then gobbled up or conscripted as a fit man to go to Raleigh. They put me in a room with 170 men. The room was so small that we lay three deep. At night we started for Raleigh with an officer. At half past eleven at night one of my guards was away and the other was snoozing. I went out on the platform. The cars were going at the rate of twelve miles an hour and I jumped off the train into a frog pond. It rained as hard as I ever saw it rain. I worked my way back to Wilmington, pretty well used up. In such ways I managed to keep out of the army. I made these efforts in opposition to the rebellion and because of my loyalty to the United States. I finally got back to my old quarters. I was in the state of Maine when my cotton was seized and I know very little about it. I escaped from this city on the 14th of November."

The court determined the value of Charleston upland cotton to be $131.20 a bale and he was awarded $4,198.40.

Hancox, Clement. Chartered his steamer *Edwin Lewis* to the Army on August 4, 1863 at $40 a day. On December 31 she was in Folly Creek, South Carolina and a government pilot was put aboard to take her up the creek at night to avoid a rebel battery at Secessionville. The master objected saying the vessel was too long for the sharp bends. The pilot went ahead, the vessel struck, sunk, and was abandoned.

She was eventually salvaged and restored to service under the charter agreement. The salvage and repair time was 129¼ days which would have paid Hancox $19,387.51. A dispute arose between Hancox and the quartermaster over who should pay for the salvage and whether Hancox was owed money for the repair period. They agreed the Army would pay for salvage and running expenses during the repair period, $5,170, and Hancox would forego the rent from the time of sinking to restoration of service. The Army paid the salvors $5,500 and Hancox the $5,170.

Hancox later felt the settlement wasn't fair and sued to recover a balance but his petition was dismissed in 1873 on the ground the compromise between the two parties was legal and he signed a receipt.

Hancox, J. W. Chartered his steamer *Hero* to the Army on April 21, 1864 at $250 a day until August 20, 1865. On June 8 the Quartermaster General reduced the daily rate to $207.90

as of 60 days after April 21 and Hancox was told the vessel would be discharged from service if he objected. Hancox replied on the 23rd that he accepted the new rate but he intended to have the vessel remeasured and felt confident that would command a higher rate at a later settlement date.

He was paid $250 a day from April through August, but $207.90 for September through November with a further reduction of $42.10 per day from June 20 to August 31 to reduce the charter rate to $207.90 after the first 60 days. Hancox accepted the payment "in full of the above account."

He had the vessel remeasured and asked the Army to reexamine the case and if they didn't accept the larger measurements he might have the boat discharged. The Quartermaster General allowed him $221.45 a day and allowed $221.46 a day for the period of 60 days after the charter. Hancox wasn't happy later and sued to recover the full amount but his petition was dismissed since he signed a receipt for payment in full.

Hardee, Ann M.

Wife of Noble A. Hardee, a Savannah cotton factor, who sued to recover on 85 bales of upland and 411 bales of sea-island cotton seized at Savannah.

A mob broke into Noble's office and destroyed all his books and papers the day after the city was occupied. Noble took President Lincoln's conditional oath of amnesty of December 8, 1863 "with reference to the emancipation of slaves" on June 30, 1865 as administered by Captain Charles H. Cox of the 75th New York Volunteers. Noble was described by Captain Cox:

"The above-named has dark complexion, gray hair, and blue eyes; is 6 feet; aged sixty years; by profession a merchant."

Noble accepted the pardon on July 31, 1867 and died on September 10. Ann was awarded $103,856.86 in 1872.

Harrison, David and Thomas.

Cotton-spinners of Staleybridge, England doing business as T. Harrison & Sons. They wrote to William Battersby & Co. at Savannah in September 1861 to purchase 1,000 bales of cotton for them and store it somewhere in the interior until the blockade was lifted. Battersby purchased 750 bales on their account and drew bills of exchange with the Harrisons who reimbursed them. The Army seized 309 bales of their upland cotton, sold it in New York, and $54,170.97 was deposited into the Treasury, which they recovered in 1870.

A total of 32,304 bales of cotton were brought to New York from Savannah.

Hart, Simeon.

An El Paso, Texas merchant who joined the Confederate service and furnished supplies, money, and transportation for the invasion of New Mexico.

Lieutenant Thomas K. Jackson was acting commissary of subsistence at Fort Bliss, Texas. He resigned his commission on April 3, 1861 to join the Confederate service.

Major John B. Grayson, brevet lieutenant colonel, was the Department of New Mexico chief commissary of subsistence. He left on April 19, 1861, proceeded to San Antonio, Texas where he joined Colonel Earl Van Dorn's command, and tendered his resignation from there.

Second Lieutenant Edward Treachy was acting assistant quartermaster and acting commissary of subsistence at Fort Craig, New Mexico where he remained until May 1, 1861. He stayed in the Army and died on February 15, 1864.

All of these folks owed money to Simeon Hart for debts incurred on flour and other goods while they were in the Army and he had five vouchers for payments owed between March 3 and June 21, 1861.

Hart filed a claim with the War Department and on November 13, 1873 it was referred to a federal court by Secretary of War William W. Belknap.

Vouchers were held to be prima facie evidence of a debt but never as conclusive evidence. In any case, the Joint Resolution of March 2, 1867 prohibited paying any lawful debt owed prior to April 13, 1861 to anyone who aided the rebellion.

Hart also relied on the unconditional pardon of December 25, 1868 but the pardon restored only civil rights, as the court said:

"A pardon restores to civil rights, to the enjoyment of property, to the right to sue, to the right to military duty, to the right to exercise the franchise, and to hold office, but it does not confer the right to take money from the Treasury of the United States, except as appropriated by Congress."

His petition was dismissed.

Hartiens, Adolph.

John and William H. Osborne were brothers who owned a large plantation in Rapides Parish on the Red River 10 miles below Alexandria, Louisiana. William was a civil engineer.

General Nathaniel Banks occupied Alexandria on March 16, 1864 with protection from Admiral Porter's fleet on the Red River.

Between May 5 and 13 U.S. military forces seized 1,000 hogsheads containing 1 million pounds of sugar, 10,000 bushels of corn, 50 mules, 14 horses, and 100 head of cattle from the Osborne plantation, all valued at $109,750. The sugar was put aboard naval vessels or Army transports on the Red River and from there its disposition was unknown. It was later shown that the Army commissary department purchased a large quantity of sugar at Alexandria on May 5 for 9 cents a pound and that $19,750 worth of Osborne goods were taken by the Army for its own use. There was no way to remove private property from the area as all vessels were under military control.

William died on December 2, 1865 leaving a wife, Mary Corinne L. A. Duval Osborne and an infant daughter, Mary Corinne Osborne. Mary married Henry H. Rogers in 1868 and died in 1872. She and Henry had no children.

On December 1, 1887 Mary Corinne married Adolph Hartiens. She died on February 8, 1892 leaving three minor children, Sidney L., William W., and Mary R. Hartiens.

John Osborne declared bankruptcy in 1869. He submitted a claim on April 18, 1884 to the House Committee on War Claims for $67,050 representing his half of the seized property. It was found that John Osborne was loyal during the war but the loyalty of William could not be firmly established and the claim was referred to a federal court under the Bowman Act.

John died before the trial and the suit was filed by his wife, Belle Osborne. The trial was held in 1890. One witness, Dennis Kelly, deposed at Alexandria, Louisiana, stated that in 1863 William was supervising the building of rafts in the Red River at Fort De Roussey 30 miles below Alexandria for the purpose of preventing the *Queen of the West* and other federal vessels from ascending the River. This was not substantiated by other witnesses and the government argued the court had no jurisdiction until the loyalty of both partners could be firmly established. The court held that William Osborne "to all intents and purposes, though not in form, has been found disloyal" and the petition was sent back to Congress on May 6, 1889 for rehearing.

In March 1906 Dennis Kelly disclaimed his former testimony in a deposition taken at Washington, D.C. Adolph Hartiens then filed suit and on December 3, 1906 the court declared William loyal and reported their findings to Congress.

Haskell, Leonidas. Sued unsuccessfully to recover on a $55,375 voucher for a shipment of mules delivered to General McKinstry at St. Louis at $119 a head. The amount was reduced by the Davis-Holt-Campbell commission to $10,546.

Hawker, James. In May 1862 Captain A. M. Huntington, assistant quartermaster at Clarksburg, Virginia, hired Hawker as wagon master to organize a 23-wagon train of farmers' teams in an all-fired hurry to bring forage to New Creek. Hawker hired nine 2-horse teams at $27 a day, two 3-horse teams at $8 a day, and two 4-horse teams at $10 a day.

Hawker got $40 a month for himself, $1 a day for his horse, saddle, and bridal, $3 a day for each 2-horse team; $4 a day for each 3-horse team, and $5 a day for each 4-horse team. The train left Clarksburg on the 27th and arrived at New Creek on July 8. The farmers were ordered to remain there until they could be paid off, which occurred on the 20th. Hawker claimed he was entitled to pay through his return to Clarksburg and sued for an additional $739 but the Army refused. He recovered $384 for his return to Clarksburg and for rations for the farmers.

Haycraft, William A. Haycraft filed suit on July 30, 1872 to recover on 100 bales of cotton seized in April 1863. The statute of limitations on claims under the abandoned or captured property act was two years after the suppression of the rebellion. The legal date of the end of the war was August 20, 1866. In court, Haycraft proudly announced he was a rebel and as such had no right to sue under the Act until he was unconditionally pardoned by President Johnson's proclamation of December 25, 1868 and that happened after the statute of limitations had expired. He claimed he had a right to sue the government under an implied contract for the actual market value of his property at the time and place it was seized.

His petition was dismissed on the ground that the pardon restored only civil rights, not monetary claims.

Hayden, Julius A. Claimed 180–190 bales of cotton seized from his farm three miles from Atlanta. Upon the approach of General Sherman he removed his wife and daughters to the south instead of toward Union lines, which he said was impossible to do. Hayden was credited with 140 bales and recovered $50,581.60.

Hayes, Philip. Owner of four bales of upland cotton and 36 barrels of turpentine seized at Charleston. He recovered $524.80 for the cotton and $1,703.52 for the turpentine.

Haym, Harry. Sued to recover the loss of 360 bales of upland and 42 bales of sea-island cotton. President Johnson's unconditional pardon of December 25, 1868 gave all who aided the rebellion the right to prosecute their claims in the federal Court of Claims. All they had to prove was the loss. Haym had a warrant of pardon from President Johnson dated March 18, 1867 valid only upon Haym taking the prescribed oath of May 29, 1865. Haym accepted the pardon on April 2, 1867 but he took the oath on July 13, 1865. The court held he did not strictly conform to the terms of the pardon but the Supreme Court's decision on the 1868 proclamation gave them no choice and he recovered $72,853.98.

The Court of Claims had dismissed December 25 proclamation claims on the ground that the pardon restored only civil rights, not monetary claims but this interpretation was reversed by the Supreme Court.

Headman, Henry D. Claimed three bales of sea-island cotton seized at Savannah. On November 6, 1961, Henry's name was entered in the poll book at Savannah as having voted for Jefferson Davis. He couldn't prove sole title to the cotton and his case was remanded to the docket until he could.

Hebrew Congregation Benai Berith Jacob. The congregation was chartered in 1862 for religious purposes under the laws of Georgia with the right to buy, sell, sue, and be sued. Three trustees, the rabbi and president Jacob Rosenfeld, Philip Dzialynski, and Harry Haym, purchased a number of bales of upland cotton for investment purposes. Seven were captured at Savannah in Dzialynski's storehouse on Bay Street.

The cotton was shipped to New York on the *L. L. Sturgis* and sold for $1,200 in gold. The congregation was awarded the net proceeds of $1,227.31.

Heflebower, John. In 1860, John purchased a 190-acre farm in Washington County, Maryland adjacent to Maryland Heights and near Harpers Ferry, Virginia. In 1861 he had about 120 acres under cultivation. From late July 1861 to the end of the war, except for short periods in 1863, about 55 acres of the farm was used by the Army as a campground, a stopping place for wagon trains for up to 1,400 teams at a time, and the Signal Corps used it as a depot for recruits.

The reasonable rental value of the land for agricultural purposes at the time it was occupied was $5 an acre per year. Heflebower would have been owed $1,100 had he ever been paid. The land was unusable for two years after the Army left due to soil compaction, pit holes, sewers, chimneys, and other debris. The estimated cost to restore the property was $550. His location was critical.

The Proclamation of July 1, 1862 declared 39 counties in western Virginia as loyal. When this territory was admitted as a new state by the West Virginia Admission Act of December 31, 1862, President Lincoln's proclamation of April 20, 1863 included nine other counties in Virginia and later Berkeley and Jefferson Counties were added to the new State by the Acts of March 10, 1866 and the Joint Resolution of June 18, 1866.

The territory was divided for legal purposes into three areas: territory never declared in rebellion, territory declared in rebellion at the start of the war but later admitted to the Union as loyal in 1863, and territory — Berkeley and Jefferson Counties — which had been declared in rebellion throughout the war and was hostile but which had later been declared as having been loyal from the beginning by the 1866 legislation. A narrow strip of Virginia, which included the towns of Alexandria and Norfolk, were initially declared in insurrection but were retaken very quickly and recognized as loyal territory as early as July 1861.

Certain parishes in Louisiana were initially declared hostile but later exempted.

Tennessee was not declared in insurrection by President Lincoln in his Emancipation Proclamation of January 1, 1863 and in the Act of July 28, 1866 Congress extended benefits of the Act of July 4, 1864 "to the loyal citizens of the State of Tennessee."

The problem for the courts was that at no time during the war there ever a "fixed and settled" line between loyal and hostile territory and hostilities ranged in the States from Pennsylvania to Texas. This became a problem in Heflebower's case with regard to a phrase in legislation, "the seat of war." His property had no strategic value but was especially suited for a campsite owing to its level terrain as opposed to surrounding land.

The Act of July 4, 1864 authorized the Quartermaster and Commissary Generals to investigate claims for "stores and supplies of loyal citizens in States not in rebellion." In February 1867 Congress restricted the Generals from settling any claim "for supplies or stores which originated in a State or part of a State declared in rebellion by the proclamation of July 1, 1862" but there was no mention in the Act of real estate.

When Heflebower filed his claim in 1885 there was no remedy in law for the loss of supplies taken by engineers or the medical department or for real property. After the war ended Congress passed 11 acts for the relief of individual owners of occupied real property: two were charitable organizations, one was an express contract, three were post-war cases, two were owners of property within the narrow strip of Virginia controlled by the loyal legislature of Virginia, one was in Tennessee, and two were in hostile territory.

Since the Act of July 4, 1864 the policy of Congress was to redeem owners for the government's use of personal property but not to pay for injured or destroyed property. The Bowman Act was another impediment to Heflebower since it barred the court from entertaining any claim "for the use and occupation of real estate by any part of the military or naval forces of the United States in the operations of said forces during the said war at the seat of war." No one knew exactly what the phrase "seat of war" meant.

The Constitution's Fifth Amendment makes no distinction between real and personal property taken for public use, nor had the Supreme Court.

On April 5, 1886 the court ruled the damage to Heflebower's property was not done for military necessity, "but were of the nature of waste under an implied tenancy, for which the Government is liable under the decision of the Supreme Court in the case of Bostwick v. The United States." (94 U.S. 53). The findings of fact were transmitted to the House Committee on War Claims on April 5, 1886.

Henderson, Robert J. A resident of Nashville who was hired on January 1, 1865 by Department of the Cumberland quartermaster J. L. Donaldson to cut and deliver 3,000 cords of wood on the Cumberland River near Marrowbone Point 18 miles from Nashville at $6 a cord. His workers had cut and piled 2,900 before March 1 when he was ordered to cease. Only 1,510 had been taken away and delivered. He sued to recover $7,253.90 but his petition was dismissed.

Henry, Ake. A resident of Cleveland, Tennessee who owned 27 bales weighing 10,000 pounds captured at Dalton, Georgia in June 1864 by Colonel Laibold's 2d Missouri Infantry. He was awarded $12,345.75.

Henry, Anthony W. Enrolled as a corporal on August 16, 1861 in Captain James Warnock's Company D, 2d Regiment of Ohio Volunteer Infantry under Colonel Charles Whittlesey. He advanced to first sergeant and on August 15, 1863 he received a second lieutenant's commission from Governor Tod of Ohio. He reported to the division mustering officer for assignment to Company D but was told there were only 62 enlisted men in Company D, not enough to warrant a second lieutenant.

Section 2 of the Act of July 22, 1861 authorizing volunteers prescribed each regiment to be composed of ten companies, each with three officers, 16 non-commissioned officers, and from 64 to 82 privates. The Act of March 3, 1863, Section 20, stated:

"That whenever a regiment is reduced below the minimum number allowed by law, no officers shall be appointed in such regiment beyond those necessary for the command of such reduced number."

Company D's only lieutenant went on temporary duty with the Signal Corps in September and was subsequently killed at Chickamauga around the 20th.

Captain Warnock and Colonel Whittlesey appealed on his behalf and were given the same reason. Whittlesey then ordered him to report to Captain Warnock, which he did, and he served until he was discharged on October 10, 1864. He was in several engagements and commanded the company at Missionary Ridge.

Henry's name appeared on the muster role as a first sergeant since it was prohibited to show him as a second lieutenant. After his discharge he applied for second lieutenant's pay and was refused. He sued and recovered $1,118.11. As the court stated with regard to these numerous cases:

"For them there is no appeal to the Supreme

Court; for the defendants there is. If this suit be decided adversely to the claimant by this court, the decision will be final against all of these soldiers. They are men who rose from the ranks by hard fighting and good conduct, earning their commissions before they got them, and working for them after they came, and it seems a strange anomaly that six years after the war ended such men should be driven to seek the fruits of their promotion in a court of justice."

Hill, Charles. A resident of Liverpool, England who wrote to William Battersby & Co. in Savannah on October 5, 1861 with an order to purchase 300–500 bales of upland cotton to be stored on the plantations or in the interior until the blockade of Savannah was lifted. Battersby got the letter on December 21 and bought a quantity of cotton at 7½ cents a pound. The company sent a bill that Hill paid in England. The cotton was stored in Savannah where it was captured and sold in New York for $37,695.95 net proceeds on 215 bales.

When Hill filed a claim to recover it was discovered that he had invested in Alexander Collie & Co. of London for the purpose of blockade running but no evidence linking any vessel with that company was found and Hill recovered the full amount in 1873.

Hill, John. Hill was a contractor who was arrested in December 1862 and held in the Old Capitol Prison at Washington City. He was released on April 29, 1863 when a $1,500 payment from Clement Hughs was made through Hill's friend, James P. Gregory, after repeated demands by government officers for the money.

Gregory got a receipt from the Judge Advocate, L. Turner:

> Received of James P. Gregory, for John Hill, fifteen hundred dollars, being money fraudulently obtained from the Government by said Hill.

No charges were ever brought against Hill while he was incarcerated nor did he ever appear before any tribunal. On January 30, 1863 Hill made what appeared to be a voluntary sworn statement while he was in prison to the effect of admitting his guilt for the purpose of obtaining his release. He stated he had a contract with Colonel Ingalls to deliver 1,000 tons of hay at $25 a ton and 50,000 bushels of oats at 54 cents per bushel. He purchased the goods from a dealer named White at Baltimore. White told him he was filling another contract and that he was adding 15 percent to the weights on the bills

of lading since he believed the government never weighed the grain "upon the Peninsula" and that he would give back one third of that percent.

The release money was deposited into the Treasury by Inspector General James A. Hardie on November 16, 1868. Hill sued to recover and in court he admitted to fraud but claimed the government used duress to secure his release. His petition was dismissed.

Hodges, Fleming. A resident of Chickasaw County, Mississippi who had 39 bales of cotton seized on his place in August 1865 by Treasury agents. Hodges had actually sold it to Dr. W. W. Humphries who sold it to the Confederate government. A receipt for 39 bales was made out by Special Agent M. S. Jay in Okolona, Mississippi on August 23.

Hodges's suit to recover was the last claim filed under the Act of March 12, 1863. His petition was dismissed in 1883 when agent Jay's receipt was found proving he didn't own the cotton.

Hogarth, William F. In 1834 Dr. Branson and his wife owned 475 acres in St. Helena Parish, South Carolina. They had no children when he died without a will and under South Carolina law she inherited one-half the property. Dr. Branson had brothers and sisters who could rightfully claim the other half but none came forward.

Mrs. Branson married Parm Wallace and the property eventually became known as the Wallace place. On March 10, 1863 it was sold by the U.S. Direct Tax Commission. After the sale Parm died. They had no children and her heirs, the Norton's, subsequently recovered the $2,375 value of the land on February 26, 1893 pursuant to the Act of March 2, 1891.

On May 23, 1893 William Hogarth, a relative of Dr. Branson, sued in federal court to recover the same money. The court stated:

> In the class of cases to which this suit belongs a right of action is given, in effect, by the Act 2d March, 1891 to owners or heirs of owners who lost their lands in two parishes in the State of South Carolina, St. Helena and St. Lukes, by direct-tax sales during the civil war. The divesture of this property, though by legal proceedings, was exceedingly pitiable, and when the harsher judgments of the war had softened and passed away Congress deemed it an act of justice as well as mercy to award something in the nature of restitution. The amount of restitution in this class of cases was $5 an acre."

Hogarth claimed as evidence the contents of a lost will, which he never produced. As the court noted:

"When the forces of the United States in 1861 appeared before these islands the terrified inhabitants fled, abandoning houses and homes and household effects. Their deeds and documents and muniments of title were forgotten or lost. Still more unfortunately, the public records of the two parishes were destroyed, and, as a general thing, conveyances and wills and all documentary evidence of title to realty in those two parishes vanished from the face of the earth."

On May 6, 1895 the court dismissed the petition:

"The court regrets that the adverse parties were not both in court at the same time, so that they might have been brought face to face and required to interplead, as in the abandoned or captured property cases. But it will be observed that the judgment in the former case was not rendered until the 20th February, 1893, and probably was not paid until some days later, and consequently that the present claimant had a period equal substantially to that which was given to owners of captured property, and that during this period and until the 23d May, 1893, they slept on their rights."

Holland, John R.

A resident of Upperville, Virginia who turned over 1,200 pounds of cotton warp, 120 yards of unbleached cotton, 400 pounds of wool, 70 yards of blanket flannel, 40 yards of fulled cloth, and 4 yards of homespun to Lieutenant H. C. Alford to keep it out of rebel hands. The goods were sold and net proceeds in the Treasury were $1,870.36. He recovered that.

Holmes, Jeremiah H.

Resident of Philadelphia and master of the 541½ ton brig *Edwin H. Fitler* who arrived at New Orleans in February 1865 with a commercial cargo from Philadelphia. Major General Edward Canby was then organizing an expedition at New Orleans for the capture of Mobile and was in great need of vessels to transport troops, supplies, and munitions. On the 8th he directed his quartermaster, Captain F. W. Perkins, to either charter or seize all the steamers and sailing vessels he could find.

Holmes entered into a charter-party with the Army on the 28th at $150 per day in order to avoid having his vessel seized. He would remain aboard as captain.

Holmes made several voyages from New Orleans to Mobile and back. In the meantime, Colonel Holabird, chief quartermaster of the Department of the Gulf, sent copies of the charter agreement to Washington. All charters were first submitted to the Returns Office at the Department of the Interior then went to the War Department's Chief Quartermaster, General Montgomery Cunningham Meigs.

On April 11 Meigs disapproved the rate Holabird authorized. Meigs had set charter rates for sailing vessels from Portland, Maine to Galveston, Texas at generally $3.50 to $4.50 per ton per month and $100 per day for sidewheel and propeller steamers.

The *Fitler* arrived back at New Orleans on May 29 and Captain Holmes was informed that his payment would be $100 per day. Holmes refused the new rate, his vessel was seized, and held until June 1st when it was released back to him. Captain Perkins then paid Holmes $9,225 for 92½ days.

Holmes sued for the remaining $50 per day and while he was at it he apparently attempted to increase the deadweight tons of the brig to 800 by the use of alternative admeasurement standards. The *Fitler* was worth about $38,000 with a commercial life of 25–30 years.

The government argued Holmes had already been compensated by receiving a charter rate well above the normal commercial rates for sailing vessels. He pointed out that competition for freight between East Coast ports was highly competitive at the time and many vessels barely broke even as shipping rates often fluctuated wildly. A roundtrip from Philadelphia to New Orleans was worth about $21,600 to the owners of a sailing vessel like the *Fitler*. The distance from New Orleans to Mobile, "bar to bar," was 75 miles and a trip typically took about 48 hours for sailing vessels under favorable conditions.

The court found Captain Perkins had full authority to make the charter agreement and that he never engaged in any type of fraud or misrepresentation in order to charter the vessel. He could simply have seized it. The court stated, in part:

"We find neither in the contract nor in the facts or in the law any right or authority of the Quartermaster General to subject this contract to the procrustean process by conforming it to any special standard he had established."

The Act of July 4, 1864 gave Army the authority to seize vessels in an emergency as the court pointed out:

"This makes the commander of the army or detachment, whose movements are to be provided for, the sole judge of when the emergency exists. And the law is not so lame and impotent in its conclusions as to allow the plans of a campaign to be thwarted, nor an army paralyzed in its movements by requiring a commander to wait for necessary transportation and supplies until all the contracts for their purchase and procurement have been submitted to and approved by the Quartermaster General.

"The contract was made in this case and fulfilled by the claimants in good faith and we can see no reason founded in justice or law why they should not be paid according to that contract."

Holmes recovered $5,062.50.

Hoover, Jonah D. In June 1861 Hoover and his wife leased a house they owned in Washington at the corner of I and 19th Streets to the Army for $160 a month for an indefinite period of time. On February 13, 1865 the Hoovers were told the building was no longer needed. The rent had been paid up to that date but upon inspection the Hoovers refused to accept the house claiming it was unlivable. On March 28 another lease was concluded with the provost marshal to commence April 1 at $2,500 a year.

The Army had agreed to the repairs and eventually spent $1,554 but these were not completed until March 28, 1868 during which time the building was uninhabitable as a dwelling.

On July 7, 1865 Quartermaster General Meigs, ignorant of the $2,500 lease, ordered the house rented at $160 a month for the Freedmen's Bureau. On October 6, 1866 the Hoovers were paid rent at $160 from April 1, 1865 to October 1, 1866. The Hoovers demanded an additional $870 on rent of $2,500 a year and during the repair period but the Army initially refused to pay. The Hoovers sued and recovered $1,095.18 on rent at $2,500 a year from April 1, 1865 till October 1, 1866.

Hosmer, Henry J. Enlisted as a private in Company B, 15th Regiment of Massachusetts Volunteers on July 12, 1861 pursuant to the President's proclamation of May 3, 1861. Under War Department General Order No. 15, May 4, 1861, and No. 25, May 26, 1861, an enlistment bonus of $100 was payable upon being honorable discharged. The Act of July 22, 1861 required two years' service and a later statute waived the longevity requirement for wounded soldiers.

Congress legalized the General Orders on August 6, 1861. Hosmer was medically discharged on January 5, 1863 but no enlistment bonus was forthcoming. He recovered $100 based on the Act of August 6, 1861. This was the first case involving this bonus and the court was mindful of the large number of future claims, the amount of money involved, and the government's right to appeal, and the claimant's inability to appeal a judgement of less than $300.

Houston, Samuel. Owner of 22 bales of cotton seized at the De Shea Landing on the Arkansas River in December 1864. It was shipped to Cincinnati on the steamer *Silver Moon* for $313.77. Houston recovered $2,225.47 in 1873.

Howe, Smith. A resident of Charleston who owned eight bales of upland cotton seized on February 17, 1865. Howe purchased the cotton in July 1864 from Frederick A. Sawyer who hid it from the rebels. Both were proved loyal and Howe was awarded $1,049.60.

Hudnal, John A. An Indiana native who moved to Galveston in 1858 and became a cotton agent. He sued to recover on 186 bales of cotton and stated:

"I left Galveston about the 10th of May 1861 on account of the order having been issued that those who would not take the oath to the confederate government and enter the service must leave the country.

"There were men owing me money all through the country, in Texas, and before going to Mexico I made arrangements with William Lake, a resident of Marlin, Texas, to receive this cotton for debts owing me from him and others, delivered there at Marlin. I had it delivered there because it was the nearest point to the planters in the country. This cotton was delivered to me and John Finley, the man whom I had employed to haul the cotton in June 1861. This cotton was stored in the warehouse of Mr. John Bush. The cotton was not marked at the time having come direct from the different plantations. On receiving the cotton, getting the weights, I instructed Mr. Bush to put the planters' initials on each bale. I received 186 bales, averaging 500 pounds per bale, thus delivered to me at Marlin."

Finley was going to take the cotton to Brownsville but his horses were confiscated by rebels. The cotton remained in the warehouse until August 1863 when he moved it to Corpus Christi and in November he was able to proceed to Brownsville. He was about 60 miles from

Brownsville when he was arrested by "pickets of the Union forces." He applied to General Dana in Brownsville for an order to release the cotton and Dana directed W. B. Leech, his aide-de-camp, to send the order via Finley to Captain Owen, the quartermaster at Brownsville who had possession of it. By the time he got to Owen the cotton had been removed and piled up near the water at Point Isabel. Finley went there and was able to get on board the steamer *Clinton* on which the cotton was going to New Orleans. He watched the cotton sold by Colonel S. B. Holabird in a lot of 404 bales. Holabird got $834,529.34 for the lot at an average net proceed of $258.58 per bale. The Act of March 12, 1863 required Holabird to send the money to the Treasury but on orders from the commander of the department, as was common, he used the money to buy supplies for the Army.

Hudnal continued:

"After leaving Houston I went to Matamoras, Mexico. I have always been loyal to the United States government and have never given aid or comfort to the rebellion in any way." After his cotton was sold, he commanded a U.S. transport and in 1865 commanded a flag-of-truce boat.

A. J. Hamilton, the governor of Texas, testified to Hudnal's loyalty. A discrepancy attended the actual number of bales and Hudnal was credited with 170 bales at $258.58 for a total of $43,958.60.

Hughes, Clement L. Hughes, Fuller & Co. proposed to deliver 250,000 bushels of corn in 56 pound bushels at 77 cents if bagged and 70 cents in bulk; oats; and 1,875 tons of hay within 45 days to either Baltimore & Ohio Railroad Baltimore wharf at Locust Point or Camden Yards, Maryland. The corn contract went awry and the company sued for $63,488.79 under breach of contract and recovered $15,321.

Hukill, Mark W. Contracted with the Post Office Department on April 28, 1858 to carry mail on Route No. 7904 between Kidron and Webber's Falls, Arkansas from July 1, 1858 to June 30, 1862 for $700 a year.

Arkansas seceded form the Union on May 6, 1861 and on that date Hukill was owed $417.75 for services from October 1, 1860.

On December 28, 1863 he enlisted in Company B, 18th Regiment Iowa Volunteers for three years at Sugar Loaf Valley. He was mustered in on January 5, 1864 at Fort Smith, Arkansas and mustered out on July 20, 1865.

On March 3, 1877 Congress appropriated $375,000 to reimburse mail contractors for money due in 1859, 1860, and 1861 within the secessionist States and Kentucky and Missouri so long as no money had been paid to the carriers by the Confederate government.

The Congress of the Confederate States of America required, in part:

"That it shall be the duty of the Postmaster General to collect all moneys due from the several postmasters within the Confederate States, and which they had not paid over at the time the Confederate States took the charge of the postal service, and several postmasters are hereby required to account to the General Post-Office of this Government under the same rules, regulations, and penalties that were subscribed by the law under which said moneys were received.

"Sec. 2. The moneys so received shall be kept separate and distinct from the other funds of the Post-Office Department, and shall constitute a fund for the *pro rata* payment of claims for postal service in the States respectively comprising this Confederacy, as may hereafter be provided."

Hukill's petition was dismissed in 1880 since he could not prove he wasn't paid by the Confederate government. Two years later Hukill was granted a new trial but he had no new evidence and his petition was dismissed.

William A. Wyatt had Route No. 7900, Lebanon, Arkansas to Forsyth, Missouri, at $319 a year and Route No. 7934 between Burrowsville and Dover, Arkansas at $299 a year. His petition was also dismissed since he couldn't prove he wasn't paid by the Confederate government.

Josephus Wallace had Route No. 5048 between Washington and Portsmouth, North Carolina via Ocracoke at $750 a year. One unhelpful witness at his hearing stated, "Wallace was as good a rebel as any of us." Others stated he continued on the route in Confederate service without interruption until June 30, 1863 when his contract expired. His petition was dismissed.

John Faulkner had Route No. 8740 between Paris and Warren, Texas at $190 a year. His petition was also dismissed since he couldn't prove he wasn't paid by the Confederate government.

Hunt, Elisha. A Chattanooga resident as described by his attorney:

"The plaintiff is one of the old hardy pioneers of Eastern Tennessee and Northern Georgia, so justly celebrated for their devotion to the

Union during the dark days of the republic. He was a Baptist preacher, was stopped preaching because he would talk Union sentiments. He was attacked by Confederate soldiers, shot in the thigh, was taken up by the vigilance committee and put in jail and then sent to Atlanta in chains with a gang of 14 other Union men. His hardships and dangers as a Union man caused him to leave his home and become a refugee in Indiana for the last two years of the war. He refused to take Confederate money at all times and on all occasions."

He recovered $8,720 on 20 bales of cotton seized at Chattanooga in June 1864.

Hunt, W. E. William Hunt was born and educated in Massachusetts. He moved his family to Frankfort, Kentucky and then acquired the La Grange, Montrose, and Belmont plantations near Greenville, Mississippi but kept his home in Frankfort. He had voted against secessionist candidates and was known to be openly opposed to secession, was in Mississippi when the war started, and left for home in Frankfort but told his slaves it would be better for them to stay at home and take care of their families and the property on his plantation "inasmuch as they would all be free in any event."

One of his sons joined the Confederate service over his strong objections and he sent another son to Germany to evade rebel service. On occasion he would take passage on U.S. naval vessels to check his property and bring food to the slaves.

In early 1862 someone reported Hunt to the Confederate authorities. General Samuel W. Ferguson, commander of the Confederate cavalry and pickets around Vicksburg, charged Hunt with disloyalty and reported him to General Earl Van Dorn at Vicksburg and Van Dorn ordered him arrested. Hunt got word that he was wanted, managed to evade arrest for some time, but was captured by Colonel Wirt Adams.

Hunt presented a claim to the Southern Claims Commission for the loss of $40,460 worth of supplies seized by General Frederick Steele in 1863 for the use of the Army: 145 mules at $250 each; 5 horses at $250 each; 3 four-horse wagons at $150 each; 1 spring wagon, $100; 3 carts, $60 each; 6 yoke of oxen, $200 per yoke; 20 beef cattle, $20 each; 1 wagon, $150; and 1 dray, $60. The claim was rejected as the commissioners were not convinced of his loyalty.

Hunt died shortly after the war ended and his executor, W. E. Hunt, petitioned Congress for relief. The Senate appropriated $40,000 under the Bowman Act of March 3, 1883 and referred the claim to a federal court for fact finding. The case was dismissed since he was found to be disloyal during the rebellion on the ground that he maintained his residence and plantations in Mississippi, moved some of his slaves to Texas, and kept his business going. Hunt filed suit again under the Tucker Act of March 5, 1887. The court found Hunt loyal and the reasonable value of the seized property to be $16,010 at the time and the facts were reported to Congress on November 10, 1910.

Irvine, David. Irvine and Colonel C. J. Field owned a plantation in Bolivar County, Mississippi. On February 20, 1863, sailors from Lieutenant Commander Thomas O. Selfridge, Jr.'s gunboat USS *Conestoga* loaded 67 bales of their cotton at Kentucky Landing.

The next day, this cotton, along with other cotton, was transferred to the merchant steamer *Rose Hambleton* and taken to Cairo, Illinois on order of Admiral Porter. The cotton was transferred to Captain A. M. Pennock, USN, who turned it over to the U.S. marshal on April 9, 1863. The United States district attorney filed a libel requesting the cotton be condemned and sold but it was sold on order from a district court before it was formally condemned at the federal level.

On June 16, B. F. Compton petitioned the district court claiming the cotton actually belonged to him. His plea was successful and he was paid $10,454.

In 1883 the heirs of David Irvine and Colonel Field filed a claim in federal court as the descendants of the rightful owners. They claimed the district court had no jurisdiction to condemn the cotton, sell it, and then turn the proceeds over to Compton.

The government maintained that since no money ever reached the U.S. Treasury, the claimants had no cause of action.

The court agreed and cited a technicality:

"It was the misfortune of the owners of this cotton that they were inhabitants of rebel territory during the war of the rebellion, and so were in law rebel enemies, and that the cotton fell into the hands of the Union naval forces engaged in actual warfare. All property so seized might have been confiscated under the statutes, or held as booty under the more rigorous rules of warfare.

But Congress, by the passage of the abandoned or captured property act of March 12, 1863, waiving to some extent the severer laws, undertook, through this court, to restore to loyal citizens the proceeds of their captured property which actually reached the public Treasury. But it went no further. It gave no remedy to those whose property, although seized by officers of the United States, was lost, stolen, or otherwise so disposed of that no proceeds ever reached the Treasury."

The Supreme Court had already ruled on this point in U.S. v. Ross (92 U.S. 281):

"It is incumbent upon claimants, under the Captured or Abandoned Property Act, to establish by sufficient proof that the property came into the hands of a Treasury agent; that it was sold; that the proceeds of the sale were paid into the Treasury of the United States; and that he was the sole owner of the property, and entitled to the proceeds thereof. All this is essential to show that the United States is a trustee for him, holding his money."

The petition was dismissed.

Jencks, Delancy. A black resident of Savannah who owned 3 bales of upland cotton. Recovered $571.29 on May 26, 1869.

Jenkins, William J. Owned 60 bales of sea-island cotton seized at his Indian Hill plantation on Saint Helena Island, South Carolina. When the island was occupied there was 75,000 pounds of cotton in the seed stored in his cotton house and about 2,500 pounds that had not been weighed. All the cotton was brought to Saint Helena and put aboard the *Mayflower*, taken to Hilton Head, then to New York.

Treasury records showed Saint Helena–Hilton Head sea-island cotton was worth an average of $161.25 a bale. Two witnesses stated that it takes from 1,250 to 1,400 pounds of seed cotton to make one sea-island bale. The average of those amounts is 1,325 pounds. In 1873 Jenkins was awarded $9,432.12½ on 58½ bales of 77,500 pounds.

Johnson, Leonard B. A resident of Sandusky, Ohio who purchased the 275-acre Bulls Island in Sandusky Bay on June 10, 1853 for $3,000 from William W. Wetherell, Francis Whitney, and Samantha Farwell. He renamed it Johnsons Island and on November 11, 1861 leased part of the island to the Army for a depot for prisoners of war at $500 a year, the rent to be paid quarterly. A wharf was also leased for 1 year at $100 a year.

The island was occupied and rent paid through March 1867 when it was abandoned but the Army had violated the lease agreement by using approximately one acre of unleased ground for a cemetery for Confederate soldiers.

In 1878 Congress appropriated $1,500 "for care and protection of the Confederate cemetery on Johnsons Island" on condition that title to the land be conveyed to the government. Johnson apparently refused so no money was spent.

In 1887 Congress appropriated $2,000 for Confederate cemeteries near Columbus, Ohio and Johnsons Island. The cemetery on Johnsons Island was enclosed with an iron fence and the mounds repaired.

Johnson sued for loss of the cemetery parcel on the ground that during the intervening years the portion of the island occupied by the cemetery—"the most beautiful portion of the island"—had become very valuable for suburban residences, summer homes, club houses, and resorts.

Witnesses placed the yearly rental value of the cemetery land at $1,000. Johnson had every legal right to remove the graves to another place and reclaim the land but he chose not to and because of that his petition was dismissed on April 6, 1896.

Johnson, Matilda. Owned a plantation near Little Rock with 65 bales of cotton and 7 more, after ginning, that was captured. When she sought to obtain proof of sales money deposited into the Treasury, the records traced the bales to a Treasury Department employee named Abbott. Of the 65, 32 had her plantation marks and these went into a lot of 238 bales shipped from Little Rock in April 1864 and sold at Cincinnati in June for $474.86 a bale. The other 33 went missing. It was explained that they were in with the 238 but all those bales were marked and only 32 were Matilda's. She was able to recover only $15,195.52 on 32 bales.

Johnson, Micajah. Owned of 225 bales of cotton at Sabine Pass, Texas. In June 1863, 30 bales were seized and sent to New Orleans. Of those, 28 were seized by a Treasury agent and sent to New York where they were sold for $2,698.94 net proceeds. The remaining 195 bales were sent to Houston where they vanished into the ether. Prior to 1878 Micajah died and his administrator filed suit and recovered $2,698.94.

Jones, George W. Jones had a contract with Colonel McKim at Cincinnati to deliver

200,000 yards of Army cloth on specific dates in 1864, the last shipment of 10,000 yards being due on or before December 15. In August the mill making the cloth for Jones burned down. The cloth was not available on the market and from August 1864 through February 1, 1865 the mills making it were at capacity. On November 23, 1864 Jones told McKim that he was unable to furnish the remaining 77,806¼ yards, asked to be released from the contract, and requested $25,538.46, the 10 percent that had been withheld from previous payments. McKim referred him to Captain Perry in Washington. In February 1865 Perry told him Congress couldn't help him, he had to furnish the goods, and if he asked Colonel Moulton, enough time would be granted to complete the contract. More time was granted and Jones contracted with F. M. Ballou & Co. to make the cloth at $2.12½ a yard. Ballou made only 51,801½ yards and on April 4 Jones again asked to be released. On the 22nd Moulton was informed that Quartermaster General Meigs would not release him and that his extended time had expired. Richmond was captured just at this time and the same dark blue cloths and Army cloths could be had there for half the price being paid in Cincinnati. It could also be obtained in New York for no more than 75 cents a yard.

At the end of April Jones delivered 25,899¾ yards to Moulton but he refused to accept it. Jones then sold the cloth on the open market for $54,503.88 and in May 1865 the $25,538.46 was paid to him.

Jones sued for the remainder of his contract but his petition was dismissed since the amended agreement was not in writing pursuant to the Act of June 2, 1862 requiring all contracts for military supplies to be in writing.

Jones, Henry. An enlisted man in the 5th Cavalry who was promoted to second lieutenant for gallantry. He made first lieutenant and on October 28, 1863 his regiment was on picket duty near Germantown, Virginia. The next morning he was ordered by Captain Leith to send out a patrol "to his front to patrol the distance of five miles outside of the lines." Jones sent a non-commissioned officer and six men while he remained with the reserves. After the patrol passed the line of videttes, he and his second officer, Lieutenant Robert H. Montgomery, rode out to the vidette on the main road. As he was instructing the first vidette, he heard gunfire

coming from the direction of the patrol. He and Montgomery rode out to within sight of the patrol but saw no disturbance and started back to the first vidette. When they were about 500 yards away, near Elk Run, they were ambushed and captured by guerillas hiding in the bush. No others were present.

They were taken to the headquarters of General Young then marched to Richmond Libby prison then held in other prisons until March 1, 1865. Jones arrived at Camp Parole at Annapolis, Maryland on the 5th having been a prisoner for 1 year, 4 months, and 12 days. Jones and Montgomery then learned that they had been dismissed from the Army on November 19, 1863 for having been captured. Montgomery, as the junior officer, was subsequently reinstated. Jones was not.

Jones applied for $1,760.11 in back pay but was refused on the ground that he was no longer an officer in the Army. He requested a court of inquiry and was refused. He sued and in court the assistant attorney general was harsh:

"The duties of a picket guard are exceedingly delicate and important. On this guard depends the safety of the camp. The negligence of an officer charged with this duty, or even of a sentinel, may lead to the destruction of an army. There is but one punishment for a sentinel who sleeps while on duty, which is death.

"The offence of Lieutenant Jones was greater than that of a sleeping sentinel. He left his guard without any commander — left them and the camp at the mercy of the enemy. He did not do this in the performance of a duty. His duty was to remain with and inspect his guard. The act was not bravery but willful rashness. Had his patrol been in distress, he could have rendered no aid. His going could accomplish no good and might have resulted in disaster to the camp.

"For this grave offense, for the inexcusable breach of military discipline, the President dismissed Mr. Jones from the service. If this court were now sitting as a court martial on Mr. Jones's case, it could not fail to confirm this order from the President."

Brevet Captain Montgomery testified:

"I was with the claimant when he was captured and in my opinion he was not guilty of any failure or neglect of duty, though he may have been guilty of an indiscretion in this, that he might have sent me to see the cause of the firing as his next junior officer and permitted me to be captured and avoided capture himself."

The court found the Army had every right to dismiss him from the service but could not withhold his pay while a prisoner of war as there was no statute to support that. From a total of $1,721.92 found due, he was awarded $1,362.72 less servant's costs: $184.00, pay; clothes, $38.33; and rations at 30 cents per day, $136.50.

Justice, Philip S.

Justice, Philip S. A Philadelphia arms manufacturer who was supplying the Army with 1,000 .58 caliber rifles with sword bayonet at $20 each plus $1.50 for the packing box, 500 to be delivered in ten days and the balance by September 1, 1861.

On August 12, 1861 he wrote to Lieutenant T. J. Treadwell, First Lieutenant of Ordnance at the Frankford Arsenal in Philadelphia, with an offer to supply 4,000 .69 caliber rifled muskets for $20 each and he sent a sample. The next day Treadwell wrote to General J. W. Ripley at the Ordnance office in Washington for advice. He said, in part:

"I have examined a sample of the musket, and it is a good, serviceable arm, caliber .69, clasp-bayonet, long-range sight, original percussion barrel, and well finished. I think it would be desirable to secure these arms."

Ripley said go ahead, and to also order 5,000 cavalry sabers, reserving the right to refuse acceptance if the lot was not delivered on time. Another manufacturer named Pondir also sent a sample of a gun that had no half-cock position. Treadwell wasn't impressed with them and Ripley told him not to accept any.

Treadwell wrote to Justice on the 17th with an order for 4,000 muskets, 20 to a box, and 4,000 sabers at $6.75 each in boxes of 50, the whole order to be filled on or before January 1, 1862 at specified delivery rates per month.

Justice delivered 2,469 .58 caliber muskets with sword bayonets and 2,174 .69 caliber rifled muskets with angular bayonet to Treadwell that he accepted but these guns were not of the same quality as the sample Justice had originally provided. It was not equal to the Springfield rifle and "were far from being a first-class arm." Nevertheless, all but 350 sword-bayonet rifles, 472 rifled muskets with angular bayonets, 362 cavalry sabers, and 10 Whitney revolving pistols with appendages were accepted and paid for.

On March 13, 1862 Treadwell wrote to Justice saying the balance not previously paid for were accepted along with 41 boxes of Whitney revolvers at $2.50 each.

The weapons had been issued to the 58th, 88th, and 91st Pennsylvania Volunteers and complaints started coming in from Camp Hamilton. Reports of condemned parts being found cobbled together, stocks made of soft, unseasoned wood with no band springs to hold the stocks and when the wood dried the stock fell off, rifle grooves cut only a few inches back from the muzzle, imitation screws cut into metal, soft iron bayonets that stayed bent, poor locks, and so on.

Treadwell wrote to General Ripley on March 28, in part:

"The bulk of those arms were inspected by Mr. Wilson, late foreman (I think) at Harper's Ferry armory, and after he left his situation here the inspection was made by Mr. Thomas Daffin, who had previously assisted Mr. Wilson. These statements show the manner in which the inspection was made, and the opinion of the inspectors as to their serviceableness and fitness for use in the field. My instructions to them were to inspect the arms, and reject all that in their opinion were not good and serviceable, and in all respects fit for use in the field. Having entire confidence in their integrity, I think these instructions were complied with. These arms were offered to me at a time when the demand for arms (especially rifled arms) was most imperative, and it was deemed desirable to accept them, to meet in part the pressing demand. Comparing the arms to those of our own manufacture, none would pass inspection and it was not supposed they should be subjected to any such standard, but that all that were passed on inspection would prove good and serviceable, was believed. Examining two boxes of these arms in store, I do not find them to have the radical defects complained of, nor can I account for the very different report of their inspection at Camp Hamilton and that made to me by my inspectors; especially I cannot understand how the arms should gauge correctly here, and be found there to vary between 65 and .70 inch in caliber. I find the sights were soldered on, but on tapping 20 of them with a hammer sufficiently hard to dent them, some were found to come off, or were started."

Assistant Inspector General John Buford reported:

These guns have been in the hands of the regiment about four months, and have been fired but little. At practice with blank cartridges one gun burst. At target practice so many burst that the men became afraid to fire them. At present it is with difficulty that the men are made to charge their arms for guard duty; those who do load them throw away part of the powder.

Colonel Thomas D. Doubleday, 4th Regiment New York Artillery stated:

You could hardly conceive of such a worthless lot of arms, totally unfit for service, and dangerous to those using them.

A new inspection was ordered and Justice appeared before the Holt-Owen commission in Washington. On June 6, 1862 the commission found the arms unserviceable and Justice in non-compliance and on the 25th decided that $15 should be paid on 2,174 rifled muskets and $20 on 2,469 rifles with sword bayonets.

On the 30th the Chief of Ordnance directed the Second Auditor to pay Justice $19,171.25. On December 8 the Auditor sent Justice a bill for $8,301.25.

Justice sued and recovered the balance due on the original price since the arms delivered were equal to the sample sent. The government appealed and the Supreme Court reversed the lower court and ordered the petition dismissed.

Kelly, Thomas W. Enlisted for three years as a private in Company D, First Battalion, 19th Regiment, U.S. regular infantry, on February 12, 1864 at Detroit, Michigan. The enlistment came with a $400 bounty paid in successive installments. Kelly received $175 before he deserted at Augusta, Georgia on October 3, 1865 to be with his ill mother. He was reinstated by Major General J. J. Reynolds on December 11 without court martial on condition that he serve the lost time. He was discharged at Fort Gibson, Cherokee Nation, on April 20, 1867 but the final $225 payment of the bounty was withheld by the paymaster and approved by Major Pinckney Lugenbeel.

Kelly sued and recovered the $225 in 1867 pending review by the Supreme Court since Kelly could not appeal, the amount in question being less than $300, and the government could. Paragraph 1358 of Army regulations, 1864 stated:

Every deserter shall forfeit all pay and allowances due at the time of desertion. Stoppages and fines shall be paid from his future earnings if he is apprehended and continued in service, and if they are adjudged by a court martial; otherwise from his arrears of pay.

Kelsey, Alexander. Kelsey put down $4,000 in forfeitable pledge money to bid on a grain contract. The deal went awry and Kelsey sued to recover. Captain E. D. Chapman explained at the trial:

"In August 1863 I was assistant quartermaster stationed at St. Louis, Missouri in charge of the forage department. On or about the 10th of August 1863 I advertised for proposals to furnish oats, corn, and hay for the government. I required two cents a bushel for each bushel of oats bid for and two dollars a ton for each ton of hay to be deposited by the bidders with their bids, to be forfeited to the government unless the parties bonded. This was a regulation of my own and was not disapproved of by my superiors and was made for the purpose of preventing straw bids. For instance, a party, a reliable one, would bid in his own name to furnish grain at say, 75 cents per bushel. They would have in two or three other bids by others in their employ ranging from 65 to 73 or 74. If no parties bid below their bid of 75 cents these straw bids ranging from 65 to 74 cents would not come forward to bond. If other parties bid below the 75 cents then they would answer to the next highest bid straw bid. And they would also purchase low bidders out of the way. For instance, they would give a low bidder a thousand dollars or more not to appear and enter into bonds, which they could well afford to do, when they would make, perhaps, $6,000 or more."

On August 29, Kelsey was awarded a contract to furnish 200,000 bushels of oats and David B. Martin got a contract for 100,000 bushels. Both put in their bonds but during the day telegrams were received from the west and northwest saying the corn crop had been severely injured by frost. The price of grain increased rapidly and Kelsey and Martin called on Chapman to cancel their contracts. Their bonds had not been executed and Chapman let General Allen decide what to do with the deposits. Allen said to refund it but by then Chapman had spent it. Assistant Quartermaster General Charles Thomas decided the two were out of luck since they failed to enter into bonds.

The court awarded Kelsey $4,000 and Martin $2,000.

Kenney, Kate. Kate Cregan was a servant girl in Charleston who invested her money in one bale of upland and one bale of sea-island cotton early in the rebellion. It was captured and sold in New York. After she married Thomas Kenney she sued to recover the loss and was awarded $368.90.

Kettler, Henry. Owned the steamboats *Bright Star* and *Wide Awake* at Washington, Missouri. One of the boats was in ferry service at Washington and the other carried passengers and cargo on the Missouri River. On September 26, 1864 Major General William S. Rosecrans at St. Louis wrote to the people of Missouri regarding Confederate General Sterling Price's advance across the Missouri River:

> After two years of barbarous and harassing war, in which every citizen, directly or indirectly, suffered loss of property and many of life, you are now invaded by Price and the recreant Missourians, who, in defiance of professional principles, have been the chief cause of your sufferings and loss. They bring with them men from other States to plunder, murder, and destroy you for adhering to the Government of your interests and your choice. Prepare them for the reception they deserve. Make this raid fatal to the enemy, and you will endure peace. Let them succeed, and you almost ruin your State.
>
> The governor of the State has been informed of the threatened raid and requested to call the militia to serve until the invaders are destroyed or driven from the State. I rely upon their courage and patriotism, and have only to say, let your assembling be prompt, and let the commissioned officers see that proper steps are at once taken to secure for their commands all needful supplies of arms, equipments, ammunition, camp and garrison equipage, and blankets.

On the 29th he issued Special Order No. 270, which read in part:

"11. The 54th and 55th Regiments E. M. M. have been consolidated and called into active service. Col. Daniel S. Gale is charged with their organization into a regiment; he will also call out all able-bodied arms-bearing men of Franklin County between the ages of eighteen and forty-five.

"13. Col. Gale will make requisitions on the chief com's'y of subsistence and on Brig. Gen. E. A. More, quartermaster general of Mo., for arms, ammunition, clothing, camp and garrison equipage."

Gale took command of the Enrolled Missouri Militia. They were paid by the State of Missouri and fed, armed, and clothed by the United States.

Gale directed his provost marshal to quickly acquire the boats to evacuate government property and save it from destruction by Confederate forces crossing the Missouri. The boats were seized and the crews remained onboard, receiving their regular pay from Kettler. One of the boats was loaded with unwanted munitions and documents belonging to the U.S. internal revenue collector and immediately left for St. Louis. On the return trip she brought back needed equipment. The other boat remained at St. Charles with steam up, loaded with stores, and ready to go if necessary. The boats were used for ten days while completely under Army control but Kettler was never paid for their use.

Colonel Gale did not have time to enter into a formal charter-party agreement with Kettler nor did he seize or appropriate the vessels for government use under the usual meaning of the terms. Kettler did not object to the use of his boats, they were returned to him unharmed, but when he sought compensation for their use he was denied. He then sued.

Colonel Gale had the right to acquire the boats as the court noted from a previous Supreme Court decision:

"The taking of private property by the Government when the emergency of the public service, in time of war or impending public danger, is too urgent to admit of delay, is everywhere regarded as justified, if the necessity for the use of the property is imperative and immediate and the danger as heretofore described is impending; and it is equally clear that the taking of such property under such circumstances creates an obligation on the part of the Government to reimburse the owner to the full value of the service. Private rights under such extreme and imperious circumstances must give way for the time to the public good, but the Government must make full restitution for the sacrifice" (13 Wallace 629).

Kettler was awarded $1,000.

Kidder, Mary W. William H. Cuthbert owned lot C, block 90, in Beaufort, South Carolina, which he held in trust for Mary W. Rhett "for her life, with power in her to appoint the same by will to and among the issue of her marriage with Edmund Rhett."

The U.S. Direct Tax of $106.74 was not paid, the property was sold at public auction on March 13, 1863 for $1,500, and the $1,393.26 surplus held in trust in the U.S. Treasury. Mary Rhett died in 1873. Her will stated:

> I direct that my house and lots in the town of Beaufort be sold, and $4,000 of the proceeds be invested by my son Stuart, as trustee of the same, for the benefit of my daughter May, she to receive the interest or dividends of the same during her life, and at her death to become the property of

such of my descendants as she may by will direct; and if she die intestate, leaving issue, to become the property of said issue; but if she die leaving no issue, then the said $4,000 I direct to be equally divided between my son Stuart and my daughter Anne. After the above sum has been disposed of as directed, I leave $6,000 to my son Stuart, who gave me this sum when I was in pecuniary difficulties, and I now return it to him. After the above bequests have been paid, should any property be returned by the U.S. Government or remuneration made therefor, I direct the same be invested by my son Stuart as trustee for the benefit of my daughter Anne, she to receive the interests or dividends of the same during her life.

Mary Kidder was executrix and Stuart Rhett trustee, but Stuart apparently declined to participate. Stuart received his half of the legacy before the estate was settled while he had a lawsuit pending against the United States as trustee for Anne S. Elliott to enforce his right to the property.

Mary Kidder filed suit as executrix and recovered the $1,393.26 surplus leaving Anne and Stuart to settle up.

Kilduff, James. Owner of 153 bales of cotton stored in his Mobile pickery. It was seized, stored in Nelson W. Perry's Planter's Warehouse, then shipped to New York on the *E. L. Thayer.*

Kilduff was described in court as "an old man, who was doing well enough under the old government and desired no change." He was awarded $28,063.26 on net proceeds.

Kimball, John H. Owner of the Bath, Maine barque *Annie Kimball*. She loaded 1,061 long tons of anthracite steamer coal at Philadelphia on April 18, 1865 for Port Royal, South Carolina under Army contract. The freight was $6.25 a ton, $100 a day for demurrage, and 21 days allowed for unloading. On May 6, the quartermaster at Port Royal, Captain John L. Kelly, refused the shipment and ordered the master to "get under way and sail to Key West." The master protested that Key West was not the contracted port and the bar at Port Royal was unsafe to cross at that time. The captain of the port reportedly said "they would put in another master and send the vessel to Key West without him." Kelly sent for a government tug and on the morning of the 8th the *Achilles* arrived two hours into an ebb tide and a heavy swell. The barque struck the bar several times, started leaking, and had to be anchored but kept taking on

water. Between 7 and 8 P.M. she was brought back to Port Royal and run ashore to keep her from sinking. The vessel was detained by the government until June 24 when she was discharged from Army service with a note, "The detention of the vessel was owing to no fault of the master or crew."

Kimball sued for $7,604 for damage and $5,600 for demurrage and was awarded $12,904.41. The government appealed to the Supreme Court where the judgement was reversed on a matter of jurisdiction.

Kirkham & Brown. This company furnished subsistence to men not yet mustered in to the 131st Regiment Illinois Volunteers under contract with the governor of Illinois. Vouchers for $7,054.29 were approved by regimental commander Colonel George W. Neely but denied by the War Department. The court held the contract with the governor could not bind the United States.

Kiskadden, Alexander. William Kiskadden, of Denver City, Territory of Colorado, contracted verbally with Captain S. H. Moer on February 22, 1862 in response to a military emergency to furnish a train of 32 teams of 4 mules or horses and a wagon and driver to transport camp and garrison equipment of Colonel John P. Slough's 1st Regiment Colorado Volunteer Infantry from Denver City to assist Fort Union in the Territory of New Mexico. Forage and food was carried for the animals and drivers and the teams were to be returned to Denver.

Thomas Pollock was wagon and forage master and James Kiskadden, Alexander's brother, went along. Colonel Slough had control over the teams, drivers, and wagons. Slough pushed the teams and heavily loaded wagons very hard under Pollock's protest. The weather was cold, windy, and snowy. The road was rough and the Raton Mountain region was barren, thinly settled, and had sparse forage.

The forage carried was hard Mexican corn, all that was quickly available in Denver City. This was dangerous food for animals without supplemental roughage like hay or fodder and that was not available on the trail except in small quantities, which were found or seized along the way.

The train reached Pueblo, Colorado in good condition but the news was not good: Colonel Canby had been defeated at Valverde, near

Fort Craig, New Mexico on February 21 and the rebels were advancing up the Rio Grande toward Albuquerque, Santa Fe, and Fort Union, the supply depot for the whole territory.

When the train was at Red River, 108 miles from Fort Union, Colonel Slough learned that the picket line at Fort Union had been breached. He ordered all the supplies unloaded and all the sick and exhausted soldiers put into the wagons. The bows and covers for the wagons were taken off and the last leg was covered in two days and one night with 60 miles covered in one day. The whole 225–275-mile trip to Fort Union was made in eight days.

On March 14, 1862 a survey board was convened at Camp Slough, near Fort Union to assess the damage to the train. The board found 36 animals were lost: 33 mules at $150 each; 1 mule at $186; and 2 horses at $283 each.

The train returned to Denver City on March 29 after losing more animals. All the animals were injured, some permanently disabled. All the wagons were damaged, the bows, covers, and some harness lost, and wood from the wagon boxes had been eaten away by starving animals or the wood was used for cooking fires.

Kiskadden was paid $13,440, the contract price for the teams, and he signed receipts for payment in full but he lost $9,702 in damages that was not included in the payment. Alexander sued after William's death and recovered the money on February 1, 1909.

Knee, H. Henry. Resident of Charleston described as "a poor and ignorant German, with little command of his native language, and almost none in English." When the war started he apparently hid in the Pickens district to avoid conscription. He was sought after, advertised for, and finally apprehended as a deserter and, as the court noted, "through much suffering steadfastly evaded the rebel military service, absent from Charleston during half the war, and when he returned, after repeated arrests, he seems to have been a shy, suspicious, reserved man, seeking concealment and not friends."

He claimed 9 bales of upland cotton he bought from Laurey & Alexander on April 21, 1863 and was awarded $1,180.80.

Knote, John. A citizen of Wheeling charged with treason and rebellion. His property was seized under the Confiscation Act of July 17, 1862, libeled in the District Court for the District and State of West Virginia, and sold for $11,000. Knote sought to recover under President Johnson's unconditional pardon of December 25, 1868. A federal court decided the pardon restored "rights, privileges, and immunities," not property, and his petition was dismissed.

Koester, Louis F. A Charleston shopkeeper who became a naturalized citizen in March 1855. He sued to recover on 107 bales and 46 pounds of upland cotton and 15 bales and 206 pounds of loose sea-island cotton seized on March 30 and May 16, 1865 at Charleston.

Koester apparently paid the Confederate authorities to allow him work at the munitions factory in Charleston making percussion primer tubes to avoid being arrested and sent into the field. Witnesses said he received little or no pay and evaded work as much as possible. He was awarded $16,025.94.

Kohns, Lazarus. A resident of Columbus, Georgia who owned 28 bales of sea-island and 4 bales of upland cotton seized from the Lower Hydraulic Press warehouse at Savannah by General Sherman's forces. Kohn bought the cotton to insure a debt owed to his brother David in New York. Kohns stored the cotton at Savannah in the belief the seaport would be captured quickly and the cotton less likely to be destroyed. Kohns's loyalty was accepted and he was awarded $5,337.12.

Kugler, Rebecca E. J. John and Rebecca leased 250.51 acres of their 450 acres near Miamisville and the Little Miami River to the State of Ohio on April 27, 1861. The federal government took immediate possession for use as Camp Dennison. When the property was returned on June 1, 1866, Kugler found a cemetery covering two acres, "imperishable rubbish" two feet deep over three acres, five acres of former farmland destroyed by deep gravel pits, washes, and privies, and five acres covered by roads of firmly packed broken rock and gravel a foot deep. The rest of the unused acreage was unplowable and adjoining fences and a large quantity of grain "were trodden down and destroyed by squads of soldiers crossing and recrossing for a short cut to Milford, or bathing places in the Miami river."

After John died Rebecca sued and recovered $15,200.

Kuper, Frederick A. A conductor on the Richmond & Petersburg Railroad who owned four bales of cotton cloth stored at the Virginia Central Railroad freight depot. Three of the bales were captured at Richmond in April 1865 when Kuper was in a Confederate reserve force. He sued to recover $691.91 and testified:

"I was never called upon at any time during such employment [as conductor] to express by act or word, any feeling I had against the United States. I was always very prudent and cautious in expressing my opinions in relation to the United States. I was in constant intercourse with the confederate military and meeting and conversing with the officers daily in the transaction of my business. I never volunteered in any military service but two or three times I was ordered out as part of the reserve force to oppose raids and I have stood guard over federal prisoners putting up breastworks around Richmond. At one time we were so employed about two weeks."

Confederate authorities at Richmond had a standing order "to arrest all persons who did not have certificates showing they were members of companies" but Kuper was unable to show the court the order was ever enforced against him and his petition was dismissed.

Lagow, John. Owned a three-story brick building near Evansville, Indiana that had been a starch factory. It was taken in March 1862 by the Army's Dr. John W. Davis as a "pest-house" for soldiers with smallpox at $13 a month. The Army vacated the building on December 4, 1862. Two days later it burned down and Lagow sued for the cost of the building. His petition was dismissed since there was no proof the Army was responsible.

Lander, John. Enlisted for three years, enrolled in Company B, 2d Arkansas Volunteers on January 1, 1864 and mustered in on the 16th retroactive to the 1st. On November 12 he deserted and was arrested on June 2, 1865. He was restored to service with the loss of all pay and allowances due or to become due during his enlistment. On August 5, 1865 he was honorably discharged.

Years later, Lander sued believing he was owed the $508.20 withheld from his pay, part of which was his enlistment bonus. The government cited the Joint Resolution of March 1, 1870 authorizing withholding the pay of all volunteer deserters and crediting the amount to the National Asylum for Disabled Volunteer Soldiers. The court held he could not be punished by a

statutue that was enacted three years after he was honorably discharged and awarded him the money in 1873.

The government appealed to the Supreme Court where the decision was reversed on the ground that the allowances forfeited included the enlistment bounty.

Lane, George W. Resident of Norfolk, Virginia who contracted on December 20, 1864 to sell 1,000 bales of his cotton to Treasury Agent Thomas Upton. Delivery was to be on January 1, 1865 at Norfolk. Supervising Purchasing Agent Hanson A. Risley's December 19 orders to Upton stated:

Sir: You are hereby appointed an agent of the purchasing agency of the United States Treasury Department for the purpose and duties hereinafter designated, viz: You will proceed on board the steamer *Philadelphia,* now lying in this port, and in the capacity of supercargo proceed to the Chowan river, in North Carolina, to such points as are designated by Mr. G. W. Lane. On arriving at the said point of destination you will deliver the cargo (a schedule of which is hereto attached) to Mr. G. W. Lane, or order, provided and upon the condition that the said Lane shall deliver to you on board the said steamer three times the value of said cargo in cotton, which you will continue to hold in your possession until the same is delivered to me in Norfolk, Virginia. And all permits granted to Mr. G. W. Lane for the bringing in cotton and taking out supplies you will hold until the aforesaid cotton is safely within the military lines of the United States."

There was a similar agreement to purchase another 100 bales and Lane had a permit from General Shepley to bring in a sum of goods at an aggregate price of $10,442.86, which included "90 pairs common boots at $5, and 505 pairs shoes at $1."

Lane and Upton boarded the *Philadelphia* for the Chowan River. The cargo was discharged and 257 bales were loaded aboard on January 10. Soon after departing the landing the steamer was stopped by the USS *Valley City,* on Chowan River reconnaissance patrol to Winton, North Carolina.

Just at this time Commander Macomb, naval commander in North Carolina, received a letter from Rear Admiral David D. Porter, commander of the North Atlantic Squadron, directing him to release vessels holding safe passage permits from generals in adjoining districts. Macomb examined her papers, contacted Shepley, and the *Philadelphia* was allowed to proceed. A report made out by Macomb reached Admiral Porter before she arrived back at Norfolk that stated, "a guard of rebel soldiers was placed on board her to take her up in safety." Porter ordered her arrested and sent "all evidence against her, to New York." She was seized by gunboat *Ceres* on February 1, 1865 and sent to Roanoke Island for needed repairs.

On the 20th Porter ordered her turned over to the Treasury Department. On the 26th Lane wrote to Secretary of the Treasury Hugh McCulloch requesting the steamer be sent to Norfolk where his cotton could be sold by Treasury agents as agreed.

On March 3 the *Philadelphia* reached Newbern, North Carolina where she was formally turned over to the Treasury Department by the Navy and the cotton was put in "proper order for shipment to the New York market." Upton protested vehemently and on the 26th Secretary McCulloch wrote to D. Heaton, special supervising agent for the 6th District:

> You are hereby directed, if the property has been turned over with charges of the nature above described, to cause it to be taken to some port within a district where an information may be filed, and the rights of all parties may be decided by a court having legal jurisdiction.

On the 16th Upton protested removing the cargo from Norfolk, "as the cargo already belongs to the seventh agency, with headquarters at Norfolk, and of which I am in charge as special agent on board said steamer."

On the 28th Heaton wrote to McCulloch to say that because of the condition and unseaworthiness of the *Philadelphia* a part of the cotton had been sent to New York where "the rights of the government in the case and that of the claimants can be fully tried." On April 30, 235 bales arrived in New York with the balance arriving on the 27th.

On May 25 the *Philadelphia* was libeled in the U.S. District Court for the District of Columbia. Lane again petitioned Secretary McCulloch and on July 11 the Secretary ordered Murray & Nephew, the government's agent in New York, to "deliver the said cotton on the payment by him of all lawful and proper charges incurred in handling, transportation, and care of the same, and on the execution by him of a paper which will protect you and all officers of the government from any legal action for the part taken in the premises." On July 22 Lane received 252 bales of cotton weighing 114,381 pounds and

Lane signed a receipt that said, in part: "I hereby release the said Murray & Nephew, and all officers of the government, from any legal action for the part taken by them, respectively, in relation to said cotton."

Cotton was then worth 46 cents a pound and Lane said he intended to sue for the difference between what the cotton was worth when it was seized and the price in New York when it was returned to him.

Meanwhile the *Philadelphia* had been released on December 13, 1865.

Lane sued for $31,620.40 and argued that if the voyage had been allowed to proceed the vessel would have arrived at Norfolk on or about January 12 where the cotton would have sold for $1.18 a pound, the current price in New York on that date, less one-fourth for the United States.

He was awarded the full amount in 1866 on the ground that he had a contract with Upton and his duty was to supervise the deal and if he put rebel troops on board to safeguard the merchandise and cotton to insure its passage on his lawful permit that was his business.

Lapene, Jules. A naturalized native of France doing business with French national Auguste Ferré as Lapene & Co. at New Orleans. On February 20, 1862 they sent their travelling clerk out to collect debts and to purchase cotton and sugar with the bank notes, Confederate money, and shinplasters collected. Cotton agents J. Numa Avegno and Oscar Bois purchased 179 bales of cotton for the company and stored it in the sheds of Coulon Devilliers.

After New Orleans was captured on April 27, Ferré obtained a military pass and a passport from the French consul and went to New York, then Europe.

The average net proceeds from the sale were $218.74 per bale. Loyalty proven, they were awarded $34,368. The government appealed to the Supreme Court where the decision was reversed:

"The agency to purchase cotton was terminated by the hostile position of the parties. The agency to receive payment of debts due to Lapene & Co. may well have continued. But Avegno was no debtor to that firm. He advanced money to their agent when it was legal to do so. With this money, and with other moneys belonging to them, while in an enemy's country, the agent of the plaintiffs bought the cotton in question. This purchase gave effectual aid to the enemy, by furnishing to them the sinews of war. It was forbidden by the soundest principles of public law. The purchaser obtained no title to the cotton, and has no claim against the Government for its capture."

La Peyre, Jean M. On June 18, 1865 La Peyre put 476 bales of his cotton on board the steamer *Bella Donna* somewhere on the Red River. The Red River is west of the Mississippi River. The cotton was consigned to a deputy Treasury agent named Cutler who was authorized to buy cotton for the government within insurrectionary districts. The vessel arrived at New Orleans on the 24th. At that time no shipments from west of the Mississippi were allowed except under consignment to Treasury agents.

La Peyre executed a bill of sale to Cutler on the 26th and on the same day, according to regulations, Cutler sold 337 bales back to La Peyre. The remaining 119 bales were sold at auction and the net proceeds of $9,955.66 were deposited into the Treasury. At the time of this transaction neither Cutler nor La Peyre had any knowledge of the Treasury Secretary Hugh MuCulloch's proclamation of May 9, 1865, approved by the President and effective June 10, amending regulations dealing with agents purchasing cotton within specific areas of insurrectionary states. The President's June 24 proclamation on the amendments wasn't published anywhere until the morning of the 27th.

The deal between La Peyre and Cutler took place after hostilities had ceased. General E. Kirby Smith, commander of Confederate forces west of the Mississippi had surrendered on May 20. Lee had formally surrendered all forces on April 9 and General Joseph E. Johnston on the 26th. The war was over.

Section 5 of the Act of July 13, 1861 prohibited all commerce between residents of the north and insurrectionary districts "so long as such conditions of hostility shall continue." On May 10 President Johnson proclaimed that, "armed resistance to the authority of the Government may be regarded as virtually at an end."

The agents were authorized to purchase products within insurrectionary districts for ¾ of their value in New York. The idea for taking ¼ the value from the owners was that the war deprived the owners from selling it and ¼ was the consideration for the privilege of doing so during wartime. That sounded like a con game to many at the time but that's the way it was.

On June 13 all restrictions on trade east of the Mississippi were lifted and on June 24 all areas west of the Mississippi were free to trade. Cutler claimed his 25 percent on the 26th, in all probability ignorant of the fact that legal restrictions to trade had been lifted two days prior. Both he and La Peyre believed the war was still on. Cutler filed his claim for the ¾ and received it. La Peyre sued in federal court to recover the 119 bales but the court could not reach a decision on when the June 24th proclamation took effect and his petition was dismissed. He appealed to the Supreme Court and a narrowly decided court held he should recover.

La Plante, Edward. A native of Bordeaux, France who lived in New Orleans before the war. He apparently returned to France in 1858 to import a quantity of wines and brandies into the port of New Orleans shortly before the war started. He purchased cotton at Summerville, Georgia through R. T. Henderson around the 1st of January 1863 while he was still in France. He came to New York that September and when Savannah was captured, 302 bales of his cotton were seized and sold in New York. He recovered $112,659.25 in 1870.

Laporte, John. Owner of 38 bales of cotton seized near Abbeville in St. Landry's Parish, Louisiana on May 4, 1863. It was sent to New Iberia, recorded by the quartermaster there, and then dropped out of sight. Of the 6,000 bales of cotton taken out of the Teche country, only about 3,000 ever reached New Orleans. The average net proceed per bale of St. Landry cotton was $192. Mrs. Laporte was awarded $7,296 in 1873.

Laws, Elijah. Laws became a third assistant engineer in the Navy on March 19, 1858. On December 1, 1860 he was promoted to second assistant engineer, and in 1863 he was at that rank aboard the screw frigate USS *Wabash*. On May 2 he was sentenced by a court martial to dismissal from the service. The sentence was approved on May 27 but on March 31, 1864 he was pardoned and reinstated by President Lincoln retroactive to December 1, 1860. On July 21, 1866 he was promoted to first assistant engineer and on March 21, 1870 to chief engineer. Laws was not paid during the time he was under dismissal and he petitioned Congress for relief. An act was passed on March 3, 1875 to award $641.95 pending fact finding in a federal court. His petition was dismissed on December 14, 1891 on the ground that he was not in "actual service" as required by the Longevity Pay Act of 1883.

Lawton, Samuel G. Owned the Lawton place and the Hill place in South Carolina. The U.S. Direct Tax Commissioners illegally assessed his property for taxes and penalties and sold both when the sale of one parcel would have paid the entire amount owed. Lawton recovered $352.66 on January 11, 1886.

Leary, Daniel D. Chartered his steamer *Mattano* to the Army on November 19, 1862 at Port Royal, South Carolina for $250 a day. The Army paid for the coal, Leary furnished the crew and provisions, and the operation and lading of the vessel was under complete control of the Army.

On May 12, 1863 the ship was at Port Royal when the harbormaster ordered the *Mattano*'s captain to move his vessel to make room for the passenger steamer *General Hunter*. The captain objected as the tide was very low and there was a brisk breeze blowing from the NNW. The harbormaster insisted on the move, the captain complied, and in the process of backing out of her slip the steamer hit a submerged mooring anchor that holed the hull and the steamer sank.

The anchor had been put in place by Army quartermaster Captain Sexton to hold a marker buoy but the buoy was carried away during a storm. There was no danger at high water.

Orlando Bennett had a contract with the War Department to perform salvage services at Port Royal. He was promptly summoned, raised the ship, removed the anchor, and brought the *Mattano* to a drydock at St. Helena. Bennett was paid by the United States but no effort was made to assess the damage to the steamer.

The *Mattano* was out of service until December 10, a total of 214 days or $53,500 on the charter-party. Leary got no response from the Army and sued. The reduction in the assessed value of the vessel after the accident was subsequently determined to be $12,000 and Leary was awarded that.

Lincoln, Cicero L. Joseph A. Harvey, of Lowndes County, Mississippi, sold 77 bales of cotton to the Confederate States of America on April 22, 1863 for $10,010 in face value Confederate bonds.

In May 1865 Harrison Johnston was appointed an assistant special Treasury agent to seize all cotton sold to the Confederate government in Lowndes and other counties in Missis-

sippi and on July 21 he seized the 77 bales "over the objection and protest" of Harvey.

Johnston seized 30,610 bales and of these 16,334 were sent to New York and sold at auction for $2,355,778.72. Net proceeds of $1,588,882.16 were deposited into the Treasury after costs, fees, and taxes of $537,829.87 making the average price per bale of $97.27.

Harvey's administrator sued to recover under the Act of March 3, 1911, which allowed the federal Court of Claims to hear petitions for goods taken after June 1, 1865 under the Act of March 12, 1863. On January 11, 1915 the petition was dismissed on the ground that no proof was furnished to show that Harvey's cotton ever reached New York.

Lindsley, James. Owned a "sand bed" near Nashville and agreed to let the Army take sand for 75 cents a load for the railroad machine shops and foundries at Nashville. They took 4,000 loads and gave Lindsley a voucher for 10 cents a load. He was paid $400. His suit for $2,600 was dismissed since he accepted the payment.

Livingston, Bell & Co. In September and October 1861, James M. Livingston's company in St. Louis sold army clothing to Quartermaster McKinstry and his successor Brigadier General Robert Allen at St. Louis. At this time the Davis-Holt-Campbell Commission was convened to examine the financial doings of John C. Frémont and payments to all vendors in his department were suspended. After a long wait, Livingston presented his $107,293.34 bill to the Commission and was told everything was approved but a few days later he was told $7,293.34 was being deducted. Livingston protested and was informed that unless he accepted $100,000 for the entire order, nothing would be paid. Livingston accepted this under protest in lieu of bankruptcy. Quartermaster General Meigs then approved a $74,000 payment claiming Livingston was a sutler with the Army and subject to military orders. No. 1002 of Army regulations stated:

> No officer or agent in the military service shall purchase from any other person in the military service, or make any contract with any such person to furnish supplies, or make any purchases or contract in which such person shall be admitted to any share or part, or to any benefit to arise therefrom.

Livingston sued. The court found the prices paid to be fair and reasonable, condemned the

Commission's arbitrariness, disregarded the alleged position of Livingston, and awarded the $7,293.34.

Lloyd, William A. Lloyd signed a written contract with President Lincoln on July 13, 1861 to serve as a spy for $200 a month. He was to "proceed south and learn the number of troops stationed in the different points and cities in the insurrectionary States, procuring plans or fortifications and forts, and gaining all other information that might be beneficial to the Government of the United States, and report the facts to the President."

He got a pass from Lincoln and was able to travel within rebel lines, was occasionally imprisoned, "ran great risks," and communicated his information from time to time. He received no pay while he was within Confederate lines. He reentered federal lines on April 27, 1865 at Danville, Virginia and reached Washington on June 15.

In October 1865 he presented a bill for salary and expenses to the Secretary of War and was paid $2,380 for his expenses with the understanding that if he accepted the money it would not affect his demand for salary due. Apparently the salary was never paid and Lloyd made no effort to collect.

On May 22, 1871 the administrator of Lloyd's estate, Enoch Totten, filed a claim for money due Lloyd from July 13, 1861 to May 13, 1865, after 46 months' of service. The government argued the 6-year statute of limitations and the fact that there was nothing to prevent Lloyd from requesting money due him at the same time he was sending information back. The court rendered a *pro forma* decision for the government based on the Supreme Court's policy forbidding the conducting any trial which would disclose confidential information or allow any confidence to be violated.

Lobsiger, Rudolph. A citizen of the Swiss Confederation living in Charleston who owned eight bales of upland cotton and 100 barrels of rosin. Seven bales were seized and he recovered $942.90 on the cotton. He could not furnish any proof the rosin was taken, sold, or money deposited into the Treasury.

Loper, Richard E. Chartered his 154-foot, 329-ton steamer *General Meigs,* of Philadelphia, under Captain G. W. Watson to Colonel G. H. Grossman on October 15, 1862 for six months at $300 a day, the Army reserving

the right to purchase the vessel after three months for $45,000 cash. The agreed value was $50,000. The agreement stated, "the above charter to commence when the vessel is reported at the quartermaster's office in Philadelphia as being ready to receive cargo." The boat was reported at Philadelphia on December 29, 1862 and was in service until May 13, 1863.

Another steamer, Anthony Reybold's *General Burnside,* of which Loper owned one-fourth, was also chartered at the same time under the same conditions.

The charter agreement was signed and sealed on the 20th. On February 2, 1863 Quartermaster General Meigs wrote to Grossman with instructions to purchase the boats as of January 15 and to cease charter payments after that date except for the ordinary running expenses from January 15 until the Army took possession. Meigs stated:

"It is believed that the arrangement now understood to exist between the owners of these steamers and the captains, whereby the latter are to provide the necessary officers (except engineers) and crew to man them for the sum of $1,000 per month, which includes provisions for all the officers and crew, will be advantageous to the government; and you are therefore authorized to make similar arrangements."

Loper agreed and wrote to quartermaster Lieutenant Colonel Herman Briggs about the sale and said, in part:

"It was also agreed that the captains should have $1,000 per month to man the boats and victual all hands; the U.S. War Department to pay engineers, firemen, and coal-passers' wages; captain to furnish board."

Nothing happened with the vessels and on March 9 Grossman's office contacted Loper to find out why the sale had not been concluded. Loper stated he refused to sell them. Meigs was notified and replied that "The report of the committee on charters recommends that no money be paid on charters in which certain parties are interested" and Meigs put the sale on hold until further notice.

On May 10 or 11 Loper was summoned to Grossman's office where he was told the vessels were to be transferred immediately. Loper protested and said the boats had increased greatly in value from 50 to 100 percent and the government owed him money from January 15 to date and he wanted the money and if he thought he could fight the government and win he wouldn't sell the boats at all, and he was very short on cash. On May 13, 1863 he delivered a bill of sale on the *General Meigs* for $45,000.

Everyone accepted October 15 as the beginning of the charter but the Army was late in payment on the agreement and when the purchase was made the owners objected to the use of October 15 as the start of the 3-month period. Loper accepted the purchase payment and a $4,000 payment for running expenses but sued to recover $3,000 in wages for the disputed dates. The petition was dismissed because Loper and Captain Watson both certified the vouchers paid as correct.

The facts in the claim of Anthony Reybold and his steamer *General Burnside* were the same as the Loper case so both were tried and dismissed at the same time. Loper was a one-fourth owner of the *Burnside*.

Love, T. L. T. L. was in the cotton business with his father at Haw River, Chatham County, North Carolina as Robert Love & Son. They had 80 bales of cotton worth over $20,000 stored at Morrisville, North Carolina. General Sherman's 15–20,000-man 15th Army Corps was camped nearby in April 1865 when the soldiers seized it for bedding. Part of the badly damaged cotton was recovered when the camps were abandoned and some of it was stolen from the Love's agents. No money was ever paid for the lost cotton.

The Love's presented a claim in 1867 but no action resulted from it. After Robert died, T. L., of Wake County, North Carolina, petitioned Congress for relief and his claim was referred to a federal court for fact finding. On June 11, 1907 he filed suit to recover $5,000 of the $20,000 loss on the ground that his father was loyal throughout the war.

Robert was elected to the convention in opposition to secession. He refused to volunteer for Confederate service and when conscripted he procured a substitute. Sometime in 1864 he and other citizens in Chatham County appealed to Confederate forces for protection and requested a company of soldiers be stationed in the county but since the Confederate military was the only protection then available the court did not consider the request a disloyal act. The court reported to Congress in favor of Love on January 6, 1913.

Low, Andrew. Low and his partner, Charles Green, began business in Savannah as Andrew Low & Co. sometime between 1847 and 1849. When the war started they were operating a store and Low's Wharf. Green left the partnership in 1861 by mutual consent and Low continued under the firm's name to collect debts and settle up with Green. Between 1862–64 Green's agents bought 2,246 bales of upland and 349 bales of sea-island cotton for him under the firm's name and stored it in his warehouses. All the cotton was seized.

On December 28, 1861 Green received $1,691.87 from Low in full settlement of the partnership. Low sued to recover his share of the cotton on the ground it was company property. At trial it was discovered that he was a commissioner who negotiated a $15,000,000 loan to the Confederacy but on April 7, 1865 he took an amnesty oath under the proclamation of December 8, 1863. In 1871 he was awarded $175.33 per bale of upland and $231.79 per bale of sea-island for a total of $474,685.89.

Lowry, William M. Claimed 47 bales of cotton worth $30,836 captured at Atlanta. The Treasury reported 10,220 pounds and Lowry recovered $9,140 on 20 bales at $457 a bale.

Lynch, John and James. Irish brothers and naturalized citizens who lived in Atlanta for about 20 years before the war. On September 21, 1864 the Army seized 108 bales of their cotton weighing 52,433 pounds and worth about $1.10 a pound. It was sent to Nashville then to Cincinnati where it was sold.

They were in a group of about 30 or 35 Union men in Atlanta, were "moneyed men" and well known. Joseph Gatius testified in their behalf:

"They were not conscripted. They commuted it by some equivalent under the rebel Congress exemption system by attaching themselves to the fire department, subject to military call on emergencies."

They convinced the court of their loyalty and were awarded $38,909.16.

Lynch, Michael. A resident of Van Buren, Arkansas who owned 50 bales of cotton purchased in the seed from Josiah Foster's gin about eight miles from Lynch's residence. Before it was marked, a portion was stolen by a Confederate provost marshal named Catterel and "issued to the poor." The rest, 30 bales was seized at the gin in February or March 1863 by the 10th Illinois Cavalry. Lynch was present at the time and protested but the cotton was loaded into wagons and carried off to Fayetteville. It went to Springfield, Missouri then to St. Louis where it was auctioned for 75 cents a pound net.

Michael's brother and clerk, Patrick C. Lynch, and Luther N. Hollins swore there were no marks on the cotton but the invoice showed an < L > mark on the bales although there was a discrepancy on the amount. In court, the assistant attorney general said Lynch was a country storekeeper "and not likely to be an uncompromising Union man" as required to recover under the Act of March 12, 1863. The court found him loyal and awarded him $8,102.22 on 600 pounds.

Lyon, Reuben E. James R. Lyon was first lieutenant of Company B, 23d New York Cavalry. On January 23, 1864 he was granted 25 days' leave but did not return until March 14. He was court martialed and sentenced to forfeit one months' pay of $51.73. On April 8 he resigned his commission because of physical disability, was honorably discharged at Newbern, North Carolina, and paid $77.80 on 819 miles travel subsistence to Providence, Rhode Island. The sentence was approved on April 30, 1865 and published on May 5.

The accounting officers said he was erroneously paid $39.62 while he was AWOL and demanded $10.31 after credits. James died and Reuben Lyon sued to recover the forfeited pay. The government did not file a counterclaim and Rueben's petition was dismissed on December 2, 1912.

McClure, Alfred A. Enlisted as a private in Company H, 21st Indiana Infantry and was discharged on December 31, 1863 so he could reenlist as a veteran volunteer, which he did on January 1, 1864 for a term of three years. On September 23, 1865 he was declared a deserter. He never returned to his company and the company was discharged on January 20, 1866. Under the Act of July 5, 1884 the charge of desertion was removed and he was declared discharged on September 23, 1865. He had been paid his $100 enlistment bounty and $260 of the $400 veteran bounty, less an advance of $25 due before his desertion. He sued to recover the $25 balance and was awarded that on March 11, 1907.

McClure, Daniel. Major McClure was paymaster at San Antonio, Texas. On or about February 25, 1861 "an armed force in charge of one of the commissioners of the State of Texas" broke into his office, forced open the safe, and

made off with $289.05. The loss was charged to McClure.

He also had $1,183.13 in government funds on deposit with A. J. Guirot, the assistant U.S. Treasurer in New Orleans. On March 30, 1861 Guirot became an assistant treasurer with the Confederate States of America. The loss was charged to McClure.

On May 31, 1861 he claimed credit for $84,415.88 in payroll expenses. Voucher No. 65, Company D, Third Infantry payroll, was over-added by $1,000 for which he also claimed credit.

On April 30, 1862 he was at Washington, D.C. when another paymaster, Major Ira L. Hewitt, took credit on a receipt for $1,432.48 from Hewitt signed by McClure and the Treasury officers charged it to McClure.

On September 9, 1862 he was at Indianapolis when another paymaster, Major S. C. Stevenson, took credit on a receipt for $125,000 from Stevenson signed by McClure and the Treasury officers charged it to McClure.

On September 26, 1862 he was at Indianapolis when another paymaster, Major V. C. Hanna, took credit on a receipt for $4,993.06 from Hewitt signed by McClure and the Treasury officers charged it to McClure.

McClure sued and recovered the money lost to the Confederacy but the court was not convinced the other money receipted for was never received by him and those claims were disallowed.

McDonald, Robert S. Robert was born on July 5, 1851 and lived on a farm in Benton County, Mississippi. His father died in 1858 leaving a wife, himself, and his brother William, born in July 1857. In the summer of 1862 personal property was taken from their farm by the Army. Their mother died in the fall of 1863 and neither parent left a will. William died and Robert petitioned the House War Claims Committee. The claim was referred to a federal court but his petition was dismissed on May 3, 1886 as barred by statutes of limitations and the Bowman Act of March 3, 1883.

McElhose, James B. An Irish subject of Great Britain who came to America shortly before the war and owned 36 bales of upland cotton and 3 bales of sea-island cotton seized at Charleston. He bought 15 bales three days before the city was captured and that upset his plans. The court was skeptical of his motives since his answers to questions were vague and he appeared to plead ignorance of American politics:

"I cannot tell what you call rebels. I cannot distinguish. I cannot say about men being rebels or not. I know nothing about American political affairs."

He was awarded $2,361 for 18 bales of upland and $712.92 for three bales of sea-island after he was forced to admit that he bought the 15 bales from a man named Cocking who was wearing a Confederate uniform at the time and he knew he was not a Union man.

McElyea, Wilford. First lieutenant in the 11th Missouri Infantry Volunteers who sued to recover three months' back pay and bounty under the Act of June 5, 1920. McElyea's petition was dismissed on May 31, 1921 as barred by the Act of December 22, 1911.

McKay, Donald. Signed a contract on August 22, 1863 to build the gunboat *Ashuelot* within 11 months. Design changes delayed delivery until November 29, 1865 — 16 months and 7 days — and cost McKay $27,424.37, which he recovered in federal court. The government appealed to the Supreme Court and on January 3, 1899 the decision was reversed on the ground that "the increased cost arose during the contract term of eleven months."

McKay, Nathaniel. On July 4, 1861 Secretary of the Navy Gideon Welles asked Congress to fund a board to obtain "floating batteries or iron-clad steamers," seek ideas, report on their findings, and oversee their construction. The board was appointed and immediately advertised for designs from naval architects. Seventeen proposals were received, all but three were rejected, and the three were built. The first ship completed was designed by the famous Swedish inventor John Ericsson. His 172' *Monitor* drew 10'-6" and was commissioned on February 25, 1862.

Galena was built by C. S. and H. L. Bushnell of Mystic, Connecticut and commissioned on April 21, 1862. She was 210' long, powerful, and had iron plating 3' thick. Her draft was 11' and, like the others, too deep for the shallow bays and rivers of the South to support troop movements.

The 230' *New Ironsides* was built by Merrick & Sons of Philadelphia and commissioned on August 21, 1862. She had 11" guns, a draft of 15'-8", and was probably the most powerful warship of her day.

Of the three, the *Monitor* was the most unique, having a turret that revolved and a low freeboard that gave her a low silhouette and minimum exposure to gunfire. The *Monitor*'s world-famous battle with the Confederate ironclad *Virginia* (ex-USS *Merrimack*) on March 9, 1862, although a standoff, proved the usefulness and ultimate superiority of Ericsson's design. Ericsson was rewarded with a contract for six *Passaic*-class monitors.

Captain Ericsson had made detailed drawings prior to beginning work on these vessels. The draft was still 10'-6" and, like the original *Monitor*, she was built by Ericsson's subcontractor, the Continental Iron Works of Greenport, New York. The *Passaic* was built in 180 days, the *Monitor* in 100 days.

In the fall of 1862 the Navy realized it urgently needed smaller, shallow-draft "river and harbor monitors" to operate in the bays and sounds of the Atlantic and Gulf coasts. Nine contracts were let for 20 new vessels, which were modified *Passaic*-class monitors. The new *Casco*-class river monitors were intended to be 225' with a 6' draft, 15" freeboard, twin-screw, a single turret mounting two 11" Dahlgren smoothbore guns, and a crew of 60. Armor was sacrificed to get the reduced draft and ballast tanks were included to lower the ship during an engagement.

To meet the emergency, Ericsson came up with general configuration drawings describing the mode of building and engine, boiler, and propeller specifications for a single-turret monitor with a draft of 6'-6½' but he did not produce any detailed plans as he had with the *Passaic*-class. He submitted his drawings on October 9 and was to act as a sort of project manager.

The Navy placed an ad dated February 10, 1863 requesting bids for "Light Draft Vessels for Rivers and Bays" which stated:

The Navy Department will receive proposals for the construction and completion in every respect (except guns, ordnance stores, fuel, provisions, and nautical instruments) of armored steamers of about seven hundred tons, of wood and iron combined, having a single revolving turret.

On personal application at the Navy Department at Washington, or to Rear-Admiral Gregory, No. 413 Broadway, New York, parties intending to offer can examine the plans and specifications, which shall be furnished to the contractors by the Department.

The average bid price of the vessels was just below $400,000. Between March, April, and May, contracts for 20 light-draft monitors were signed. The Navy's liaison man between Erics-son and the contractors was Navy Chief Engineer Alban C. Stimers. Stimers set up shop in the New York office where he and his assistants frequently consulted with Ericsson. Ericsson did not make all the calculations and detailed plans for the vessels and, probably believing it to be a fairly simple matter, left the details to Stimers. Stimers had not only worked with Ericsson on the *Monitor,* but he had been an engineer on the ship during the engagement with the *Virginia.* He also witnessed the Navy's assault on Confederate-held Fort Sumpter by seven monitors in the spring of 1863.

An important question was raised when Stimers consulted with other Navy engineers and planners. In going forward with new construction, should the Navy build vessels according to set-in-stone plans, get them built and in service, or should the plans and specifications be modified during building whenever navigational or actual combat experience showed a better way? They chose the latter. This philosophy was impractical from the builder's standpoint because it delayed construction, increased costs dramatically, bankrupted some shipbuilders, and often resulted in unproven ideas. The decision would wreak havoc for decades.

In addition to this, the Navy Department decided they wanted the boats built in Portland, Maine instead of Boston.

The first of the 20 vessels completed were the *Casco* and the *Chimo,* both launched in May of 1864. *Casco* was built by the Atlantic Iron Works of Boston. Once in the water, it was immediately apparent that a miscalculation of displacement had occurred. The ships had only 3" of freeboard without the turret, guns, or stores. The two boats were ordered to be converted to torpedo boats, never saw service, and were decommissioned and laid up in June the next year. *Chimo* was built at South Boston by Aquila Adams, launched on May 5, 1864, and commissioned on January 20, 1865.

The firm of Nathaniel McKay & George Aldus of East Boston responded to the ad and McKay visited the New York office to view the plans. A $395,000 contract was subsequently signed on May 5, 1863 to build the *Squando.* The vessel was to be completed on or before November 4, 1864 and the Navy was to supply all the plans and specifications.

The company did not receive the promised plans and wrote to the Navy on the 5th and 25th of May requesting the plans and specifications. In the meantime, they began constructing the sheds and support buildings they would need.

When McKay and Aldus finally got their plans they noticed significant differences from the drawings viewed in the Navy's offices. Changes were also made from time to time before the keel was laid and as construction progressed. These changes dealt with every part of the ship until a virtually new vessel was created. Because of all the changes, the completion date had passed and on June 23, 1864, work was stopped by the Navy for about three months while they contemplated further modifications. Without the modifications the company would have completed the ship on time. McKay and Aldus's expenses continued to accrue during the stop-work period and they could not let any journeyman workers go due to a shortage of skilled workers.

The *Squando* was finally completed in 23 months on April 4, 1865.

The Navy and the contractors had agreed to the cost of four major modifications: improved bulkheads, $1,547.52; pilot house cover, $1,000.00; port stoppers, $300.00; and raising the hull 22 inches, $90,000. The total amount received by the contractors for all the modifications was $194,555.70. Of this, $14,220.09 was paid to McKay for the installation of machinery and materials from the *Chimo;* using parts from two of the *Modoc's* gun carriages, $182.40; fitting magazines at the Boston Navy Yard, $153.92; and installing other equipment at the Navy Yard, $304.82.

McKay and Aldus claimed they were still short by $41,375 on the original settlement and, because of increased costs of labor and materials during the war, they were also behind by $60,462 due to all the delays. All this was too much for the firm and McKay and Aldus filed for bankruptcy in 1868. The major creditors were Edward Page, J. A. Richards, and Dwight Foster. A public sale of the company's assets was held on July 29, 1871 at the auction house of Samuel Hatch & Co., No. 3 Morton Place. The creditors had an unadjudicated claim against the Navy for $142,793.76, which Nathaniel McKay purchased from them.

McKay claimed the total cost to him to build the *Squando* was $414,696.44. The Navy Department had already paid $194,555.70 for the extra work but he was still owed $225,000. Not being forthcoming, he sued. The court stated:

"The particular grievance complained of upon the part of the contractors was, the alleged delay of the officers in charge in furnishing drawings and plans, with sufficient facility to enable the parties to prosecute the work with diligence and complete the same within the time specified by the agreement. The work was not completed until April 1865, nearly two years after the date of the agreement. This was an extraordinary delay, considering the fact that the vessel was intended for use in the war which was then flagrant.

"During the period of its construction the contractors were continually complaining to the officers in charge because of the delay, and while so delayed exercised reasonable diligence to prevent increased cost in the value of material and labor."

McKay recovered $115,157 but nothing for the shops and sheds required to build the ship.

Another shipbuilder, George W. Lawrence & Co. at Portland, Maine contracted for $386,000 to build the *Wassuc*. He experienced the same difficulties and his widow, Thankful M. Lawrence, recovered $36,385.08 on February 15, 1897.

John Souther, president of The Globe Works, got a $395,000 contract to build the *Suncook* at his marine engine plant at South Boston. Work began on the original plans, then the Navy Department insisted he build it in Portland. As with the other builders, numerous design changes were made and the contract renewed with later completion dates. In August 1863 he began constructing shops in Portland but the vessel was apparently completed in Boston. When finished it was declared unseaworthy and was never used. Globe recovered an additional $198,674.30 for alterations and design changes.

Donald McKay recovered $231,068.20 on his *Nauset* contract. The Atlantic Works built the *Casco* and recovered $73,058.50.

Alexander Swift and Seth Evans, doing business as Alexander Swift & Co., of Cincinnati were awarded a contract on March 26, 1863 to build the *Klamath* and *Yuma*, delivered to Cairo, Illinois within six months at $395,000 each. They subcontracted with S. T. Hambleton, also of Cincinnati. Swift's petition was dismissed on the ground the contract authorized the Navy to make changes and alterations and the company was paid the contract price. Neither vessel was ever commissioned

The Navy finally decided that five of the 20

vessels would be converted into torpedo boats to give them a shallower draft and the other 15 should have their freeboard increased by raising the deck 22" higher than designed. This would put them lower in the water, defeating the initial purpose of the boats, but increase their effectiveness as monitors. It appears that only two were converted to torpedo boats and only five were raised the 22-inches. Most of these boats were never commissioned and none saw any significant service.

It was probably inevitable that such things would happen, given the tremendous advances, innovation, and invention during this time of the Industrial Revolution, but no doubt the *Casco*-class monitors were the most expensive part of the Navy's learning curve up to that time. The hurried need for the *Casco*-class monitors only added to the problem and their failure to enter the war as designed might have delayed the inevitable and cost many more lives and lost property.

McKay, William. A subject of Great Britain living in Charleston. He sought to recover $10,498 on 15 bales of cotton that was seized on March 8, 1865. At the trial, the British consul, H. Pinckney Walker, esq., testified that McKay was the steward of the Charleston Club until the time of its abandonment after which he became a "petty trader." He stated, as did other witnesses, that he was pretty sure McKay was never in Confederate service. His legal advisor, R. W. Seymour, esq., would say only that his client was "strictly neutral."

The court was not impressed with the knowledge of the plaintiff's witnesses. The government was able to show that he was one of a number of individuals who attempted to run the openly loyal Charles J. Quimby out of town, that he was a purchasing agent for the Confederacy, rejoiced in their victories, and "dressed in a garb well understood to mean sympathy with the Confederate army." McKay's petition was dismissed.

McKee, Henry E. Brigadier General John M. Thayer was commander of the District of the Frontier at Fort Smith—the Indian Territory south of Kansas and west of Arkansas—and Captain Greene Durbin was chief quartermaster. During most of 1864 it was impractical to supply General Thayer's command at Fort Gibson with grain via the Arkansas River due to low water. The nearest supplies were at Fort Leavenworth and Fort Scott in Kansas but the route from there was long and difficult to protect from Confederate raids. Fortunately, timothy and prairie grass was abundant in the Territory so Greene advertised for bids to supply 3,000 tons of hay at Fort Gibson, Cherokee Nation.

McKee proposed $30 a ton of merchantable timothy or prairie hay delivered to Fort Gibson or $22 a ton stacked within seven miles of the Fort or to any other place designated at the same price with delivery to start on or before July 15. This was accepted and a contract was signed on June 20, 1864.

On July 17, Durbin got a note from General Thayer at Fort Smith demanding 4,000 tons of hay immediately "at Cabin Creek, 40 miles from Fort Gibson, & at Hudson's Crossing on the Neosho River, 70 miles from the fort; two thousand tons to be delivered at each of said points."

Durbin contacted McKee and ordered the additional hay and asked him if he would accept an amended contract. McKee replied that he would "on condition that the necessary military protection be furnished at those points."

During July, August, and September, the only permanent troops in the Territory was the Indian Brigade and most of the time they were inside the forts. Other troops were on temporary duty in the region and Thayer had to keep a supply route open between Fort Smith and Fort Scott, about 250 miles away. Along this route was Fort Gibson, Cabin Creek, and Hudson's Crossing. Cabin Creek was 55 miles north of Fort Gibson, Hudson's Crossing 85 miles north. Fort Gibson to Fort Scott was 105 miles.

Continual skirmishes were fought along these routes and because of this General Thayer wasn't always able to provide timely protection to every contractor working outside the posts although it was against regulations for working parties to go outside the posts without protection. McKee's subcontractors were protected as best they could under the circumstances but many days were spent waiting for escorts. One of the subcontractors, Cohen, was attacked on September 2 about seven miles from Fort Gibson. About 600 tons of stacked hay at $22 a ton and 200 tons of unstacked hay at $19 a ton, $12,600 worth of hay, was destroyed along with animals, machinery, and stores worth $1,100 causing an 8-day delay. McKee presented his claim for the lost hay to the Third Auditor, the Second Comptroller concurred, and he was paid.

McKee still had 400 tons to deliver under his original contract but other haymakers had

experienced attacks 12 miles from Fort Gibson and the post commander there forbid the contractors from working outside the post.

On July 17 McKee delivered 1,128 tons to Cabin Creek at $30 a ton. On September 19 a rebel force destroyed 115 tons of hay worth $15,674 and $1,100 worth of equipment there belonging to George H. Stotts. When word of this reached another party cutting hay at Hudson's Crossing, Lieutenant Colonel John R. Wheeler of the 13th Kansas Volunteer Infantry ordered work stopped and the workers and their guards into Fort Scott leaving 70 tons of hay on the ground. After the attack no contractors were allowed at either place. McKee again submitted a claim and was paid $6,285 on the 115 ton lost at Cabin Creek and the 70 ton abandoned at Hudson's Crossing. He also got $945 for the hire of teams used to abandon Hudson's Crossing.

McKee was paid a total of $16,774 and on September 26 he got a note from Durbin saying the contract was being terminated since the garrisons needing hay were small and it was too dangerous to continue. McKee would have made $6 a ton on 400 tons under the June 20 contract; $7 a ton on 757 tons for Cabin Creek, and 1,930 for Hudson's Crossing.

McKee sued to recover money owed on the June 20 contract but was denied. He was awarded potential earnings of $29,557 on the terminated July 17 contract. The government filed a counterclaim and got back $12,000 already paid on hay that was destroyed by rebels under the June 20 contract but were denied that lost under the July 17 contract. McKee was awarded $16,957 in 1876.

William J. Chandler, another hay contractor in the area at the time, recovered $3,200 in 1881.

McMahon, John. Owned 8 bales of upland cotton seized at Charleston and he sued for $1,649. He was described as a "violent Union man" and testified:

"I have done something to aid Union prisoners here from the time Corcoran came here till they left the race-course. I contributed at every call made upon me. I took the carpeting and matting off my floor and gave it to them to make shelter. I sent them socks, &c., indeed went beyond the means I had, almost. I did nothing to aid the rebellion, being perfectly opposed to it from the very first. Prior to the arrival here of the Union troops I had eight bales of cotton — it was the best upland cotton. I had it stored on my own place, 398 King street. It was marked J. McM., those being the initials of my name. I had owned this cotton for some time before the Union troops came here. I bought the cotton as an investment and for no illegitimate purpose nor for the purpose of running the blockade. I did not buy this cotton to enable parties who were rebels to get it off their hands."

McMahon bought the first lot on January 5, 1865 for 3 cents a pound and a second lot on January 25 for 5 cents a pound. General Sherman left Savannah on January 22 but no proof was presented that he knew of this and he was awarded $1,049.60.

Mahan, Eliza Jane. P. R. Nicholls married Eliza Jane's mother, Sophia G. and the family owned and lived on the Palatine Hills cotton plantation in Mississippi. A life estate and ownership of the Palatine Hills plantation in Mississippi was vested in Eliza Jane. Nicholls died and Sophia married James H. Mitchell and James became Eliza Jane's stepfather and guardian. Since he received the profits from the plantation, he became indebted to Eliza Jane under the terms of the life estate in the amount of $24,701.24. To secure the debt, a mortgage was executed on February 23, 1841 on certain personal property, Palatine Hills, and slaves, which became due when Eliza Jane reached the age of 21, when she married, or when she called for the money at any time after that.

James Mitchell died on September 23, 1862.

In December 1862 General Van Dorn ordered all cotton moved at least ten miles from the Mississippi River to prevent its capture and any cotton left behind would be burned. Sophia moved the cotton to Kingston, near Natchez, where it was stacked and covered. In the early summer of 1863 Sophia conveyed ownership of 116 bales of cotton to Eliza Jane at 20 cents a pound in partial satisfaction of the mortgage but there was no weighing, no paperwork, no payment, and no physical delivery. In August was captured at Kingston.

Eliza Jane Mitchell claimed ownership of the cotton after it was seized and asked to have it released to her but it was shipped to Natchez and sold.

Eliza Jane married Richard H. Mahan in Mississippi in March 1865. In court, Richard and Eliza Jane claimed they raised, ginned, and baled the cotton at Palatine Hills but this was proved untrue. They were supporters of the Confederacy and had subscribed to the Confederate loan. Sophia Mitchell's testimony was contradictory and she was declared disloyal. Eliza Jane was declared loyal but she could not prove ownership of the cotton and her petition was dismissed in 1870.

Sophia filed suit in 1885 but her petition was dismissed on June 1, 1886. She could have sued herself under the Act of March 12, 1863 anytime before August 20, 1868. Her claim was barred by statute of limitation and the Bowman Act.

Maine, State of. The State appropriated $1 million in general obligation bonds to raise 10 regiments. They expended $1,027,185 and sued to recover the interest paid on the bonds. On November 28, 1901 the State was awarded $131,587.20.

Malone, Benjamin. A volunteer assistant paymaster appointed March 23, 1863. On the afternoon of February 22, 1864 he withdrew $70,000 in large bills, all over $20 denomination, and in sheets of fractional currency to pay troops in and around Culpepper, Virginia and Fort Washington, Maryland. He took the money to a third floor hotel room serving as his office at No. 401 C Street, Washington City that was also occupied by his father and his son. The Hon. Isaac Newton also resided in the building. Malone's intention was to start paying troops on the 7:30 train the following morning.

During the afternoon and until around midnight he and his son, who helped for part of the time, cut up the sheets of fractional currency and arranged the money. Malone went to bed before his father. The father put the money into a government trunk, locked it, and placed it at the foot of the bed occupied by Malone and his son. While he was undressing for bed, and before the son had fallen asleep, a messenger arrived with a telegram. He took the message then locked the door and went to bed.

Sometime during the night burglars entered the room, removed the trunk, took it to a stable at the back of the lot where the building stood, and removed the money. Malone and his son discovered the theft around 6 the next morning. Malone immediately reported the theft to the chief of police of Washington City and he assigned two detectives to the case. War Department detectives got involved along with Colonel Wood, superintendent of the Old Capitol

Prison. Wood discovered the robbery had been planned by an employee of the Secret Service, Christopher V. Hogan, and carried out by Al Burtis, a professional burglar from New York, who was assisted by Matthew Kinney and John Dugan. The money was taken to John Murphy's house in Washington City, where he received his share, and the rest was taken to New York and divided among the others.

About $1,800 was recovered from Murphy and some postal currency was found in the stable but none of the rest of the money was ever found.

Malone was charged with $68,800 by the War Department. He sued and was awarded the loss.

Mann, William D. Colonel Mann held a patent on a type of knapsack. On March 18, 1865 the War Department placed an order for 5,000 knapsacks at $2.85½ each to be delivered within 40 days. On the 23rd, 1,000 were delivered. On the 22nd Mann was instructed to make the remaining 4,000 and on the 25th Quartermaster General Meigs suspended the contract. This notice was received by Mann on the 29th or 30th but the order was filled by then and Meigs refused to pay pursuant to No. 1002, Army regulations. Mann sued for $14,275 and was awarded $13,975.

Mannahasset. A schooner owned by various investors under Captain Richard Ryder. On August 29, 1863 Commodore Henry H. Bell, Commander of the Western Gulf Squadron aboard *Pensacola,* chartered her at $50 a day to load 325 tons of coal at New Orleans and deliver it to other Louisiana and Texas ports as directed by the Navy. The government furnished a $13,000 war risk insurance policy and the Navy paid all pilotage, towing, and quarantine fees.

The *Mannahasset* left New Orleans with 360 tons of coal on September 3. On the 8th she arrived at Sabine Pass and reported to the commander of the fleet there. He directed Captain Ryder to anchor six miles offshore and the warships would come alongside for coal as needed. Soon after this order, Ryder was directed to move nine miles offshore. By the 28th he had discharged 240 tons of coal. While lying on a single anchor that afternoon in pleasant weather, a storm suddenly approached. Ryder immediately got his yards, light spars, and sails down. He let go his sheet anchor and let out both anchor cables to their full lengths.

From 8 P.M. on the wind blew a full gale with periods of hail. Around midnight the sheet anchor chain broke and the schooner began dragging in toward shore. The stream anchor was let go and its cable let out fully but the vessel continued to drift to within 1½ miles of shore.

Sometime between 3 and 4 A.M. her anchors caught bottom and held but the sheet anchor was lost. The wind was still too strong and his position too perilous for Ryder to make sail.

Ryder hoisted a distress signal at daylight to attract the fleet's gunboats. The signal went unnoticed in the fleet but a rebel battery on shore saw it and commenced firing. The second shot blew the stream anchor cable apart and the schooner was blown ashore. A rebel boarding party quickly captured the ship, cut the masts down, and hauled everything of value off.

The schooner's owners contended their vessel was lost due to enemy action but the government refused to pay. In court the government argued the vessel was lost through the negligence of Captain Ryder who should have gotten his ship out to sea when the storm arose, should have known that Confederate shore batteries were in the vicinity, and, if he couldn't get out to sea, it must have been because his vessel was "not sufficiently staunch or well manned or appareled" which would render Captain Ryder guilty of negligence.

The court noted the Navy had placed Captain Ryder nine miles from shore where he could not observe any batteries or movements of batteries and no evidence was presented that showed he knew about any batteries or should have expected to be fired on and no failure of equipment or negligence on the part of Captain Ryder was found. The court held the loss of the schooner was due to enemy action and the owners were awarded $13,000.

Maple Leaf. Charles Spear and John H. B. Lang of Boston chartered their steamboat to the Army on September 1, 1862 at $550 a day, an exorbitant rate, and included 33 percent profit per annum on the $50,000 appraised value of the vessel, minus operating expenses. On August 19, 1863 the charter was renewed but Quartermaster General Meigs reduced the rate to $300 a day retroactive to April 22 with a provision that when the payments reached $50,000 her ownership would pass to the government. On June 22 the rate went to $250 a day.

The *Maple Leaf* was part of a group of transports sent up the St. John's River in Florida "on a very hazardous military expedition" and when returning on the night of April 1, 1864 she struck a torpedo in the river and sank.

The owners applied to the Third Auditor for compensation. The Auditor's account stated $50,000 for the value of the vessel; 33 percent profit on $50,000 for 9 months, 8 days, and 16 hours, $12,750.40; running expenses including 6 days and 8 hours to return the crew to Boston, $20,681.50; repairs, $2,572.63; and credit of $66,125, leaving a balance of $19,887.93. The balance was paid and accepted without protest by the owners. They later claimed to be owed a total of $116,125 — the value of the vessel plus $66,125 in earnings. The owners were paid a total of $86,012.93, the earnings and charter balance, but claimed an additional $30,112.07 for the vessel. Their petition was dismissed because the owners accepted the final settlement. In the 1869 decision one judge stated:

"I regret as much as anyone the conduct pursued by the Quartermaster's Department, toward claimants, about these charter-parties. The whole proceeding of that department toward this claimant and others, as I think, was in violation of law. It would seem from the many and repeated notices and objections by this and other claimants, that advice should have been sought from the law officers of the government as to the legality of their action. If the defendants should be made to suffer for the wanton wrong of its officers in disregarding the obligation of contracts, it is their fault, and not the fault of the law."

Markham, Marcellus O.

William Markham, of Fulton County, Georgia, owned the Johnson House and the Washington Hall Hotel — known as the Markham House — and several stores in Atlanta that were seized and occupied by the Army as enemy property. He also lost some cotton.

On June 25, 1867 he recovered $3,602.70 for the cotton that was seized. He died and his heir petitioned Congress under the Tucker Act to recover $10,250 for the use and occupation of the buildings. Congress approved it and referred the case to a federal court for fact finding.

The government claimed Markham was actually disloyal during the war and had they evidence not available at the trial to recover the cotton sale proceeds. The assistant attorney general claimed Markham was a soldier in the Georgia State Militia and had furnished supplies to the Confederate government. On April 12, 1909 the court reported the facts to Congress.

General Sherman stayed at the 150-room Washington Hall from September 1 to November 16, 1864. The charge for that was $3,750 at $1,500 a month.

Martin, Edmund H.

Owned a plantation in St. Landry Parish, Louisiana. He had 350 bales on the plantation from the crop of '61; 32 bales from the recently ginned '62 crop were hidden in a corncrib, and the rest was hidden away in different buildings. Just prior to the arrival of General Banks, he sold about 100 bales of cotton to the Confederate States to support his family. All payments were in Confederate money or bonds

About 150 bales were discovered by the Army, including those sold, but before they could be removed a group of rebel soldiers burned them up. The 32 hidden bales were seized in May 1863 and sent to Barre's Landing on Bayou Corlableau. Exorbitant shipping rates were charged in taking cotton from Barre's Landing to New Orleans, to Boston, then to New York. A total of 2,644 bales were shipped from Barre's Landing in 1863 and netted the Treasury $622,148.81 for an average of $235.26 a bale.

Martin had sent one of his sons to Europe for the duration, his loyalty was sufficiently sustained, and he recovered $7,427.52 on the 32 bales.

Martin, Milton.

Chartered his steamer *Sylvan Shore* at $200 a month. The rate was reduced to $100 a month and Martin sued for $24,750. His petition was dismissed since he accepted a settlement without formal protest.

Mason, William.

Mason's Taunton, Massachusetts works had built cotton machinery since 1842 and locomotives since 1852. On January 6, 1862 Assistant Secretary of War Thomas A. Scott requested the Chief of Ordnance, General James Ripley, to order 50,000 Springfield rifled muskets at $20 each from Mason of if he could make them in his own plant. Ripley ordered the guns plus 50,000 more. On May 30, the Holt-Owen Commission recommended amending the contract to 30,000. Mason asked for 75,000 but the Commission said 30,000 and he signed the new contract. He delivered 30,000, was paid for them, and then sued for $500,000 for breach of contract. His petition was dismissed on the ground that he accepted the new terms.

Massachusetts, State of. The State issued 5 percent war-loan bonds in 1861 to borrow money to raise troops, protect its harbors, and fortify its coast. The bonds were payable on July 1, 1871. Commonwealth law required paying the interest on State bonds in gold and silver coin but there was no federal or moral obligation to make payments in coin rather than in less expensive currency. A total of $886,389.68 in premiums for gold and silver coin was spent to pay the interest and principal on the bonds. In 1864, $1 in gold was worth $1.80 in greenbacks.

In 1863 the State borrowed $200,000 to fortify its coast. The State filed many claims with the Treasury Department to recover the principal. These were denied so the State petitioned Congress. The Treasury Department examined the claim, certified to Congress that the State spent $209,885.61, and the money was appropriated and paid.

On October 10, 1902 the State filed another claim with the Treasury Department to recover the interest it paid on the bonds issued to fortify the coast. That was rejected. The Act of July 27, 1861 authorized reimbursement to the States only for money expended to raise troops.

The State sued in federal court to recover the $886,389.68 premium it paid for gold and was awarded that on April 9, 1917 while the claim for interest and premium paid for coin for seacoast fortification bonds was dismissed. The court stated:

"If Massachusetts deemed it proper to protect her good reputation and credit for the future, no one could object, but surely she could not expect the Federal Government to pay the bill for a benefit so personal to herself. As well say that because she had a reputation for generosity to her citizens and, seeking to perpetuate it, she placed upon the breast of each of her soldiers a diamond pin. No one would deny her the right nor dispute the wisdom of such means of accomplishing her purpose; but who would say that a diamond pin was a necessary part of a soldier's equipment and a proper item for reimbursement under a statute agreeing to indemnify for 'expenses properly incurred in aiding to suppress the insurrection'?"

Mayers, Jacob. A Philadelphia merchant and sutler in the Army who employed his brother, David Mayers, an Atlanta merchant, to collect his large debts throughout the South and to invest what money he could collect as best he could. The debts were paid in Confederate money, which David had no way of converting to U.S. currency, so David bought 71 bales of Georgia cotton. David took 21 bales and stored them at his residence in Newman, Georgia but Jacob lost 50 bales when they were seized at Savannah in January 1864.

J. R. Hayes testified that Jacob Mayers resided in Philadelphia during the war and was loyal. Aaron Wilbur and C. B. Wesolowsky testified the claimants had clear title to the cotton. Mayers was awarded $9,523.50.

Means, Anne S. Thomas and Anne Means owned the 1,254-acre Means plantation on St. Helena Island, South Carolina. The State taxed 754 acres as usually cultivated land and the remaining 500 acres were taxed at 20 cents an acre as uncultivated land.

On March 12, 1863 the property was sold to pay $60.82 in U.S. direct taxes and on December 8, 1866 Anne purchased 160 acres of the plantation from the government for $1,850.

Thomas died in 1876 leaving Anne and a daughter. The daughter subsequently died without having children.

On February 1, 1892 Anne sued to recover $5 per acre under the Act of March 2, 1891 plus the $1,850 she paid to repurchase the 160 acres. On May 2 her claim was amended to drop the repurchase amount and on October 24 she was awarded $3,328.52 for 594 cultivated acres at $5 an acre and $1 per acre for 500 uncultivated acres.

She recovered the $1,850 on March 23, 1896.

Medway, Louisa C. A subject of Great Britain residing at Wilmington, North Carolina who owned 130 bales of cotton stored on the west bank of the Cape Fear River opposite Wilmington. The cotton was watched over by a man named Knox who felt indebted to Louisa for her assistance to his family during an outbreak of yellow fever. Knox put her cotton at the bottom of, and inside, a large pile of 1,000 to 1,500 bales to help insure its not being stolen or burned by rebels. On February 22, 1865 the pile was set on fire by rebels evacuating the city. The Army put out the fire and managed to save 400–500 bales from the pile including all of Louisa's. It was then seized and sent to New York and sold.

In court, Dr. Merriweather testified that she gave him hospital supplies and was very helpful at the North-East River hospital in caring for "about 4,000 hospital patients, United States prisoners and exchanged prisoners, as appeared on our rolls. We called them returned prisoners" and further stated:

"One of my officers on the Lenapee, since deceased, reported to me that during the war, he with many others was captured near New Berne, North Carolina and while waiting at the Wilmington, North Carolina depot for transportation to a southern prison, many of them wounded and sick and all in a half-starved condition, they were surrounded by a large crowd of insolent rebels who refused to give them food or refreshments of any kind, when the plaintiff discovered them and in opposition to the wishes of the crowd and their threats of personal violence, purchased a large quantity of provisions and gave them to the Union prisoners. This report was afterward verified by citizens of Wilmington, North Carolina.

"I know of her giving large quantities of medicines and provisions to the Union sick, wounded, and distressed, and that she did all in her power in behalf of the United States during my stay in the Cape Fear River.

"Three or four thousand sick prisoners from Columbia, South Carolina and Andersonville, Georgia arrived in the hospitals with various contagious and infectious diseases. She administered to them in every way in her power and was untiring in her attendance upon them, freely risking her life in the cause."

She also kept the sick in her home and helped them recover until they were able to travel north. She was serenaded by Union sailors at one time. After the war, she was "so shunned by the disloyal society of Wilmington that she was compelled to move to Illinois, where she still resides."

Unfortunately, someone else produced a letter she had written to Jefferson Davis dated February 10, 1865 in which she said she had offered her services to him in a letter dated January 2 but had received no response. She ended with:

"I am so sorry I could not have seen you, for I have much to tell, and do not dare to write, but it is now too late. I pray earnestly that you may have the strength to bear the burden and heat of this fervid day, your reward being the independence of this people, who, however they flag and falter now, have certainly sustained themselves against the most terrific odds and most vindictive adversary on record."

The courts noted that no one proved whose handwriting the letter was in or where it came from but apparently Louisa admitted to writing and signing it. It tested the rules of evidence but in the end the court dismissed her petition.

Meldrim, Ralph. Joint owner with James Doyle of 31 bales of cotton seized on March 23, 1865 from Doyle's storehouse at Bay and Whitacre Streets in Savannah. James moved to New York after Savannah was captured and applied for a presidential pardon. This was granted on October 18, 1865 but he died on October 27 never having formally accepted it as the law required. He was survived by his wife, Margaret, who joined Meldrim in a suit to recover the cotton proceeds.

Margaret's petition was dismissed and Meldrim was awarded $2,717.61.

Meriwether, Elizabeth Avery. On March 10, 1862 Minor Meriwether's property in Memphis was seized and on that day he executed a deed-poll to his wife, which said, in part:

"Being desirous to provide for the comfortable support of my wife and children, and the liberal education of the latter, I convey to my wife, Lizzie Avery Meriwether, all the following described property, viz: One lot of ground containing 4.29 acres, more or less, lying east of Memphis, adjoining the lot upon which W. B. Waldron now resides, known as lot No. 6 of the Harvey subdivision of a part of the Rice grant, being the same which I purchased of A. Fike and Elizabeth Fike on 24 October, 1853 ... one lot of ground, containing 4.96 acres, more or less, or Kerr avenue, south of Memphis, known as lot No. 2 of Stewart and Latham subdivision, being the same which I purchased of Louis Selby, on 27 April 1860 ... one lot of ground fronting 69 feet on Jefferson street, Memphis; on' fronting 74 feet on Second street, known as part of lot 258 on the plan of the city of Memphis, being the same which I purchased of L. P. Carathers, on the 9th April, 1859 ... my half interest in one lot of ground fronting 39¾ feet on Jefferson street, and fronting 74 feet on Second alley ... being the same purchased by A. M. Clayton and myself of Charles Jones, on 13 December 1859 ... one lot of ground on the north side of Union street, Memphis, which I purchased of S. H. Lamb, Estelle Lamb, and Wm. T. Avery, trustee, on the 10th

March, 1857 ... one lot of ground on Union street, Memphis, which I purchased of Wm. Farris on 23rd March, 1857 ... one lot of ground, being a part of the old Union street, Memphis, which I purchased of S. H. Lamb on 24th July, 1855. All of the above described seven pieces of ground are in Shelby County, Tennessee. I also give and hereby convey to my wife, Lizzie Avery Meriwether, the following named Negroes, viz: One negro man named Henson, light-black color, aged about 20 years; one negro woman named Louise, light-black color, aged about 18 years; one negro woman named Rose, black color, aged about 20 years; one negro child of woman Rose, aged about four months. All the above-described land and negroes I give to my wife, Lizzie Avery Meriwether ... But I require as a condition of this gift that my wife shall pay at its maturity my note given to my brother, Owen Meriwether, for $6,200, due 3d July, 1865, with six percent. interest per annum from 3d July 1860. And if my wife should die intestate, then all this property, with its increase or its proceeds and reinvestments, if she shall have disposed of it, shall revert to me; or, if I am dead, it shall descend to our children; and if they be dead also, leaving no child or children, then my brother shall inherit it."

The will was witnessed by S. H. and Estelle Lamb.

After the property was seized the Army collected rents amounting to $2,166.71 and after September 30, 1864 rent amounting to $1,329.55 was collected by the Treasury Department for a total of $3,496.26 which was paid into the abandoned or captured property fund.

Elizabeth sued to recover the rents with her husband as co-claimant. There was no statute in Tennessee which gave a wife the right to hold property and to sue or be sued but in practice she could own real or personal property without the need of a trustee and obtain property from her husband "as from a third person." The court held the deed valid and Elizabeth recovered $3,496.26 in 1877.

Minor Meriwether's petition was dismissed.

Merrill, Lewis.

Merrill was a captain in the regular army when the war started and left to become colonel of the 2d Regiment Missouri Volunteer Cavalry known as Merrill's Horse. He served until December 1865 and returned to regular service. His lawsuit was in the class of

officers who held commissions in the regular army, retained their rank upon discharge from volunteer service, and sought the three months' pay bounty authorized by the Act of March 3, 1865. Congress recognized early in 1865 the war was all but won and felt it necessary to induce volunteer officers to remain in the service for the final push. If enough officers left, it might reduce the regular ranks to below levels necessary to win the war so they offered three months' extra pay for staying in.

Specific requirements stated, "all officers of volunteers below the rank of brigadier general" who were in service on March 3, 1865 and whose resignations were presented and accepted, or who were mustered out at their own request, or otherwise honorably discharged from the service after April 9, 1865 pursuant to the Act of July 13, 1866.

Merrill was one of several hundred regular officers in volunteer units who believed the offer pertained to them as well. By 1867, most of the officers entitled to the benefit had been paid but Colonel Merrill's claim was rejected on the ground that he was an officer in the regular army and not a volunteer.

He sued and the government's deputy solicitor stated, "He left his regiment and sought, as a personal privilege, to be transferred to the volunteer service, with its added rank and its increased pay." A volunteer cavalry regiment was just then being formed at St. Louis and he was welcomed by the commanding general and the governor of Missouri. Merrill was technically on furlough and "his continuing absence only winked at," and "he was never merged, nor was this officer capable of freeing himself for an instant from his obligations in the regular army. He was not of those to whom any bonus or premium could be offered to induce him to continue in the military services until the end of the war. He could not be mustered out of the service in any legal sense so as to become entitled to any such extra three months' pay. It would be a mere gratuity in his case and an unauthorized illegal addition to his pay and emoluments in the regular service, into which he at once leaped on throwing off this anomalous colonelship."

The court stated in response:

"The statement that Colonel Merrill was, when the war commenced, and is an officer of the regular army is not denied. But we fail to see how that fact can affect his right of recovery. The law was made for 'officers of volunteers' at the time when the law was passed, namely, March 3, 1865. At that time Colonel Merrill was in commission as an officer of volunteers, duly mustered. His pay and emoluments were never questioned. His rank was universally conceded. He was in active military service as a volunteer officer only. He had no pay in the regular service, and no functions of an officer to discharge therein.

"To insist that the claimant was an officer in the regular service, when he had ceased to act or be paid as such, is only equaled in absurdity by the converse proposition that he was not in the volunteer service after he had been regularly commissioned and mustered therein.

"Had the Congress intended to prohibit officers of the regular army who were commissioned in the volunteer service from participating in the benefits of this law, why did it not give expression to that intention? There is no exception."

The court recognized the validity of the government's argument and the significance of the claims by regular officers. Merrill was awarded $330 on the ground that the government could appeal the decision to the Supreme Court but Merrill could not, owing to the small amount of money involved.

The government appealed to the Supreme Court where the judgement was reversed on the ground that his military service continued uninterrupted as either a regular or volunteer.

Mezeix, Justine. Marguerite (Margaret) Justine Belhomme Marchand Benoist, 44, a native of Angouleme, France, was a milliner who purchased a store with residence above at 88 Main Street in Natchez, Mississippi on June 15, 1858 from Corrina E. Miller for $3,576.

On December 2, 1860 she married her third husband, Claudius Mezeix, a native of Lyon, France and late of New York. Claudius was in the business of buying and selling cotton. When the war started Justine's business dropped off so she rented the premises to another milliner, Eliza C. Elbingham and Mrs. Pfister. She and Claudius moved to Blowburn Cottage on the 80-acre Blowburn plantation on Old Palestine Road outside the picket lines about 4 miles from Natchez near Washington, Mississippi.

Natchez was occupied in July 1863. The store and residence was seized on August 1, 1864 on the ground that Claudius and Justine had contributed flags and uniforms to the Confederacy and later that month Claudius was found to be in possession of a packet of letters addressed to Confederate authorities. He was arrested, jailed for two weeks, fined $1,000, and his horse and buggy were confiscated by Major George D. Reynolds, provost marshal at Natchez. Claudius was also banned from Natchez for about six months.

Elbingham and Mrs. Phister were evicted and the Army rented the property to Goldman & Aiken (Akin), dry goods merchants, and William J. Morgan for $100 a month. Justine made repeated, unsuccessful attempts to retrieve her property on the ground that she was a French subject. She received no rent money or compensation for the use of her property.

The mortgage holder on Justine's property was Patrick H. McGraw, owner of an adjoining drug store on Main Street. Justine was allegedly ordered to satisfy the mortgage by General Mason Brayman at Natchez and when Claudius was away from home she appealed to Charles Findlay to assist her in paying off the $2,767.16 debt. Findlay asked McGraw if he would accept "greenbacks"—U.S. Treasury notes—but he refused saying he preferred "the security of his mortgage to the money offered him." Apparently this resulted in a civil suit between the parties and when Brayman heard of this on December 2, 1864 he declared the Mezeixes and McGraw disloyal and ordered the $2,767.16 paid into the Treasury.

On February 24, 1865 Claudius, 40, was reportedly shot and killed by McGraw on Washington Road about 3 miles from Natchez.

In the summer of 1865 William J. Lyle, Justine's agent, took over the rental of the property for her occupation and use. The rent was $50 a month, later raised to $100. The property was returned to her on October 1, 1865. Justine sold the property to Abraham Meyer on March 9, 1866 for $6,000 and then sought to recover the mortgage loan money from the Treasury. She couldn't prove the money was hers, her petition was dismissed, and Charles Findlay was awarded $2,767.16 in 1870.

Justine died on July 31, 1879 in Natchez.

Millar, William S. An Irish subject of Great Britain who resided at the British consulate in New Orleans.

W. M. Burnet, assistant special U.S. Treasury agent in Natchez, deputized A. Van Camp on January 14, 1864 to purchase 250 bales of cotton in Claiborne, Jefferson, Wilkinson, and Adams Counties in Mississippi within 30 days. His permit was renewed from time to time after that to make other purchases.

In May Millar purchased 60 bales of cotton from A. W. Sutphin's plantation in Jefferson County and on the 13th he registered his property at the consulate. Sometime in early June he purchased 44 bales from Mrs. Valentine and another lot of cotton from Judge Baldwin, both plantation owners in Claiborne County.

On June 6 Millar obtained a permit from Burnet to purchase 500 bales of cotton in Jefferson and Claiborne Counties and to bring it out via the Mississippi River to New Orleans.

On June 27 he registered 140 bales he had purchased and stored on Judge Baldwin's plantation and 92 bales on Mrs. Valentine's place. Millar claimed he made all these purchases under his permit.

On June 13 he had contracted to purchase 140 bales of cotton in Jefferson County but "owing to the unsettled condition of the country" he could not immediately remove it to New Orleans. The cotton was stored about 16 miles from the river.

On July 15 1864 Van Camp appointed William Millar as his agent to buy cotton.

On February 23, 1865, 100 bales of Millar's Jefferson County cotton were brought to Cole's Creek Landing and put aboard the steamer *Mittie Stephens*. The other 40 bales were brought to Rodney and picked up there. Millar was aboard the steamer to take charge of his cargo and it was received in New Orleans by his agent, George Coppel, who was also the acting British consul at New Orleans.

On March 2 and 14, 40 bales were sold to O. N. Cutler, the U.S. purchasing agent at New Orleans for 70 cents a pound and on the 17th 100 bales were sold at 63 cents a pound for a total of $25,563.50. Coppel was required to pay a drawback tax of 25 percent of the gross proceeds, which amounted to $13,614.24.

Coppel protested but was told the money was for deposit into the captured and abandoned property fund. Millar sued to recover claiming duress and the fact that he bought the Jefferson County cotton on Van Camp's permit but his petition was dismissed.

Miller, Cornelius B. Miller and J. B. Fellows were in the clothing business in New York as C. B. Miller & Co. and in Mobile as J. B. Fel-lows & Co. When the war started, Fellows sold out his stock and bought 100 bales of upland cotton. When Union forces were approaching Mobile the rebels wanted to burn all the cotton. That caused an uproar so permission was given to remove any cotton 100 miles into the interior. The cotton was moved upriver, hid, and then brought back to Mobile where it was seized on May 12, 1863.

Miller's loyalty was unquestioned and Fellows was able to prove his night service in the home guard at Mobile was involuntary and forced upon him and the duty was of a police rather than a military nature and they recovered $18,825.

Mills, Thomas R. A buying and shipping merchant at Savannah in partnership with his brothers J. G. and Charles F., president of the Marine Bank. They were compelled to sell their ships owing to the blockade. One was in port, the others overseas. The proceeds were invested in 751 bales of cotton that was captured at Savannah.

The court noted they were singled out as strong Union men by the Rattlesnake Club but weren't bothered. Thomas and J. G. both subscribed $1,000 to the Confederate loan and the Marine Bank loaned $200,000 to the Confederate government but these were excused as being under duress.

Witnesses said the captain of a British ship was "tarred and feathered for showing favor to a Negro man" in Savannah, a Yankee schoolmaster was tarred and feathered, and another man received 100 lashes and sent north in critical condition.

The Mills brothers recovered $131,146.84.

Mims, Aseriah. Administrator of the estate of Jacob Redwine, owner of two bales of cotton weighing 695 pounds seized at Atlanta. Although Redwine's three sons were in the Confederate army, two as officers, Jacob was proven loyal and Mims recovered $719.88.

Minor, Rebecca A. G. Wife of William J. Minor and owners of the Hollywood and Southern sugar plantations in Terrebone Parish, Louisiana. They had 354 hogsheads of sugar, 900 barrels of molasses, and 523 molasses barrels seized. William died after the war and Rebecca recovered $20,481.71 on 241 hogsheads of molasses and on 640 barrels.

Mintz & Fass. Joseph Mintz, a Russian naturalized citizen, and Simon Fass, an Austrian, were Charleston merchants. They claimed 13 bales of cotton seized at No. 489 King Street and 13 bales seized in Saint Bartholomew's Parish: 7 at Risher's plantation and 6 at Willis's plantation. They were credited $1,443.20 on 10 bales of upland and 1 bale of sea-island cotton.

Mix, James. Deputized by the Treasury Department in June 1862 to buy cotton. He bought 300 bales from Robert W. Smith for delivery at Grand Junction, Tennessee but prior to delivery rebel forces burned all but 24 or 25 bales. The original deal was cancelled and they agreed on a price of 30 cents a pound for the remaining bales. This was seized by the Army and Mix recovered $5,378.27.

Molina, Ramon and Francis E. Citizens of Spain who operated a store in the Scriven House in Savannah and who owned 24 bales of upland cotton stored in the cellar there. It was seized on February 25, 1865 and sold in New York. They recovered $4,207.92.

Montgomery, Robert H. A British subject, businessman, and resident of New Orleans since 1845. On July 17, 1862 he took the oath of allegiance pursuant to General Benjamin Butler's Order No. 41 of May 6, 1862.

On September 9 he purchased all the sugar, molasses, and rum from J. W. Burbridge & Co. of New Orleans, the agent for Leo L. Johnson's Lafourche Parish plantation known locally as the "Webster place." Johnson was a resident of Arkansas and owed Burbridge $130,000 for loans and supplies.

On November 9, General Butler ordered the sugar seized and taken to New Orleans via the Baton Rouge, Grosse Tete & Opelousas Railroad in two separate shipments. Montgomery could not provide proof of his identity at New Orleans so the goods were sold and the net proceeds of the first lot, 426 hogsheads at $37,351.49, were paid into the Treasury but the $22,018.97 second lot proceeds on 278 hogsheads were turned over to him. Montgomery sued for the first lot but his petition was dismissed based on technicalities involving weighing and measuring pursuant to Louisiana laws on the transfer of property and as a violation of the Non-Intercourse Act.

Moore, Lida. Lida was a minor whose mother died in 1853, her 8-year-old brother in 1858, and her father, William Moore, in May 1861. She inherited a plantation in Newton County, Mississippi on which 59 bales of cotton were stored.

Joseph G. Moore, Lida's uncle and administrator of her father's estate, attempted to sell the cotton to Charles Baskerville, a Confederate cotton agent, but the sale was never completed because Mississippi law prohibited property belonging to a minor to be sold by a guardian or the administrator of an estate without authorization from a probate court and no court order was ever obtained.

In June 1865 the cotton was seized. Her new guardian, Oliver H. Long, a resident of Drake County, Illinois until 1866, filed suit on her behalf. Apparently he was known to the family and was appointed guardian because he was loyal to the Union and could successfully sue to recover the $5,640.50 Lida was awarded in 1871.

Moore, Sophia B. William P. Moore, Sr., his daughter Sophia, and her brother, William P. Moore, Jr., lived in New Berne, North Carolina.

On July 10, 1862 the Treasury Department seized the Moore property, rented it out, and $2,547.50 in revenue was subsequently paid into the Treasury. Commodore Stephen Rowan seized 2,000 barrels of rosin and 50 casks of turpentine, put them in with a large lot, shipped the lot to New York, and filed a libel in the U.S. District Court as a lawful prize of war on behalf of the United States. A man named Ellis claimed ownership of the whole lot and it was released to him.

William, Jr. died in October 1864 and left a will bequeathing everything after debts and funeral expenses to Sophia. Sophia was still a minor and her father was appointed her guardian. He subsequently died and John Hughes was appointed. Sophia sued in 1868 to recover $13,497.50 on the goods sold into the Treasury under the Act of March 12, 1863 but her suit was dismissed on the ground that the proceeds from property captured on land by naval and land forces, removed to a loyal state, libeled prior to the Act of July 17, 1862 and sold could not be recovered under the abandoned and captured property act.

Sophia married Charles Duffy and on September 11, 1888 she petitioned Congress for relief. Her case was referred to federal court for fact finding where she presented a complete claim:

2,000 barrels of rosin	$40,000
50 casks, spirits turpentine	2,500
28 barrels of tar	140

10,000 barrels of rosin	100,000
43 months' rent of hotel stables	8,000
43 months' rent of distillery	4,300
43 months' rent of Gaston House	12,000
43 months' rent of three warehouses	43,000
43 months' rent of seven houses and lots	5,000
43 months' rent of house	4,300
	$223,240

Large quantities of turpentine were shipped from New Berne to New York and Philadelphia and condemned as prize. Rosin sold at auction for an average price of $7.46 per barrel and turpentine $7 per barrel.

On April 29, 1889 she recovered $15,270 on 2,000 barrels of rosin, the 50 casks of turpentine, and no rent money.

Mordecai, Moses C. A resident of Charleston, South Carolina who contracted on October 3, 1860 to deliver mail between Charleston, and Key West, Florida via Savannah, Georgia with his steamer *Isabel* twice a month for $40,000 a year from October 15 to June 30, 1864. The contract provided, "that the Post Master-General may curtail or discontinue the service in the whole or in part, he allowing one month's extra pay on the amount dispensed with."

South Carolina seceded on December 20, 1860, Florida on January 10, 1861. Mail service became disorganized prior to the secession of the Southern states but most routes on U.S. contracts remained open until the Confederate government became fully organized.

On January 2, 1861 First Assistant Post Master-General Horatio King notified Mordecai the route was being discontinued and he would receive the extra pay. The *Isabel*'s last trip commenced December 31, 1860 from Key West and ended January 4, 1861 at Charleston.

Mordecai was never paid any money from Richmond and no money was forthcoming from Washington. He remained in Charleston until July 1865 and filed a claim in 1881 pursuant to the Act of March 3, 1877.

He filed suit on January 16, 1883, the accounting officers figured he was owed $3,333.33, but his suit was dismissed by statute of limitation and because he continued service for 13 days after South Carolina seceded.

Morgan, Thomas P. Owner of the steamer *Tappahannock* who signed a charter agreement at Brazos, St. Igao, Texas on March 1, 1865 for $182.25 a day. In July she was loaded with a cargo for New Orleans and a government

pilot was put aboard. The quartermaster ordered the vessel to sea but it was low tide so she was put under tow of a government tugboat to drag over the bar. The master and pilot both protested that the vessel could pass over the bar only at high tide but the quartermaster ordered the vessels out. The tug passed over but the steamer struck and the towline parted. The *Tappahannock* returned to port damaged and the quartermaster ordered another attempt. This time the tug was able to drag the steamer over the bar but caused great damage and she had to be escorted all the way to New Orleans.

She was drydocked at New Orleans on August 5 and emergency repairs continued around the clock for 20 days since there was an urgent need for transports. Complete repairs were made from November 8 to December 4, 25½ days. Only partial payment was made on the repairs and Morgan sued for $8,833.21. The court ruled the vessel's damage was due to marine risk, not war risk, and the petition was dismissed.

Morse Arms Manufacturing Co. A company organized in New York City on February 17, 1848. In 1856 George W. Morse, of Louisiana, was awarded patent No. 15995 for a breech-loading musket, patent No. 15996 for a "metallic cartridge intended to be used as a gas check," and later, patent No. 20503 for a cartridge extraction mechanism.

Morse brought his weapon to the attention of the War and Navy Departments and on March 5, 1857 Colonel Craig, chief of ordnance, advised Major William H. Bell, commander of the Washington Arsenal, that Morse would bring his civilian-marketed gun in for evaluation. Bell reported the weapon's machinery was complicated but might be as useful for military purposes as it was for civilians.

On August 12 a board of officers met at West Point to evaluate and test various breech-loading rifles and to decide which was the most suitable for military use. The board found that "the breech-loading rifle submitted by A. E. Burnside, of Rhode Island, is suited for military service." Ambrose E. Burnside was an Army officer who resigned his commission to work on his inventions.

Morse wrote to Secretary of War John B. Floyd on November 12:

> Now, sir, I only await your leisure, and from your known knowledge of firearms confidently expect to prove to you the truth of my assertion that mine is the best gun in the world.

On December 9 Secretary Floyd wrote to Colonel Craig:

The colonel of ordnance will direct Maj. William H. Bell to have a gun made at the Washington Arsenal upon the plan of Mr. Morse's gun after either of the patents which have been exhibited, or a combination of them, the work to be executed under the supervision of Mr. Morse himself, if he chooses.

On January 27, 1858 Colonel Craig requested Morse to send one of his guns, with ammunition, to Lieutenant General Scott for testing.

On February 26 Morse wrote to the board of officers to use brass cartridges as "I do not depend upon the gun for a tight joint at the breech, but upon the cartridge, which seals it perfectly, and is renewable after each discharge, so that it can never wear out."

On March 5 Secretary Floyd ordered 100 of Morse's guns at $40 each to be paid for in lots of 25.

In May Floyd requested the House Committee on Military Affairs to recommend a $100,000 appropriation to modify old muskets and rifles into breech-loading weapons. An act was passed on June 12 to appropriate $20,000 for breech loading guns. Morse was paid, and $2,500 was paid to William Mont Storm to modify 2,000 breech-loading guns using his ideas.

On August 5 the board of officers that met at West Point reported to Secretary Floyd that they had picked Morse's gun:

"Inasmuch as it differs from the others by including the new and untried principles of a primed metallic cartridge, which may, on actual trial, be found of advantage."

On September 9 Morse authorized the War Department to modify 2,500 old guns using his plans for $5 each. Secretary Floyd accepted the offer for 2,000 guns and wrote:

Let Mr. Morse have an order for three United States flintlock muskets, of the latest model, and for three United States percussion rifles, seven groves, to alter after his plan, for patterns. When these patterns are ready let an order be given for the alteration, according to the pattern arms, of 2,000 muskets of the same model at either United States armory, as he may designate. The arms so altered to be rifled and sighted at the armory, and Mr. Morse to have the privilege of superintending the process of alteration and to be required to state that the work is done in a satisfactory manner to him before the altered arms are issued for trial. Let a written grant of the privilege to alter 2,000 arms at the rate proposed be obtained from

Mr. Morse, payment to be made to him ($10,000) out of the special appropriation when the agreement is signed, which agreement is to include all his patent privileges.

On September 13 Morse wrote:

In consideration of the sum of $10,000, paid to me by warrant on the Treasury of the United States, I hereby grant, sell, and convey to the said United States the right and privilege to alter 2,000 of the muskets now belonging to the United States.

On February 6, 1859 Morse and a man named Anderson wrote to Secretary Floyd about changing the order to 100 carbines at $40 each and "instead of it to sell the Government the right to manufacture 1,000 carbines according to the particular plan thereof which has been applied in the alteration of the United States rifles" for a fee of $3 per gun. This offer was accepted on the 9th and Morse forwarded a license.

Sixty of Morse's guns were made prior to November 12, 1859 and he was paid $13,000.

In February 1861 Morse wrote to Jefferson Davis:

In pursuance of my understanding with you respecting the machinery for arms, I shall have the satisfaction of knowing that my exertion and honest endeavors to benefit the Confederacy will be crowned with success.

In March he wrote to Leroy P. Walker, Confederate Secretary of War:

If success does not attend the efforts now being made for the establishment of a Southern armory, these arms can be manufactured in Europe or anywhere else at about the same cost as those of the ordinary kind. I shall be happy to make a trial of them before you at any time you may indicate.

P.S.— It seems to me the adoption of a single plan of breechloader, with one caliber, for both the army and navy, would be advantageous.

On April 6 he wrote to J. C. Grubb & Co. about making 1,000 Morse guns in Europe for the State of Texas:

I enclose you a circular in reference to this gun, and I doubt not that if I can get its manufacture under way that any number of them will be sold in the South, where some models of it have been in use for sometime past by Major McColloch, and shown all over the country.

On April 11 Morse left Washington for Louisiana.

On July 18 he wrote:

Hon. L. Pope Walker
Secretary of War, C. S.
Sir: In accordance with your suggestion, I submit the following as a list of machines which I hope to obtain for the purposes set forth in a letter

from the governor of the State of Tennessee to his excellency President Davis:

1 trip hammer, with such special tools for welding gun barrels as are at hand; 2 small planers; 1 screw machine; 1 cone machine; 2 small lathes; 1 profiling machine; 2 drilling machines with 3 or 4 spindles each; 8 milling machines; 1 rifling machine; 1 nut-boring machine; 1 smooth-boring machine; 1 barrel-turning lathe; 1 punching press; 1 horizontal milling machine for ramrods; 1 old breech-screw cutting machine; 1 old index machine.

It is the loan of these tools only which is asked for, the value of which may be fairly estimated at from eight to ten thousand dollars. There are several good reasons why the request should be granted, and one of them is, that under the representations of Gen'l Polk that it would be done, the State of Tennessee has purchased buildings and grounds for an armory.

Another is that at Nashville workmen from Louisville and St. Louis are easily obtained to duplicate them and make more of the same kind.

Still another reason is, that the State has purchased large supplies of war material, and the Confederate Government has not only already availed itself of a part in this in the form of percussion caps, but will want large supplies of powder from her mills. All of which is respectively submitted for your consideration.

I am, sir, your ob't servant,

Geo. W. Morse
Supt. Tenn. Armory

The patent for the cartridge expired on October 28 1870 but Congress extended the patent term for the gun to November 29, 1879. Between July 10, 1875 and November 29, 1879 the War Department modified or manufactured 54,864 breech-loading guns.

Morse sued for patent infringement claiming he "the lawful patentee of a device for sealing a breech joint of a breech-loading gun, purposely made open, by the expansion of a yielding metallic cartridge case, purposely made to fit loosely in the chamber." The court determined $1 per gun and 25 cents per gun for the ejection mechanism would be reasonable royalties.

Comparisons were made between a Confederate Morse gun built on his original patents captured during the war, the Springfield rifle, Model 1856 and 1873, and a Winchester repeating rifle. On June 20, 1892 the court found the state of the art in 1856 would not support patents for an expanding metal cartridge in a breech-loading gun or a cartridge extracting mechanism especially when compared with the Lefaucheux sporting gun. The inventions lacked novelty and Morse's petition was dismissed.

Mott, John N. John owned 53 bales of cotton stored in a warehouse at Mobile that was seized on May 13, 1865 and sold in New York for an average of $183.33 a bale. His loyalty was proved and he was awarded $9,716.49.

Mott, John W. Mott's agent chartered his small steamer, the *Washington Irving,* to General Marsena A. Patrick, Provost-Marshal General of the Army of the Potomac, on August 9, 1864 to use her as a dispatch boat. The Army provided war risk insurance on the boat and Mott bore the marine risk insurance.

On December 26, General Sharpe, assistant provost marshal, ordered the vessel to depart from City Point on the James River and go upstream on a very dark night in dense fog to Bermuda Hundred with urgent messages. The master, first assistant engineer, and chief engineer were not available. A government pilot and the second assistant engineer were aboard and they protested, believing the trip to be very hazardous.

Sharpe had information that "the rebels were about to turn the line of the Army," a situation he considered urgent, so he ordered the vessel to get underway immediately. The *Irving* had a lookout posted and was going ahead slow but a wrecked canal boat drifting down with the current was unseen and it smashed into the steamer's port bow.

Both insurers declined to pay. Mott petitioned Congress and the claim was referred to a federal court. In 1874 the court ruled that Mott's vessel had been hired to carry dispatches and the proximate cause of the wreck was entirely a marine risk.

Mott, Randolph. Joint owner with Edward Padelford of 1,293 bales of cotton stored at Savannah. The cotton was seized, sent to Simeon Draper, the cotton agent at New York on 11 different vessels, sold at auction, and $246,277.71— $190.47 a bale — in net proceeds were deposited into the Treasury.

At the trial, Thomas M. Hogan, Columbus, Georgia postmaster, said Mott told him he would "prefer to give up all his slaves rather than that the Union should be dissolved." Mott apparently had declared that the four acres of his residence in Columbus had not seceded and this was "the talk of the town." Hogan said Mott had been a mail contractor prior to the war but refused to carry Confederate mail.

General James H. Wilson, who captured

Columbus, testified that he knew of Mott as a loyal Union man. He said the eldest of Mott's two sons was a lieutenant in the Confederate service, out of a sense of duty, "having been educated at a military school in Georgia" but Mott took his other son out of a military company and sent him to Europe before the war.

Each owner received $123,138.85.

Mount, Elijah. Owned a plantation and gin house on Mount's Bayou, Issaquena County, Mississippi. On March 31, 1868 Mrs. Mount filed a claim to recover the loss of five bales of cotton seized in August 1863. On January 6, 1874 it was shown that the cotton was owned by Elijah and a motion was filed to make him the claimant through his administrator, William G. Mount. By that time the two-year statute of limitations on suits under the Act of March 12, 1863 had expired and the petition was dismissed.

Mowry, Albert L. The Pacific Railroad of Missouri did not have the number of cars needed for immediately transporting troops and supplies in Missouri. On September 22, 1861 Mowry signed a $76,250 contract with Quartermaster McKinstry to build 50 boxcars and 50 platform cars delivered to the tracks of the railroad company. Fifty cars were to be delivered in 18 days and the other 50 in 30 days.

The Davis-Holt-Campbell Commission reduced the amount to $58,750, which was paid to Mowry under protest. Mowry sued and recovered $17,500.

Murphy, John. A merchant in business with Patrick O'Neil in Charleston as Murphy & O'Neil. During the war they owned 14 bales of cotton and 30 barrels of turpentine stored at Kennedy's farm near Charleston. It was seized after the war and sold for $2,501.86. Patrick left Charleston some time before the city was captured and was a government employee at Hilton Head, South Carolina when he died. Murphy recovered the money in 1878.

Murphy, William R. Mustered in as first lieutenant of Company F, 29th Pennsylvania Volunteers on September 10, 1861. Two or three days before the Battle of Ball's Bluff, Major General Banks ordered Colonel Murphy, commander of the regiment, to appoint an officer as acting commissary of subsistence and one enlisted man as clerk. Murphy and Joseph E. Sailer of Company G were detailed to the duty. They were temporarily stationed at Camp Muddy

Branch near Darnestown, Maryland where Murphy was put in charge of the beef cattle. He sold hides, tallow and byproducts, food to the officers, and purchased supplies.

They moved to Frederick City on December 2 and left there on February 22, 1862. On the 24th his command "took the field," was constantly on the move, and as a result his quarterly reports to Washington were delayed. He and Sailer kept their records as best they could.

On May 24 his train was captured in Frederick County, Maryland and he lost vouchers for herding, forage, and payroll amounting to $4,006.04, and $60.99 in cash. Murphy was personally assessed with damages of $4,003.60 and sued under the Act of May 6, 1866. Sailer testified:

"We started on the march about half-past eight and about 1 o'clock the rebel cavalry cut the train in two and seized our wagons between Middletown and Newtown. I was present at the capture and saw it myself. I was alongside of the wagon. This wagon had our mess, desk, and Captain Murphy's trunk containing $341. I saw Captain Murphy place this money in the trunk. He remarked, 'It would be safer here than on my person.' We had the night previous counted how much money belonged to the government and found it to be $60.99. This desk contained every voucher and paper that belonged to the department from the time Captain Murphy was detailed."

Murphy recovered $4,003.60.

Murray, Charles E. John Murray owned a lot in Beaufort, South Carolina the U.S. Direct Tax Commission assessed at $1,000. The $16 tax, $8 penalty, and $1.49 in interest was not paid so the lot was condemned and sold to the United States. John died leaving his wife Isabella and their minor children Walter L., Charles E., and Anna, and James, an adult son.

The lot was sold to Isabella Murray for $1,505 and a surplus of $1,489 was deposited into the Treasury. Isabella, James, and Anna died leaving Walter L. and Charles E. Murray. Walter died leaving his wife Julia M. Murray and a minor child, Walter L. Murray.

Charles sued to recover the surplus under the Act of March 2, 1891 and was awarded $1,489 on May 28, 1894.

Myers, Abraham C. General David E. Twiggs was a native of Georgia who distinguished himself during the War of 1812 and the

Mexican War. After the Mexican War Congress presented him with a sword for his faithful service and shortly afterwards the State of Georgia and the City of Augusta, Georgia followed suit, each presenting him with a sword.

Twiggs joined the Confederate army and was at New Orleans when Major General Benjamin Butler's forces closed in. He had his 7-year-old son, John Washington Twiggs, from his first marriage in 1854, and the two fled on the morning of April 25, 1862. Before he left New Orleans he wrote a note to a 19-year-old girl in the presence of her mother and other witnesses:

I leave my swords to Miss Rowena Florance and box of silver.

D. E. Twiggs

N. O. 25th April, 1862

The silver belonged to his family and came mostly from his first wife's father.

General Butler received information that Twiggs had fled the city and left his swords and silver with a young woman. She was soon located and brought before Butler. After initial resistance and protest Rowena produced the swords and the silver. Butler sent them to President Lincoln "to be placed in public possession, as a memorial of Federal success." Technically, they were "passed to the United States as munitions of war"—instead of abandoned or captured property and out of reach of the provisions for recovery under the Act of March 12, 1863—"and it was left to the sovereign grace of the Government to determine what should be the disposition of them ultimately."

In 1869 Rowena filed an unsuccessful suit in a New York court against General Butler to recover the swords. None of the Twiggs heirs came forward to claim them until 1878.

Rowena married Joseph Guedalla, a London solicitor. On March 3, 1887 Congress authorized President Cleveland to return the "Twiggs swords" to their rightful owner and directed Secretary of the Treasury Charles S. Fairchild to deliver the swords to whoever the owner was at the time they were seized after fact finding by a federal court.

Twiggs had fled via the Mississippi to Augusta, Georgia where he died on September 16, 1862. Twiggs had a daughter, Marion, by his first wife who married Colonel Abraham C. Myers in 1887. Myers was executor of Twiggs's estate and guardian of his minor child. He filed a claim on March 15, 1887 followed by Rowena Guedalla on the 31st. She was then living in London and

her letter claiming them as a gift arrived on April 19. John Washington Twiggs claimed the swords as heir.

Rowena knew Twiggs through her friend, Belinda Adams, a schoolmate and the niece of Twiggs's second wife. The second wife died in 1855 and Belinda died in 1861. Marion lived with her father and her half-brother after 1855 and there apparently was little, if any, social contact between her and Rowena. In March 1862 Marion went to Virginia.

The court had to decide if the swords were delivered to Rowena under a bailment for safe-keeping or were a gift. The General's motive for turning them over to a 19-year-old girl—possibly his mistress—was questioned. The court decided on May 13, 1889 that Twiggs was the owner of the swords when they were captured and it was certified to the Secretary of the Treasury that they should be turned over to Colonel Myers for the benefit of the heirs.

Myers, Adam. Sergeant in Company F, 3d Missouri State Militia Cavalry. On June 10, 1864 the company's captain, George L. Herring, died. On August 6, First Lieutenant James M. Roberts was promoted by the governor of Missouri to captain retroactive to July 8 and Sergeant Myers was commissioned first lieutenant. Myers was never mustered in as first lieutenant but served in that rank and performed all the duties of it until April 14, 1865 when he was mustered out of the service.

During this entire time, both the regiment and Company F were below the minimum personnel levels authorized for a captain and first lieutenant under the Act of March 3, 1863.

General Order No. 96 of November 7, 1861 stated, in part:

"Authority to raise a force of State Militia, to serve during the war, is granted by direction of the President, to the governor of the State of Missouri. This force is to co-operate with the troops in the service of the United States in repelling the invasion of the State of Missouri and in suppressing rebellion therein. It is to be held, in camp and in the field, drilled, disciplined, and governed, according to the Regulations of the United States Army and subject to the Articles of War. But it is not to be ordered out of the State of Missouri, except for the immediate defense of the said State."

The troops were to be "armed, equipped, clothed, subsisted, transported, and paid" by the

United States in accordance with regulations. The field officers of a regiment authorized and appointed by the governor, were one colonel, one lieutenant colonel, and one major. A company had one captain, and one first and one second lieutenant.

On March 3, 1865 the Missouri State Militia had 158 commissioned officers who remained in the service until April 9, 1865. One of the 158 had been dismissed from the service on June 30, 1863. Prior to the Act of June 3, 1884, 65 commissioned officers of the Missouri State Militia received three months' additional pay authorized by the Act of March 3, 1865. Myers was paid $575.35 for his service. The total pay of a first lieutenant of cavalry for the same service time, including the additional mustering out pay, would have been $1,258.98. Myers sued for the difference but he waited a little too long.

Myers's petition was dismissed on April 27, 1885 since he was commissioned after June 20, 1863 pursuant to the Act of June 3, 1884.

Nelson, Elisha. Nelson, John G. Owen, and Richard G. Thomas claimed to own a large number of bales of cotton seized by the Army at Jackson, Tennessee in February 1863 to build breastworks. After a few weeks it was removed and put in storage. Sometime later all but four bales were returned. These were held by the provost marshal and were never returned on the ground the government was "short" four or five bales and were needed to make up for the shortfall. They were never accounted for, Elisha waited too long to sue, and her petition was dismissed on March 21, 1887 barred by statutes of limitation and the Bowman Act.

New Bedford Propeller Co. Chartered their steamer *Thorn* on April 5, 1864 to the Army at $150 a day for 30 days or as long as she was required. The appraised value was $40,000. On March 4, 1865 she hit a rebel torpedo in the Cape Fear River and sank. The company was paid $28,602 and they sued for the $11,397.64. The action was rejected for the same reasons in the *Maple Leaf* case.

New Hampshire, State of. On June 25, 1863 the War Department had set up a pay schedule under General Order No. 191 to pay reenlisting veterans installment payments totaling $402 after three years' service.

On October 17, 1863 President Lincoln called on the governors of the states to recruit 300,000 men for military service for enlistments of three years. Quotas were established for each State and a pay advance, premium, and enlistment bounty was offered. If voluntary enlistments failed, the draft would commence on January 5, 1864.

On October 24, 1863 Provost Marshal General, Colonel James B. Fry, issued an order:

If the government shall not require these troops for the full period of three years, and they shall be mustered out of the service before the expiration of their tem of enlistment, they shall receive, upon being mustered out, the whole amount of bounty remaining unpaid, the same as if the full term had been served. The legal heirs of recruits who die in service shall be entitled to receive the whole bounty remaining unpaid at the time of the soldier's death.

On November 3, 1863, Circular No. 98 outlined the bounty schedule for new recruits enlisting under the President's call: one months' pay in advance and bounty and premium amounting to $302.

On November 4, New Hampshire's total quota of 3,768 from the three Congressional districts was announced and a breakdown by towns and wards was subsequently published. The same day, Governor J. A. Gilmore and Daniel Clark sent a telegram to Secretary of War Edwin M. Stanton:

Concord, N. H., November 4, 1863
Hon. E. M. Stanton:
Sir: If to secure its quota of men under the last call of the President for 300,000 men the State of New Hampshire or the various towns should pay cash to each man mustered the amount of the bounty offered by the general government, and take an assignment of his claim for a bounty, will the government pay these bounties to the State or towns instead of to the men, at the time and in the manner they are to be paid to the soldiers respectively? If this can be done we all concur that we can raise our full quota speedily. Answer by telegraph.
J. A. Gilmore
Dan'l Clark

Colonel Fry replied the next day with an approval of the proposition. The quota was easily raised and each new recruit was paid $302 and each veteran $402 in cash and the State took an assignment on his right to the bounty.

On November 11, 1863 Major O. A. Mack wrote to Colonel Fry at the War Department from Concord, New Hampshire:

"Colonel: From conversations held with Governor Gilmore I learn that he has had some correspondence with you respecting the State advancing the amount of bounty offered by the general government to recruits and receiving an assignment from them of their claims. The governor has obtained your consent to this on behalf of the government; but I believe it was found that additional legislation would be necessary for the State to carry out this plan, and the governor has in his proclamation recommended the towns and cities to adopt it, and it appears now that many, if not all, of them will adopt it. The governor seems to be of the opinion that the government would pay the bounty in the stipulated installments even if the recruit deserted. I do not think this would or should be done, and I have so informed such parties as have consulted me. I respectfully ask instructions on this point.

I have also been asked that in case the State does not furnish her full quota under this last call of the President, and a draft is ordered in January to fill it, whether the towns that have filled their quotas by voluntary enlistment will be exempt from that draft.

Since the receipt of your telegram of the 5th instant, saying that if a State filled her quota under this call no draft would be ordered in January, I have been of the opinion that the same principle would be applied to the towns so far as practicable. I think this would be proper and have a beneficial effect, stimulating all the towns to work earnestly in the recruiting business. I respectfully submit the suggestion to your consideration.

O. A. Mack
Major and Aid-de-Camp
Acting Assistant Provost-Marshal-General

On the 19th, a reply was written:

War Department
Provost-Marshal-General's Office
Washington, D. C., November 19, 1863
Brig. Gen. E. W. Hinks, U.S. V.,
Acting Assistant P. M. G. for New Hampshire,
Concord, N. H.:
General: I am directed by the Provost-Marshal-General to acknowledge the receipt of your communication of the 11th instant, relative to the State advancing the amount of the bounty offered by the general government to recruits and receiving an assignment from them of their claim. In reply I am instructed to inclose herewith copy of a telegram to Governor Gilmore of the 5th instant, and to state that if the recruit deserts after delivery to the general rendezvous and muster into the United States service the government is alone responsible.

As far as possible, towns, &c., will be exempted from draft if their full quota is furnished.

I am, general, very respectively, your obedient servant,
Samuel B. Lawrence,
Captain, Sixteenth Infantry,
and Assistant Adjutant-General

Governor Gilmore applied to the Secretary of War for repayment of the bounty money on January 12, 1864 after the State's quota had been reached and $563,027.67 was paid. The government repaid all the bounty money owed to State recruits, which they could have claimed for themselves, to those who served out their enlistments but no money was paid to deserters who failed to comply with the terms of his enlistment.

The State sought to recover from the Secretary of the Treasury an additional $350,000 paid out during 1863 and 1864 on those already paid but who did not serve out the term of enlistment or deserted. The Secretary referred the claim to a federal court to answer two questions: did New Hampshire have a contract with the United States, and did the United States have an obligation to reimburse the State for soldiers who did not complete their enlistment as provided for in the law?

The court stated, in part, in its June 1, 1885 decision:

"This correspondence between subordinate officers of the War Department does not make a contract with the State of New Hampshire. No officer nor representative of the State is a party to it. So far as appears, they learned of its existence many years after it took place. No copy of it is found in the archives of the State. Governor Gilmore, in his letter to the Secretary of War, asking for the repayment of the bounties after the State had furnished its quota, dated January 12, 1864, makes no mention of this correspondence. He incloses a copy of the telegram of November 5, and relies upon that and nothing else as constituting the agreement.

"The Government has already paid to the State the full amount of bounties that could have been claimed by the volunteers had there been no assignment. That amount, in the opinion of the court, is all that the State is entitled to claim within the terms of the agreement.

"Whether these telegrams constitute a contract binding upon the government, and, if not, whether they were subsequently ratified by an act of Congress, under the above ruling of the court are no longer material questions. The government, in the opinion of the court, has done all that its officers engaged it should do, and whether in so doing not now concern the claimant.

"The court, therefore, answers both questions propounded by the Secretary in the negative."

A copy of the ruling was transmitted to Secretary of the Treasury.

On November 28, 1901 the State recovered $104,967.94 it paid on interest it paid on bonds to raise troops.

New Mexico Mounted Volunteers, Company K.

On November 21, 1861, 13 volunteers were mustered into Company K as privates, 3d Regiment New Mexico Mounted Volunteers at Fort Craig. Each had his own horse and horse equipment. A board of officers appraised the value of each horse and equipment and each volunteer was allotted $8 a month for forage for his animal.

On February 8, 1862 the volunteers were assembled in a line with their horses and equipment. They were ordered to remove the saddles, bridles, lariats, and spurs and put everything in a pile on the ground. The horses were inspected and the fattest and those in the best physical shape were brought into the fort. Wagons were sent to pick up the equipment and it was taken into the fort.

Companies F and H of the 3d Regiment were transferred to the 2d New Mexico Volunteers and Company A and Company K of the 4th Regiment New Mexico Volunteers were put on garrison duty at Fort Craig.

The horses taken into the fort were purchased from their owners, branded, and issued to mounted volunteers in other companies. The rejected horses were sent to a grazing camp on the Bosque River near San Antonito about 60 miles from Fort Craig. Security for the camp was under Lieutenant Pantaleon Archuleta of the 1st New Mexico Volunteers and the guards under him were 60 "non-effectives of the different volunteer companies." On February 23 the horses were captured by a rebel raiding party and never recovered.

No money was paid to the owners for the captured horses or for any of the equipment that was taken. A six-year statute of limitations existed for filing claims against the government of which the soldiers were ignorant. When they learned of it after the time had expired, they petitioned Congress for relief and their case was referred to a federal court where they recovered in 1880.

The claimants, value of horse, equipment, and award:

Baca, José, $65, $11		$76
Barranca, Juan, $35, $9.50		$44.50
Blea, Amada, $40, $8		$48
Ceballos, Tomas, $60, $12		$72
Dominguez, Cayetano, $55, $12		$67
Gallegos, Guadalupe, $32, $7.50		$39.50
Gonzales, José Yldefonso, $45, $10		$55
Lerma, Neponisena, $67.50, $10		$77.50
Lucero, Marcelino, $62.50, $12		$74.50
Martinez, Tomas, $40, $9		$49
Romero, David, $27.50, $10		$37.50
Sanchez, Antonio, $52.50, $6		$59
Valdez, Mariano, $40, $5.50		$45.50

Company A was formed at Fort Marcy in the fall of 1861. The Company was stationed at Santa Fe, Albuquerque, and Polvidera. On February 13, 1862 they were ordered to Fort Craig and arrived there on the 18th. The next day they were dismounted and their horses and equipment disposed of, as was Company K's.

The Company arrived just in time for the Battle of Valverde during which, or prior to, 26 members— about one third— of Company A deserted. When José A. Crispin, Manual Apodaca, Victor Giron, and Tomas Ortega presented their claims along with Company K, the evidence presented was inconsistent and sometimes contradictory to their loyalty and their petitions were dismissed.

Antonio Tapia also sought to recover but it was shown conclusively that he deserted and his petition was dismissed.

New York, State of.

President Lincoln requested Governor Edwin D. Morgan to buy arms and equipment and raise troops but the State had no money in its treasury that was not already appropriated for State needs.

On April 15, 1861 the legislature passed an act under chapter 277 designating the governor, lieutenant governor, secretary of state, comptroller, State engineer and surveyor, and State treasurer as officers responsible for expending up to $3 million to enroll and equip volunteers. The Act also imposed a tax not to exceed 2 mills on each dollar of the assessed value of real and personal property that would begin October 1. The State also issued 7 percent interest-bearing bonds and borrowed $1,623,501.19 from the canal fund at 5 percent interest. The tax rate of 1860 allowed the State to collect $2,039,663.06 for the canal fund.

The State had approximately 20,000 men already in military service in New York. Between April 22 and July 4, 1861 the State enrolled 30,000 volunteers into 38 regiments for enlistments of two years. Between April 1861 and January 1862 the State spent $2,878,501.19 to raise the troops. From that total, $91,320.84 was paid in interest on the bonds and $48,187.13 in interest was paid to the Canal Department. During the same time the State made $8,319.95 from its own interest-bearing bank accounts.

On July 25, 1861 Secretary of State William H. Seward telegraphed Governor Morgan:

Buy arms and equipments as fast as you can. We pay all.

On August 10, Secretary of War Simon Cameron telegraphed:

Adopt such measures as may be necessary to fill up your regiments as rapidly as possible. We need the men. Let me know the best the Empire State can do to aid the country in the present emergency.

On September 5, 1861 the War Department ordered the officers of the State to assemble all the troops and to place them under the command of Governor Morgan to be reorganized and made ready in all respects for the service of the United States. On the 28th Morgan was commissioned a major general of volunteers and put in command of the Department of the State of New York.

On February 11, 1862 Secretary of War Edwin M. Stanton telegraphed Morgan:

The Government will refund the Sate for the advances for troops as speedily as the Treasurer can obtain funds for that purpose.

The bonds matured, the State paid them off, and the money borrowed from the Canal Department was returned with interest.

The State presented claims to the Treasury Department totaling $2,950,479.10 for reimbursement, including interest charges on the canal fund loan. They were reimbursed $2,775,915.24 to cover the principle on both loans but the Treasury Department refused to refund the canal fund interest charges. The State claimed a balance due of $174,504.22, which was disallowed, as of January 3, 1880. The State then presented an amended claim for $131,188.02, which Secretary of the Treasury Charles S. Fairfield referred to a federal court for fact finding. The amount represented $91,320.84 interest paid on the bonds and $39,867.13 interest paid to the Canal Department after deducting the $8,319.95 the State made on its own interest-bearing bank accounts.

Due to statutes of limitations, Congress passed an Act to refund the "cost, charges, and expenses properly incurred by said State for enrolling, subsisting, clothing, supplying, arming, equipping, paying, and transporting troops."

On June 8, 1891 the court dismissed the petition for $39,867.13 interest paid to the Canal Department and awarded $91,320.84 in bond interest paid as a legitimate expense.

Noble, Samuel. A resident of Rome, Georgia who purchased 247 bales of upland cotton from the Roswell Manufacturing Company on March 25, 1863 that he stored at Savannah. On December 8 he purchased 162 bales of sea-island cotton from John W. Anderson also in Savannah.

On January 6, 1865 he was appointed a Treasury Department special agent by Supervising Special Agent Hanson A. Risley pursuant to the Act of July 2, 1864. This allowed owners to dispose of their cotton legally and possibly save it from destruction, capture, or theft.

Noble told Risley that he owned between 7–8,000 bales of cotton—about 800 in Selma, Alabama, 1,256 in Mobile, 200 in Rome, Georgia, 1,800 around Savannah, and between 4,000 and 5,000 around Augusta. He had deals in the works to buy more cotton and agreed to deliver 250,000 bales to Fernandina, Pensacola, Port Royal, Mobile, Huntsville, Jackson, Savannah, Brunswick, Chattanooga, and New Orleans before January 1, 1866. Risley also had a subagent, George W. Quintard. Risley agreed to receive the cotton and after all the expenses were paid and the cotton sold, remit to Noble ¾ of the net proceeds.

On January 19 Noble purchased 62 bales of sea-island and 50 bales of upland cotton from William Duncan at Savannah. On March 11 he purchased 203 bales of sea-island and 69 bales of upland cotton from the Home Insurance Company.

All the cotton was subsequently captured at Savannah, sent to New York and sold for $144,922.85. The cotton purchased from Roswell and Anderson sold for $82,434.76. In Savannah, 879 bales of his cotton were seized and in Selma, General James H. Wilson ordered 294 bales of his cotton burned and another 100 at Columbus, Georgia.

Noble claimed damages of $309,795.67 as the result of the seizures and destruction but his petition was dismissed because he mixed cotton purchased as an agent with cotton clearly seized under the Act of March 12, 1863.

Norfolk County Ferry Committee. On May 14, 1862 the Army seized one of the company's ferryboats that ran between Norfolk and Portsmouth, ran the boat as before for a period of almost four years, and kept the fares and revenue for itself. Military supplies, troops, stores, munitions, and animals were carried along with the usual civilian passengers and cargo. No money was paid to the company and they waited until the late 1880s to petition Congress for the revenue collected. Their claim was referred to a federal court by the House Committee on War Claims. It was dismissed on December 10, 1887 as barred by statutes of limitations and the Bowman Act.

Norris, Henry L. Henry and Richard Norris were railroad locomotive builders in Philadelphia as Richard Norris & Son. On October 29, 1863 they signed a contract with the Pennsylvania Railroad Company to build 10 passenger locomotives at $14,500 each and 10 freight locomotives at $15,000 each plus the 3 percent U.S. excise tax on or before August 1, 1864. The first delivery was due in March 1864 but by the first of the year in was becoming evident that the price of labor and materials was increasing to the extent that the company would not make a profit on the existing contract. At the same time there was a great military need for locomotives in Tennessee and on January 11 the company began talks with Department of the Cumberland general manager of railroads. On February 24 they wrote to the Secretary of War:

> "We beg to inform you that we have now well under way ten locomotives, ordered for Penn. R. R. Co., which cannot be altered. Ten more, not yet much done to them, material all on hand. Ten more for the Illinois Cent. R. R. Co., material partly on hand. If the requirements of the government be such as to make it important for early delivery, if you will cause us to be released from the contracts for ten of the engines for Penn. R. R. Co., and eight for the Illinois Cent. R. R. Co., we can commence delivery of four or five locomotives per month in May next. At all events, government work shall have precedence over all other work, if you will save us harmless."

Brigadier General Edward Canby replied on March 8 that Colonel McCallum in New York was the manager of the railroads in the Department of the Ohio and the Military Division of the Mississippi and that his orders for locomotives would constitute a contract with the government "and that you will be indemnified for any damages that may result from taking locomotives ordered for other railroad companies."

On March 16 Canby ordered 18 five-foot gauge locomotives and the company replied the same day:

> "Dear Sir: We will, with much pleasure, conform to your order of this date, and will take 13 of the locomotives now under way for Pennsylvania Railroad Company; the same to be made to a gauge of five feet, with four 54 driving wheels and copper flues; two pumps on each engine; tenders on eight wheels; all complete, for the sum of $18,231; each machine complete; cash on delivery of each on cars at our works for transportation.
>
> We will also, in due course, construct five more of same description, and at same price and terms, in all 18 complete locomotives and tenders, suited to a gauge of five feet. The whole number of 18 to have precedence of all other work whatsoever, and to be finished with all possible dispatch. A No. 5 injector, with adjustable nozzle, to be put on the left side of each locomotive."

Thirteen of the Pennsy engines being constructed were altered and another five were built with materials already purchased for other commercial engines contracted for. Had the company not built government engines they would have fulfilled the Pennsy contract as required. Only seven were delivered prior to August 1 and the other 13 after August 1. Each time the company delivered an engine to the government a statement was attached with the amount due on the indemnification for non-performance on their civilian contracts. The War Department refused to pay on this until all the engines had been delivered. This was a problem with other manufacturers and the Department decided that no more than $25,750 would be paid in full for each locomotive. The War Department paid the company $338,002.74 or $18,777.93 each. The company's total payment under this rule would be $463,500. On April 8, 1865 the company was paid $104,581.65 for indemnity on 15 locomotives when the company was expecting $114,949.87. There was also a dispute over the amount owed on the remaining three locomotives and the company began writing letters. They got no response and on June 8, 1865 they wrote again to say the company was owed $20,916.21 "to place us on the same footing all others were, which you will agree we are entitled to." This bill was paid on December 30. The $10,547.39 for indemnification was paid on January 22, 1866.

On the same day, Norris wrote to Secretary of War Stanton to say the company was still owed $10,250 reimbursement for the 3 percent tax. The company sued and the case was dismissed on the ground that the tax was included in the indemnification payment.

North, Alfred A. Commissioned captain
of Company M, 10th Regiment Illinois Cavalry
on May 3, 1864 retroactive to April 26. He was
in Springfield at the time but the regiment was
in Little Rock, Arkansas. Shortly after he left to
join up with them he became ill and returned to
Springfield. He remained at Camp Butler as
recorder on a board of inspection for new recruits until October 15. He was never mustered
in as captain because regulations required him
to actually join his unit before mustering in.

North claimed pay from May 3 to October
18 under the Act of June 3, 1884. His company
and regiment were not below the minimum
number of personnel required but North could
produce no records to show that he actually performed the duties for which he was commissioned and his petition was dismissed on January 11, 1886.

Northup, Mary E. George W. Northup
enrolled as captain of Company B, 23d Regiment Kentucky Volunteer Infantry on September 12, 1861 at a general rendezvous. He was paid
as captain from November 11 and first appeared
on the muster roll on December 31. In 1908 Mary
Northup sued to recover his pay from September 12 to November 11. Her suit was dismissed
on December 20, 1909 on the ground that she
couldn't prove he was a captain when he joined
and the Auditor of the Treasury for the War Department records showed captain's pay from December 31.

Norton, Lemuel B. A first lieutenant in
the 10th Pennsylvania Volunteer Reserves Corps.
He was detailed for temporary duty with the signal corps by order of Major General George B.
McClellan to serve as acting assistant quartermaster at the signal corps school at Georgetown.
Part of his duty was to pay teamsters, laborers,
and employees. He estimated his expenses for
August and September 1862 would be $1,000 and
reported this to the Quartermaster General's
Office. Several days later he received warrant No.
2070 on the U.S. Treasury. On September 29 he
paid out $562 and put $208 of the $438 balance
in his trunk and $230 in his pocketbook, which
he carried for paying teamsters who came to collect money due. While he had this money on
him he was thrown from a horse and seriously
injured. He was taken to his tent and put in his
bed and his clothes were removed and placed on
a chair beside his bed with the money "remaining in the pocket of his pantaloons." In a short

time five other officers came to visit him and
Norton removed some money from his pocketbook and gave it to Lieutenant Wonderly to purchase some food Norton wanted. He put the rest
of the money back and Wonderly returned in
about an hour with the food and Norton's
change. When he went to put the change back
into the pocketbook he discovered the rest of the
money was gone. The tent was searched but no
money was found. None of the officers were
searched and the money was never seen again.
The loss was charged to Norton and he sued to
recover.

Major Norton's explanation was that it
must have been stolen as a result of "the thiev-
ing propensities of some of his professed friends,
who had called to condole with him in his afflic-
tion."

One of the officers present was Adin B.
Capron and he said he was present during the
entire time and said it must have been stolen.
Norton normally kept cash hidden in his bed
when he slept. The other officers were questioned and suspicion began to fall on one of
them but this one was not questioned.

He was reimbursed the $230 in 1866.

Nugent, Terrence, Jr. Claimed ten bales
of upland and seven bales of sea-island cotton
captured at Savannah. Nugent's sole obstacle
was whether or not he voted for Davis-Stevens
in '61. A poll worker entered "T. Nugent, Jr." on
the roll but the court held it could not use that
as irrefutable proof they were one and the same
person for the money involved. Nugent recovered $2,273.34.

O'Keefe, James. A subject of Great
Britain and resident of Savannah whose 18 bales
of upland cotton were stored at Thomas
Daniels's house at 148 Broughton Street along
with cotton belonging to Daniels. While a military guard was present at the house a fire broke
out in the cellar. All the cotton was removed
with some bales burned, wet, or broken. It was
all taken away, repacked, and sold. O'Keefe was
credited with 10 bales and paid $1,904.70.

Oliver, W. T. A free black shoemaker in
Charleston who had never been a slave. He
owned one bale and three packages of upland
cotton seized at Charleston. He was awarded
$262.60.

Osborne, Belle. John and William H.
Osborne, a civil engineer by profession, were

brothers who owned a large plantation in Rapides Parish on the Red River 10 miles below Alexandria, Louisiana. General Nathaniel Banks occupied Alexandria on March 16, 1864 with protection from Admiral Porter's fleet on the Red River. Troops were being assembled there for an assault on Texas.

Between May 5 and 13 U.S. military forces seized 1,000 hogsheads containing 1 million pounds of sugar, 10,000 bushels of corn, 50 mules, 14 horses, and 100 head of cattle from the Osborne plantation, all valued at $109,750. The sugar was put aboard naval vessels or Army transports on the Red River and from there its disposition was unknown. It was later shown that the commissary department of the Army purchased a large quantity of sugar at Alexandria on May 5 for 9 cents a pound. There was no way for owners to remove private property from the area as U.S. forces were evacuating Alexandria and all vessels were under military control.

It was later shown that $19,750 worth of goods were taken by the Army for its own use.

William died on December 2, 1865 leaving a wife, Mary Corinne L. A. Duval Osborne and an infant daughter, Mary Corinne Osborne. Mary married Henry H. Rogers in 1868 and died in 1872. She and Henry had no children.

On December 1, 1887 Mary Corinne married Adolph Hartiens. She died on February 8, 1892 leaving three minor children, Sidney L., William W., and Mary R. Hartiens.

John Osborne declared bankruptcy in 1869. He submitted a claim on April 18, 1884 to the House Committee on War Claims for $67,050 representing his half of the seized property. It was found that John Osborne was loyal during the war but the loyalty of William could not be firmly established and the claim was referred to a federal court under the Bowman Act. John subsequently died and the suit was filed by his wife, Belle Osborne. The trial was held in 1890. One witness, Dennis Kelly, deposed at Alexandria, Louisiana, stated that in 1863 William was supervising the building of rafts in the Red River at Fort De Roussey 30 miles below Alexandria for the purpose of preventing the *Queen of the West* and other federal vessels from ascending the River. This was not substantiated by other witnesses and the government objected the court had no jurisdiction until the loyalty of both partners could be firmly established. The court stated that William Osborne "to all intents and purposes, though not in form, has been found

disloyal" and the petition was sent back to Congress on May 6, 1889 for rehearing.

In March 1906 Dennis Kelly disclaimed his former testimony in a deposition taken at Washington, D.C. Adolph Hartiens then filed suit and on December 3, 1906 the court declared William loyal and reported their findings to Congress.

Overton Hotel Co. A building in Memphis, Tennessee that was taken for use as a Confederate hospital in November 1861 just prior to its completion as a hotel. It was used as a hospital until June 6, 1862 when it was captured by the Army. It was then used for the care of the Confederate patients already there and new Army patients who were admitted during the war. It was returned to its owners in September 1865.

In the late 1880s the company petitioned the House Committee on War Claims for rent for the use and occupation of the property from January 1, 1863 through September 1865. The claim was referred to a federal court for fact finding but the petition was dismissed on March 19, 1888 as barred by statutes of limitations and the Bowman Act.

Pacific Railroad Co. of Missouri. In October 1864, 13 bridges on the railroad's main line in Missouri were burned by General Sterling Price's invading forces. Major General William S. Rosecrans, commander of the Department of the Missouri, met with Pacific Railroad officials and said rebuilding the bridges was an immediate military necessity. He expected them to get the work done and any work they could not, or would not do, would be done by the Army and the charges for the work withheld from payments for carrying government supplies and troops "for such outlays as in law and fact it should be found entitled to have repaid." The company said it would do it they could to quickly rebuild but they believed some of the bridges had been burnt by "proper military authority" of the United States and they expected the government to rebuild those at its cost.

Rosecrans said the company might have a case but it was too early to worry about it and he expressed a desire for fairness in the future. The company got busy rebuilding and Rosecrans fired off a telegram:

Hdgrs., St. Louis, Mo., Oct. 12, 1864
Hon. Edwin M. Stanton,
  Sec. of War:
The rebuilding of the bridges on the Pacific R. R., recently burned by the rebels, are essential and

a great military necessity in the defense of this State. The railroad co. is unable to replace them.

Please authorize Col. Myers to have them rebuilt at once, the U.S. to be reimbursed the cost out of freight on the road.

W. S. Rosecrans,
Maj. Gen.

Stanton referred the matter to Quartermaster General Meigs. Later that day Meigs notified Stanton that he approved the plan and recommended Rosecrans be informed that Brevet Brigadier General D. C. McCallum, superintendent of military railroads, would be directed to get it done and enclosed a draft of approval for McCallum with instructions to use St. Louis quartermaster Colonel William Myers as he saw fit.

The directors of Pacific Railroad had no knowledge of these communications or decisions but they found out soon enough. On November 1, Pacific Railroad president G. R. Taylor wrote to Colonel Myers, which was transmitted to McCallum:

> The delay on the part of the War Dept. in providing for the repairing and rebuilding of the bridges on this road has prompted the company to unusual resources for some of them, and I therefore beg to say that we are constructing the Gasconade and Moreau bridges ourselves, and expect to have them ready by the 25th of this month, leaving only the Osage to be replaced. In view, then, of the avoiding any misunderstanding on the part of General McCallum in the premises, may I request that you immediately communicate the facts by telegram, as those with whom he has contracted may be led into error. I repeat that the only bridge on the main line to be replaced by the government is the Osage, 1,200 feet in length, this company having replaced all the smaller and are now replacing all the larger ones.
>
> I learn that McNairy, Claflin & Co., with whom Gen. McCallum contracted, are at Cleveland, Ohio.

The Osage bridge was ordered destroyed on October 5 by Brigadier General Egbert Brown, commander of the central district of the Missouri, acting under orders from Rosecrans to "use every means in his power to prevent the advance of the enemy." The cost to replace the bridge was $96,152.65. The Moreau bridge was also ordered destroyed by Brown. The company began rebuilding but a freshet in the river washed the new construction away. The company didn't have the money to complete the project so it was rebuilt by the government at a cost of $30,801.

Two bridges on the southwestern branch across the Maramec River were burned by rebels and they were rebuilt by the government for $54,595.24 or a total of $181,548.89 for the four bridges. Pacific Railroad rebuilt the other nine bridges. All the bridges were rebuilt between the spring of 1865 and June 28, 1867.

The Army never took control of the railroad at any time before or after the bridges were destroyed and the company continued to carry military freight and passengers on contract as before.

The company sued to recover $130,196.98 that they felt was spent by the government and charged to them without their consent. The government counterclaimed for the cost of the Moreau bridge and other work. On March 2, 1885 the company was awarded $44,800.74 and the government retained $85,396.24.

Padelford, Edward. Padelford was born in the north but became, along with other northern men, a prominent, wealthy director of the Marine Bank of Georgia in Savannah. The bank made a $200,000 loan to the Confederate government and invested in Confederate bonds under the threat of removing any director who dissented and replacing him with another who would "give up the whole capital of the bank to the confederate government — this ruining the shareholders and giving tenfold as much aid to the rebel cause." The bank could have loaned $3 million. Every other bank in Savannah except Marine was increasing its funding of the rebellion.

Padelford and Randolph Mott owned 1,293 bales of cotton seized in December 1864. Net proceeds of $246,277.70 were paid into the Treasury. Both sued for his half and Mott successfully recovered.

The government argued that Padelford was under no coercion whatsoever, had two sons in the rebel army, owned cotton presses and large stock in a Georgia railroad, contributed at least $102,000 in aid to the rebellion, and voluntarily lived and did business in the South. The court noted:

> "In the early part of 1861 a subscription for a loan of $15 million to the Confederate government was opened in the city of Savannah, and all persons were expected and required to subscribe to it who were able to do so, and declarations and threats were publicly made to all who did not subscribe voluntarily should be made to

subscribe. These threats were openly made at the place of subscription and by persons influential with the populace. Mr. Padelford's name was mentioned, his absence was remarked upon, and inquiries were made as to where he was and it was publicly threatened that if the Marine Bank, of which he was a director, did not subscribe it should be pulled down."

Padelford subscribed $2,000 to the loan but sold the stock two weeks later.

Lewis A. Bennett testified:

"Mr. Padelford was no more exposed than others to molestation — probably not so much so, from the very high position he had reached in the community. I never was frightened for myself, although other men were taken up and carried out, whipped, and tarred and feathered for their Union political sentiments. These were the acts of organized bodies composed of the lower classes of society. This state of things continued until early in the year 1862 when the military night police was established by the commanding general of the Confederate forces."

The court held that Padelford acted "not voluntarily but under a reasonable fear of violence to his person and property" and he was awarded $123,138.35.

Pargoud, John Frank.

John Frank, of Louisiana, was no scalawag. He aided the rebellion any way he could and admitted it later when he sought to recover the proceeds of 85 bales of his cotton seized in the summer of 1865 "after the surrender of all the rebel armies and the suppression of the armed rebellion." His case in December of 1868 was the first to be heard in the Court of Claims under the Act of March 12, 1863 after all the presidential amnesty and pardon proclamations had been issued. John Frank took a loyalty oath under the Proclamation of May 25, 1865 and received his conditional pardon from President Johnson on January 11, 1866. The court dismissed his petition on the ground the Act required loyalty to recover money, that "crime is effaced by amnesty and pardon," and the court was not a criminal court authorized to prosecute crime, and therefore could not recognize pardons. The Supreme Court reversed the judgement as in John A. Klein's case: "The proclamation of the 25th of December 25, 1868 granted pardon unconditionally and without reservation. This was a public act of which all courts are bound to take notice, and to which all courts are bound to give effect" (13 Wall. 128).

Parish, Joseph W.

In September 1861 Parish received a note from General McKinstry, the quartermaster at St. Louis:

"You are authorized to purchase for a regiment of cavalry, to be called the McKinstry Guard, to be raised in Central Illinois, 1,158 horses, at prices not to exceed $110 each. They must be rigidly inspected by a board appointed by the colonel of the regiment previous to being received. To be delivered at Peoria, Illinois."

Parish bought and delivered the horses, they were accepted, and he received vouchers totaling $127,380. Parish presented the vouchers, they were reviewed and approved by a commission headed by Captain Philip Sheridan, and also approved by Major Allen. Parish turned the vouchers over to Sturgis & Son, of Chicago for collection. Sturgis submitted them to Quartermaster General Meigs where they were reduced to $105 per horse or $121,590.

Parish sued and recovered $5,790.

Parish was doing business with William L. Huse under the name of J. W. Parish & Co. In January 1863 Parish responded to an advertisement for bids from Henry Johnson, the U.S. Army Medical Storekeeper, to furnish ice for the Medical and Hospital Department at Hilton Head, South Carolina; New Berne, North Carolina; Fortress Monroe, Virginia; Pensacola; Nashville and Memphis; New Orleans, St. Louis, and Washington D.C. through January 1, 1864. Bidders were asked to state the amount of ice they could furnish.

Parish said he could deliver ice to Memphis, Nashville, St. Louis, and Cairo, Illinois. A contract was signed on March 5 and the Assistant Surgeon General's office at St. Louis ordered 5,000 pounds at St. Louis and Cairo and 10,000 pounds at Memphis and Nashville "for the use of the sick of the armies in the field, and should be furnished without delay." Three days for unloading at each destination was allowed. The Army was not very well prepared to receive the ice and Parish was requested to provide icehouses to store it, which he did at St. Louis for $1,500 and at Cairo for $500. He was reimbursed for these expenses.

Parish delivered 4,174 pounds to St. Louis, 1,388 to Cairo, 6,456 to Memphis, and 750 to Nashville. He purchased 23,000 pounds of ice between March 25 and April 2, 1863. Of that, 10,000 pounds was purchased at Lake Pepin, Minnesota. During April the water in the Mississippi River was low but if Parish had steamers and barges at Lake Pepin ready to go he probably would have been able to ship the ice south but he had no boats or barges and none could go up and the ice he purchased melted.

Parish sued to recover the lost ice but his petition was dismissed since the order from the Surgeon General's office was not part of the contract. Parish appealed and the Supreme Court reversed the decision on the ground that Parish purchased the ice on a valid order from the Assistant Surgeon General.

On the ice delivered, the government requested the company to discharge the ice from the boats and pack it in the icehouses. This delayed the boats and barges, which caused Parish to pay demurrage charges of $11,230.50 under the charter agreements. Parish and Huse sued to recover and were awarded the amount in 1866.

Parkhurst, Hiram S. Enlisted as a private in the Army as Hiram S. Smith on July 30, 1861 and was mustered into Company B, 3rd New York Cavalry Volunteers. He was promoted to sergeant, reenlisted as a veteran volunteer on January 5, 1864, and discharged on July 9 to accept a second lieutenant's commission.

On June 19 he was thrown from a horse and the horse fell on him injuring his lower back. He was declared unfit for duty but not confined to his tent. He went home to Mexico, New York prior to receiving orders on June 20 from the governor of New York appointed him second lieutenant in the 24th New York Cavalry Volunteers retroactive to the 15th. He received the orders about three weeks later but never reported to the commander of the 24th and remained at home without leave until the end of the war. He never sent in a monthly report of his medical condition as required by Army Regulations.

On December 30, 1864 John Hutchinson was appointed second lieutenant in his place.

Parkhurst applied to the War Department for pay and bounty as a second lieutenant pursuant to the Acts of June 3, 1884 and February 3, 1887. On November 25, 1890 the Medical Department certified him as a second lieutenant to the Second Auditor of the Treasury from June 20, 1864 to June 17, 1865. Parkhurst was told to apply at the Treasury Department for any money due. He did and was denied. He sued and his petition was dismissed on May 28, 1894 on the ground that his actions amounted to a resignation of his commission.

Patten, George. Owned a warehouse at Savannah to store cotton. In December 1864 he had 30 bales of sea-island and 252 bales of upland cotton. Ten of the upland bales were his and were marked "P." All the cotton was seized and sold. George's cotton netted $1,753.30.

George sued to recover the proceeds on the 252 bales on the ground that he held liens on it for freight, insurance, and storage. He couldn't prove the amount of the liens and received $1,753.30.

Payne, George E. Owned a 1,982-acre sugar plantation in St. Charles Parish, Louisiana on the Mississippi River about 29 miles above New Orleans. He purchased one plantation in 1856 and an adjoining one in 1860. Between July and December 1862 the Army seized $6,770 worth of his stores and supplies for their use.

On November 5, 1862 the Army occupied St. Charles Parish and on the 9th, General Benjamin F. Butler issued General Order No. 91 declaring all property west of the Mississippi except Plaquemines and Jefferson Parishes sequestered. A military Sequestration Commission would work and control all plantations in the new District of La Fourche, as Butler named it. On December 5 Butler appointed John S. Woodward manager of Payne's plantation for one half of the sugar and molasses produced for the United States. The property and everything on it was to be returned eventually in good order to Payne.

The net proceeds from the crop of 1862 was $6,688.13. No money was ever paid to Payne.

When the property was seized there was about 450 arpents of "very heavy and fully-ripe sugar-cane standing in the fields" worth about $30,000. Payne could have realized about 500 hogsheads of sugar and 750 barrels of molasses. The production cost would have been about $3,000 and the sugar and molasses would have been worth from $40–$48,000.

The government operation under Woodward managed to produce about one third of the amount of sugar and molasses that Payne could have made.

Sometime between February 15 and September 1863 Colonel Holabird, chief quartermaster of the Department of the Gulf, turned the plantation and all its equipment over to Benjamin F. Flanders, Treasury Department supervising special agent at New Orleans, as captured and abandoned property. Flanders and his manager, S. W. Cozzens, of the Freedmen's Bureau, made 254 hogsheads of sugar and 351 barrels of molasses from the 1863 crop. All was shipped to New Orleans and sold at auction for $33,820.49 and that amount was deposited into the Treasury on February 29, 1864. Flanders reported his production expenses as $16,809.66 leaving a net profit of $17,010.83, which on Payne's demand was paid to him. Payne claimed the reasonable production costs were $8,201.17 and he claimed the balance of $8,809.66.

On January 23, 1864 Flanders turned the plantation over to William Spear, of Ohio, until January 1, 1865. Neither Cozzens nor the employees on the plantation recognized Spear and in the spring of 1864 Cozzens plowed up all the ratoon cane, supposedly to plant cotton. All the seed cane, dwellings, shops, machinery, stables, fences, and bridges were also destroyed. The damage estimate to Payne's property was $103,000.

Flanders refused to return what was left of Payne's plantation to him when Spear's lease was up unless he signed a receipt releasing the government from any claim for damages. Payne refused and his property was turned over to the Bureau of Refugees, Freedmen, and Abandoned Lands. It was held by them until January 1, 1866 when Payne got it back. He also received about $1,500 in like goods from the $6,770 seized in 1863, leaving a balance due of $5.270.

Payne never presented his claim to the Southern Claims Commission. He waited until the 1880s to sue for $132,980.17 for the use and occupation of his property from December 8, 1862 to January 1, 1866 and the destruction of the place.

Payne argued that St. Charles Parish was never insurrectionary and was excepted in President Lincoln's Emancipation Proclamation of January 1, 1863. The President and the courts held the Parish to be loyal and as such would not be subject to the rule of military occupation "at the seat of war" within Section 3 of the Bowman Act. Nor was it abandoned or captured property and, in fact, it was held by agents of the Treasury Department. Payne sued too late and his petition was dismissed on March 14, 1887 as barred by the Bowman Act.

Payne subsequently died and William R. Irby, executor of his estate, petitioned Congress to recover and by a special act the case was referred to a federal court. On January 9, 1922 Irby was awarded $21,818.13 for $5,130 worth of goods; the $6,688.13 1862 crop; and $10,000 for two years' rental of the property at $5,000 per

year on the ground that Payne was loyal. The $5,270 claim for property was not allowed since its disposition was unknown.

Paynter, Henrietta M. She had a life interest in a one-acre country lot on Auction Street in Memphis "with remainder to her children" and then to her husband, Henry H. Paynter, upon her death. Her only child was C. W. Paynter.

The Direct Tax Commission designated it lot 520 and assessed taxes of $25.49. This was not paid and it was sold to William J. Smith and Fielding Hurst for $300 and a surplus of $274.51 was deposited into the Treasury.

Henrietta refused to leave the premises and no effort was made to evict her. She later turned it over to someone named "Walt."

She filed suit to recover the surplus and was awarded $274.51 on April 5, 1886.

Pennsylvania, State of. On June 30, 1874 the State presented the last of nine claims to the Treasury Department totaling $100,780.45 for raising troops. The claim included $47,129.47 the State paid to various individuals and corporations for damage done to grounds and buildings while housing troops. The State recovered $45,239.90 on June 16, 1902.

Phelps, Lorenzo A. Major Phelps, 5th Regiment Virginia Volunteer Infantry, was court-martialed at Charleston, West Virginia on a series of charges and found guilty on April 24, 1863. He was ordered home by Colonel R. B. Hayes: "proceed to Ceredo, West Virginia and there remain under arrest to await the decision of the court-martial in his case." He left and went to a "residence notorious for rebel sympathizers" at Guyandotte, ten miles from Ceredo, and was arrested on September 7.

Phelps stated he left home because "it became dangerous to remain there any longer, owing to the proximity of rebel troops and the absence of United States troops."

The sentence was originally announced on May 17, which was "dismissal from the service and forfeiture of all pay and allowance then due or thereafter to become due."

He was paid up to the date the sentence was published and sued to recover. The court found no valid reason for his leaving home and dismissed his petition.

Phillbrook, Harry B. Enlisted in the Army for three years on August 4, 1862. On February 10, 1865 he was discharged "by reason of having received an appointment as clerk in the Adjutant-General's Office." He sued to recover the $50 bonus authorized by the Act of July 28, 1866, which provided for a $50 bounty for enlisting after April 14, 1861 for not less than two years.

He was denied the bonus on the ground that he didn't serve his full term. The court agreed and his petition was dismissed.

Pollard, William.

A "colored drayman in the city of Savannah, possessed of property real and personal and of good credit and reputation in business." He bought 60 bales of upland cotton in the fall of 1864 from Erwin & Hardee "known to the vendee as having been in the Confederate service" and stored it at his residence on Bryant Street. Erwin was a captain in the Confederate army but left in 1862 for health reasons. Hardee was collector of the port of Savannah.

Erwin testified:

Q. Had you heard, at the time of the sale of this cotton to this claimant that the United States military forces under the command of General Sherman were advancing towards Savannah?

A. I had at the time I made that sale the general impression in Savannah, which was that he would cut across from about Marion and strike Beaufort, little thinking he would come here. Property was being run into Savannah from all quarters for safety."

Evidence was presented to show that Pollard harbored Union prisoners, helped them escape, and "assisted Union men escaping from serving in the rebel army and helped them get through the lines."

The Secretary of the Treasury reported that all the upland cotton seized at Savannah netted $176.56 a bale at auction. No evidence was presented that Pollard attempted to defraud the government and he was awarded $10,020.

Potter, Eliza.

Wife of Lorenzo T. Potter, lived in Charleston, and owned 29 bales of upland cotton stored at No. 17 Wentworth Street. The Army seized 28 bales on March 30 and sold it.

Eliza testified:

"During the war my husband and myself were loyal to the United States and opposed to the rebellion. Neither he nor I ever gave any voluntary aid to the rebellion. I was in the daily habit of attending to the Union prisoners. It was my sole occupation during the war. We were much troubled by the rebels, even to our chil-

dren. My boy had a United States flag and his fellows found out about it and asked him to give it up. I told him, 'My boy, you must never give up that flag. Some day or other you will raise it in Charleston here in glory.' He said, 'I don't want to give it up, only, I tell you the boys will whip me.' Two days after, taking off his jacket and shirt, I found he had been lacerated from head to foot. He said nothing to me about it and when I asked him he simply said they had whipped him because he would not give them the stars and stripes to spit upon. 'I have not given it either and I won't,' he added. He was about 14 years old then. He went back to school fighting his way, but one day, while ascending the steps from the ground to the school, he looked around and received a blow in the head with a heavy brickbat thrown by one of the boys. He never recovered and we buried him soon after. In these ways they persecuted every one who waited on the prisoners they starved or showed any love for the Union. My attendance on the hospitals excited their hate and anger against us. Mr. Potter placed $11,000 to my use saying, 'I don't ask you what you do with it, do what you please, only don't tell me.' I understood what the money was for, of course. He did this so if they forced him to say whether he had himself aided the prisoners they could not fix it on him and imprison him or confiscate what we had. I made my way to our boys in the hospitals and camps by bribing the officials. What I spent in money altogether was about $17,000. It was all confederate money to be sure, but in 1862 it was not so valueless. We had to take it in payment of debts, dollar for dollar, and it would buy anything from real estate up."

Eliza was awarded $3,665.28 on 28 bales of upland cotton.

Powell, James W.

Lieutenant Powell was a surgeon in Major General Hooker's 71st New York Volunteer Infantry. He was placed in charge of a hospital at Bottom's Bridge, Virginia. A surgeon was allotted two horses but Powell was "mounted with three horses and equipments, prepared for field service."

On or about June 30, 1862 he was taken prisoner during the Seven Days' battles in the Peninsula campaign near Bottom's Bridge. He lost the three horses and their equipment worth $535, and swords and pistols worth $130.

He presented his claim to the Third Auditor but was denied. He sued and recovered $344.74.

Pratt, Leonard B. A resident of Buck-sport, Maine and owner of the self-propelled, 182-ton steam derrick *Dirigo*. When he was at the port of Newbern, North Carolina on January 15, 1863 he chartered the vessel to Colonel Herman Biggs through Captain James C. Slaught for $200 a day for 30 days "or as much longer as the government saw fit to keep her." She proceeded to Beaufort and then secretly to Hilton Head and then transported "heavy guns" from Stone River to Morris Island.

The Quartermaster General approved the charter but on July 11 he ordered the rate reduced to $100 a day retroactive to June 17. Pratt threatened to remove his boat from military service but the Army said it wouldn't be released. Pratt then applied for the $100 a day rate but the quartermaster refused unless he signed a new agreement. Pratt refused and the boat remained in Southern waters until it was eaten up by worms and sank on June 10, 1864. The Army paid Pratt for the charter term at $100 a day but demanded a release "in full of the above account." The release was executed by Pratt's agent as irrevocable.

The vessel was assessed at $25,000 but Pratt maintained her true value was $75,000. Pratt was required to keep the vessel "tight, staunch, and strong and well and sufficiently manned, victual led, tackled, appareled, ballasted, and furnished in every respect fit for merchant service."

He sued for $102,000: $100 a day from June 17, 1863 and the full value of the vessel but was awarded $35,700 for the 347 days at an additional $100 a day.

Price, Edwin M. Owner of 176 bales of cotton seized in northern Georgia in May and June 1864 and taken to Kingston, Adairsville, Nashville, then Cincinnati. It was mingled and co-mingled along the way with many lots and great effort was required to determine the average sale price at auction. Price was awarded $480.51 per bale on 143 bales for a total of $68,712.93 in 1871.

Price, Hawkins. Owned 32 bales of cotton seized at Kingston, Bartow County, Georgia in May and June 1864 apparently along with Edwin Price's cotton. He recovered $15,376.32 at $480.51 per bale.

Price, Joseph W. Lieutenant of Company C, 39th Iowa Volunteers from November 24, 1862 to January 6, 1865. He joined at Davenport, mustered out at Savannah, was transported to New York, but refused travel pay home to Adel on the ground that he was a volunteer. He sued under the Act of July 22, 1861 giving commissioned volunteer officers equality with regulars and recovered $234.

Price, Theresa. Thomas Price purchased six bales of upland cotton on July 21, 1864 and shipped it to Savannah on the Central of Georgia Railway. It was seized and sold into the Treasury for $1,051.96. Thomas died and his wife recovered $1,051.98.

Prime, Frederick E. Major Prime was General Grant's chief engineer and engineer disbursing officer and had an office at the large supply depot at Holly Springs, Mississippi in which $1,725 was securely stored. Prime was ordered to Memphis on December 14, 1862 and his clerk, A. J. Halleck, left for St. Louis with the major. The money was left in the care of Sergeant H. B. Douglas who was specifically detailed to the office. The depot was raided on the 20th by Generals Van Dorn and Price. Prime returned on the 26th and found the office in shambles and all the money gone. None of it was ever recovered.

Grant severely censured all the officers in charge, held Prime liable for the loss, and withheld an equal amount from his pay.

Prime sued and when Sergeant Douglas testified he claimed he had no knowledge of the money in the office. He said he was taken prisoner when the depot was raided but released that afternoon and allowed to return. He was awarded all the money withheld pursuant to the Act of May 9, 1866.

Provine, James M. Owner of six stores in Memphis the Army converted into hospitals in February 1863. Eight buildings were taken including two belong to a lady named Talbot. Provine recovered $7,485 for damages to the premises.

Pugh, Edward. Owned a sugar plantation in Assumption Parish, Louisiana for many years but left it on the advice of his physician and went to Texas when the war started, leaving it to a manager to run. The Army seized the property on October 15, 1862. The place was leased to a third party during 1864 and 1865 and molasses and sugar worth at least $15,000 per year were produced.

Pugh returned in November 1865 and sued to recover $72,508 plus interest on the ground of trespass and destruction rather than a Fifth Amendment taking for the public good or under the Act of March 12, 1863. He claimed the Army occupied the place in the mistaken belief that he had abandoned it and $42,508 worth of his property was carried away or destroyed.

Pugh emphatically denied that he abandoned the property. The Act of July 2, 1864 described abandoned property as when "the lawful owner thereof being absent therefrom, and engaged, either in arms or otherwise, in aid or encouraging the rebellion." This also Pugh denied.

The court was divided but his petition was dismissed.

Pullen, Nancy M. Albert Johnson, of Panola County, Texas, owned 13 bales of cotton seized there. He filed suit to recover but became very ill and could not pursue the claim so he sold it to Martin Tally of Shreveport, Louisiana. Albert died shortly thereafter and on December 25, 1863 his wife, Nancy, was qualified as his executrix. Nancy then married Franklin Pullen and on December 7, 1871 filed suit to recover the proceeds of the cotton for Martin Tally.

The original 13 bales were compressed into nine bales at New Orleans and sold in a lot of 70 bales in New York for an average net price of $46.88½ per bale or $421.96 for the nine, which she recovered.

Queyrouze, Simon. A citizen of France who lived in New Orleans and owned 102 bales of upland cotton seized in St. Landry Parish, Louisiana in the spring of 1863. Simon died and his son Leon was appointed administrator on May 10, 1869. The value of cotton seized from this area was fixed at $192 a bale. Leon recovered $14,592 on 76 bales.

Quigley, E. J. A Georgia native and merchant in Dalton who moved to Indiana when the state seceded. He gave power of attorney to B. F. McKenna to collect his debts and invest the money. He sued to recover $356.66 on the proceeds of two bales of cotton captured at Savannah, which was awarded in 1877. He was regarded as a refugee by the court.

Quinby, Charles J. A Rhode Island native who was a photographer and well-known Union man in Charleston who owned 437 bales of upland and 131 bales of seized sea-island cotton. Quinby was jailed by the Confederate provost marshal for refusing to serve in the rebel army then joined the fire patrol. He and others purchased the *Louisa* with the intention of loading her with cotton and running the blockade on a one-way trip where the proceeds of the cotton would be overseas and "beyond the control of the Confederate authorities." The others bought the *Aries* instead, loaded her with general merchandise, and sailed her to Charleston. Quinby immediately sold out. He recovered $76,293.60 on 366 bales of upland and 119 bales of sea-island cotton.

Ramsdell, George W. Resident of Washington, D.C. who wrote a note to Secretary of War Simon Cameron on October 31, 1861 claiming to represent Samuel B. Smith, of California:

> I propose to fill the order of the department in July last to C. K. Garrison for 10,000 rifled muskets, which he has failed to execute, with an arm equal in every respect to the one he agreed to furnish, and at a price $6 less per gun than the price named in his order. A sample of the gun I propose to supply is in General Ripley's office.

Ripley was Chief of Ordnance. On November 16 Lieutenant Colonel William M. Maynadier replied to say he had been given authority to buy the 10,000 guns and pointed out that Garrison's price was $27 each.

The next day Ramsdell wrote a note witnessed by James Burns:

> Samuel B. Smith, of the State of California, having agreed to furnish me with 10,000 guns, according to sample deposited by me in the United States Ordnance Office, I hereby authorize him to deliver to the general government, in my name, the said number of 10,000 guns, as per order of the Bureau of Ordnance to me directed, bearing date November 16, 1861, and signed by William Maynadier, lieutenant colonel of ordnance; and I give to him, the said Smith, full and complete authority to collect and receive from the United States government the money due or to become due upon the delivery of said guns, and to sign all necessary receipts and vouchers in the premises to the government for me, in my name, or otherwise.

Smith placed an order with Boker & Co. of New York to import guns from Europe at about $13 each. On January 13, 1862 Ramsdell told Ripley that all the guns had arrived in New York, that Samuel Smith was his agent, and to deal with him directly.

On the 17th Ripley told Major Hagner, Bureau of Ordnance chief in New York, that Ramsdell had said the guns were ready for delivery anywhere designated and that he was sending him the sample of the gun Ramsdell had supplied.

The gun was carried to New York by W. K. Mehaffy "wrapped in paper and sealed with the seal of the Ordnance bureau." It was delivered to Smith who took it to Captain Crispin of the Ordnance Bureau who was in charge while Major Hagner was away. The guns were stored in a warehouse under Hagner's control. They were inspected by Captain Crispin and he reported the guns were so inferior he refused to accept them unless ordered to.

On March 13, the new Secretary of War, Edwin M. Stanton, appointed Joseph Holt and Robert Dale Owen "to audit and adjust all contracts, orders, and claims on the War Department."

Smith went to see Stanton to say he needed the guns to be accepted and paid for at once. Stanton told Smith to furnish a copy of his contract "with all his proof, before the commission; and that the department would not act until the commission had decided upon the matter."

On March 15 Major Hagner reported that Crispin felt a mistake had been made as he had purchased the same weapon for $7.50 to $10 each, "that it was evident from the first order to Garrison that there was a mistake, as Garrison's arms were to be French, (Leige make), and, as General Frémont stated, much better than the Enfield or any others that he had seen."

On the 18th Smith wrote to Holt and Owen advising them that he was Ramsdell's agent, he had ordered the guns from Europe, admitted the price was high, but hoped the government would honor the agreement as he "was pressed to make payment for the guns, and was unable to make it until the government should pay him, and that by further delay he should be ruined." Holt–Owen invited him to suggest a reduction in his price and on May 2 Smith offered to sell the guns for $14.50 each. The Commission then concluded that no more than $11 should be paid. This was formally stated on the 9th, Smith accepted, the guns were accepted, and Smith was paid $110,000. Ramsdell then filed a claim for $100,000 for the balance on the original agreement of $21 each.

It was then learned that Smith had approached a man named Duffy to help him procure the arms. Duffy was an associate of Garrison but Smith didn't want his name to appear anywhere so he substituted Ramsdell, with his permission, and Ramsdell later admitted to this.

The government argued that neither Smith nor Ramsdell had any standing in court, the Act of February 26, 1853 prohibited the assignment of claims against the government, and the assignment of contracts was prohibited by the Act of July 17, 1862.

Smith's original contract was made without advertising for bids but there was a "public exigency" then existing. There were no guns to be had in the market and no means of obtaining arms quickly other by importation.

In awarding Ramsdell $100,000 the court stated:

"The contract made may have been, from subsequent circumstances or otherwise, a disadvantageous one for the government, but it was made with due legal authority by the Secretary of War acting through the Ordnance Department, according to statute, and, for the reasons stated, the court think it valid against the United States, and that Mr. Smith is entitled to the balance of his contract price unpaid."

Ravenel, William Parker. The U.S. Direct Tax Commission placed a total valuation of $9,076 on the Cherry Point, Cherry Hill, and McTureous tract plantations on St. Helena Island, South Carolina. The tax was not paid and on March 10, 1863 they were sold at auction for $1,605 and the net surplus after deducting the taxes, interest, penalties, costs, and commissions was $1,302.27. Cherry Point and Cherry Hill were bought by E. S. Philbrick. The McTureous tract was bought by the United States.

The owners of Cherry Point were Mary C. De Sanssure, Susan H. and William H. Peronneau, Elizabeth Coffin Ravenel, and Ann B. Du Bose as tenants on common.

The owners of Cherry Hill were Elizabeth, William, Daniel, Elias P., and Mary Coffin Ravenel and Mary S. De Sanssure and her children Mary C. De Sanssure, Susan H. Peronneau, and Ann B. Du Bose who owned one-fifth of the plantation.

Elizabeth C. Ravenel owned one-fifth of McTureous tract.

Elizabeth C. Ravenel died in 1870 and William Ravenel was appointed administrator of her estate. Ann B. Du Bose died in 1873, William Peronneau in 1874. Henry H. Peronneau was appointed administrator of their interests. Elias Ravelel died in late 1886 and William Ravenel was appointed administrator of his estate.

In the late 1880s William Ravenel was joined by Susan H. Peronneau in a lawsuit to recover the surplus, which they calculated at

$1,429, and said the Tax Commission deducted $2 for every $100 of assessed value while the plaintiffs said it should have been $1.17.9 per $100.

The Act of August 5, 1861 fixed the assessed value of South Carolina for direct tax purposes at $363,570.67. Not having the official records, the Direct Tax Commission fixed it at $30,833,322.10.9.

The court computed the surplus to be $1,429 pursuant to the Act of June 7, 1862 and each claimant was awarded one-fifth of that amount on March 26, 1888.

Reeside, John E. Resident of Washington, D.C. who had five contracts totaling $65,586 a year to deliver mail in Arkansas, all of which expired on June 30, 1862. The contracts specified that the Postmaster general could discontinue his service at any time with one months' notice.

On May 27, 1861 Postmaster General Montgomery Blair suspended mail service in the insurrectionary States and the next day Reeside was notified his routes were suspended.

This affected all of his routes and he asked Blair to annul his contracts but this was refused. Reeside was told they would remain in force and service would resume "when it was should be safe to do so." Reeside had property including stagecoaches in the affected areas but no notice was given to him about the anticipated suspension of service. Arkansas seceded from the Union on May 6, 1861 and it would have taken him 20 days to secure or dispose of his property. President Lincoln had declared a state of war had existed as of April 15, 1861.

No payments for the suspended contracts was offered. Reeside sued but the court was divided over Reeside's rights under the circumstances and rendered a *pro forma* decision in favor of the government in 1866. Reeside appealed and was awarded one month's pay, $5,464.

Reilly, James. Mary Reilly was an industrious resident of Savannah who astutely invested her husband's personal property and notes in cotton, which she purchased in her own name, while he was away, apparently in the service of the Confederacy. She bought 30 bales, stored it at the Central Cotton Press, and 30 bales stored at home in their stable and in the yard. All 60 bales were seized and shipped to New York.

She initially sought to recover under her own name but her attorney, with her consent, substituted her husband as the plaintiff since his assets were used to purchase the cotton. The court had to consider Georgia law, specifically Section 1700:

"In this State the husband is the head of the family, and the wife is subject to him; her legal civil existence is merged in the husband, except so far as the law recognizes her separately, either for her own protection or for her benefit or for the preservation of public order."

Section 1701 provides that, "all the real estate of the wife, and all her personalty in possession, or which may be reduced to possession by the husband during his life, shall vest in and belong absolutely to the husband, except that such property shall not be liable to the payment of any debt, default, or contract of the husband existing at the time of the marriage . . ."

Section 1708 makes certain allowances:

"The wife, by consent of her husband, evidenced by notice in a public gazette for one month, may become a public or free trader, in which event she is liable as *feme-sole* for all her contracts, and may enforce the same in her own name. In such cases the acquisitions of the wife become her separate property."

The Reilly's never conformed to Section 1708 so James had the right to sue in his name and, as the court stated:

"He is purged of his former treason by the President's amnesty granted in his proclamation, and he may now prosecute this suit with no other proof of loyalty than the amnesty granted in the proclamation of December 25, 1868."

They recovered $10,310.80 in 1871.

Reils, Benjamin. Resident of Charleston whose 32 bales of upland cotton and two bales of sea-island cotton were seized by the Army. Reils was especially commended by the court for his "generous assistance to federal prisoners by feeding them and contributing largely of his means to enable them to return to their friends and to duty." He was awarded $4,542.48.

Benjamin's mother-in-law, Eliza Hilborn, 58, owned seven bales of upland cotton that was stored with his and was also taken. Eliza was from Maine and had lived in Charleston for 15 years. Her loyalty was attested to by Robert H. Hearney, "a respectable, intelligent, and wealthy colored man:"

"She was often at my house and I at hers.

From her frequent conversations I know she was a loyal woman. I could not tell how many times I heard her talk — times without number. I mean very often. She would speak in favor of the Yankee forces, saying that some day or other they would get here and give some ease from the distresses we were laboring under. I regarded her as a Union woman during the war. I have never heard her talk in favor of the confederacy and never heard her talk against the United States. I am a colored man.

"I have heard other people speak of her as a Union woman. I do not know of her visiting hospitals. I talked with her very often. I ought to be a Union man if I was not. I do not know anything but the Union. She always wanted the Union troops to win. I owned large property and bought some of our people out on time to prevent them being sold into other slavery. Some of them I afterwards gave their time to and some of them paid for it themselves."

Mrs. Hilborn was awarded $918.40 and the court stated:

"Though in humble life and moderate circumstances, she contributed again and again 'the widow's mite' to the relief of Union prisoners. Union officers escaping from southern prisons found a hiding place and shelter under her roof."

Reybold, Anthony. Chartered his sidewheel steamer *Express* of Delaware City, Delaware on November 17, 1863. On January 6, 1865 he sold one-quarter interest in the boat to George F. Needham and one-quarter to Asa Needham. The vessel was at Washington sheathed in iron 12-inches above the waterline forward and six-inches the rest of the length as protection against ice.

On the 20th quartermaster Captain E. S. Allen was at his office at the Sixth Street wharf, 60 yards from the Potomac in Washington. The river was frozen six to eight inches thick from bank to bank, very dangerous, and closed to commercial navigation. Government steamers, ferryboats going between Washington and Alexandria, and the natural current kept a channel open but masses of thick ice floated down. Allen ordered the master of the *Express* — which the master regarded as an unquestionable military order — to take 75 men downstream to Giesboro the next morning, pick up 80 horses, proceed to City Point, discharge the men and horses, and return to Washington. The weather was wet, cold, and ice was building.

When the vessel was about 28–30 miles downriver, about opposite Glymont and just above Indian Head, heavy ice broke the hull abaft the starboard wheel and at the bow and she sank in 3½ fathoms about three hours later. The men and animals were taken off by the *City Point* and *General Rucker*. The *Express* was abandoned and remained about six weeks until wreckers hired by the owners salvaged her, brought her to Baltimore, and spent $42,384.13 to rebuild her.

The owners sued to recover as a war risk loss but the court held the master never protested and the loss was clearly a marine risk.

Reynolds, Edward. A naturalized Irish resident of Charleston whose 30 bales of upland cotton were seized. Reynolds proved that he secretly kept Sgt. James O'Donnell and Martin McDonald of the 26th New York in his home after they escaped from the prison camp at the race-course. Reynolds recovered $3,936.

Reynolds, Elizabeth C. Thomas F. Reynolds enlisted in Company A, 126th Illinois Infantry Volunteers on July 31, 1862 for three years. On April 21, 1864 he was promoted to first lieutenant of the company, mustered in on September 13, and honorably discharged on July 31, 1865. He was due a $25 enlistment bounty immediately after enrolling and another $75 after two years' service. He never got it, never claimed, it and his widow, Elizabeth sued to recover. On December 7, 1903 her petition was dismissed. As the court stated:

"The offer of the bounty of $100 was intended to encourage men to enlist, as well as to secure their services for a definite period, while in case of their promotion before the completion of that period, the honor of being a commissioned officer, coupled with the emoluments attached thereto, was deemed sufficient to induce them to accept the same in lieu of the bounty so offered."

Reynolds, William. Captain Reynolds was summarily discharged by General Ord on March 28, 1865 and was restored to duty on July 20. Reynold's claim for back pay was dismissed.

Rhett, James M. Rhett's land in South Carolina was assessed $12.50 by the U.S. Direct Tax Commission. It was not paid and it was sold to the United States for $190 and the $177.50 surplus deposited into the Treasury. Part of the land was later sold for $343 and another ten acres was made into a national cemetery as directed by President Cleveland on September 16, 1883.

Rhett redeemed one third of the property under the Act of June 8, 1872 and sued to recover the whole $190, less taxes and costs. Rhett recovered $118.33 on two-thirds of the surplus on May 18, 1885.

Rhine, Abraham. Samuel Rhine was a dry goods merchant in Clarksville, Texas. His brother Abraham was in the same business 120 miles away in McKinney, Texas. Both owned and operated their businesses independently but were partners as A. & S. Rhine in buying dry goods from northern manufacturers and exchanging the merchandise for cotton in the south. After the war started they closed up their stores. Samuel was killed in March 1863 when he was employed by the Confederate government to purchase cotton. At the time of his death he reportedly had about 1,500 bales in 40 parcels stored on the plantations where he had bought it for their partnership.

Abraham employed Moses Steinlein, a storekeeper in Jefferson, Texas, to look after the cotton and in the summer of 1865 he was given the bills of sale for all the cotton, all of which was seized by deputy Treasury agent John Reed and sent to New Orleans. Abraham filed suit on July 23, 1868 but the testimony of Steinlein wasn't heard until March 12, 1873. His store burned down in March 1871 along with it all the receipts for the cotton. All Abraham could prove was that he and his brother dealt in large amounts of cotton but not whether as individuals, partners, or as agents of the Confederate government. All he could prove was that he had 31 bales stored on Mrs. Record's plantation in Lamar County, Texas, it was transported to Jefferson, Texas and seized there by Reed. He could not show that any proceeds from a sale ever reached the Treasury and his petition was dismissed in 1878.

Rhode Island, State of. The State borrowed money to raise and equip troops. They were reimbursed $231,478.51 on October 18, 1861 for the principle but not for the interest paid and the U.S. Direct Tax contributed was not accounted for. The State sued to recover $252,861.11 in additional expenses and on January 27, 1902 was awarded $146,154.45 as a recomputed amount.

Richardson, Andrew J. Richardson's sidewheel steamer *Niagara* was on the ways undergoing repairs at the Allison shipyard in Jersey City, New Jersey in November 1862 after duty in the McClellan Expedition when he heard that vessels were being sought for another expedition and he put in an application.

A secret operation known as the Banks Expedition was being put together. It would require a large number of vessels and to carry out the procurement of vessels without arousing suspicion Secretary of War Edwin M. Stanton approached Cornelius Vanderbilt, esq., of New York City, "a gentleman of large wealth, of long and practical experience as a navigator and shipowner, to accept some official position by which he could make his knowledge and experience available to the government in fitting out and sending forth the expedition." Vanderbilt refused outright any official appointment but offered his services free of charge and went hunting for vessels of superior quality for use as transports. Commodore Gershom J. Van Brunt, USN, was detailed and Charles S. Haswell, port inspector for the port of New York, "and an eminent naval engineer and surveyor for the underwriters of New York city" was employed to assist Vanderbilt and to inspect the vessels and machinery.

The *Niagara* was built for lake navigation with projecting guards and sponsons and had been in passenger service for some time between New York City and Sag Harbor, Long Island. A New York board of underwriters had classed the *Niagara* A 1½, an unusually high rating for a very sound vessel. Richardson's application was accepted, he signed a charter agreement, but was never told the purpose of the charter or the vessel's specific destination. The charter agreement, made by Vanderbilt, stated only, "to any port of the United States, the gulf of Mexico, or the West Indies."

Because the ship was for secret service the law required a special inspection regardless of the vessel's civil rating. Van Brunt and Haswell looked at the ship while in drydock at the request of General Nathaniel Banks and Commodore Vanderbilt and the two pronounced her fit for the secret mission, of whose nature they had full knowledge. She was also surveyed by John M. Weeks, a local government steamboat inspector, who pronounced her sound. Improvements were made to pumps and fireproofing.

The charter was signed on November 26 for $600 a day and the vessel went into service the following day with her normal officers and crew.

Richardson assumed all operational costs. About 150 tons of coal was loaded aboard at New York along with a large quantity of stores.

In December, about 440 troops of Lieutenant Colonel John W. Locke's 50th Massachusetts embarked and the *Niagara* left New York on the 15th. The first night out the port sponson filled with water, which caused maneuvering and steaming problems. Because of her deep draft, the blowpipe was more than a foot underwater and the resulting discharge pressure caused it to burst while they were off the Delaware breakwater. The troops became alarmed at this and a petition was drawn up and signed by the expedition's officers and presented to the captain:

On board Steamboat *Niagara*,
December 15, 1862

The undersigned, officers of the 50th regiment Massachusetts volunteer militia, after due deliberation and taking full and true testimony of competent witnesses, do judge and decide this transport is unseaworthy, with her present freight and passengers, and that we ought to make the nearest port, and furthermore do protest against going to sea.

They put in at Philadelphia and when Vanderbilt found out what happened he ordered her returned to New York but the War Department had already ordered her retained in Philadelphia. In January, Richardson applied to the War Department to have her returned to him. He was referred to Quartermaster General Meigs who refused the request. Further requests were also rejected. In early March 1863 she was ordered back to New York and on 12th she was returned to Richardson by order of Secretary Stanton. She was kept a total of 106 days but she was not used for any service after reaching Philadelphia. Richardson sought to recover money due on the charter from the time she reached port until she was returned to him but his claim was disallowed by Meigs. A number of vessels had problems during the expedition and Congress got involved. Meigs explained to Stanton why he rejected Richardson's claim:

"A special committee of the Senate reported that, in the opinion of the committee, the government was absolved from the obligation of the charter, and that it could not be doubted that the owner was fairly chargeable by the government with the damages consequent upon delay, disembarkation of troops, &c. They further reported that of the unseaworthiness of the *Niagara*, and of her unfitness for the service for which she was chartered, there was little room for doubt."

Richardson sued in federal court. The government argued his vessel was not in the shape required to be by the charter, the United States was not bound by the inspection made by government officers, Richardson knew the language of the charter regarding destinations, and he was bound by the terms of the charter.

Richardson argued his vessel was perfectly suited for the purposes she was built for, the government inspectors pronounced her fit for their intended purpose — which was kept secret from him — and she was grossly overloaded by the Army.

The court found that no legal charter agreement was made when the vessel was hired but on December 15, 1863 Vanderbilt concluded a formal agreement with Richardson. The court dismissed this on the ground that Vanderbilt had no authority at that time to make a charter on behalf of the government since "His agency in the matter had been closed, and his authority in the premises exhausted." All matters relating to the charter were thrown out.

The next question was whether or not Richardson misrepresented the qualities of his vessel in any way. Vanderbilt was questioned about the vessel:

A. The application of the *Niagara* lay there among those of the other steamers. It lay on my desk. The owner one day applied for a charter for her.

Q. What was his name?

A. A. J. Richardson, I believe. He represented her as a first-quality vessel. After he so represented her I spoke to the inspectors, but you have not got to the inspectors yet. There were inspectors appointed by the War Department, as I understood, to inspect these vessels. Whenever I took a vessel I always took it subject to that inspection by these people, who should go out and inspect them. If they did not bear inspection, of course the vessels were not chartered. It relieved me from some trouble. When this *Niagara* came, and the men reported her to me, I asked these gentlemen to go and inspect her and see if she was what the man reported her to be and whether she was fit for this expedition. They did go and so inspect her and reported to me that she was.

Lieutenant Colonel Locke had testified before the Senate committee and stated that the *Niagara* was in fair weather for 24 hours after leaving New York, the port sponson sprung a leak and the blowpipe burst. He had also discovered that one beam and some carlines in the after cabin were very decayed and it was obvious, to him, that the vessel was unseaworthy.

Locke's testimony before the committee was accepted by stipulation.

Charles Haswell testified about his inspection and stood by his report.

Commodore Van Brunt was asked about Haswell's report:

Q. Do you know whether Mr. Haswell examined particularly the timbers and hulls of these vessels?

A. Yes, sir. I went on board with him. I saw her on the ways, in the first place, when she was putting her sponsons on. I went over there and she was on the ways at Jersey City and Mr. Haswell examined her. I was with him. Her bottom appeared fair, and was, no doubt. The sponsons on that vessel were put on tight, as was supposed, and the subsequent difficulty arose, as I suppose, from the fact that her sponsons leaked before she got to Philadelphia and filled with water. The vessel became logy. The men got frightened and they run into Delaware breakwater. Any man who knew anything about this subject would tell you that if they had taken a plank off so as to allow the water to run in and out that difficulty would have been overcome because these sponsons were simply to break the sea off of the guards and if they had taken a plank out she would have been perfectly seaworthy. There was no evidence of weakness about her. I went around her and if I had discovered any evidence of weakness I would have noticed it. I believed she would have performed her voyage.

Q. To New Orleans?

A. Yes, sir. I believe she could. That is my opinion about it. I examined her particularly. I was on board her particularly when she sailed. I went aboard to see that she was not overloaded. There were about 100 men then alongside and a large amount of freight was also lying there in a lighter — barrels &c. I said to the quartermaster, 'You are loading this vessel too deep. You must not put those men on board, neither must you put that material on board because it is too large a quantity. I think she now has enough on board.' She then had 440 men as near as we could ascertain. At my request they were taken away from her and placed on another vessel and she went out with only those men aboard her. That vessel could easily have taken 500 men if she had not been overloaded with stores. She had no room for that number. The great difficulty is that they crowd all these vessels with stores from the quartermaster's, commissary's, and medical departments. It is one of the most difficult things to keep them in order."

Captain J. Langdon Ward gave his account:

I knew the steamer *Niagara*. I was on board her in December 1862 on the occasion of taking a part of the 50th regiment of Massachusetts volunteer militia to Philadelphia. I was a captain in the regiment. The vessel went from this city to the Delaware breakwater. I don't know where she started for. I can't tell you why she went to the breakwater of my own knowledge. While I was on board of her I saw evidence of her unsoundness. The first thing I saw was some rotten wood in some beams in the lower cabin aft, which ran athwartship. I don't remember how many. I should think about two or three. On the way down the sea was very still. There was very little wind, if any, and we ran along very slowly. The ship seemed to labor considerably. I think we left here about 1 o'clock Saturday afternoon and got back to the breakwater about 10 o'clock next morning. Do not know the distance. She was heavily loaded. Her after-guards at the gangway were not more than three feet above the water.

The thing which astonished me most was that after we got to Philadelphia one of my men sent for me into the lower after cabin, where they were, and put the small end of his ramrod right through the side of the ship, put one of his fingers on the other end and pressed the ramrod right through the side of the vessel. I went up on the main deck and stopped and looked under the guard and saw the end of it sticking out. I saw no hole there.

Another witness, George H. Willis, 41, a shipbroker from Orange, New Jersey who had gone to sea at age 14 and commanded sailing vessels, but no steamers, often saw the *Niagara* in port and went aboard to see his cousin, Captain Duncan, the master, testified:

Q. State whether, from the examination you made of the vessel, you were able to come to any conclusion or not as to her seaworthiness or whether she was a vessel adapted for navigating the ocean, being sent with troops and freight or stores to any port in the United States, Gulf of Mexico, or West Indies.

A. As near as I can remember I expressed the opinion at that time that I did not think she was suitable to carry troops outside. I judged from her appearance that she was not built for that purpose. For the purpose for which I supposed she was built I should think she was seaworthy. I supposed from her appearance that she was built for river and sound navigation.

Another witness, Thomas D. Taylor, also expressed the same opinion. Haswell was recalled to the stand and asked about his inspection of the vessel after she returned:

A. I again inspected the vessel in March or April, soon after her return from the Banks expedition, at the request of Brigadier General Van Vliet, quartermaster at this place, and in the discharge of my duty as surveyor of steamers. I made a report at that time to General Van Vliet, to the underwriters, and a communication to Mr. Richardson. My report to General Van Vliet was on the 11th of May.

The report stated:

This vessel is effectively sound, the exceptions to entire soundness being confined to some of the inner faces of the wales, abreast of the boiler and when they lie against the frames, and one of her clamps at a scarf where it has been exposed to weeping from a wheelhouse.

As a whole, the frame of this vessel is very heavy and very sound. Her waterwheel guards are sponsoned forward and slatted aft and she is suitably fitted with an independent steam, fire, and bilge-pipe, hose and ground tackle.

Philadelphia port inspector Samuel Zane testified:

I found her in very bad condition. I visited her with my colleague who was the boiler inspector, James W. Waples. We received instructions from the Secretary of the Treasury to visit all transports that came into this port to see whether they complied with the inspection laws. We visited the *Niagara* shortly after her arrival while lying near about opposite the navy yard or a little above may be. We, after we had boarded her, found on her larboard side aft of the wheelhouse, that two or three deck planks had been knocked out. Also on the starboard side we found the deck pretty well rotten in one place. My colleague went to look after the boiler and engine while I went in the after cabin to examine the hull of the vessel. She was pretty well loaded down with commissary stores. I called for a light and got one. I found her beam and carline, after I took the casing off, in very bad condition, so much so that I pulled a piece out two feet in length and could have pulled it all away. This was out of one of the main beams. I examined the carlines where they rested on the clamps. All I examined were pieced out. I came upon deck and asked for the captain. I think I saw the captain. I told him he must not go to sea in that vessel in her present condition. I went to the district attorney and related the case to him. He told me to telegraph to the Secretary of War "For God's sake not to let that vessel go to sea." He gave me a note to take to the captain, a protest. I went aboard and delivered it to the captain. I went aft to the quarters where the officers were quartered. I found all the officers were dissatisfied with the vessel. I went around the side of her in a small boat under her guards to make an examination there. She was pretty well down in the water. I found nothing there that looked different from her general appearance.

Machinery and boiler inspector Waples reported that her engines and boiler were OK. Ship joiners gave varying and sometimes conflicting testimony as to the vessel's condition. Shipyard owners were particularly careful not to offend the sensibilities of vessel owners by being too critical.

Charles B. Arnold, an "engineer and manufacturer" stated:

I know the steamer *Niagara,* formerly owned by Mr. Richardson. I first saw the boat in the Genessee river at Charlotte near Rochester. This was about the first of June, 1862, or within a few days of it. I took charge of her and brought her around to New York, down the rapids of the St. Lawrence, through the Gulf, and around to New York by sea. We had on that voyage quite a good deal of rough weather. The ship behaved well. She gave evidence of being a good sea boat, staunch and strong.

Conflicting evidence continued to be presented as to the vessel's soundness. In May 1863, Richardson offered his boat for sale to the Quartermaster's Department at a very low price, "owing to the injury done her reputation by the report of the Senate committee." according to Samuel Churchman, a civilian employee of the department who inspected the vessel. Churchman found the vessel "to be in very excellent condition" and she was purchased in May of 1863 at what he thought was a very low price, $30,000, and served continuously for two years.

Assistant Secretary of War John Tucker testified about Richardson's desire to release the *Niagara* from the charter in late '62 or early '63, which was denied.

Shipmaster Wickham S. Havens testified:

I was formerly a ship master and ship agent. From 1828 to 1844 I was constantly at sea. From 1844 to 1855 I was ship agent, a commission merchant, and ship chandler to 1859. From 1859 to 1864 a steamboat captain. During a part of the time from 1859 to 1864 I knew the *Niagara,* belonging to Richardson. I had command of her from July 8th, 1862 until about September 14th, 1862. A part of this time I was running her from New York to Sag Harbor, and a part of the time she was employed on the McClellan expedition, so-called, conveying troops from the Peninsula to Aquia creek and Washington and Alexandria. During this time I had good opportunities of knowing the qualities of this vessel. I knew all about her. In my opinion, vessels of her class are not calculated for ocean navigation. She was better suited to rough water than any other of her class I knew of. I knew the vessel particularly at the time she was chartered for the Banks expedition. I considered her at that time a seaworthy vessel in the sense of her being sound and having sufficient strength for the purpose of navigation. I never saw any weakness in her whatever. There was no spring in her. She was built and had a frame like a ship. I told Mr. Grimes, of the Senate committee on Banks expedition charters, that I could go around the world in her if her guards were reduced. I saw her on her return from the Banks expedition. I had charge of her from the 10th of January to the 12th of March, 1863 while on this expedition. I knew her to be as seaworthy then as she was before. When she returned from the Banks expedition I saw the condition she was in. I saw a beam and two or three carlines that were decayed. The decayed beam and carlines did not affect the seaworthiness of the vessel or weaken her materially. After this vessel was sold to the government in May, 1863, I took her to New Orleans. We went around Cape Hatteras in a northeast gale. We were two days in it. I don't think there is any worse place for a vessel on the globe. She behaved well.

The court stated, in part:

"Upon this state of facts we cannot see how a recovery can be resisted. Vanderbilt had authority to hire the vessel. He did employ her at a fixed compensation. She was fit for inland or short coast service. The claimant was entirely unaware how she was to be employed or where sent. How could he be responsible that she should be suitable for that of which he had not the remotest idea she was to be employed in? The government made their own selection and inspection, and, unless there was fraud or concealment on the part of the claimant, are liable for the hire while they had the vessel in possession. There is no evidence whatever of fraud, and none can be presumed.

"But why she was kept for more than 100 days, lying idle at the Philadelphia wharf, passes all comprehension when she ought to have been redelivered to the claimant within ten days and her pay stopped if found to be unfit for the service for which she had been chartered. The claimant during all that time was at the expense of fuel for his vessel, her officers and crew were kept full, their hire was paid, same as if actively employed, the time of the vessel was totally lost if not paid for by the government.

"The price at which the vessel was chartered must be regarded as the fair market value of such services as she was fitted to perform. But her full expenses lying in port, although with fires constantly kept up, were less than on active duty. The wear and tear of her machinery would be saved, her risks would be smaller, although her insurance was probably the same. For these a deduction is to be made. That deduction, in our judgement, ought to be one-third the com-

pensation. Then to the balance is to be added the cost of repairs for the damage committed by the soldiers on the run of the vessel to Philadelphia. The proof is that those repairs coast claimant $1,335."

Richardson was awarded $63,600 for 106 days' charter at $600 a day, minus $21,200 in deductions, making $42,400 to which the repair costs were added for a total award of $43,735.

Richmond, Sarah A. Richmond & Wilmot was a Savannah jewelry firm. Wilmot had left for Bridgeport, Connecticut prior to the war as it was his custom to spend the winter in Savannah and the rest of the year up north. Richmond carried on with the business and also served as a clerk in the Confederate commissary department. In 1863 he purchased 82 bales of sea-island cotton under his own name. On December 31, 1864 he took a loyalty oath under the of December 6, 1863. On February 25, 1865 he assigned the interest in the cotton for the sum of $1 to Wilmot. Richmond died in 1870 and Sarah, with Wilmot's consent, filed suit as tenants in common and Richmond & Wilmot were awarded $19,006.76 in 1871.

Robertson, Charles F. Contracted with Quartermaster E. C. Wilson on June 14, 1862 to deliver 250 horses at $114 each to Perryville, Maryland on or before the 30th reserving the right to change the place of delivery to Washington, D.C. with the extra expense paid by the government. Wilson ordered 100 horses to Perryville then to Washington and the rest were delivered to Washington or to points around Washington. Wilson failed to pay the additional cost. Robertson sued for $2,000 and recovered $750 in 1866.

Roddin, Jane. Jane Knight, of Charleston, bought four bales of upland cotton from John Larkin while she was a widow. The bales were brought down on the South Carolina Railroad, officially weighed, brought to her house on the corner of Line Street and Railroad Avenue, and rolled into her yard shortly before the city was captured.

She married Bernard Roddin on April 17, 1865. Bernard lost five bales of upland cotton at Charleston, four of which were Jane's, and then died sometime after that. Jane sought to recover the loss under the Act of March 12, 1863.

A woman who married in South Carolina forfeited her property to her husband. If he died she had to bring suit through an administrator to retrieve it. Mr. W. A. Rook initially acted as her representative but his name was removed from the claim. She was then advised to sue in federal court under own name but the court upheld the laws of South Carolina and declared the claim dead along with her husband since she had no administrator.

Roman, Charles. On June 13, 1865, 142 bales of Roman's cotton were seized at New Orleans, 107 bales were returned to him, and he sued to recover on the 35 bales sold. He recovered $3,971.96 but was ordered to pay the 2 percent internal revenue tax of $846.94.

Ross, George W. A resident of Athens, Tennessee who enlisted in the Army in October 1863 and served until the end of the war. He owned 31 bales of cotton that were stored in a warehouse in Rome, Georgia. It was seized on May 18, 1864, loaded on wagons and taken to a warehouse on the railroad tracks near Kingston, put on the train and taken to Chattanooga with 11 other bales from Rome. The lot arrived at Nashville on August 24 and the whole lot sold for net proceeds of $20,806.69. Ross was awarded $15,356.78 at $495.38 a bale.

The government appealed to the Supreme Court where the assistant attorney general argued:

"There is absolutely nothing but conjecture to establish any connection between Ross's 31 bales and the 42 bales shipped from Kingston in August 1864 and a grossly improbable conjecture at that. How was Kingston situated? It lies a dozen miles east of Rome, and the branch road from Rome strikes the Great Western & Atlantic Railway at Kingston so that the cotton coming over this little branch of a dozen miles or so was but a drop in the bucket to that which came over the trunk-line extending via Atlanta to the seacoast at Savannah and Charleston in one direction, and to Mobile and New Orleans in the other, with ramifications throughout the cotton States. Thus, Kingston was in the heart of the cotton country."

The decision was reversed on the ground that there was no evidence to show any of the cotton actually belonged to Ross or that the proceeds from the sale of any of his cotton ever reached the Treasury.

Royse, C. R. C. R. was the administrator of Felix G. Royse's estate and sued as one of the Kentucky Draft case plaintiffs.

In 1863 all of the loyal States were divided into enrollment districts generally corresponding with Congressional districts. Each district was required to supply so many draftees based on population. Sparsely settled areas were subdivided into units composed of a number of counties. Credits were given to each district based on voluntary enlistments, reenlistments, and new enlistees.

In the spring of 1864 Confederate forces under General Morgan invaded and conducted raids in Kentucky that interfered with the mustering of troops in the 4th through 9th Congressional districts and there were "uprisings in the State hostile to the Union after the President's proclamation."

On March 1, 1864 the authorities in Kentucky suggested a redistribution of the credits because of irregularities in the credits given.

On the 14th a draft call was issued by President Lincoln for 200,000 men and it was found necessary to draft men from Kentucky. The credit revision was ordered by the provost marshal general on April 12 but was not carried out until July 21. Many draftees called during this period from Adair, Butler, Casey, Crittenden, Grant, Grayson, Green, Jefferson, Lincoln, Mercer, Ohio, Pendleton, or Taylor Counties claimed to have been illegally drafted under the call of March 14 after it was determined that at the time of the call the counties had already fulfilled or exceeded their quotas.

Ludwell McKay originally petitioned Congress regarding the matter long after the fact. He was joined by Felix G. Royse of Adair County, one of the draftees who avoided military service pursuant to the Act of February 24, 1864. On May 27, 1910 Congress passed a resolution authorizing and directing the Secretary of the Treasury to reimburse over 2,000 illegally drafted men identified as having paid the $300. Of these, 141 surviving draftees, their heirs or administrators, came forward from Kentucky to present claims.

The War Department stated their records were incomplete at the county level but the State as a whole furnished 9,186 drafted men under the call of March 14. Of those, 421 actually served; 531 furnished substitutes; and 3,241 paid substitutes.

A total of 16,805 were drafted in Kentucky under the call of July 18, 1864 of which 1,439 served; 1,981 furnished substitutes; and 24 paid commutation money.

On April 1, 1912 the court dismissed the petitions:

"The conclusion of the court upon the whole case is that the claims of the respective claimants are not founded upon any obligation of the Government, legal or equitable; that the payments made by the respective claimants as set forth in the findings were made at their own requests and for their own benefit, and that the Government, by accepting the money in lieu of the military service of the claimants, assumed no responsibility and incurred no liability."

Rubey, Thomas P. A deputy Treasury agent from St. Louis who was authorized to buy cotton within certain counties in Mississippi pursuant to section 5 of the Non-intercourse Act of July 13, 1861. Eleven bales were purchased for him by C. E. Hovey and stored while awaiting shipment. They were seized by soldiers and sent to Vicksburg. Hovey found them there before they were sent to Cincinnati where eight of the bales were sold at auction for $1,210.49. Hovey and Rubey proved loyalty and Rubey was awarded $1,210.48.

Rudolph, James. A black resident of Charleston who invested surplus earnings in cotton. He sued and testified:

A. I was born free. Before and during the war I was a drayman. When the Union army came in here I owned five bales of cotton. I had it in Mary's street opposite the school. It was not where I lived. I had it stored there. I purchased this cotton of C. C. Clacius about 1863. I bought it with gold and silver of my earning. I kept it till the Union army came here. I reported it to General Hatch and Captain Sturdivant at No. 10 Broad street. It was taken away and carried to the custom-house. I have been loyal to the United States all the time. I never did anything to aid the rebellion. I sold all my drays, discharged all my men, and kept but one dray to drive myself and I had a certificate from the doctor that I was not fit for service. I did what I could with money for the Union prisoners. Sent them coffee and things. I took up a collection and sent my son to them. I can say under oath that I was always loyal to the United States and opposed the rebellion. I had every reason to be. They were going to free my race. They were losing their lives fighting for my race and I had a right to feel for them.

On cross-examination he stated:

Q. What did you purchase the cotton for?
A. I had $1,375 in the Charleston Bank and when the war broke out I heard they were giving people confederate money so I went and got the money and bought the cotton. I had an idea that I could always sell my cotton for good money. I bought it of C. C. Clacius. I knew the confederacy was going up.
Q. What made you think the confederacy would fall in 1863?
A. It was my faith God was going to deliver his people and that the time had arrived.
Q. Had you not more faith in the shells than in anybody else?
A. I think it was all the working of God.

James was awarded $525.04 for four bales of upland cotton.

Ruggles, George D. Major D. Colden Ruggles was an additional paymaster in the Army. From about September 15, 1864 he had made payroll payments to soldiers in Washington, D.C. hospitals through the first week of October.

On October 12 he withdrew $115,000 from the Treasury and the next day boarded a Baltimore & Ohio train with $108,000 in cash and $2,088.25 in vouchers to pay off General Sheridan's troops at Winchester, Virginia. On the train with Ruggles was paymaster Edwin L. Moore, also en route to pay Sheridan's troops with $64,236.30 in payroll vouchers and $136.30 in cash in a tin box. The railroad was within Sheridan's lines at the time and considered safe. The guards had been removed and the B & O was maintaining a regular schedule. Somewhere between Harper's Ferry and Martinsburg the train was captured by Moseby's guerillas and Ruggles was held prisoner until he died.

None of the money was ever recovered and Ruggles's estate was charged with the loss. His administrator sued to recover.

A witness stated he saw the major with the money in his traveling bag and his clerk stated he took the regimental muster rolls with him.

George was awarded $110,080.25 in 1866.

None of Moore's money was ever recovered and he was charged with the loss. He sued to recover and was reimbursed in 1866.

Russell, John H. Sought to recover $111,859.33 on the value, damage from overloading, and use of his steamboats, *J. H. Russell, Liberty,* and *Time and Tide* when seized by the government. He recovered $41,355.33.

Rutherford, R. A. Co-owner of 27 bales of cotton seized at Brownsville, Texas on May 31, 1865. That summer, 514 bales and 489 sacks of cotton — all equal to 563 bales — was shipped from Brownsville to New Orleans. All the cotton was repacked into 523 bales and of these 79 bales were held on order of the U.S. circuit court as evidence in a lawsuit; 105 were sold in New York for $14,180.71; and 339 sold for $58,574.89. The 79 bales were a part of the repacked 523 bales and were equal to 85 bales of the original 563. The sale of 478 bales produced a fund of $72,735.81 or $152.20 per bale.

Rutherford sued on behalf of himself and his partners, a common practice with claims under the Act of March 12, 1863 to eliminate needless duplication. A decision was rendered and the parties were left to settle up between themselves. Rutherford was awarded $4,100 on 27 bales at $152.20 a bale in 1873.

John D. Grissett sued to recover the proceeds of 78 bales of his cotton later found in this lot. He recovered $11,746.02 in 1873.

Sainte Marie, Henry B. On April 20, 1865 Secretary of War Edwin M. Stanton put a notice in newspapers announcing a $25,000 reward "for the apprehension of John H. Surratt, one of Booth's accomplices" and also said that "liberal awards will be paid for any information that shall conduce to the arrest of either of the above-mentioned criminals or their accomplices." There was no time limit on Stanton's offer but it was rescinded by President Johnson on November 24.

In April 1866 Ste. Marie and Surratt were zouaves "in the military service of the Papal government." Ste. Marie furnished information on the whereabouts of Surratt and was duly awarded $10,000. He sued for the full amount but his case was dismissed since he didn't actually arrest Surratt.

Sampson, George T. and Augustus. Shipbuilders in Boston who signed a $75,000 contract with the Navy Department on September 9, 1862 to build the hull of the 205-foot, 974-ton wooden paddle-wheel, double-ended gunboat *Mattabessett* and deliver it 200 miles away to Allaire Works, the engine builder in New York, on or before 126 days from the signing of the contract. Delivery to the Navy was to be on or before 50 days after reaching the engine builder. Launching was scheduled for January 13, 1863 but the Navy failed to furnish the required drawings, made numerous alterations and additions throughout the building process, and even after the move to New York they ordered changes and alterations to the hull. The Navy extended the contract by 50 days to March 4 but the vessel

was still not completed until January 18, 1864. The hull reached New York on May 2, 1863.

The increased cost to the Sampsons was $19,703.24. The Navy paid them $500 for the trip to New York and $3,723.70 for extra work but they claimed they were still owed $487 for hurricane deck awnings and $1,325 more for getting the hull to New York. The total amount paid out was $79,223.70. They petitioned Congress for relief on March 16, 1864 to no avail but because of the numerous claims from contractors building ships for the Navy during the Civil War, Congress passed a joint resolution on March 9, 1865 establishing the Selfridge Board to examine 1862 and 1863 contract over-runs and report to the Senate. The Board was composed of Commodore Thomas O. Selfridge, Chief Engineer Henderson, and Paymaster Eldridge.

The Sampsons filed a claim for $83,239.08 with the Board on June 29, 1865 claiming a balance owed of $4,015.38. The Board accepted this and forwarded their recommendation to the Senate on January 30, 1866.

Augustus died in 1894. The brothers had been in business together at Boston from 1862 to 1875.

Congress authorized the payment on June 17, 1902 under the Tucker Act of March 3, 1887 pending findings of facts by a federal court. George filed suit on April 10, 1907.

Their loyalty was established and George wanted reimbursement for additional expenses not authorized by the Board. The court said it had no jurisdiction to award an amount over the $4,015.38 under the Tucker Act and he was awarded that on May 6, 1907.

Sams, J. Julius. J. Julius and Horace H. Sams owned about 200 acres in St. Helena Parish near Beaufort, South Carolina called Sams Pine Land, and another 650 acres on the 1,300-acre Datha Island known as Datha Inlet Land.

Sams Pine Land was bordered on the north by Jenkins Pine Land, on the south by the Capers place and Ashdale; on the east by Oakdale, Ashdale, and the Capers place; and on the west by the Wegg place and Joe Johnson's place.

Dr. Berners Barnwell Sams purchased one-half of the land owned by Horace Sams when he made a down payment of $2,000 on February 1, 1860.

South Carolina taxed Sams Pine Land as uncultivated land and the Datha Inlet Land as cultivated land.

On March 10, 1863 the Direct Tax Commission condemned properties in St. Helena for non-payment of taxes and caused them to be surveyed into 640-acre sections without regard for existing legal boundaries. These one-square mile sections were then subdivided into 10-acre plots.

The Commission valued Sams Pine Land at $800. The taxes, penalties, and interest charges amounted to $26.69. The United States bid $40 for the property leaving a surplus of $13.31 deposited into the Treasury. The United States sold the property on February 24, 1864 to heads of families, loyal citizens, soldiers, and sailors.

Taxes, penalties, and interest charges on Datha Inlet Land amounted to $86.73. It was sold to the government for $450 leaving a surplus of $363.27. The surplus was paid over to the Sams by judgement of a federal court. A total of 995.37 acres was sold on Datha Island. Buyers were Cyrus Andrews, 160 acres; H. P. Kellum and W. T. Colkins, 547.37 acres; and J. B. Case, 288 acres.

B. Barnwell Sams owed $3,650.28 on the mortgage when the land was seized and sold.

J. Julius Sams sued to recover the tax surplus on the Pine Land and a $5 per acre bonus on cultivated land and a $1 per acre bonus on uncultivated land pursuant to the Act of March 2, 1891.

Horace Sams died prior to March 14, 1892 when a decision awarded J. Julius Sams $1,625 on $5 per 650 acres, less one-half the surplus, $181.64, and less $26, one-half the taxes held in reserve for the State of South Carolina, for a total of $1,417.36. He also received $1 per acre for 200 acres of uncultivated land, less taxes withheld, for a total of $1,509.36. B. Barnwell Sams was awarded $1,417.37; Grace L. Sams, C. Whittle Sams, and Fannie Sams, heirs of Horace Sams, were awarded $92 for $1 per acre on $200 acres of Sams Pine Land.

Sanderson, Harriet A.

Sanderson, Harriet A. Edwin C. Lawson enrolled on August 21, 1861 at Carlinville, Illinois as a private in Company C, 32d Regiment Illinois Infantry for three years. He was promoted to captain on September 24, 1864, wounded on December 10, granted 30 days' leave, and honorably discharged on February 25, 1865 at New York City.

Lawson's claim for travel pay home to Carlinville was denied on the ground that his point of discharge was near his place of enlistment.

The distance from New York to Carlinville was 1,060 miles. A captain's travel pay — one days' pay for every 20 miles — would have been 53 days less $3.18 of income tax and amounted to $100.75. On July 25, 1904 the comptroller allowed him $60.42 for "commutation for subsistence for traveling 1,060 miles" less the tax.

His wife Harriet had remarried after Edwin died and wanted the travel pay but her suit was dismissed on March 12, 1906 on the ground that she couldn't prove he wasn't transported home on government transportation:

"For this reason we think it would be very dangerous to establish the precedent, at this late day, that in such cases the Government should be compelled to assume the burden of proving that transportation had been furnished."

Scharfer, Frederick M. Owner of 13 bales of sea-island cotton seized at Charleston. Recovered $1,705.60.

Schirling, John. A German citizen who owned a quarry at North Vernon, Indiana. When he heard a new arsenal was being built at Indianapolis he proposed in writing to furnish blue limestone at $2.40 a cubic yard for dimension stone and $1.40 a cubic yard for rubble stone. His offer was verbally accepted but before a formal contract was drawn up he realized his prices were too low and he withdrew the offer. In October 1863 he signed a contract for dimension stone at $3 a cubic yard and $2.40 a cubic yard for foundation stone. He delivered 368 cubic yards of foundation stone and 68 cubic yards of dimension stone and was paid $1,087.20. He was still unsatisfied with these prices and a new contract was executed on July 1, 1864 under which he delivered 1,224½ cubic yards of material at $5 a cubic yard, enough to complete the project. This included 25 yards of foundation stone for which the accounts credited him $2.40 a yard and he was paid $6,057.80. He disputed the calculation of the amount and the price and alleged that he signed the contract without fully realizing its contents owing to his poor English. He petitioned Congress but before any legislative action was taken he filed suit and recovered $1,377.50.

He brought a second suit in 1875, which was dismissed. He went back to Congress and on March 3, 1883 his claim was referred to a federal court with a dismissal of any statute of limitations.

The court found he delivered 950 cubic

yards of stone over and above the 1,538 yards used for the building and its fair market value was $12.50 a cubic yard, worth $11,875. Schirling had already been paid $8,522.50. The court added $7,549 to the 1,538 building stone and he was awarded $10,901.50 on March 29, 1886.

Schreiner & Sons. John C. Schreiner and his son S. A. Schreiner were subjects of the North German Confederation and the Duke of Saxe-Coburg-Gotha. Another son, Hermann L. Schreiner, was a U.S. citizen. They owned a store at the corner of Congress and St. Julien in Savannah selling music and musical instruments. S. A. Schreiner had been conscripted into Confederate military service but escaped and made his way to New York.

Hermann sued to recover $7,203.36 on 43 bales of cotton seized at Savannah in February 1865 and sent to New York on the bark *Atlanta*.

W. G. Engelke testified that Hermann was instrumental in forming a Confederate German volunteer company but when it was actually called up he refused to go and other members of the group threatened to shoot him if he didn't join them. Other witnesses, Vincent Czurda and G. S. Obens, said the Schreiners sold "certain pieces of music designed to encourage the rebellion, military goods, drums, and buttons." Others said the goods sold to rebels were "music, fancy soaps, perfumes, and toilet articles."

Hermann was unable to prove his loyalty and his petition was dismissed.

Schultz, Alexander. Signed a contract with the Quartermaster of the Army of the Potomac on December 31, 1861 to run his steam ferryboat *Tallacca* between Georgetown, District of Columbia, and Fort Corcoran in Virginia for $115 a day for at least seven months and thereafter for as long as the government required the service. Schultz was to furnish the crew and to keep the boat available at all times, day and night and, "He shall also maintain the landings and in every respect bear the costs of running a very busy ferry service."

Service began on January 9, 1862. On April 11 the boat was fully loaded with government stores and property, the weather windy and stormy. The quartermaster ordered Schultz to tow three schooners from Budd's Ferry to Walloman Creek on the Potomac. The master of the steamer objected, claiming towing duties were not a contractual obligation, the vessel was already loaded to capacity, and any additional load

would likely cause the vessel to break down. The quartermaster insisted so the tow commenced but the master was forced to drop anchor due to inclement weather. They apparently reached their destination without further trouble but two days later, in pleasant weather and with a light cargo, the vessel's machinery broke down and completely disabled the boat. She was towed to Washington and from there to Baltimore. The repairs took 65 days and cost $683. She returned to service on June 16th and stayed in service until October 1st. Schultz was paid $13,355 for service under the contract but the Army did not compensate him for the lost days of service or the cost of repairs, which Schultz claimed was caused by the Army. His claims were repeatedly denied so he sued.

The court found the government liable for the $383 damage plus $30,475 for service from January 9 to October 1st. The court deducted $129 for $20 a month crew and steward wages Schultz saved during the repair period; $2,064 for coal not used during the repair period and for coal furnished by the government for 83 days of the 172 days at $12 per day; and the $13,355 already paid was deducted.

The final award of $15,609.01 was made in December 1867.

Scott, Isaac. Resident of Macon, Georgia and partner in the firm of George Parsons & Co. He and Edward Padelford owned one-fourth interest in 206 bales of cotton captured at Savannah. Scott applied for amnesty under the proclamation of May 29, 1865 and accepted the pardon in October 1865, which was dated August 29, 1865 and signed by Secretary of State William H. Seward. There were complications with the oath he took as it was not specifically under the proclamation by which he was granted amnesty. In 1873 he recovered $9,029.49 on 51½ bales. He was also awarded $18,234.32 on 104 bales and $62,242.15 on 355 bales for claims previously filed.

Seabrook, Cato A. A resident of rural South Carolina who recovered $203.19 on January 11, 1886 after the Direct Tax Commission illegally assessed his property and penalties at a higher rate than allowed.

Sevier, John V. Owner of a plantation in Tensas Parish, Louisiana from which 37 bales of cotton were seized on February 1, 1864 by Brigadier General Ellett's Mississippi Marine Brigade. Sevier recovered $5,181.48 in 1871.

Shaw, John S. Owner of the $70,000 steamer *Robert Campbell, jr.* of St. Louis. The Army requested Shaw to carry cargo to Memphis and Vicksburg but he declined so on September 17, 1863 she was impressed into government service against his will. She was loaded with military supplies, left St. Louis on the 25th for Vicksburg under Captain Shaw and his crew, and caught fire and burned up near Milliken's Bend.

Shaw had $25,000 worth of insurance, which he was paid, and applied to the Third Auditor for the $45,000 difference. The Auditor valued the boat at $57,000, deducted the $25,000 already paid, and sent him a check for $32,000. Shaw later accepted it under protest then sued under the Act of March 3, 1849 to recover the $13,000 balance on the value and the $25,000 insurance money on behalf of the insurance companies. The court held he could not recover on a loss by fire under that Act if he was operating his own vessel under a charter agreement and he could not recover the insurance money.

Sheppard, James. Owned a cotton plantation near Pine Bluff, Arkansas. In April 1864, there were about 600 bales of cotton in Pine Bluff collected from various plantations. The entire amount was sent to Little Rock for use in fortifications. A total of 273 bales were used in Little Rock but only 248 were taken out, most in very poor condition with owners' marks obliterated. All were sold at a net profit of $259.53 a bale. Sheppard was credited with 182 bales and awarded $42,908.32 in 1873.

Shrewsbury, William S. General Carleton, commanding in New Mexico, needed a million pounds of supplies not available locally so Colonel M. R. Morgan authorized the transfer of supplies from Forts Leavenworth and Riley to Fort Union. Shrewsbury signed a contract on March 27, 1865 to transport up to 15 million pounds of supplies from Leavenworth to Union during 1865. He subsequently transported 14,202,811 pounds leaving 797,189 pounds on his contract.

When Carleton needed corn in a hurry, before winter set in, to feed Indian prisoners of war, Morgan signed a contract with A. N. Fuller and John Tierman. The corn was part of 800,000 pounds consigned to Shrewsbury. Fuller & Tierman transported 10,000 bushels of shelled corn at $8.54 a bushel. The corn cost $1.25 a bushel at Fort Leavenworth and $7.29 was for transportation.

Shrewsbury said it was part of his contract but Morgan denied the claim. He sued for $24,000 in unliquidated damages claiming fraud but his petition was dismissed on the ground that the delivery was in the nature of an emergency.

Sierra, Joaquina. Joseph Sierra was the U.S. collector of customs, superintendent of lights, and an agent of the marine hospital at Pensacola from April 21, 1853 to April 9, 1861 when he resigned and continued the same duties in voluntary Confederate service throughout the war. He died on May 14, 1867 with the U.S. government owing him $3,704.68 for duties performed prior to the war.

His wife applied for the money but was barred by the Joint Resolution of March 2, 1867. Joaquina sued in the Court of Claims under the unconditional pardon of December 25, 1868 but her petition was dismissed by statute of limitation. The court decided the last day she had to file was April 2, 1872, six years after the proclamation of April 2, 1866 which declared the rebellion over in Florida. She filed on May 16, 1872. The statute of limitations in the Court of Claims was six years.

Silliman, Robert F. Silliman, Matthews & Co. of New York owned four 2-deck barges: The *R. D. Silliman,* 165 tons, Captain D. D. Askins; *L. P. Gardiner,* 155 tons, Captain H. Silliman; *Saint Nicholas,* 211 tons, Captain James Lynch; and the *A. S. Perry,* 214 tons, Captain James Weaver. On April 1, 1863 the barges were chartered to the Army for $38 a day each. On June 2 Quartermaster General Montgomery Cunningham Meigs instructed Major Stewart Van Vliet, the quartermaster at New York, that all double-decked barges used for transporting cattle and horses then in service and after March 1 should be chartered at rates not to exceed $4 per registered ton per month.

When Silliman and Matthews were notified they replied their barges had been measured as single deck, the proposed rate was unacceptable unless they were allowed to include the upper deck, and rather than accept the reduced rate they would prefer to withdraw the barges from service. Van Vliet reported this to Meigs and Meigs told him to discharge the barges as quickly as he could and procure others on the new terms. Van Vliet replied on July 22 that there were no other barges available at that rate based on the registered tonnage, which measured only the hold and not their actual carrying capacity. The Army held the barges as before until December 10 when Meigs told Van Vliet to pay at the reduced rate after December 1. Silliman said he would not let them for $4 a ton per month and he wanted them back. On the 28th Meigs issued a circular letter to all quartermasters saying that no payments on barges due after March 31, 1863 would be made to owners at any rate other than that proposed on June 2.

Silliman then went to Washington to confront Meigs personally. He demanded his barges back and Meigs told him the Army needed them and would keep them and the money due him for the charter. Silliman went back to New York and to see Van Vliet but his hands were tied. He couldn't pay Silliman without authorization from Washington and that wasn't going to happen unless Silliman agreed to the new rates.

On January 8, 1864 Silliman wrote to the Secretary of War to complain about the treatment he and his partner had received and said, in part:

"We desire to sell, if we cannot have our barges or obtain money for their use, as we cannot meet our obligations to our captains and crews without money to do it, and hope you will act favorably for us at an early date."

On March 5, the partners notified Meigs they would accept the new rates as of the nearest first-of-the-month. Meigs replied their new rate would be in effect as of April 1. The partners wrote back, in part:

"We have been paid to November 1, 1863, and if we have to go back to April 1, 1863, we shall have to stop payment, as we have depended on this money to keep along in our business. We have been told by other parties that they dated new charters from December 1, and we can see no reason that they should be favored above us. We cannot go back to April 1, 1863."

Meigs said too bad so Matthews went to Washington to see him and was again told that he had "laid down the rule" and that he would keep the barges and not pay for them unless the partners agreed to the terms. Matthews then met with Colonel Clary and made the new agreement on May 16 under protest.

In March 1863 the *Gardiner* was in the Potomac under tow when gale force winds came up. The tug captain anchored the barge close in to shore against the wishes of Captain Silliman. The barge's anchor couldn't hold and the barge was driven ashore and damaged. The Quarter-

master then deducted $389.36 from the rent for 18 days and 7 hours of lost time while the barge was being repaired at a cost to Silliman & Matthews of $1,351.15.

In May 1864 the tug towing the *Perry* was struck by a sailing vessel in the Potomac and then ran into the barge causing damage and in September she collided with the government tug that was towing her when the tug went aground causing further injury. The company was charged $245.97 for 9 days and 6 hours of lost time for repairs, which cost the company $528.65.

The total cost to the partners to repair their four barges was $1,913.34. They sued and recovered $3,653.85 in 1876.

Silverhill, Simeon W. Claimed two bales and six bags of upland cotton seized at Savannah in early 1865. Before the cotton was removed he sold it to J. Schiffer & Co. as payment on a debt. When the suit was filed Samuel Schiffer of New York was the surviving partner. The court could find no evidence linking Schiffer to the cotton since it was in the possession of the United States when Silverhill was supposed to have sold it. The case was remanded to the docket instead of being dismissed.

Silvey, John. Owner of 77 bales of cotton seized in Atlanta. At an average weight of 500 pounds per bale, he recovered $27,715.38.

Simons, John H. Owned a lot and dwelling in Charleston at No. 6 Lynch Street which he rented. The U.S. Direct Tax Commission valued the property at $18,000 but he never paid the $184.80 tax. On May 6 William Lucas paid the tax including $40.80 in interest at 10 percent per year and Simons was allowed to collect rent again. Simons subsequently repaid Lucas and on August 23, 1882 he decided he wanted the interest back and decided the tax was collected illegally. The Treasury Department didn't agree. Simons sued and the court held the interest was charged illegally since it accrued prior to the assessment of the property and he recovered the $40.80 in 1884.

Slawson, Hamilton, Jr. A resident of Charleston, South Carolina who bought the light-draft steamer *De Kalb* at an auction there in April 1863. Slawson had been the vessel's agent for the previous owner. Prior to and after this sale the Confederates had impressed the vessel to transport men, arms, and supplies around Charleston Harbor.

On the evening of February 16, 1865, right before Confederate forces evacuated the city, the rebels ordered the *De Kalb* to proceed from her wharf to one or more islands in the harbor to evacuate personnel and supplies. Slawson did not want to risk losing his new boat on this hazardous mission so he suggested to the engineer that they disable the vessel to keep it from being used. The engineer agreed and wrecked the boiler so it could not be fired.

Rebels set fire to the boat, cut the mooring lines, and set her adrift in the stream during the evacuation of Charleston with a Navy gunboat and other craft nearby. Slawson got on board with assistance from friends, extinguished the fire, and got the boat to James Island.

General Alexander Schimmelfennig had placed Navy Chief Engineer George B. N. Tower in charge of captured steamers in Charleston Harbor. Slawson appealed to Tower to get his boat back and the two made an informal agreement to place the vessel at the service of the United States. No fee was discussed and Tower did not see the boat but he said he would help put the steamer back in service, get her back to Charleston, and pay whatever she was reasonably worth under a charter-party agreement. Things went awry, possibly over questions concerning Slawson's loyalty, and shortly after that Tower turned the boat over to the Army quartermaster.

The Army salvaged the boat, repaired it at Charleston at a cost of $15,000, and used it there for 104 days. No formal agreement had been drawn up due to the urgent need for the steamer. Neither Tower nor the Army ever formally seized the vessel, she was not considered captured property during the time of her use, and Slawson was at all times recognized as the rightful owner of the boat to whom money would eventually be due. A total of 402 days was eventually agreed to but after her service the Army sold the boat as captured property for $3,963.83. Pleas to the War Department went unheeded so he sued.

Slawson professed loyalty and sought compensation at $75 a day for each day of her use by the United States and claimed $30,150 less $150 for the repair work done at Charleston under the verbal agreement he and Tower had made.

On March 2, 1865 Slawson took President Lincoln's oath of amnesty of December 8, 1863.

In court, the assistant attorney general questioned Slawson's right to recover since he had, in his opinion, given aid and comfort to the rebellion through the use of his steamer prior to the evacuation of Charleston and said the steamer was rebel property during the 3-year siege of Charleston and pointed out:

"That from and after the 16th day of August, 1861, the citizens resident within the limits of the States embraced in the President's proclamation of that date became public enemies, and that this condition attached to the loyal as well as disloyal."

Concerning the Act of March 12, 1863 he stated:

"It treated all the property of the citizens of the rebellious States as lawful prize of war, and appointed officers to receive and dispose of such property for the use of the United Sates, reserving to those persons who were not enemies in fact, a right to the proceeds of property taken from them, upon bringing themselves within the provisions of the 3rd section of that act."

The other problem was Chief Engineer Tower. Tower did not have the authority to enter into a contract with Slawson. This was somewhat irrelevant since no contract existed in any case but, because of this, Slawson had no standing in court. Neither could Tower, being a naval engineer, enter into agreements on behalf of the Army. The Act of July 4, 1864 vested that authority in the "3d division of the Quartermaster's office" and the Army never signed a contract with Slawson.

The court dismissed Slawson's claim citing lack of jurisdiction.

Smith, Andrew D. Doing business as A. D. Smith & Brothers who owned the barges *Lake Erie No. 13*, *Lake Erie No. 34*, and *Lake Erie No. 38*. The Army quartermaster at Cincinnati impressed the barges for government service between September and December 1864 at $6 a day per barge. They were used to transport hay, grain, wood, coal, and bridge timbers on the Mississippi and its tributaries. *No. 38* was on the books until March 24, 1865, the *13* until April 30, and the *34* until July 31. Then they disappeared. A search was made in March 1866 for the *13* and *34*. It was concluded that the *34* was lost in a storm in March 1865 but no sign of the *13*.

Smith was paid $2,928.80 for the hire of the barges but they were never found and never returned. The accounting officers were at a loss so Smith sued. He stated in his petition the barges were worth $700 each and that's what he got even though the court found their value was considerably more.

Smith, Samuel B. On December 10, 1861 Smith offered Secretary of War Simon Cameron 40,000 rifles at $20 each delivered to New York on or before June 1, 1862 and sent a rifle for examination and testing. The next day Cameron agreed pending approval by the Chief of Ordnance. On the same day, Brigadier General James W. Ripley, Chief of the Ordnance Office, wrote to Smith to order the same rifles as the sample, subject to inspection, along with "one screwdriver and one cone wrench and one wiper for each arm, and one spring vise and one ballscrew for every ten arms."

Smith acknowledged the order and regarded these communications as a contract.

On January 29, 1862 Edwin M. Stanton, the new Secretary of War, wrote a memo forbidding the purchase of any foreign-made items and to require anyone claiming to have a War Department contract to respond within 15 days with the particulars of their contract and to submit a written, signed copy of it.

Smith had intended to purchase his guns abroad.

On March 13, 1862 Stanton appointed Joseph Holt and Robert Dale Owen to audit and adjust all contracts. On the 18th, Smith contacted the Holt-Owen board and sent a copy of his contract with the German-owned firm of H. Boker &. Co. of New York. Smith met with the commission, his contract was voided, but he offered to furnish block sights for rifles instead of leaf sights, which was approved but apparently never ordered or paid for.

Five years later he sued for breach of contract and his petition was dismissed.

As a court noted:

"About this time, or before the date of the transaction, the government was sorely in need of arms. A vast army of patriotic men stood ready to defend their country, but they had not weapons. Hence contracts were made at exorbitant prices, and, upon the supposition that the public exigency justified it, more arms were contracted for, and yet undelivered, in the first months of 1862, than our armies would require in two years."

Smith, Thornton. Captain Smith was a volunteer assistant quartermaster until September 3, 1862 when he was summarily dismissed from the service for being absent without leave while his unit was in the field. He was reinstated on February 13, 1864 when the order was revoked. On June 11, 1864 he resigned his commission due to disability sustained in the Red River campaign. He recovered $2,344.50 in back pay in 1866.

Smoot, Samuel S. Awarded $20,000 for breach of contract on the sale of 2,500 horses at St. Louis. The government appealed to the Supreme Court where the decision was reversed.

Spencer, Horatio N. Owner of the Highland place cotton plantation in Carroll Parish, Louisiana where a 390-bale crop was raised in 1862. Of these, 240 had been ginned by McCorkle, the overseer, and 200 were compressed into bales. The 200 bales were hidden in a cane thicket for safety but they were found and burned by rebels. McCorkle left in February 1863 and foreman James Bland took control. Bland and the slaves compressed the remaining ginned cotton into another 40 bales. About 150 bales of seed cotton were left in the gin house.

The slaves took the 40 bales to Mrs. C. A. Blackburn and stored them in her backyard as she promised to care for it. A witness later stated the slaves did this "to save it for their old master who had been kind to them."

Mrs. Blackburn then shipped the cotton to Treasury agent Thomas H. Yeatman at Memphis. The cotton was in bad shape on arrival and was rebaled into 35 bales by Mrs. Blackburn's agents, Lacey, Able & Co., and sold at auction for $6,628.49. The slaves found out and went to Memphis where they claimed the cotton as their own. A compromise was made whereby they were paid $2,000 with the balance of $4,628.49 going to Mrs. Blackburn.

Spencer attempted to recover in federal court but his petition was dismissed on the ground that no money from the sale ever reached the Treasury. The court stated:

"The facts of this case, which are drawn out with some particularity, forcibly illustrate the loose and reckless manner in which the Treasury agents and others charged with the duty of collecting 'abandoned or captured property' executed the laws of the United States under which they claimed to act. Their conduct was not only often rude, but in many cases without authority of law, and the injuries thus done to private rights wholly irreparable. The law authorizing the capture of private property on land was of itself severe enough, but it lost much of the dignity of law, and more of its justice and beneficence, in the hands of irresponsible officers and agents intrusted with its administration."

Yeatman, of Cincinnati, was replaced by James M. Tomeny in early 1864. These Treasury agent appointments could be highly political. Tomeny was regarded by some as under the influence of Southern sympathizers.

Sprott, Walter D. Purchased 300 bales of cotton for 10 cents a pound from an agent of the Confederate government in Claiborne County, Mississippi in March 1865. The agent's job was to raise money for munitions but Sprott was never told of this and he considered the deal a matter of honest business although he knew the cotton was owned by the Confederate government. The cotton was seized, the scheme uncovered, and Sprott sued to recover claiming he was the true owner. The court held the Confederate government was an unlawful assembly with no corporate power "to take, hold, or convey a valid title to property, real or personal" and that Sprott must have known the agent's purpose. Sprott appealed to the Supreme Court where the decision was upheld. Said Justice Miller of his position:

"The government of the Confederate States can receive no aid from this course of reasoning. It had no existence except as a conspiracy to overthrow lawful authority. Its foundation was treason against the existing Federal Government. Its single purpose, so long as it lasted, was to make that treason successful. So far from being necessary to the organization of civil government or to its maintenance and support, it was inimical to social order, destructive of the best interests of society, and its primary object was to overthrow the Government on which these so largely depended. Its existence and temporary power were an enormous evil, which the whole force of the Government and the people of the United States was engaged for years in destroying.

"When it was overthrown it perished totally. It left no laws, no statutes, no decrees, no authority which can give support to any contract or any act done in its service, or in aid of its purpose, or which contributed to protect its existence. So far as the actual exercise of its physical power was brought to bear upon individuals, that may, under some circumstances, constitute a justification or excuse for acts otherwise indefensible, but no validity can be given

in the courts of this country to acts voluntarily performed in direct aid and support of its unlawful purpose. What of good or evil has flown from it remains for consideration and discussion of the philosophical statesman and historian."

Stanton, Huldah L. Frederick and Huldah owned the La Marque plantation in Concordia Parish, Louisiana. In the spring of 1862 there were about 1,000 bales of cotton on the farm when Confederate authorities ordered it burned but the plantation overseer managed to remove and hide about 250 bales in a canebrake about 1½ miles away. It was found and seized in October but 196½ bales had been destroyed by water and exposure. Frederick died and Huldah became the tutrix of their minor children, Elizabeth H., Frederick, and Newton H. She and the children recovered $51,696.16 on 196½ bales of cotton.

Stark, William H. A native of Lyme, Connecticut who resided in Savannah for half the year while conducting business. He claimed $68,975.25 on 136 bales of upland and 91 bales of sea-island cotton. Stark stated:

"I am a native of the state of Connecticut and still retain a home there. At all times I have been true and loyal to the United States and opposed to the rebellion. There never has been a time when I saw a reason to change my first view, that it was uncalled for, would result unfavorably, and was wrong. I never voluntarily aided the rebellion. I never did in any way subscribe to Confederate loans, organize companies or soldiers to fight the United States. I once sent to Cuba for 56 pounds of Cuba coffee, 55 pounds of sugar. I never brought in anything else. That was for the use of my family. I never had blockade stock or anything of that kind. I never did anything of that kind to help the Confederate government. I did my best to keep Mr. Richmond from going into the rebel army. I do not know that I had any opportunity to aid Union prisoners here. I saw none that I knew. I believe northern men here were all watched and a general surveillance exercised over them. Northern men here were under constant dread and had to be very cautious what they did and what they said to escape public violence. There were clubs and other organizations here who used to watch out and take those suspected of disloyalty to the Confederacy. I heard some were lynched but I did not see them. There was a perfect reign of terror here and I thought I would better be cautious. I got into difficulty in Augusta in a friendly conversation with a friend in a store there. I was overheard by a clerk and reported to a vigilance committee. They came down in force and to run me off but let me go on the terms that I would leave town. They had before that lynched a man but for some cause or other I got off. I was in the store of Mr. Conley at the time. The conversation was a Union conversation in which I expressed strong hostility to the Confederacy. They came, about six or seven of them, armed with sticks. I was told I'd better be very cautious. I think I was watched by the Rattlesnake Club here, that they were following me and on my trail. I employed one of that club in my store to avoid the surveillance of the club a little time after.

"I was a member of a firm when the war commenced and endeavored to sell out and get away. They thought I would sell out at any price and placed so low an estimate on it that I turned round and bought them out. I insisted upon our northern debts being paid after the ordinance passed here prohibiting it and I did pay the debts by an underground railroad. I paid every dollar the firm owed north. I attended no meetings to incite men to join the rebellion. I did nothing intentionally to incite rebellion. I did nothing but what I thought necessary to avoid danger. All Union men here had to act the hypocrite more or less. There was no time during the war when a Union man could express his Union sentiments at a Union meeting or anywhere else with safety.

I bought and sold and went on with the citizens of Savannah as before the war. My yearly transactions during the war continued and accumulated, I should say, to $200,000 the first year, during subsequent years, in inflated currency, to $500,000 or $600,000 a year."

The court stated.

"The proof of claimant's loyalty wholly fails. The ordinary presumption of complicity with the rebellion, by voluntary residence within the Confederacy, applies with ten-fold force to the case of a citizen and a resident of the north voluntarily remaining absent from his northern home, in the south, from motives of gain."

Stern, Henry. A resident of Union Springs, Alabama whose disloyalty prevented him from recovering $1,700 worth of goods taken by the Army in April 1865. His suit was dismissed on June 24, 1897.

Stern & Oppenheimer. Jacob Stern owned six bales of sea-island cotton and Karl M. Oppenheimer owned 11 bales of upland and eight bales of sea-island cotton. Ten witnesses failed to convince the court of their loyalty and their petition was dismissed. No place of residence for them is shown.

Stevens, Simon. A partner of financier J. Pierpont Morgan. In August 1861 Stevens sold Major General John C. Frémont 2,000 smooth bore Hall's carbines, appendages and packing boxes at $22 each for a total of $3,695. All negotiations were by telegraph. Frémont wanted the guns sent express instead of fast freight and said he would pay the extra charges. He also wanted ammo and told Stevens to hurry.

Stevens said he could send the guns immediately as smooth bores for $1 less apiece or he could rifle the lot in 10 days for the stated price. Frémont said OK, but hurry.

By previous arrangement, the $55,550 voucher for the first 2,500 carbines was made out by Captain F. D. Callender of the Ordnance Bureau to Morgan. Morgan presented it to Ketchum, Son & Co. for redemption and the voucher was paid in full on September 10, 1861.

Frémont received the lot, the guns were distributed to the troops before September 26, 1861, and a second voucher was issued for $58,175, as before. When it was presented to the war Department for payment it was sent to the Holt–Owen Commission. On June 12, 1862 the amount was reduced to $11,000 but Ketchum, Son & Co. refused to accept it.

Stevens sued. The carbines were found to be of good quality and the sale price was a fair market value. The court found a valid military urgency existed which would authorize Frémont to purchase arms and supplies on the open market without advertising for bids and Stevens was awarded $58,175 in 1866.

Stoddart, Alexander. A naturalized citizen from Scotland and wealthy Mobile businessman who retired in 1859 due to "feeble health and advanced age." He moved north, first to Brooklyn, then Baltimore, and finally to Ypsilanti, Michigan leaving Thomas Henry as general manager. On June 9 he gave Henry power of attorney to close up his business, sell his real estate, and collect his debts, the whole amounting to around $50,000. The war disrupted this and Henry accumulated $30,000 in Confederate money. He used $19,000 to purchase 260 bales of cotton in his name as an investment. The cotton was seized from Nelson W. Perry & Co. and sent to New York on the steamers *E. S. Thayer* and *Monterey* and netted $183.32 per bale. Stoddart sued to recover $47,673.60.

Henry said he had to buy the cotton under his own name or it would have been seized by rebels as enemy property. Stoddart's claim was dismissed since he didn't own the cotton. Stoddart appealed, a new trial was granted, and a divided court awarded him $24,394.86 on 133 bales.

Stovall, George A. Owned a building in Memphis. He conveyed the title to his wife, Laura J. Stovall, on February 22, 1862, "for and in consideration of the love and esteem I entertain for my wife to her sole and separate use, free, released, and discharged from all my liabilities or control." He then joined the Confederate army. On June 15, 1862, about a week after the city was captured, the Army seized the building as enemy property for use as a hospital. Rent was assessed and paid on buildings only on proof of the loyalty of the owners. Laura took the oath of allegiance on June 17, 1863 applied to Quartermaster General Meigs for rent but she could not produce the deed. George had taken the deed and other important papers to Laura's mother in Mississippi for safekeeping. Payment of rent was authorized on September 14, 1865 from July 29, 1865 when Laura produced the deed. The reasonable rent was $250 per month.

Several alterations were made in the building including the cutting of new doorways and removal of walls and partitions. The cost to restore the building was $1,015.54. Laura presented a claim for this and for $10,950 in rent to Meigs. It was refused on the ground that only claims from loyal citizens arising before April 2, 1866 in states not declared in rebellion could be considered by the War Department.

Laura subsequently died and George sued to recover but his petition was dismissed on March 16, 1891 as barred by statutes of limitation and the Bowman Act.

Sweeney, Thomas C. Sweeney's steamboat *Ben Franklin* was at Louisville when quartermaster John H. Ferry urgently needed steamers. He offered Sweeney $175 a day, Sweeney demanded $200, then attempted to avoid a charter agreement altogether. Ferry persisted and a charter was signed on March 3, 1863 at $175 a day. Sweeney called on Colonel Swords and got

his $200 a day and this was paid to March 20 when all payments stopped. The boat was released on September 17. Sweeney sued to recover $9,955 but his petition was dismissed.

Sykes, Emma P. Owned one half of a plantation in Mississippi before her marriage. Her husband purchased the other half and they jointly owned the land, slaves, buildings, and produce as tenants in common. The husband died in January 1865. In July, 85 bales of cotton were seized after it was learned the husband had sold the cotton to the Confederate government. Proceeds into the Treasury were $79.19 a bale for a total of $6,704.72.

Emma was worried that a federal court wouldn't recognize her rights under Mississippi law, so she moved to have the State's constitution recognized as foreign law. According to the Revised Code Mississippi, 1857, Article 23:

"Every species and description of property, whether consisting of real or personal estate, and all money, rights, and credits which may be owned by or belong to every single woman, shall continue to be the separate property of such woman as fully after her marriage as it was before."

Article 24 allowed her to "hire out her slaves, rent her land, or make any contract for the use thereof."

She recovered $3,352.36 in 1872.

Tait, James. A naturalized Scot and trustee for Hanford & Browning Co. of New York who had resided in Mobile since 1838, bought their goods, and collected their debts in the South. When the war started he owed the company about $13,900. In November 1862 he bought 55 bales of cotton at Pickensville, Alabama where it was stored but subject to damage from spring flooding. On April 1, 1864, 46 bales worth about $12,000 were removed to Mobile. One year later Confederate authorities started collecting all the cotton in the city and burning it at Orange Grove. Tait obtained permission from the Confederate commander to put his cotton aboard the schooner *Thistle* and run it upriver. He was ordered to go 100 miles but when they were about 20 miles up the vessel stuck at a creek and remained there until the cotton was returned to Mobile and seized in May of 1865. Tait recovered $8,707.34.

Talbert, William. District of Columbia resident and shipwright at the Washington Navy Yard off and on between 1833 and 1882. In 1860, while not employed at the Navy Yard, he entertained the idea of opening his own shipyard — a small one on available land on the Eastern Branch of the Potomac River near the Navy Yard.

Upon surveying the site, he found the water too shallow to allow a marine railway of sufficient length to be built without obstructing the river channel. Thinking about this caused him to invent an improvement for hauling out vessels and for which he eventually obtained a patent.

While in the process of designing his new marine railway the war began and he was recalled to work at the Navy Yard. In the course of fitting out vessels for wartime service, he, and the officers at the Navy Yard, realized the lack of water depth at the end of the existing marine railway was insufficient for hauling out the larger, deep-draft gunboats that would soon be needed. Vessels 200 feet or longer and drawing more than 3 feet could not be hauled out. Vessels drawing 5 feet and 150 feet long could be hauled out but not far enough to work efficiently on them as the stern grounded on the riverbed. In 1862 the officers in charge hired a man named Bishop to refit the existing railway but during the first use of his device it was crushed by the forefoot of the trial vessel and completely wrecked.

Talbert then came forward with his idea and during the winter of 1862–63 he constructed it after directing his attorney to apply for a patent, which was done in March 1863.

Talbert's method was put in place under a verbal agreement between himself and Rear Admiral Joseph Smith, Chief of the Bureau of Yards and Docks. Talbert would be allowed compensation if the device worked, based on what the Navy would have paid for "outside prices" at private shipyards absent his invention. If it failed, Talbert was to pay all costs. Talbert requested that his device not be used until his patent came through but Admiral Smith said the national emergency required its immediate installation and told him to proceed at once. He completed construction prior to receiving Patent No. 41452 on February 2, 1864.

His invention worked and allowed 250-foot vessels drawing 13 feet to be completely hauled out. Gunboats were repaired with an efficiency that could not have been attained at private yards and could not have been repaired at Washington at all without Talbert's system.

The Yard used his method during and after the war and on February 27, 1869 Talbert applied for his compensation. He was refused when Secretary of the Navy Gideon Welles wrote to him:

> It appears that you were in the employ of the Government when you suggested the use of your appliance, and it was used while you were so employed. Employés of the Government are prohibited from receiving compensation, unless by special act of Congress, for any inventions that the Government may use.
>
> This Department would not be authorized to grant you compensation.

He applied again directly to acquaintances in the Navy Department and was again turned away for essentially the same reasons. He then appealed to Congress.

His invention continued to be used at the Navy Yard during all this time. It consisted of one, two, three, or more "movable blocks or cars" running on the existing tracks, stacked together at the lower end. The vessel was brought up to the first car, and its forefoot placed on it. As the vessel was hauled up, the other cars were pulled up with connecting chains set at preset intervals to the length of the ship and which took up the keel and the weight of the vessel until it was hauled completely out of the water and onto the existing keel blocks.

The existing railway at the yard had consisted of three heavy, parallel timbers with iron rails on top. The two outside timbers were 14 inches wide and the middle one was 28 inches wide. The grade up from the water was five-eighths of an inch to the foot for a length of 450 feet, 200 feet of which was under water at high tide. Talbert improved the system by removing the existing large timber cradle that ran on the outside rails and all but the upper 100-feet of the heavy, stationary, 2-foot high blocks placed five feet apart along the whole length of the center cradle. The tops of his movable cars were flush with the tops of the existing bilge blocks along the sides of the cradle. He also placed a cast iron track and pawl assembly on the center rail attached to the forward car. All this simply lowered the hauling mechanism so it would engage the larger vessels as they floated lower in low water.

Talbert retired from the Navy Yard in 1882, got tired of waiting for his promised money, petitioned Congress, and was referred to a court on June 30, 1886 to assess the value of his claim. He never sought to capitalize from his invention nor was the idea used anywhere else.

In court, the assistant attorney general cited a device patented on January 18, 1857 by an English inventor, Robert Turnbull of Harwich, Essex County, that was remarkably similar to Talbert's but which, on close examination, would have produced an unacceptable degree of weakness in a typical cradle structure since Turnbull cut the cradle itself into moveable sections and connected them with long rods. Talbert constructed his device on the existing, structurally sound railway cradle. The government also questioned Talbert's right to be paid public money in the form of royalties since he was a government employee and the government bore the costs of building an unproven device. If anything, he was due a license fee, and nothing more, since there was no implied or written contract for a royalty. Assistant Attorney General Cotton summed up his argument:

"The use of a patented machine by the Government does not constitute a taking of private property for public use within the meaning of the Constitution."

The court found that Talbert's device was "the product of original thought and inventive skill" and therefore the patent was valid and that he also had a valid claim based on an implied contract with Admiral Smith that recognized the invention was Talbert's private property.

The court countered the government's argument regarding Talbert's employment status:

"It may first be noted that the claim here is not for preparing the cradle, or for placing the device upon it, for which the plaintiff was paid by wages as a shipwright, but it is for the use of a patented invention with knowledge of the plaintiff's claims, without adverse contention as to his alleged rights and with his consent. Further, it appears that the invention was made by plaintiff at a time when he was not in Government employ and without intention at that time that it should be used at the navy-yard, and that it was made for the purpose of facilitating the taking up of vessel's at the plaintiff's projected private ship-yard.

"Talbert was not assigned to the task of devising, preparing, or making the device in question. The Government bore no expense of the experiment incident to the invention, and when the device went upon the cradle it was complete, not experimental; nor when he made the invention was plaintiff an officer or employé of the Government, nor was he assigned to select a device to accomplish a desired result; that duty fell

upon commissioned officers of the Navy; nor was this a transaction growing out of plaintiff's official service or position."

The court cited other cases where the value of an invention was determined relative to the government's use of it. Admiral John A. Dahlgren invented the Dalghren gun, adapted howitzers for shipboard use, and established the Naval Gun Factory. Efforts were made by his heirs to collect on his devices and on which a court ruled:

"The materials for estimating the damages, or, in the language of the statute, the amount of compensation which Admiral Dahlgren's estate is justly entitled to receive from the United States, are meager. The patented articles have no market value, inasmuch as the United States is the only consumer. Therefore the inventor has lost no profits in the ordinary sense of the term. The inventor has made no license to any one, and had therefore no fixed royalty. The claimant, it is true, attempted to establish the reasonable worth of such a royalty on the basis of the weight of metal in the pieces; but the effort failed. The United States have not dealt in the articles, and have not used them to gain a profit in the ordinary commercial sense of the term. We are therefore thrown back upon the rule laid down in Suffolk County v. Hayden and must find the measure of the claimant's compensation in the utility and advantage of the invention to the United States over the old modes or devices that had been used for working out similar results.

"Estimating upon this theory, the value to the Government of plaintiff's invention during its existence of the patent, we find it to have been $6,544.30, and award judgement in his favor for this sum."

Talbot, Samuel H. Chartered his schooner *Keokuk* to the Navy's Ordnance Bureau on October 26, 1864. The charter provided for the vessel's discharge at Hampton Roads, Virginia. She was at anchor in Beaufort Channel, South Carolina loaded with explosives on Christmas Day when Commander West ordered the harbormaster to have the schooner towed from her anchorage into Moorehead Channel. The harbormaster directed Captain Roundtree's Navy steam tug *Berberry* to move the schooner, and "do it by daylight since it would be almost impossible to do it in the dark." Parts of the channel were only 150 feet wide. The schooner's master vehemently protested when Roundtree proceeded to tow the schooner that night "through a narrow and tortuous inner channel at low water, the tide setting across it, and a strong wind blowing at the time." The schooner grounded about ½ to ¾ of a mile from her anchorage.

Admiral Porter ordered the schooner discharged from naval service at Beaufort on Valentine's Day, 1865. The Ordnance Bureau refused to pay the balance of the charter to get to Hampton Roads or for the damage. Talbot sued for $3,000 and was awarded $1,500 for repairs, $500 in permanent depreciation, and $128 service time to Hampton Roads.

Tayloe, Benjamin Ogle.

A resident of the District of Columbia who owned a plantation in Alabama run by his overseer, R. A. Morgan. A son, Edward Thornton Tayloe also owned a plantation in Alabama and lived there. Morgan was also his agent. Morgan had around 200 bales of Benjamin's cotton on his plantation and 73 bales stored at Hatch's warehouse in Arcola.

In 1863 Edward decided to subscribe 150 bales of cotton to the Confederate cotton loan and he directed Morgan to give a bill of sale for 150 bales of Benjamin's cotton to the Confederate cotton agent with a promise to deliver them to Demopolis on order of the Confederate Secretary of the Treasury.

In June 1865 all the cotton at Hatch's warehouse was seized, including Benjamin's. In February 1866 Morgan shipped 378 bales to Mobile. In June 77 of those were seized and 19 bales were given to an informant, 8 were given to another person in payment for a claim, and 50 were sold in New York. The 73 bales from Arcola were divided with 57 going to New York and the rest unaccounted for but they were probably given to an informant.

Confederate accounts showed the loan cotton as belonging to B. O. Tayloe but Benjamin never gave Morgan permission to sell any of his cotton. Benjamin died and his widow, Phoebe, filed a claim for the estate. Benjamin disowned his son in his will and Edward was adjudged to be disloyal. Benjamin was not and Phoebe Ogle recovered $11,379.31.

Tebbetts, Horace B.

Horace moved south in 1859 to live on his Sauvterre, Boedin, and Hollybrook plantations in Carroll Parish, Louisiana. When the Army arrived in March of 1863 he left for New York and remained there for the rest of the war. Soldiers seized 92 bales of cotton that were sold at Memphis in a lot of 919 bales, which netted $216.14 a bale.

The claim was assigned to John C. Tebbetts and he was awarded was $19,384.38.

Ten Brook, Jane C.

William L. Ten Brook enrolled on May 16, 1861 for three years and was mustered in on June 20 as a musician in Company B, 4th Michigan Infantry Volunteers. He was medically discharged on September 6 and on December 10 he enrolled again for three years and was mustered in to Company A, 4th Michigan Infantry Volunteers as a private. He was promoted to corporal on July 1, 1862, reenlisted on December 29, 1863 as a veteran volunteer and promoted to sergeant on September 1, 1864. On August 20 he was mustered in as a first lieutenant and on February 9, 1865 as captain.

On January 15, 1866 he was granted 50 days' leave but never returned to duty. His regiment was disbanded on May 26 and on February 26, 1867 he was granted an honorable discharge but paid only to May 26. He filed a claim with the War Department for three months' pay and was denied.

On February 7, 1899 the War Department certified to the Treasury Department that his official discharge date would be May 26, 1866 and on May 24, 1901 his discharge was changed to dishonorable, as he was absent without leave.

His widow sued to recover and was awarded $180 on December 2, 1912.

Terrill, A. T.

A resident of Lexington, Tennessee who enlisted in the Army and was mustered into Company A, 7th Tennessee Cavalry, on August 8, 1862. He furnished his own bay horse and equipment valued at $125, and one sorrel mule and equipment valued at $150. On June 20, 1863 he lost his mule and saddle in battle at Mount Pinston, Tennessee and was never reimbursed. On March 24, 1864 he lost his horse and saddle in battle at Union City, Tennessee and was never paid.

He was honorably discharged on August 9, 1865. He filed a claim with the House Committee on War Claims under Section 3482 of the U.S. Revised Statutes allowing $200 for the loss of a horse or equipage in battle.

The claim was referred to a federal court for fact finding. On June 19, 1893 the court held that Terrill's claim was barred by lack of jurisdiction under the Bowman Act of March 3, 1883 and there was no appeal on claims under $300.

Terry, James C. A cotton planter with James A. Carnes as Terry & Carnes in Mississippi in 1861 and '62. In August 1862, Army troops from Helena, Arkansas seized 190 bales of cotton from the partner's property. Eleven of the bales were burned up while in the custody of the quartermaster and the remainder was mingled with 21 bales belonging to others. In November 48 of their identifiable bales were sold in New York for $11,295.20, 116 were sold in January 1863 for $24,976.95, 26 were lost by the Illinois Central Railroad while in transit, and 10 bales received at the forwarding house of Able & Co. at Cairo, Illinois were never accounted for. Terry & Carnes recovered $32,460.39 on 146.78 bales at 221.15 per bale in 1871.

Terry, Nathaniel. Chartered his steamer *Ocean Wave* on April 22, 1864 for $200 a day, the vessel to be returned to New York. On August 4, 1865 the steamer was ordered to New York where she arrived on the 10th. Terry was notified on the 23rd that the charter was terminated as of the 4th. By custom, the masters of vessels under charter reported to Captain John R. Jennings in General Van Vliet's office each day for orders.

The government said the master never reported between the 10th and the 23rd. The charter rate was paid up to the 11th and Terry was denied money he felt was due from the 11th through the 23 rd. He sued and recovered $1,458 at a reduced rate of $121.50, which he apparently asked for.

Thomas, Henry G. A "colored citizen, resident of Charleston, South Carolina" who owned one bale of upland cotton seized by the Army during the capture of Charleston, sent to New York, and sold as enemy property. In court, Thomas testified:

"My sentiments were opposed to the Confederate States, knowing that our freedom depended upon the success of the United States, and that if the rebels gained, I, though a freeman, might be made a slave. All of us might."

Thomas was awarded $131.20 in 1867.

Thomas, Mary W. John H. Thomas owned a plantation on Poketa Lake on the north side of the Yazoo River about seven miles from Yazoo City, Mississippi. He claimed he had 112 bales of cotton seized in July 1863 by the United States and taken to Vicksburg. John died on May 20, 1865 and on August 19, 1868 — the very last day allowed by the Act of March 12, 1863 — Mary brought suit in her own name claiming falsely that she was the owner. Under Mississippi law a wife owned property acquired only before marriage. Her petition was denied and a motion was made later to place W. Calvin Wells as administrator of the estate. Her petition was dismissed in 1877 again since she had no title to the cotton and Wells could claim no ownership.

Wells was appointed administrator of John Thomas's estate on March 18, 1875. When he filed suit for $21,554.04 it was shown that the cotton was actually stored in a shed and was burned by rebels in June 1863. The petition was dismissed for the last time in May 1883.

Thompson, John A. On March 9, 1865 General George Thomas, commanding the Army of the Cumberland, decided he needed mules in a hurry and there was no time to advertise for bids on the open market. Thompson was a well-known "mule-grower and dealer" and was offered a contract to deliver to Nashville, on or before April 20, 1,000 mules of not less than 14½ hands at prices ranging from $165, $167.50, and $175 a head depending on their height. Fulfilling the order required great effort and about $140,000 in cash or good credit.

By April 10 Thompson had acquired 900 mules, had delivered 25 with another 100 at Nashville ready to deliver, had 200–300 in railroad cars between Lebanon, Kentucky and Nashville, and another 570 in corrals at Lebanon waiting for transportation. On that date he was told Richmond was captured, General Lee had surrendered, and the Army wouldn't need any more mules and in fact they had an excess. The market was saturated with broken and seasoned mules for months afterwards with no fixed price for them. Thompson sold the undelivered animals at $42.50 a head.

The Army said it wasn't paying for mules never delivered. Thompson sued, arguing that he had a contract for 1,000 mules. The court awarded him $108,750 based on an average price of $167.50.

Thorne, Quentin M. Chartered his steam tug *Rescue* to the Army on March 6, 1862 at $50 a day. The rate was reduced to $40 a day on August 1, 1863 and Thomas claimed $760 to October 16 when she was sold to Morgan & Rheinheart. His petition was dismissed.

Todd, James. James and Robert A. Todd owned a plantation on Bayou America near

Berwick City, Louisiana where a certain amount of cotton belonging to Smith & Hines was stored. On November 6, 1862 Captain George W. Kendall, commander of the U.S. gunboat *Diana,* removed 255 bales of the cotton with Todd's consent on order of Lieutenant Commander Thomas McKean Buchanan. The *Diana* took it to Brashear City where Buchanan's command was set up. On the 7th Todd appeared at Brashear City and executed a bill of sale to Buchanan for the cotton and swore that he was always loyal to the United States and that the rebels were going to burn his cotton.

On November 14 Buchanan sent part of the cotton on the USS *Calhoun* to Colonel Schaefer, the quartermaster at New Orleans. Schaefer turned it over to the Sequestration Committee established by Major General Butler.

On December 6, Buchanan wrote a letter:

> U.S. Gun-boat *Calhoun,*
> Off Brashear City, December 6, 1862
> To Lieut. Col. Kinsman & Major J. M. Bell:
> Gentlemen: On the 6th of November I seized 255 bales of cotton in Bayou America, from the plantation of Mr. Tod, at his own request, he going along with the *Diana* to show where it was, to prevent it from being burned by the enemy.
> Mr. Tod came down and offered to sell the cotton, and stated that he was a loyal citizen and wished to take the oath. Not having seen the order of Maj. Gen. Butler, or aware that a commission had been appointed, I purchased it from Mr. Tod, as I thought it would be returned to him on proving himself a loyal citizen. He has taken the oath of allegiance, and is represented by the planters here as a Union man.
> If you consider my claim is just, and you can, consistent with your duty, let me have the cotton, I would be obliged to you if you would turn it over to Col. A. J. Butler, whom I have appointed my agent and who has a bill of sale from Mr. Tod to me."
> I am, respectfully, y'r ob'd't serv'nt,
> Tho's McK. Buchanan
> Lt Commander

The cotton had already been sold by the Sequestration Committee for $52,569.55. A. J. Butler was Buchanan's attorney and on December 16, 1862 the money was turned over to him at New Orleans. None of the money was ever paid into the U.S. Treasury so the petition was dismissed.

Turner, George W. A resident of Natchez and owner of a plantation in Tensas Parish, Louisiana. He moved to New York in 1853 and left the management to his brother-

in-law William Poyntell. He intended to go to Europe in August 1860 but the death of his brother and sickness in the family delayed him until April 26, 1861. He remained abroad until late 1864 when Confederate forces burned about 1,000 bales of cotton on his farm as they considered him an "alien enemy."

He managed to hide 68 bales and 22 bags of ginned cotton but this was seized by the Army. The bales were sold for $26,815.14. Twelve bales were made from the 22 bags and were sold for $4,596. There were charges totaling $4,107.47: at Vicksburg, $963.24; freight to Cairo, $12 a bale, $960; at Cairo, $40; freight to Cincinnati, $3 a bale, $240; 0.1 percent duty on auction sales, $26.81; customhouse fees on 31,682 pounds, $1,267.28; storage and insurance, $203.50; city weigher, $4.42; 1.5 percent for incidental expenses, $402.22; and 2 percent to internal revenue, $633.64. These were deducted and Turner was awarded $22,074.03.

Updegraff, H. On October 24, 1864, Captain M. H. Insley, assistant quartermaster, hired Updegraff's two-horse team at $10 a day to haul supplies. Two days later a "pressing military exigency" arose when Major General Curtis contacted Insley:

> Fort Scott, Kans., October 26, 1864
> Capt. M. H. Insley, Depot Quartermaster:
> You will immediately send forward to the army in the field in pursuit of Price's army, 50,000 rations of old corn, in half-loaded wagons, and 50,000 rations in commissary stores, in half-loaded wagons, with directions to drive day and night till the army is overtaken."

Updegraff was on the move for 48 days until December 10 and received a voucher from Insley for $460.80 dated November 30, 1864. Updegraff sold the voucher to Daniels, Millington & Co. who transferred it to William B. Daniels. Daniels sent it to Colonel J. A. Potter at Fort Leavenworth who sent it on to Quartermaster General Meigs at Washington. A board of examiners was convened and reduced the amount to $240. Daniels accepted it under written protest through his agents, Rittenhouse, Fowler & Co.

Updegraff sued on behalf of Daniels to recover a balance of $220.80, which was awarded in 1873.

Vance, William L. In business with Robertson Topp as Topp & Vance in Memphis. The partners purchased 170 bales of cotton from Mary A. Butler's plantation on Frenchs Bend on the Yazoo River, in Sunflower County, Mississippi. The cotton was stored on her plantation when Topp applied to General S. A. Hurlbut for permission to bring it out. Permission was granted and Topp hired the steam tugs *Allen Collier, Belfast, State Bank,* with barges, and steamers *Dove,* and *Emma No. 2* with tugs. He applied to the Treasury Department in Memphis on October 31, 1863 and their permission was granted the same day. In January or February 1864 Topp applied to the military authorities at Vicksburg for permission to send one of the steamers up the Yazoo with Colonel J. H. Coates's expedition but this was refused. General Sherman's purpose for the expedition was stated:

"To produce a diversion; punish certain parties who were hostile, and bring out cotton to indemnify the Government and certain friendly parties on the Mississippi River, who had been robbed by the Confederate authority."

All of Topp's cotton and 72 bales of Mary Butler's cotton was seized on February 20, 1864 by Coates within Confederate lines "west of the Mississippi Central Railroad."

There was no evidence that Mrs. Butler's farm was enemy territory and Topp & Vance were loyal.

The cotton was sent to Vicksburg with other lots of seized cotton.

On March 13 General Sherman ordered 1,000 bales captured by Coates's expedition turned over to the Treasury Department and the balance placed under control of a board established by Major General McPherson at Vicksburg.

The partners went to Vicksburg and appeared before the board in April to get their cotton back. They proved the cotton was theirs and an order was issued to release it to them after the payment of freight and storage costs but before the order was received the cotton was turned over to deputy Treasury Agent Joseph Nolan, taken to New Orleans and sold on his account. Mary Butler appeared before the board and her cotton was returned to her.

On May 5 Major General McPherson ordered all the cotton turned over to Nolan as reimbursement for 600 bales taken from him for use on cottonclad gunboats and vessels running past the blockade at Vicksburg in 1863. The cotton was worth about $136,000. Less transportation, internal revenue tax, and expenses totaling $7,139.50, the cotton's net worth was $128,860.50.

Topp & Vance never pursued the claim until 1886 when Vance sued as the surviving partner. His petition was dismissed on June 7, 1886 as barred by statutes of limitations.

William died in Memphis and George T. Vance and Guy P. Vance, William's sons, petitioned Congress to recover $128,860.50 on the 170 bales weighing 85,000 pounds. They were granted relief on April 20, 1892 under the Bowman Act and the case was referred to a federal court. The court found no new evidence to reverse their previous decision and this was reported to Congress.

Villalonga, John L. A Savannah cotton factor who personally owned 196 bales of cotton. He also had possession of cotton used as collateral on loans, which he advanced in Confederate money. When the city was captured in December 1864 he had custody of 70 bales of sea island and 227 bales of upland cotton on which he had advanced $51,153.17 in Confederate notes.

All the cotton was seized and sold. His cotton sold for $34,364.68 net. The cotton he held was sold for $56,026.21. Villalonga was entitled to hold the others' cotton, he could sell it to repay his loans, and hold liens on it. He recovered $175.33 a bale on 473 bales of upland cotton and $231.79 a bale on 70 bales of sea island cotton adding up to $90,389.89.

The government appealed to the Supreme Court where the decision was reversed, the money advanced in Confederate money ordered reduced to the value of United States currency at the time the advances were made, and reduced Villalonga's award only to the 196 bales he personally owned.

Wagner, Leonard. A subject of the Kingdom of Bavaria who recovered $1,563.40 on five bales of sea-island and five bales of upland cotton seized at Charleston.

Walker, Samuel P. Resident of Memphis who was appointed a U.S. purchasing agent by President Lincoln on March 6, 1865.

John Scott, of Mobile, was the chief agent of produce loans for the Confederate government in Alabama and East Mississippi. He purchased 3,405 bales of cotton from 37 growers in Alabama and Mississippi for the Confederate government. The Confederate government always needed money and Scott's job was to sell cotton to raise money. On April 6, 1865 he sold all the cotton to D. O'Grady, of Mobile, for $1 a pound in Confederate money.

Walker had claimed to own "products of the insurrectionary States, near Grenada and Canton, Miss., and Montgomery and Selma, Alabama..." and had deals to buy other goods, which he proposed to buy and deliver to the United States.

On April 12 Walker bought the cotton from O'Grady. All the cotton was stored on plantations within Confederate military lines. The custom of the region was to exchange planters' receipts for cotton sold without physical delivery to the buyer.

F. W. Kellogg, a U.S. purchasing agent, agreed to purchase 3,500 bales of cotton from Walker, who agreed to deliver it to Mobile, so Walker was given a safe conduct pass.

Mobile was captured on April 12. Between June 30 and December 1, 1,922½ bales of the cotton was seized. On May 5 General Taylor surrendered all Confederate forces in Alabama and Mississippi and all the plantations where the cotton was stored came under the control of General Canby. On May 10 Canby prohibited the sale or transfer of any cotton in East Louisiana, Mississippi, Alabama, and West Florida except by U.S. agents.

Walker sued to recover the proceeds of the 1,922½ bales but his petition was dismissed. Said the court:

"Walker's title and right of possession, as against the United States, were trebly defective; first, in his own purchase in violation of the non-intercourse acts; second, in the illegal purchase by O'Grady from the enemies of the Union in hostile organization, of which he had notice; and third, in being himself obliged to claim through transfers, orders, and licenses from that hostile organization."

Waltjen, Ernest. A resident alien from the free city of Bremen, Germany residing in Charleston who owned 22 bales of upland cotton seized there. He was awarded $2,886.40.

Waples, Rufus. U.S. district attorney for the Eastern District of Louisiana at New Orleans who filed a libel against the New Orleans real property of Charles M. Conrad on August 7, 1863 under the Confiscation Act of July 17, 1862. Conrad was accused of aiding and abetting the rebellion. The property consisted of 10 lots with two lots between St. Joseph and Delord Streets. There was a four-story brick store, a three-story "brick dwelling house," and a "three-story brick building and convenient stable erected thereon,

situate on the western side of Carondalet street, between Hevia and Poydras streets, in the suburb of St. Mary..."

The property was condemned on August 8 in Judge E. H. Durell's court and turned over to the U.S. Marshal James Graham. Waples got $1,520 in fees for his trouble. The trial to libel the property was scheduled for 11 a.m., Friday, February 3, 1865. Conrad was convicted and his property ordered sold at auction at the Merchants and Auctioneers' Exchange, 18 Royal Street. The highest bidder was Rufus Waples who received three deeds for $10,225.

Charles Conrad died and on June 26, 1874 his son, Lawrence Lewis Conrad, filed a lawsuit against Waples on the ground of prior title and for wrongful seizure of property "as possessors in bad faith." Waples won. Conrad appealed to the Supreme Court where the decision was reversed.

Waring, James J. Recovered $2,629.95 under amnesty on 15 bales of cotton seized at Savannah.

Warren, Isaiah. Trustee of the Old Dominion Pork House & Distillery in Wheeling, West Virginia.

Veteran Reserve Corps Captain E. P. Hudson, and superintendent of the recruiting service, took possession of the building on March 6, 1865 as a rendezvous for recruits without Warren's knowledge or consent. On the 20th Hudson agreed to a $125 monthly rent. The building was occupied until September 6 and Warren recovered $1,350 for damage to the premises.

Waters, John H. Owner of the Union Hotel in Georgetown, District of Columbia who leased it at $500 a month for a hospital. Recovered $1,200 for damage and missing articles.

Watt, Sarah. A "widow lady of English descent" and "a woman of some means" who owned a shop or store in Charleston. She contributed $13–20,000 in Confederate money to "the succor and relief of suffering and starving Union prisoners in and around Charleston." She owned 7 bales of upland cotton and 2 bales of sea-island cotton, purchased after the fall of Savannah, which was seized. She was awarded $131.20 a bale for the upland and $327.64 for the sea island.

Wayne, Henry. A black livery stable keeper in Savannah who purchased 33 bales of upland cotton with Confederate money on December 10, 1864, suspiciously close to the city's capture. Sixteen bales were seized on the 21st. He was barred by Georgia law from buying real estate but could purchase commodities. He recovered $2,047.52.

Weed, Cornwell & Co. Henry D. Weed and G. F. Cornwell were hardware dealers in Savannah. In late 1861 the business began to decline so the partners invested in cotton and by the end of 1863 they had about 1,600 bales. They sold bales when they needed money and by December 1864 they had about 1,420 bales of upland and 2 bales of sea-island. These were seized. Weed was holding 79 of the bales in trust for the children of Mr. C. S. Dunning but they were purchased in the company's name. Weed & Cornwell recovered $249,432.18 in 1872.

West, Henry. A "colored citizen of Charleston" who owned 3 bales of captured cotton. He testified:

"I was always a freeman. I owned cotton before the Union army came in — three bales. I bought it up in King street, out of a wagon. I do not know the man's name. I paid for it at the time I bought it, half money and half salt. I carried it to my house in Cannon street. I kept the cotton there until the Union army came here and they went up there and took it. The Union officers did. They took it to the custom-house. I reported the cotton to Lieutenant Dodge. I never saw the cotton afterwards. I hid under the house a week rather than work on fortifications. I then went on the railroad and worked as fireman until about three days before the Union army came in. I did not raise any men to fight the United States. I gave the travelling Union prisoners coming here food. I gave them what little money I had off and on, coming on from Savannah here. I gave it to them to help them out. If you had seen them coming down the Savannah railroad, it would make the heart of a stone cry."

He was able to document the sale of only 2 bales into the Treasury and recovered $262.52.

White, Robert Cornell. Owned the 1853-built inland steamer *Wyoming*, in service between New York and Elizabethport, New Jersey. In February 1864 she left New York for Hilton Head, South Carolina where Charles H. Campbell, White's agent, executed a charter party on March 7.

On May 16 she left Saint Helena Sound under Captain R. S. Parker as the leading transport with Brigadier General William Birney's ex-

pedition for the Ashepoo River to cut the Charleston & Savannah railroad. Birney chose Bennett's Point to land the troops and sent Navy Captain John C. Dutch with the *Wyoming* to oversee the landing. Captain Parker objected to the landing spot but at high tide the vessel was moored to objects onshore, broadside to the bank, and gangways were sent over. Another vessel was moored outboard of the steamer and men, horses, and supplies were sent ashore. When everything was unloaded General Birney ordered Captain Parker to move his vessel out into the stream and then he left to post his troops and reconnoiter the area. When he came back to the landing in an hour or so the *Wyoming* was still at the landing and all the other vessels were out in deep water. Birney repeated the order and told Parker his vessel would need to remain at the scene for several hours. Parker didn't budge and five hours later the boat tipped over and went hard aground almost on her beam ends. Her seams opened and continual pumping was necessary to keep her from flooding. She was pulled off at high tide by the other vessels, returned to Hilton Head with them, and then went to Saint Helena Island where temporary repairs were made at the government shops. During the 15-day repair period Captain Parker was replaced by Captain White on government orders and he was involuntarily paid $75 by Campbell.

In July she embarked on another expedition with troops from Beaufort and Hilton Head to St. John's Island for an attack on James Island. Due to some delay in executing orders, Major General John G. Foster, commander of the expedition, replaced Captain Parker with Captain Hardy. The *Wyoming* was tied to a wharf, another transport moored outboard of her, and a battery of artillery was brought ashore across her decks. She also sat on the bottom for a second time at low tide.

In November part of her structure was cut away and the bulwarks removed to unload a cargo of artillery pieces. This did not damage the hull but did weaken her upperworks.

The boat was returned to White at his request on February 6, 1866 at Port Royal, South Carolina. She was in very bad condition and was repaired in New York for $17,000.

The government charged White $5,425 against the charter for the month of August due to the damage and repair period: $1,257.21 for government repairs at St. Helena; $1,140.80 for quartermaster stores; $352.24 for commissary stores, and $2,486.45 for 14 days and 5 hours of lost time. White's agent protested the deductions on December 14, 1864 but was told that no payments would be made without the deductions. White then accepted a balance of $188.30 for the month of August. He sued to recover the $5,425 withheld on the charter. His petition was dismissed since Captain Parker had to be replaced for failing to carry out commands promptly.

White, Samuel and Elizabeth. Residents of West Feliciana Parish, Louisiana who owned the 172-ton steamer *Red Chief No. 1* and a flatboat. Samuel purchased the steamer at Shreveport from Captain N. M. Wood who was engaged in transporting supplies for the Confederate Army. Two or three days after Samuel bought the boat, it and the flatboat were seized by a Confederate quartermaster to transport supplies. White remained aboard to safeguard his $35,000 property. On or about July 1, 1863 White regained control of his vessels when they were no longer needed by the retreating Confederates. He ran them up Thompson's Creek a few miles from Port Hudson leaving a crew on board to look out for them. The flatboat was loaded with 50 hogsheads of sugar and 60 barrels of molasses.

On July 8 the *Red Chief* was seized by the Army at Bayou Sara as enemy property when Port Hudson was taken. The flatboat was captured by the USS *Essex*. Technically, both vessels and cargo were seized by General Nathaniel Banks.

The sugar weighed 1,200 pounds per hogshead, for a total of 60,000 pounds, and was valued at 25 cents a pound. The molasses was in 40-gallon barrels totaling 2,000 gallons at 50 cents a gallon. Everything together was worth $169,300.

The Army used the steamer between Bayou Sara and Port Hudson. The goods on the barge were loaded on the *Essex* and all of it disappeared into the ether and no money for the value of the goods was ever deposited into the U.S. Treasury.

Samuel sued Colonel S. B. Holabird, chief quartermaster for the Department of the Gulf, on June 3, 1864 in the U.S. District Court for the Eastern District of Louisiana for demurrage on the steamer. The court ordered the boat returned to the Whites. The district attorney appealed to the circuit court but there was no judge at that

court to hear the case so it languished and the Army retained the boat.

On October 12, 1865 the *Red Chief No. 1* was sold by mistake at auction in Mobile for $7,000—$2,000 over its assessed value. Secretary of War Edwin M. Stanton ordered Quartermaster General Meigs to turn the proceeds over to the Whites on condition they drop all further claims against the United States. The Whites agreed and were paid on March 16, 1866. After Samuel died Elizabeth appealed to Congress to recover the loss of earnings on the *Red Chief No. 1.*

On February 12, 1887 the House Committee on War Claims referred Elizabeth's case to a federal court under the Bowman Act of March 3, 1883. A preliminary hearing on April 11, 1892 found the White's were loyal citizens during the war and remained so throughout.

In court, the government argued the property was taken under the Act of March 12, 1863 and the White's had settled with the government when they got the $7,000 and therefore had no claim. The petition was dismissed on January 16, 1893.

The court reviewed the case again the next year and once again dismissed the claim, this time casting some doubt on Samuel White's loyalty:

"In 1863 the steamer *Red Chief* was captured at Port Hudson. She had been in the military service of the enemy, navigated by the decedent, her owner, and manned by his crew. She had been in the Confederate service under a former owner. The excuse offered on the trial of the issue of the decedent's loyalty was that he had so acted, in navigating his vessel, to save the boat from Confederate confiscation, she having been seized and impressed without his consent. This condition of affairs, this involuntary action of the owner, which was held to excuse him for his personal service, does not help the case when it is considered with reference to jurisdiction.

"The first section of the Abandoned or Captured Property Act expressly declares 'that such property shall not include any kind or description which has been used, or which was intended to be used, for waging or carrying on war against the United States, such as arms, ordnance, ships, steamboats, or other water craft,' and it leaves such property subject to the operation of the laws of war and the confiscation act.

"The *Red Chief* continued in the military service of the Confederate States until resistance at Port Hudson was about to cease. Then, when she was no longer needed, the owner ran her into a creek nearby. On the day of, or the day after, the surrender she was seized, as all other property which had been in the service of the enemy was seized, and turned over to the Quartermaster Department."

The case was dismissed for the final time.

White, Thomas G.

Administrator of Joseph D. Edings's estate. Edings owned real estate in South Carolina that was sold in March 1863 for unpaid U.S. direct taxes. Edings died after the sale and prior to President Johnson's unconditional pardon of December 25, 1868.

The statutes allowed an executor, as the sole claimant of an estate, to recover the sale surplus deposited in trust into the Treasury. White sued and the government argued that no one could prove that Edings "at all times bore true faith and allegiance to the government of the United States and had not in any way voluntarily aided, abetted, or given encouragement to rebellion against the said government..." as the law required.

The court held the unconditional pardon would extend to an executor and White recovered $189.98 in 1884.

Whiteside, W. H., & Co.

The company signed a contract with Treasury Assistant Special Agent A. B. Miller at Camden, Arkansas on November 10, 1865 to seize a certain lot of cotton about 65 miles away in Lafayette County, establish evidence of government ownership, and transport it to Camden in return for one-half the net proceeds. Supervising Special Agent O. H. Burbridge had some misgivings after learning of the deal and attached an endorsement on March 23, 1866 stating, "Subject to the approval of the Secretary of the Treasury..."

During November and December they removed 225 bales of the Harvey cotton, 71 bales of Thomas Trigg's cotton, and 226 bales of the Jones cotton and took it to Camden. On January 9, 1866 General May, commander of the Quachita River District at Camden, seized the Harvey cotton and returned it to C. M. Harvey as the lawful owner.

Secretary of the Treasury Hugh McCulloch apparently had heard things were getting out of hand and he telegraphed General May on December 14, 1865:

> Agents are instructed to take only cotton on Confederate lists as its property, or other cotton shown to be such, and that belonging to blockade running companies. If any agent does more than this he transcends his authority and I will thank you to apply such remedy as you can to stop the abuse.

Major General Reynolds received the same instructions the same day.

It cost the company $9,471 to haul the bales by wagon from Lost Prairie to Camden at $2 a bale, $4,510 for rebaling, new bagging, rope, and hauling to press at $10 a bale, and $3,375 for ginning 225 bales at $15 a bale for a total of $10,350. The company sued for a total of $17,356. Their petition was dismissed in record time.

Whitfield, Gaius.

Colonel Whitfield, of Marengo County, Alabama, sold 177 bales of cotton to the Confederate government for $15,651.60 worth of 8 percent Confederate bonds amounting to $15,500 plus $113.72 in Confederate money.

The cotton was seized on September 1, 1865 by assistant special Treasury agent Leslie Ellis. Whitfield appealed to the supervising special agent. An agreement was signed whereby Ellis would keep two thirds of the cotton and Whitfield could keep one third. Ellis then ordered Whitfield to deliver 118 bales to the master of the steamer *Huntsman* on November 13. The cotton was shipped to New York where $14,817.26 was paid into the Treasury.

Whitfield sued on the ground his cotton was seized after the war was long over. His petition was dismissed since he had sold the cotton and had been paid in full for it.

Whittelsey, Henry M.

General Sherman took Atlanta in September 1864. In November General Henry W. Slocum's 20th Corps was hurriedly preparing to leave on Sherman's "march to the sea."

Captain Whittelsey was acting chief quartermaster with the Corps and needed $5,000 for payroll and supplies. The 20th Corp's chief commissary, General Bullock, normally had large sums in his possession and supplied the quartermasters with money on drafts. Bullock told Whittelsey that he had taken all the money to post commissary Captain Blair's office in the Railroad Bank building in Atlanta about ¾ of a mile away and that he would go with him to get the money. Bullock, Whittelsey, and Whittelsey's orderly rode out to Blair's office. At this time there were many officers present and great commotion and hurry in the office as the Corps prepared to leave

Atlanta. Blair wrapped the money in a piece of paper, wrapped it again in brown paper, and tied it up with red tape to make a bundle about 3–4 inches thick. Whittelsey put the package in the one pocket of his uniform coat and buttoned the coat. Whittelsey, Bullock, and the orderly rode rapidly back to Bullock's quarters and Whittelsey and the orderly rode on another ¼ mile to their quarters. When they turned from the street into their encampment, Whittelsey put his hand to his breast and suddenly exclaimed that the money was gone. Whittelsey told the orderly to go back to Blair's office and see if the money was there while he retraced their steps along the route but the money was never found.

Whittelsey reported the loss to Colonel Asmussen, 20th Corps inspector general, and requested he use his spies and scouts to help find the money and this was granted. Whittelsey also posted a notice of the loss, offered a reward, and reported the loss to General Slocum. Slocum convened a board of inquiry. Whittelsey had an excellent reputation. The board found that Whittelsey had no other place to put the money and it was inferred that he did not actually put it securely into his coat as he thought. The board exonerated him of any blame but the War Department charged him with the loss. He sued to recover and was awarded $5,000 in 1869.

Wilbur, Aaron. Colonel Ransom seized 102 bales of Aaron's cotton at Savannah and turned it over to Treasury agent Marmaduke Hamilton. Hamilton entered in his ledger book:

21st Feb., 1865, ship *Sandusky* — A. Wilbur, marked A. B., 121 @ 122 —102 bales upland, weighing 49,664 lbs.

On February 18, 1868 the War Department confirmed 102 bales were seized and Wilbur recovered $17,883.66.

Wilcox, Edward W. Contracted to immediately furnish 1,000 horses in West Virginia at a price not to exceed $165 a head. He was paid $150 a head and sued for the difference. The award was made to the First National Bank of Pomeroy, Ohio.

Wilde, James. Sued to recover on 10 bales of cotton seized at Charleston and recovered $862.82 on 7 bales.

Wilkinson, Selina. The widow of a "deceased colored citizen, resident in Charleston" who purchased 5 bales of upland cotton early in the war. It was seized by Captain Sturdivant and

sold in New York. She was proved loyal and recovered $656.

Willis, Dr. Francis. A Savannah physician and president of the Augusta & Savannah Railroad. The Augusta & Savannah was leased to the Georgia Central Railroad so Willis's position as president was nominal. His 134 bales of upland cotton were captured at Savannah. The court noted he had two minor sons in the Confederate military but he was found to be loyal and recovered $23,494.22.

Wilson, Harvey J. Mustered into Company F, 15th Regiment Missouri Cavalry Volunteers on November 1, 1863 and served until July 1, 1865. He furnished his own horse and horse equipment, which he claimed as his own, for 285 days from June 19, 1864 to April 1, 1865.

On March 29, 1869 he submitted a $114 claim to the Treasury Department for the "use and risk of the horse and equipments" at 40 cents per day. This was allowed and paid on January 19, 1870.

In 1886 he applied under the Act of June 16, 1880 for the $100 bounty awarded to the enlisted men of the 15th and 16th Missouri Cavalry Volunteers who served continuously for one year or longer. Wilson served 20 months.

The government then filed a counterclaim for the $114 on the ground that no one was allowed to use his own horse after April 1, 1865. Each soldier was given the choice of sending his horse home or selling it to Captain Owen, the 15th's assistant quartermaster. Captain Owen's records were obtained and Wilson's name was on the list of purchased horses but there was a heavy line drawn through the entry and a note written in the margin: "Void — horse proven away as stolen."

The court gave Wilson the $100 bounty on January 17, 1887. The government's counterclaim was dismissed since the notation did not establish proof that Wilson stole the horse and was paid money for an animal he did not rightfully own. It could have meant the horse was stolen away from the camp.

Wilson, Joseph. Signed a contract on July 2, 1864 to deliver 500 mules to Washington, D.C. — 200 within 5 days and 300 within 25 days at $170 each. The first 200 were received without incident. Wilson had 170 mules from Kentucky at Beltsville, Maryland, about 10 miles from Washington. On the morning of July 12 Wilson's agent and muleskinners started toward

Washington with 52 animals and between 6 and 7 a.m. they reached the picket line, about 4 or 5 miles from the city's mule corral. The sentry refused to allow the mules or the men to pass under orders from Military Governor and Provost Marshal M. N. Wiswell, dated that day, in response to the imminent capture of Washington by General Jubal Early. The order prohibited anyone from entering Washington, Georgetown, or the camps without a permit. The agent informed the sentry the mules were for the government and requested permission to go in and get a permit but was refused. He said the rebels were close by and if he had to return to Beltsville they would be captured. Too bad, orders were orders. The mules were taken back to Beltsville where they arrived between 10 and noon. Another muleskinner named Bowden was getting ready to bring the remaining 118 mules to Washington and he was told not to bother so no effort was made to deliver the animals.

The next morning Bowden took the train to Washington where he obtained a permit, returned around noon just in time to meet the new Confederate cavalry commander, and by 1 p.m. all the mules had been captured.

Wilson immediately notified the Quartermaster General's Office, claimed pay for them, and asked to be relieved from the contract. Both requests were denied. Wilson, then hopping mad, went after the rebels and managed to reclaim 80 mules but another 90 were quickly driven away and never recovered. Wilson delivered the 80 recaptured mules and the balance of animals due on the contract within the required time but he was still out the 90 mules.

Wilson sued to recover at $170 each but his petition was dismissed on the ground that the Quartermaster General, with whom he had contracted, did nothing to prevent Wilson from delivering the mules.

Wilson, Victor F. A northern native who moved to Vicksburg in 1849. He became wealthy in the ice and coal business, owned slaves, and the steamboats *Capitol, Ike Hammett,* and *Victor F. Wilson.* The *Capitol* was used for towing ice barges out of the Illinois River until the war began. He opposed the war and sent the vessels north but the *Wilson* was captured by Confederates and later sunk in the Yazoo River.

He owed money to creditors in Pittsburgh but couldn't pay them in Confederate money so in the fall of 1862 he bought over 600 bales of Louisiana upland cotton and stored it at his warehouse with the intention of shipping it north to sell when the Mississippi was free. From time to time Confederate authorities took some of the cotton for use in hospitals.

He freed his slaves shortly after the Emancipation Proclamation and gave them money to live on.

When Union forces approached Vicksburg his cotton was forcefully taken for fortifications around the city. After the city's surrender on July 4, 1863 the *Capitol* and *Hammett* were returned to him and he applied to Memphis for permission to bring his cotton out but it was seized by personal enemies until a hearing ordered by General James Birdseye McPherson restored it to him. He then served with two federal officers on a court appointed by McPherson and when the court was dissolved he became collector of the port of Vicksburg. He swore allegiance under President Lincoln's amnesty proclamation of December 8, 1863. In the meantime his cotton was taken to St. Louis and sold for $125,300. He died shortly after the war ended.

The administrator of his estate, John A. Klein, sought to recover the proceeds and was awarded $125,300 on 560 bales of upland cotton at $223.75 a bale.

Wilson, William N. Enlisted as a private in the 5th Regiment Delaware Militia. On October 10, 1862 the War Department ordered Major Henry B. Judd, the mustering officer at Wilmington, to muster the existing 16 companies of Delaware volunteers raised by Colonel Henry S. McComb and to organize 10 companies into one regiment to be known as the 5th Delaware Volunteers. The remaining six companies were temporarily attached to the 5th until such time as sufficient volunteers were available to form a second regiment. Wilson was in this group and on November 6, 1862 they were mustered in for nine months then sent home to resume their normal activities until called for service.

On June 19, 1863, Colonel McComb received orders from Major General Robert C. Schenck, commander of the 8th Army Corps at Baltimore, to call out and equip five companies of the 5th Delaware Infantry and send them to Brigadier General Schoepf's command at Fort Delaware. New volunteers were recruited into what became the 5th and 6th Delaware Home

Guard. On June 26, Major Judd received a telegram from Schenck:

Headquarters Middle Department
Eighth Army Corps
Baltimore, June 26, 1863
Col. H. S. McComb
Wilmington, Del.

Major: Your telegraph is received. I am glad to hear of the ten extra companies of the Fifth Delaware. Let them be called out and put on the Philadelphia, Wilmington and Baltimore Railroad by all means, and at as early a moment as possible. The force there is, I know, too small. Take steps for obtaining these troops as soon as possible and post them on the road at once without further order, leaving one-third of what will then be the whole force, and concentrate at Havre de Grace and the crossing of the Susquehanna.

The next day, Wilson reported for active duty and served until he was mustered out on August 6, 1863.

On August 7, Major Judd telegraphed the War Department to ask whether the Home Guard should be paid for the whole nine months or just for time served. He was advised by Assistant Adjutant General Thomas M. Vincent that their pay would be only for time actually on duty. The payroll was made out to reflect that and the soldiers paid. Wilson and others signed their payroll receipts without formal protest although they complained vocally at the time. The accounts were settled at the Treasury Department and there they sat until Wilson demanded his total salary plus a $25 bounty due upon enlistment authorized on December 16, 1886. The Second Auditor reviewed the claim and sent them on to the Second Comptroller but before the comptroller reached a decision the claim was sent to Secretary of the Treasury Fairchild who referred the claim to a federal court for fact finding.

The court held that his claim was barred by statutes of limitations, the Bowman Act, and on April 28, 1890 his case was sent back to Secretary Fairchild.

Winchester, Josiah. John C. Jenkins owned a plantation in Wilkinson County, Mississippi. He died in Adams County, Mississippi in 1855 and left a will instructing the plantation be operated for the benefit of his children.

Cotton was seized from his place by naval forces and a receipt given:

U.S. St'r *Era No. 5*, Wilkinson Co., Miss.,
Plantation J. C. Jenkins' Heirs,
Feb. 18, 1863
Seized by the order of Col. Charles Rivers Ellet,

comd'g Miss. River ram fleet, 168 bales of cotton for the use of the United States Government, belonging to the heirs of the estate of J. C. Jenkins, dec'd.

Asgill Conner
Capt. Co. K. 18th Ill's Volunteers

The cotton was loaded aboard the steamer *New Era No. 5* and taken to Johnson's Landing where it was unloaded and taken to Milliken's Bend on the Mississippi River. It was combined with 258 bales and one bag of other cotton and put aboard the steamer *Rowena* and sent to Cairo, Illinois on order of Admiral Porter and turned over to the U.S. marshal on April 9. On April 17, a libel against the cotton was filed by Fleet Captain A. M. Pennock, USN. Pennock wrote a note to the U.S. attorney for the Southern District of Illinois:

Sir: I hereby file information against the following property, to wit: 258 bales and one bag cotton, 130 bales of which was seized by order of Admiral Porter from Mrs. Twitty, at Wilson Mitchell's Landing, Miss'ippi River, by the U.S. gunboat *General Bragg*, and the balance was sent from the Yazoo River by Admiral Porter as prize-cotton, to be turned over to the U.S. marshal and sold for the use of the Government of the United States, the whole being seized as being the property of rebels.

The cotton was ordered sold by the marshal and the $41,649.90 was paid to the clerk of court. One-half went to the Treasury and one-half to Captain Pennock. Pennock delivered $58,744.56 of Mississippi Squadron prize money to Admiral Porter.

A total of 407 bales from this combined Army/Navy operation were sold at Cairo.

Benjamin S. Compton filed a claim for 8 bales, for which he received $1,397.30, W. R. Musgrave filed a claim for 6 bales as the lawful owner, and W. P. Halliday was paid $13,432.23 on 82 bales on order of the court.

Admiral Porter's money was divided among the crews of 17 public vessels: *Forest Rose,* $2,644.83; *Curlew,* $2,277.78½; *General Pillow,* $436.36; *New Era,* $513.83; *Louisville,* $5,066.79; *Mound City,* $5,066.79; *Conestoga,* $4,094.94; *Marmora,* $4,531.94; *Signal,* $5,417.02; *Pittsburg,* $5,069.79; *Cincinnati,* $5,069.79; *General Lyon,* $268.47; *Romeo,* $2,341.51; *Carondelet,* $5,066.79; *Taylor,* $8,850.21; *Petrel,* $2,039.38; and *Black Hawk* and tugs, $2,986.34.

Josiah Winchester recovered $25,106.80 in 1878 as the sole surviving executor of John Jenkins's estate.

John D. Jones, a mechanic from Carrolton,

Kentucky, "having become somewhat embarrassed" moved his family to Chicot County, Arkansas during 1859. He worked as an engineer in a sawmill and was paid in Confederate money. The family had no way to get out after the Mississippi was blockaded until Memphis was taken. An acquaintance, William P. Haliday, advised Jones to buy cotton with his worthless money and take it out with him so Jones bought 23 bales of first-class cotton. He got passage on a gunboat to Vicksburg to get a permit from Admiral Porter but he became ill and was taken to a hospital in Cairo. His son, John L. Jones, heard his father was ill and went to see Porter and Porter gave him the permit to bring the cotton to Cairo. The family came up to Cairo and shortly after, John D. died. Before arrangements could be made to bring the cotton out it was seized. John D. claimed the 23 marked bales weighing 10,245 pounds and they were released to him.

Dr. Stephen Duncan owned several plantations in Issaquena County, Mississippi. In February 1863, 120 bales of his cotton were seized on two of the plantations and put in with the Cairo lot. Captain James M. Pritchett's gunboat *Tyler* took Duncan's cotton to the mouth of the Yazoo River where they were transferred to the *Black Hawk*, Porter's flagship, on February 20, 1863. On March 6, 157 bales, including all of Duncan's, were put aboard Captain R. E. Birch's *General Lyon* (ex-*De Soto*). The *Lyon* got underway the next day for Cairo, Illinois and arrived there around the 17th.

Duncan sued and recovered $19,543.79 on the ground that the seizure of his cotton was never made by any executive authority.

Winchester & Potomac Railroad Co.

A 32-mile road that ran from Winchester to Harpers Ferry, Virginia. In 1863, 22 miles of track were in the new state of West Virginia. Most of the company's capital stock was owned by investors in loyal states.

On September 11, 1861 company president William L. Clark signed a contract with Confederate States Army acting quartermaster Captain Frank P. Clark to transport supplies, troops, and munitions.

On March 24, 1862 the U.S. Army took the railroad and held it until May 25 when it was retaken by Confederate forces and held until June 11. The Army operated it until September 3 when Confederate raiders captured it again. Confederate forces retreating down the Shenandoah Valley after the Battle of Antietam tore up all the rails and destroyed the bridges from Halltown, 6 miles from Harper's Ferry, all the way to Winchester.

In March 1864 Lieutenant John R. Meigs, chief engineer in the Department of West Virginia, recommended repairing the road as a valuable military asset. On August 14 the Army military railroad department formally took control of the railroad and ran it as a business, kept all the tolls and revenues, transported government freight, and performed all the maintenance. From August 14–19 repairs were made on the 6 miles from Harper's Ferry to Halltown and from November 2–24 the 28 miles to Stevenson were repaired. The road was used between November 2–24 to supply General Sheridan's forces in the Valley of Virginia.

During repairs the original strap rails were replaced with "T" rails taken from the Manassas Gap Railroad and the Orange & Alexandria Railroad. The strap rails were stored at Alexandria, Virginia.

On November 16, 1865 Winchester & Potomac's president Robert Y. Conrad wrote to Secretary of War Stanton to have his railroad returned and to Brevet Brigadier General D. C. McCallum, director of military railroads at Washington, to have the strap rails returned. The letter requesting the rails was given to J. J. Moore, general superintendent at Alexandria, who reported to McCallum the next day there was 501.1940 tons of strap rail identified as belonging to the W & P. Conrad was never notified and the Army sold the rail and captured rolling stock for a total of $2,248,825.41. W. J. Middleton bought 506.25 tons of strap rail at auction for $30,340 the next month. The Army kept the money and used it to defray the expenses of the military railroad department.

On December 14, 1865 Secretary Stanton directed the Quartermaster General to return the railroad to its owners. On January 1, 1866 the company leased all of its road and rolling stock to the Baltimore & Ohio. The property was formally returned on January 20 but no formal lease was signed until July. The B & O extended the line 162 miles to Lexington, Virginia as the Harper's Ferry and Valley Branch of the B & O.

After the war Manassas Gap Railroad demanded the value of their "T" rails from the W & P. Winchester refused, Manassas sued, and in 1873 or '74 the companies agreed on a settlement of $25,000.

On May 11, 1885 the B & O filed a claim with the War Department to recover 507 long tons and 1,940 pounds of iron rail belonging to the Winchester & Potomac. The request was forwarded to Quartermaster General Samuel B. Holabird on November 10 for a report. Holabird recommended approving the claim and forwarding it to the Third Auditor but correcting the company's claim to 501 tons and 1,940 pounds at a value of $60.55 a ton for a total of $30,387.99.

Secretary of War William C. Endicott forwarded the claim and on March 4, 1887 Third Auditor John S. Williams denied it on the ground it should have been presented directly by the W & P and not through the B & O. The claim was amended by William A. Clark, acting president, and Frank P. Clark — now attorney for the W & P — and Robert Garrett, president of the B & O.

On April 18, 1887 the Third Auditor again rejected the claim and sent it to Second Comptroller Sigourney Butler. Butler recommended sending the claim to the Court of Claims for fact finding. On June 24, 1889 the W & P filed suit in Washington, D.C. and the company was awarded $30,340 on November 7, 1892.

The government appealed to the Supreme Court where the decision was reversed on May 18, 1896 on the ground that the claim was a "war claim" and barred from the Court of Claims's jurisdiction by the Act of March 3, 1887.

Winters, Gilbert E. Appointed captain and volunteer commissary of subsistence on March 14, 1863. On December 31 he was summarily discharged from the service without cause. He was reinstated on March 3, 1865 and sued for back pay. The court found he was illegally discharged and he was awarded $1,703.

Witkowski, Simon. A naturalized native of Prussia, traveling peddler, and speculator with family in New York. He was in Fort Gaines, Georgia in 1862 but had no permanent residence. He bought 128 bales of cotton in Macon and had it shipped to Erwin & Hardee at Savannah for storage. Erwin & Hardee sold ten bales on his order to cover the storage costs and the rest was captured. His petition was dismissed in 1870 but on appeal he was awarded $20,688.94 on 118 bales.

Woodruff, Cornelius V. John K. Elgee and Josiah Chambers, of Alexandria, Louisiana, owned the Artonish, Loch Leven, and Lochdale plantations in Wilkinson County, Mississippi as Elgee & Chambers Company. Their agent was William C. Gordon.

On July 31, 1863 Gordon contracted with special Treasury agent Charles S. Lobdell to purchase 2,100 bales of their cotton at 10 cents a pound in currency, to be delivered to Fort Adams, and to be paid for after weighing there. Lobdell would pay for bagging and baling, Dasilva & Co. would ship it to New Orleans, and after arrival it would be at Lobdell's risk. Lobdell lived in West Baton Rouge, Louisiana.

Gordon and Lobdell supervised the storage of the cotton under boards at Buffalo Bayou, about 10 miles from the Mississippi River at a place known as "The Rocks" or "Felter's Plantation," and there were about 20 bales of unbaled cotton in the gin house. After the sale Lobdell employed J. M. Morris, a local resident, to watch over the cotton and for some reason it was never moved from there.

In October, Dr. Haller Nutt, of Natchez, then within Union military lines, hired Captain Truman Holmes to purchase cotton for him. Holmes obtained the required permits and met with Elgee to arrange to buy as many of the 2,100 bales as could safely be gotten out at £20 a bale to be paid at Liverpool, England with Elgee assuming the risk until the cotton was out. Chambers was present and assented, although he had given control of the cotton to Elgee. A contract was sent to Holmes at Alexandria on October 8. Nothing happened and in December Elgee wrote to Gordon, the agent, and told him to tell Holmes that since he hadn't heard from Holmes since October the deal was off. Holmes replied to Gordon the following spring and Gordon gave him the message from Elgee.

On March 15, 1864 C. V. Woodruff and Adolph Bouchard, doing business as C. V. Woodruff & Co., made a contract with Lobdell to buy the cotton. Lobdell had since moved to New Orleans, where Woodruff also lived. Morris, the caretaker, was informed of the sale to Woodruff and was continued on as caretaker.

On April 2, B. F. Camp, a U.S. Treasury agent, took control of 572 bales of the cotton over the objection of Morris who told him it had been sold. Camp proceeded to put 500 bales on board the steamer *Venango* and 72 bales on the gunboat USS *Champion,* on which he had been traveling. The 72 bales were later transferred to the *Venango* and the lot taken to Natchez where it arrived on April 9 and stored in a yard under control of General Tuttle. A short time later the rest of the cotton was burned up by rebel raiders.

Gordon accompanied the cotton and met with General Tuttle to tell him the cotton was neither Confederate nor abandoned but Tuttle wouldn't release it. Gordon met the next day with Dr. Nutt and told him the whole story. Nutt advised him to tell Tuttle the cotton had been sold to Truman Holmes on October 8 with Union papers and that might release it. Gordon presented a letter to that effect to Tuttle and on May 2, 1864 Tuttle allowed all 572 bales to be loaded aboard the steamer *Olive Branch* and shipped to St. Louis, the very same day Elgee took the loyalty oath.

Elgee filed suit in the Circuit Court for Saint Louis County, Missouri and the U.S. Circuit Court for the District of Missouri. He lost in both courts and the U.S. Supreme Court affirmed the decisions. The 572 bales were sold on July 4 at public auction for net proceeds of $366,170.83. By that time about 50 pounds per bale had been lost in weight.

By the time all this was sorted out, Elgee and Dr. Nutt had died. Cornelius Woodruff, Julia A. Nutt, Dr. Nutt's wife, and Bessie Elgee Gansen, Elgee's executrix, and Elgee's heirs, carried on the legal action in federal court.

The 1871 judgement awarded $137,882.62 to the Elgee's on 1,528 bales; $155,922.26 to Woodruff; and $72,365.96 to Lobdell on 572 bales at 20 cents a pound plus interest. Julia Nutt's petition was dismissed on the ground that Dr. Nutt never acquired any actual interest in the cotton and the contract was made in violation of the Non-Intercourse Act.

The government appealed to the Supreme Court where the Woodruff, Bouchard, and Nutt decisions were reversed and a judgement in favor of Elgee was ordered.

Wormer, Daniel.
Contracted with Captain James A. Ekin, Cavalry Bureau chief quartermaster, to deliver 1,200 cavalry horses to the government stables at St. Charles, Missouri on or before March 26, 1864. The deal went awry,

Wormer sued and recovered $9,000. The government appealed to the Supreme Court where the judgement was reversed on the ground that his damages were "voluntarily sustained."

Wylie, William G. and Dr. James G.
William was a Louisiana Supreme Court judge, James a physician. They owned 144 bales of cotton stored on their Louisiana plantation on the east side of Bayou Mason near Joe's Bayou. In the fall of 1862 they feared the cotton would be found and destroyed by rebels so they moved it to E. O. Ross's plantation on the west side of Bayou Mason in Carroll Parish and then apparently fled the country and went to Mexico.

A Union force under Colonel W. T. Wood found and seized 80 bales of which $20,130.34 in proceeds from 74 bales made their way into the Treasury.

There was conflicting testimony as to their presence in Mexico but the court awarded them $20,492.81.

Zellner, Benjamin H.
A Monroe County, Georgia planter who ginned and packed 42 bales of cotton in November 1865. It was hauled to Macon for storage but 12 bales were sold to pay freedmen. The remaining cotton weighed 13,317 pounds. In the spring of 1866, Treasury assistant special agent Clifton T. Wharton seized the cotton and proceeds of $1,760.33 were deposited in the Treasury.

In court the government was unable to prove Zellner aided the rebellion and Zellner was unable to prove he was loyal. The court stated:

"The only other witness who has anything to say about the loyalty of the claimant is Yorke Zellner, who calls himself a farmer and preacher. This witness has been the slave of the claimant, had known him from childhood, and served him throughout the rebellion. Yet Yorke Zellner says, 'I do not know whether Mr. Zellner was a Union man or not. I never heard him say anything about it.'"

Zellner's claim was dismissed.

Appendix I:
1860 Census Data

Seceding Slaveholding States

	Total Population	White Males	White Females	Free Colored Males	Free Colored Females	Male Slaves	Female Slaves	Number of Slaveholders	Number of Farms and Cash Value (Millions)
AL	964,201	270,190	256,081	1,254	1,436	217,766	217,314	33,730	50,064/$175.8
AR	435,450	171,477	152,666	72	72	56,174	54,941	11,481	33,190/$91.6
FL	140,424	41,128	36,619	454	478	31,348	30,397	5,152	6,396/$16.4
GA	1,057,286	301,066	290,484	1,669	1,831	229,193	283,005	41,084	53,897/$157.0
LA	708,002	189,648	167,808'	8,279	10,368	171,977	159,747	22,033	17,281/$204.7
MS	791,305	186,273	167,626	372	401	219,301	217,330	30,943	37,007/$190.7
NC	992,622	313,670	316,272	14,880	15,583	166,469	164,590	34,658	67,022/$143.3
SC	703,708	146,160	145,140	4,548	5,366	196,571	205,885	26,701	28,456/$139.6
TN	1,109,801	422,779	403,943	3,538	3,762	136,370	139,349	36,844	77,741/$271.3
TX	604,215	228,585	192,306	181	174	91,189	91,337	21,878	37,363/$88.1
VA	1,596,318	528,842	518,457	27,721	30,321	249,483	241,382	52,128	86,468/$371.7

Non-seceding Slaveholding States and Territories

	Total Population	White Males	White Females	Free Colored Males	Free Colored Females	Male Slaves	Female Slaves	Number of Slaveholders	Number of Farms and Cash Value (Millions)
DE	112,216	45,940	44,649	9,889	9,940	860	938	587	6,588/$31.4
KS	107,206	58,806	47,584	286	339	0	2	2	10,108/$12.2
KY	1,555,684	474,193	445,291	5,101	5,583	113,009	112,474	38,645	83,689/$291.4
MD	687,049	256,839	259,079	39,746	44,196	44,313	42,876	13,783	25,244/$145.9
MO	1,182,012	563,131	500,358	1,697	1,875	57,360	57,571	24,320	88,552/$230.6
NE	28,841	16,689	12,007	35	32	6	9	6	2,533/$3.8

Kansas and Nebraska were territories
Source: (2004) Historical Census Browser. Retrieved 2–15–2005, from the University of Virginia, Geospatial and Statistical Date Center

Appendix II:
Military Regulations
Regarding Pay and Expenditures

U.S. Revised Statutes, Section 3482

That any field, staff, or other officer, mounted militiaman, volunteer, ranger, or cavalryman engaged in the military service of the United States who sustains damage, without any fault or negligence on his part, while in the service, by the loss of a horse in battle, or for loss of equipage, in consequence of the loss of his horse, shall be allowed and paid the value thereof, not to exceed two hundred dollars.

Army Regulation No. 1002

No officer or agent in the military service shall purchase from any other person in the military service, or make any contract with any such person to furnish supplies, or make any purchases or contract in which such person shall be admitted to any share or part, or to any benefit to arise therefrom.

Army Regulations Section 1053

[Required "rigid economy in the expenditure of public money."]

Army regulations, 1864, Paragraph 1358

Every deserter shall forfeit all pay and allowances due at the time of desertion. Stoppages and fines shall be paid from his future earnings if he is apprehended and continued in service, and if they are adjudged by a court martial; otherwise from his arrears of pay.

War Department General Order No. 15 of May 4, 1861 and No. 25 of May 26, 1861

[Authorized an enlistment bonus of $100 upon being honorably discharged. The Act of July 22, 1861 required two years' service and a later statute waived the longevity requirement for wounded soldiers. Congress legalized the General Orders on August 6, 1861.]

War Department Assistant Adjutant General's Office General Order No. 82 of June 20, 1863

I. Under the requirements of section twenty of the act "for enrolling and calling out the national forces, and for other purposes," approved March 3, 1863, it is ordered that the following rules shall govern whenever a regiment is "reduced below the minimum number allowed by law" but is of a strength above half the maximum.

1. *Infantry* — Each regiment will be deprived of the colonel and one assistant surgeon. Each company — provided it is reduced below the minimum — will be deprived of the second lieutenant.

2. *Cavalry* — Each regiment will be deprived of the colonel, one major, and one assistant surgeon. Each company — provided it is reduced below the minimum — will be deprived of the second lieutenant.

3. *Artilley* — Each regiment will be deprived of the colonel, one major, and one assistant surgeon. Each company — provided it is re-

duced below the minimum — will be deprived of the additional officers authorized to be added at the President's discretion. (See G. O. 110, A. G. O., 1863)

There being no minimum for artillery fixed by existing orders, the minimum for the object herein named will be 1,044 aggregate for a regiment and 86 aggregate for a battery.

General Order No. 191 of June 25, 1863

[Set up a schedule to pay reenlisting veterans one months' pay in advance, $13, a first bounty installment of $25, and a premium of $2 upon enlistment. After two months' service another $50 was paid; after six months' $50; after one year, $50; after 18 months, $50; after two years, $50; after 2 1/2 years, $50, and after three years' service, $75, for a total of $402.]

Circular No. 98 of November 3, 1863 pursuant to the Proclamation of October 17

The following regulations are established, with the approval of the Secretary of War, and will govern mustering and disbursing officers in their payments of the advance bounty, premium, and advance pay to recruits (not veterans) enlisted by recruiting officers, to serve for three years or the war, in old regiments now organized, whose term of service expire in 1864 and 1865:

To all recruits enlisting as above required there will be paid one months' pay in advance, and, in addition, bounty and premium amounting to $302, as follows:

One months' pay before leaving the recruiter's office or depot, $13; first installment of bounty, $60; and a $2 premium.

After two months' service	$40
After six months' service	$40
After the first years' service	$40
After eighteen months' service	$40
After two years' service	$40
At the expiration of three years' service, or to any soldier enlisting under this authority who may be honorably discharged after two years' service, the remainder of the bounty will be paid	$40

War Department Order of April 1, 1865

[The War Department prohibited cavalry soldiers from using their own horses after this date.]

General Edward Canby's General Field Order No. 39 of May 10, 1865

[Prohibited the sale or transfer of any cotton in East Louisiana, Mississippi, Alabama, and West Florida except by U.S. Treasury agents.]

Appendix III:
Acts of Congress, Joint Resolutions, Presidential Proclamations, and Administrative Directives Frequently Cited by U.S. Courts

Act of February 28, 1795 (in part)

An act to provide for calling forth the Militia to execute the laws of the Union, suppress insurrections, and repel invasions; and to repeal the Act now in force for those purposes.

Section 1. *Be it enacted by the Senate and House of Representatives of the United States of America in Congress assembled,* That whenever the United States shall be invaded, or be in imminent danger of invasion from any foreign nation or Indian tribe, it shall be lawful for the President of the United States to call forth such number of the militia of the state, or states, most convenient to the place of danger, or scene of action, as he may judge necessary to repel such invasion, and to issue his orders for that purpose, to such officer or officers of the militia, as he shall think proper. And in case of insurrection in any state, against the government thereof, it shall be lawful for the President of the United States, on application of the legislature of such state, or of the executive, (when the legislature cannot be convened,) to call forth such number of the militia of any other state or states, as may be applied for, as he may judge sufficient to suppress the insurrection.

Sec. 2. *And be it further enacted,* That whenever the laws of the United States shall be opposed, or the execution thereof obstructed, in any state, by combinations too powerful to be suppressed by the ordinary course of judicial proceedings, or by the powers vested in the marshals by this act, it shall be lawful for the President of the United States, to call forth the militia of such state, or of any other state or states, as may be necessary to suppress such combinations, and to cause the laws to be duly executed; and the use of the militia so to be called forth may be continued, if necessary, until the expiration of thirty days after the commencement of the then next session of Congress.

Sec. 3. *Provided always, and be it further enacted,* That whenever it may be necessary, in the judgment of the President, to use the military force hereby directed to be called forth, the President shall forthwith, by proclamation, command such insurgents to disperse, and retire peaceably to their respective abodes, within a limited time.

Act of March 3, 1849 (in part)

An Act to provide for the Payment of Horses and other Property lost or destroyed in the Military Service of the United States.

Be it enacted by the Senate and House of Representatives of the United States of America in Congress assembled, That any field, or staff, or other officer, mounted militia-man, volunteer, ranger, or cavalry, engaged in the military service of the United States since the eighteenth of June, eighteen hundred and twelve, or who shall hereafter be in said service, and has sustained, or shall sustain, damage without any fault or negligence on his part, while in said service, by the loss of a horse in battle, or by the loss of a horse wounded in battle, and which has died or shall die of said wound, or, being so wounded, shall be abandoned by order of his officer and lost, or shall sustain damage by the loss of any horse by death or abandonment because of the unavoidable dangers of the sea when on board an United States transport vessel, or because the United States failed to supply transportation for the horse, and the owner was compelled by the order of his commanding officer to embark and leave him, or in consequence of the United States failing to supply sufficient forage, or because the rider was dismounted and separated from his horse and ordered to do duty on foot at a station detached from his horse, or when the officer in the immediate command ordered, or shall order, the horse turned out to graze in the woods, prairies, or commons, because the United States failed, or shall fail, to supply sufficient forage, and the loss was or shall be consequent thereof, or for the loss of necessary equipage, in consequence of the loss of his horse, as aforesaid, shall be allowed and paid the value thereof, not to exceed two hundred dollars: *Provided,* That if any payment has been, or shall, made to any one aforesaid, for the use and risk, or for forage after the death, loss, or abandonment of his horse, said payment shall be deducted from the value thereof, unless he satisfied, or shall satisfy, the paymaster at the time he made, or shall make, the payment, or thereafter show, by proof, that he was remounted, in which case the deduction shall only extend to the time he was on foot: *And provided, also,* If any payment shall have been, or shall hereafter be, made to any person above mentioned, on account of clothing to which he was not entitled by law, such payment shall be deducted from the value of his horse or accoutrements.

Act of February 26, 1853 (in part)

An Act to prevent Frauds upon the Treasury of the United States.

Be it enacted by the Senate and House of Representatives of the United States of America in Congress assembled, That all transfers and assignments hereafter made of any claim upon the United States, or any part or share thereof, or interest therein, whether absolute or conditional, and whatever may be the consideration therefore, and all powers of attorney, orders, or other authorities for receiving payment of any such claim, or any part or share thereof, shall be absolutely null and void, unless the same shall be freely made and executed in the presence of at least two attesting witnesses, after the allowance of such claim, the ascertainment of the amount due, and the issuing of a warrant for the payment thereof.

Act of June 23, 1860 (in part)

An Act making Appropriations for the Legislative, Executive, and Judicial Expenses of Government for the Year ending the thirtieth of June, eighteen hundred and sixty-one.

Sec. 3. *And be it further enacted,* That all purchases and contracts for supplies or services in any of the departments of the government, except for personal services, when the public exigencies do not require the immediate delivery of the article or articles, or performance of the service, shall be made by advertising, a sufficient time previously, for proposals respecting the same. When immediate delivery or performance is required by the public exigency, the articles or service required may be procured by open purchase or contract at the places and in the manner in which such articles are usually bought and sold, or such services engaged between individuals. No contract or purchase shall hereafter be made unless the same be authorized by law, or be under the appropriation adequate to its fulfillment, except in the War or Navy Departments, for clothing, subsistence, forage, fuel, quarters, or transportation, which, however, shall not exceed the necessities of the current year. No arms, nor military supplies whatever, which are of a patented invention, shall be purchased, nor the right of using or applying any patented invention, unless the same shall be authorized by law, and the appropriation therefore explicitly set forth that it is for such patented invention.

Proclamation of April 15, 1861

WHEREAS the laws of the United States have been for some time past, and now are, opposed, and the execution thereof obstructed, in the States of South Carolina, Georgia, Alabama, Florida, Mississippi, Louisiana, and Texas, by combinations too powerful to be suppressed by the ordinary course of judicial proceedings, or by the powers vested in the marshals by law:

Now, therefore, I, ABRAHAM LINCOLN, President of the United States, by virtue of the power in me vested by the Constitution and the laws, have thought fit to call forth, and hereby do call forth, the militia of the several States of the Union, to the aggregate number of seventy-five thousand, in order to suppress said combinations, and to cause the laws to be duly executed.

The details for this object will be immediately communicated to the State authorities through the War Department.

I appeal to all loyal citizens to favor, facilitate, and aid this effort to maintain the honor, the integrity, and the existence of our national Union, and the perpetuity of popular government, and to redress wrongs already long enough endured.

I deem it proper to say that the first service assigned to the forces hereby called forth will probably be to repossess the forts, places, and property which have been seized from the Union; and in every event the utmost care will be observed, consistently with the objects aforesaid, to avoid any devastation, any destruction of or interference with property, or any disturbance of peaceful citizens in any part of the country.

And I hereby command the persons composing the combinations aforesaid to disperse and retire peaceably to their respective abodes within twenty days from this date.

Deeming that the present condition of public affairs presents an extraordinary occasion, I do hereby, in virtue of the power in me vested by the Constitution, convene both Houses of Congress.

Senators and Representatives are therefore summoned to assemble at their respective Chambers, at twelve o'clock, noon, on Thursday, the 4th day of July next, then and there to consider and determine such measures as, in their wisdom, the public safety and interest may seem to demand.

In witness whereof I have hereunto set my hand and caused the seal of the United States to be affixed.

Done at the city of Washington, this fifteenth day of April, in the year of our Lord, one thousand eight hundred and sixty-one, and of the independence of the United States the eighty-fifth.

Proclamation of April 19, 1861

WHEREAS an insurrection against the Government of the United States has broken out in the States of South Carolina, Georgia, Alabama, Florida, Mississippi, Louisiana, and Texas, and the laws of the United States for the collection of the revenue cannot be effectually executed therein conformably to that provision of the Constitution which requires duties to be uniform throughout the United States:

An whereas a combination of persons, engaged in such insurrection, have threatened to grant pretended letters of marque to authorize the bearers thereof to commit assaults on the lives, vessels, and property of good citizens of the country lawfully engaged in commerce on the high seas, and in waters of the United States:

And whereas an Executive Proclamation has been already issued, requiring the persons engaged in these disorderly proceedings to desist therefrom, calling out a militia force for the purpose of repressing the same, and convening Congress in extraordinary session to deliberate and determine thereon:

Now, therefore, I, ABRAHAM LINCOLN, President of the United States, with a view to the same purposes before mentioned, and to the protection of the public peace, and the lives and property of quiet and orderly citizens pursuing their lawful occupations, until Congress shall have assembled and deliberated on the said unlawful proceedings, or until the same shall have ceased, have further deemed it advisable to set on foot a blockade of the ports within the States aforesaid, in pursuance of the laws of the United States and of the law of nations in such case provided. For this purpose a competent force will be posted so as to prevent entrance and exit of vessels from the ports aforesaid. If, therefore, with a view to violate such blockade, a vessel shall approach, or shall attempt to leave either of the said ports, she will be duly warned by the commander of one of the blockading vessels, who will indorse on her register the fact and date of such warning, and if the same vessel shall again attempt to enter or leave the blockaded port, she will be captured and sent to the nearest convenient port, for such proceedings against her and her cargo as prize, may be deemed advisable.

And I hereby proclaim and declare that if

any person, under the pretended authority of the said States, or under any other pretence, shall molest a vessel of the United States or the persons or cargo on board of her, such person will be held amenable to the laws of the United States for the prevention and punishment of piracy.

In witness whereof, I have hereunto set my hand, and caused the seal of the United States to be affixed.

Done at the city of Washington, this nineteenth day of April, in the year of our Lord one thousand eight hundred and sixty-one, and of the Independence of the United States the eighty-fifth.

Proclamation of April 27, 1861

WHEREAS, for the reasons assigned in my Proclamation of the nineteenth instant, a blockade for the ports of the States of South Carolina, Georgia, Florida, Alabama, Louisiana, Mississippi, and Texas was ordered to be established:

And whereas, since that date, public property of the United States has been seized, the collection of the revenue obstructed, and duly commissioned officers of the United States, while engaged in executing the orders of their superiors, have been arrested and held in custody as prisoners, or have been impeded in the discharge of their official duties without due legal process, by persons claiming to act under authorities of the States of Virginia and North Carolina:

An efficient blockade of the ports of those States will also be established.

In witness whereof, I have hereunto set my hand, and caused the seal of the United States to be affixed.

Done at the city of Washington, this twenty-seventh day of April, in the year of our Lord one thousand eight hundred and sixty-one, and of the Independence of the United States the eighty-fifth.

Proclamation of May 3, 1861

WHEREAS existing exigencies demand immediate and adequate measures for the protection of the national Constitution and the preservation of the national Union by the suppression of the insurrectionary combinations now existing in several States for opposing the laws of the Union and obstructing the execution thereof, to which end a military force in addition to that called forth by my Proclamation of the fifteenth day of April in the present year, appears to be indispensably necessary:

Now, therefore, I, ABRAHAM LINCOLN, President of the United States, and Commander-in-Chief of the Army and Navy thereof, and of the Militias of the several States when called into actual service, do hereby call into the service of the United States forty-two thousand and thirty-four volunteers, to serve for the period of three years unless sooner discharged, and to be mustered into service as infantry and cavalry. The proportions of each arm and the details of enrollment and organization will be made known through the Department of War.

And I also direct that the regular army of the United States be increased by the addition of eight regiments of infantry, one regiment of cavalry, and one regiment of artillery, making altogether a maximum aggregate increase of twenty-two thousand seven hundred and fourteen, officers and enlisted men, the details of which increase will also be made known through the Department of War.

And I further direct the enlistment for not less than one or more than three years, of eighteen thousand seamen, in addition to the present force, for the naval service of the United States. The details of enlistment and organization will be made known through the Department of the Navy.

The call for volunteers, hereby made, and the direction for the increase of the regular army, and for the enlistment of seamen hereby given, together with the plan of organization adopted for the volunteers and for the regular forces hereby authorized will be submitted to Congress as soon as assembled.

In the mean time I earnestly invoke the coöperation of all good citizens in the measures hereby adopted, for the effectual suppression of unlawful violence, for the impartial enforcement of constitutional laws, and for the speediest possible restoration of peace and order, and, with these, of happiness and prosperity throughout the country.

In testimony whereof, I have hereunto set my hand and caused the seal of the United States to be affixed.

Done at the City of Washington, the third day of May, in the year of our Lord one thousand eight hundred and sixty-one, and of the Independence of the United States the eighty-fifth.

U.S. Postmaster General Montgomery Blair's Notice of May 27, 1861

All postal service in the States of Virginia, North Carolina, South Carolina, Georgia, Florida, Alabama, Mississippi, Louisiana, Arkansas, and Texas, will be suspended from and after the 31st instant.

Letters for offices temporarily closed by this order will be forwarded to the dead letter office, except those for Western Virginia, which will be sent to Wheeling.

Act of July 13, 1861 (in part)

An Act further to provide for the Collection of Duties on Imports, and for other purposes.

Sec 5. *And be it further enacted,* That whenever the President, in the pursuance of the provisions of the second section of the act entitled "An act to provide for calling forth the militia to execute the laws of the Union, suppress insurrections, and repel invasions, and to repeal the act now in force for that purpose," approved February twenty-eight, seventeen hundred and ninety-five, shall have called forth the militia to suppress combinations against the laws of the United States, and to cause the laws to be duly executed, and the insurgents shall have failed to disperse by the time directed by the President, and when said insurgents claim to act under the authority of any State or States, and such claim is not disclaimed or repudiated by the persons exercising the functions of government in such State or States, or in the part or parts thereof in which said combination exists, nor such insurrection suppressed by said State or States, then and in such case it may and shall be lawful for the President, by proclamation, to declare that the inhabitants of such State, or any section or part thereof, where such insurrection exists, are in a state of insurrection against the United States; and thereupon all commercial intercourse by and between the same and the citizens thereof and the citizens of the rest of the United States shall cease and be unlawful so long as such condition of hostility shall continue; and all goods and chattels, wares and merchandise, coming from said State or section into the other parts of the United States, and all proceeding to such State or section, by land or water, shall, together with the vessel or vehicle conveying the same, or conveying persons to and from such State or section, be forfeited to the United States:

Provided, however, That the President may, in his discretion, license and permit commercial intercourse with any such part of said State or section, the inhabitants of which are so declared in a state of insurrection, in such articles, and for such time, and by such persons, as he, in his discretion, may think most conducive to the public interest; and such intercourse, so far as by him licensed, shall be conducted and carried on only in pursuance of rules and regulations prescribed by the Secretary of the Treasury. And the Secretary of the Treasury may appoint such officers at places where officers of the customs are not now authorized by law as may be needed to carry into effect such licenses. Rules, and regulations; and officers of the customs and other officers shall receive under this section, and under said rules and regulations, such fees and compensation as are now allowed for similar service under other provisions of law.

Section 5 was gradually relaxed by proclamation to allow "a partial restoration of commercial intercourse" between citizens of previously insurrectionary states and loyal states as the military advanced. In this way the South was opened up to commerce but applying the law in areas where the military lines constantly shifted was impractical so in claims filed under the Act of March 12, 1863 the court looked to the claimant's loyalty.

Act of July 22, 1861

An act to authorize the Employment of Volunteers to aid in enforcing the Laws and protecting Public Property.

WHEREAS, certain of the forts, arsenals, custom-houses, navy yards, and other property of the United States have been seized, and other violations of law have been committed and are threatened by organized bodies of men in several of the States, and a conspiracy has been entered into to overthrow the Government of the United States: Therefore,

Be it enacted by the Senate and House of Representatives of the United States of America in Congress assembled, That the President be, and he is hereby, authorized to accept the services of volunteers, either as cavalry, infantry, or artillery, in such numbers, not exceeding five hundred thousand, as he may deem necessary, for the purpose of repelling invasion, suppressing insurrection, enforcing the laws, and protecting and preserving the public property: *Provided,* That the services of the volunteers shall be for such time as the President may direct, not exceeding three years nor less than six months, and they shall be disbanded at the end of the war. And all provisions of law applicable to three years' volunteers shall apply to two years' volunteers, and to all volunteers who have been, or may be, accepted into the service of the United States, for a period not less than six months, in the same manner as if such volunteers were specially named. Before receiving into service any number of volunteers exceeding those now called for and accepted, the President shall, from time to time, issue his proclamation, stating the number desired, either as cavalry, infantry, or artillery, and the States from which they are to be furnished, having reference, in any such requisition, to the number then in service from the several States, and to the exigencies of the service at the time, and equalizing, as far as practicable, the number furnished by the several States, according to Federal population.

Sec. 2. *And be it further enacted,* That the said volunteers shall be subject to the rules and regulations governing the army of the United States, and that shall be formed, by the President, into regiments of infantry, with the exception of such numbers for cavalry and artillery, as he may direct, not exceed the proportion of one company of each of those arms to every regiment of infantry, and to be organized as in the regular service. Each regiment of infantry shall have one colonel, one lieutenant-colonel, one major, one adjutant, (a lieutenant), one quartermaster, (a lieutenant), one surgeon and one assistant surgeon, one sergeant-major, one regimental quartermaster-sergeant, one regimental commissary-sergeant, one hospital steward, two principal musicians, and twenty-four musicians for a band, and shall be composed of ten companies, each company to be consist of one captain, one first lieutenant, one second lieutenant, one first sergeant, four sergeants, eight corporals, two musicians, one wagoner, and from sixty-four to eighty-two privates.

Sec. 3. *And be it further enacted,* That these forces, when accepted as herein authorized, shall be organized into divisions of three or more brigades each; and each division shall have a major-general, three aides-de-camp, and one assistant adjutant-general with the rank of major. Each brigade shall be composed of four or more regiments, and shall have one brigadier-general,

two aides-de-camp, one assistant adjutant-general with the rank of captain, one surgeon, one assistant quartermaster, and one commissary of subsistence.

Sec. 4. *And be it further enacted,* That the President shall be authorized to appoint, by and with the advice and consent of the Senate, for the command of the forces provided for in this act, a number of major-generals, not exceeding six, and a number of brigadier-generals, not exceeding eighteen, and the other division and brigade officers required for the organization of these forces, except the aides-de-camp, who shall be selected by their respective generals from the officers of the army or volunteer corps: *Provided,* That the President may select the major-generals and brigadier-generals provided for in this act, from the line or staff of the regular army, and the officers so selected shall be permitted to retain their rank therein. The governors of the States furnishing volunteers under this act, shall commission the field, staff, and company officers requisite for the said volunteers; but, in cases where the State authorities refuse or omit to furnish volunteers at the call or on the proclamation of the President, and volunteers from such State offer their services under such call or proclamation, the President shall have the power to accept such services, and to commission the proper field, staff, and company officers.

Sec. 5. *And be it further enacted,* That the officers, non-commissioned officers, and privates, organized as above set forth, shall, in all respects, be placed on the footing, as to pay and allowances, of similar corps of the regular army: *Provided,* That the allowances of non-commissioned officers and privates for clothing, when not furnished in kind, shall be three dollars and fifty cents per month, and that each company officer, non-commissioned officer, private, musician, and artificer of cavalry shall furnish his own horse and horse equipments, and shall receive forty cents per day for their use and risk, except that in case the horse shall become disabled, or shall die, the allowance shall cease until the disability be removed or another horse be supplied. Every volunteer non-commissioned officer, private, musician, and artificer, who enters the service of the United States under this act, shall be paid at the rate of fifty cents in lieu of subsistence, and if a cavalry volunteer, twenty-five cents additional, in lieu of forage, for every twenty miles of travel from his place of enrollment to the place of muster — the distance to be measured by the shortest usually travelled route; and when honorably discharged an allowance at the same rate, from the place of his discharge to his place of enrollment, and, in addition thereto, if he shall have served for a period of two years, or during the war, if sooner ended, the sum of one hundred dollars: *Provided,* That such of the companies of cavalry herein provided for, as may require it, may be furnished with horses and horse equipments in the same manner as in the United States army.

Sec. 6. *And be it further enacted,* That any volunteer who may be received into the service of the United States under this act, and who may be wounded or otherwise disabled in the service, shall be entitled to the benefits which have been or may be conferred on persons disabled in the regular service, and the widow, if there be one, and if not, the legal heirs of such as die, or may be killed in service, in addition to all arrears of pay and allowances, shall receive the sum of one hundred dollars.

Sec. 7. *And be it further enacted,* That the bands of the regiments of infantry and of the regiments of cavalry shall be paid as follows: one-fourth of each shall receive the pay of and allowances of sergeants of engineer soldiers; one-fourth those of corporals or engineer soldiers; and the remaining half those of privates of engineer soldiers of the first class; and the leaders of the band shall receive the same pay and emoluments as second lieutenants of infantry.

Sec. 8. *And be it further enacted,* That the wagoners and soldiers shall receive the pay and allowances of corporals of cavalry. The regimental commissary-sergeant shall receive the pay and allowances of a regimental sergeant-major, and the regimental quartermaster-sergeant shall receive the pay and allowances of a sergeant of cavalry.

Sec. 9. *And be it further enacted,* That there shall be allowed to each regiment one chaplain, who shall be appointed by the regimental commander on the vote of the field officers and company commanders on duty with the regiment at the time the appointment shall be made. The chaplain so appointed must be a regular ordained minister of a Christian denomination, and shall receive the pay and allowances of a captain of cavalry, and shall be required to report to the colonel commanding the regiment to which he is attached, at the end of each quarter, the moral and religious condition of the regiment, and such suggestions as may conduce to the so-cial happiness and moral improvement of the troops.

Sec. 10. *And be it further enacted,* That the general commanding a separate department or a detached army, is hereby authorized to appoint a military board or commission, of not less than three nor more than five officers, whose duty it shall be to examine the capacity, qualifications, propriety of conduct and efficiency of any commissioned officer of volunteers within his department or army, who may be reported to the board or commission; and upon such report, if adverse to such officer, and if approved by the President of the United States, the commission of such officer shall be vacated: *Provided always,* That no officer shall be eligible to sit on such board or commission, whose rank or promotion would in any way be affected by its proceedings, and two members at least, if practicable, shall be of equal rank of the officer being examined. And when vacancies occur in any of the companies of volunteers, an election shall be called by the colonel of the regiment to fill such vacancies, and the men of each company shall vote in their respective companies for all officers as high as captain, and vacancies above captain shall be filled by a vote of the commissioned officers of the regiment, and all officers so elected shall be commissioned by the respective Governors of the States, or by the President of the United States.

Sec. 11. *And be it further enacted,* That all letters written by soldiers in the service of the United States, may be transmitted through the mails without prepayment of postage, under such regulations as the Post-Office Department may prescribe, the postage thereon to be paid by the recipients.

Sec. 12. *And be it further enacted,* That the Secretary of War be, and he is hereby, authorized and directed to introduce among the volunteer forces in the service of the United States, the system of allotment tickets now used in the navy, or some equivalent system, by which the family of the volunteer may draw such portion of his pay as he may request.

APPROVED, July 22, 1861.

Act of July 27, 1861

An Act to indemnify the States for Expenses incurred by them in Defence of the United States.

Be it enacted by the Senate and House of Representatives of the United States of America in

Congress assembled, That the Secretary of the Treasury of the Treasury be, and he is hereby, directed, out of any money in the Treasury not otherwise appropriated, to pay to the Governor of any State, or to his duly authorized agents, the costs, charges, and expenses properly incurred by such State for enrolling, subsisting, clothing, supplying, arming, equipping, paying, and transporting its troops employed in aiding to suppress the present insurrection against the United States, to be settled upon proper vouchers, to be filed and passed upon by the proper accounting officers of the Treasury.

APPROVED, July 27, 1861

Act of August 5, 1861 (in part)

An act to provide increased Revenue from Imports to pay Interest on the public debt, and for other purposes.

[The first seven sections establish the import duty on various commodities.]

Sec. 8. *And be it further enacted,* That a direct tax of twenty millions of dollars be and is hereby annually laid upon the United States, and the same shall be and is hereby apportioned to the States, respectively, in manner following:

To the State of Maine, four hundred and twenty thousand eight hundred and twenty-six dollars.

The rest of the States are assessed in no particular order. For some reason it was thought necessary to add a fractional value to the last dollar of some States and this is stated as "and one-third dollars" or "and two-third dollars."

In one case the court reported the assessed value of South Carolina for direct tax purposes at $363,570.67. In the following value-oriented list of the States and Territories the fractional values are shown as .34 or .67:

New York, $2,603,918.67; Pennsylvania, $1,946,719.34; Ohio, $1,567,089.34; Illinois, $1,146,551.34; Virginia, $937,550.67; Indiana, $904,875.34; Massachusetts, $824,581.34; Missouri, $761,127.34; Kentucky, $713,695.34; Tennessee, $669,498; Georgia, $584,367.34; North Carolina, $576,194.67; Alabama, $529,313.34; Wisconsin, $519,688.67; Michigan, $501,763.34; Maryland, $466,823.34; Iowa, $452,088; New Jersey, $450,134; Maine, $420,826; Mississippi, $413,084.67; Louisiana, $385,886.67; South Carolina, $363,570.67; Texas, $355,106.67; Connecticut, $308,214; Arkansas, $261,886; Califor-

nia, $254,538.67; Vermont, $211,068; New Hampshire, $218,404.67; Rhode Island, $116,963.67; Minnesota, $108,524; Florida, $77,522.67; Delaware, $74,683.34; Kansas, $71,743.34; Oregon, $35,140.67.

District of Columbia, $49,437.34.

Territory of New Mexico, $62,648; Territory of Utah, $26,982; Territory of Colorado, $22,905.34; Territory of Nebraska, $19,312; Territory of Washington, $7,785.34; Territory of Nevada, $4,592.67; Territory of Dakota, $3,241.34.

Sec. 13. *And be it further enacted,* That the said direct tax laid by this act shall be assessed and laid on the value of all lands and lots of ground, with their improvements and dwelling-houses, which several articles subject to taxation shall be enumerated and valued, by the respective assessors, at the rate each of them is worth in money on the first day of April, eighteen hundred and sixty-two; *Provided, however,* That all property, of whatever kind, coming within any of the foregoing descriptions, and belonging to the United States or any State, or permanently or specially exempted from taxation by the laws of the State wherein the same may be situated at the time of the passage of this act, together with such property belonging to any individual, who actually resides thereon, as shall be worth the sum of five hundred dollars, shall be exempted from the aforesaid enumeration and valuation and from the direct tax aforesaid: *And provided further,* That in making such assessment due regard shall be had to any valuation that may have been made under the authority of the State or Territory at any period nearest to the said first day of April.

[Section 49 levied a 3 percent income tax on incomes over $800 a year beginning on January 1, 1863. Section 52 taxed the residents of rebellious areas at 6 percent per year plus interest from January 1, 1863 until paid.]

Act of August 6, 1861

An Act to confiscate Property used for Insurrectionary Purposes.

Be it enacted by the Senate and House of Representatives of the United States of America in Congress assembled, That if, during the present or any future insurrection against the Government of the United States, after the President of the United States shall have declared, by proclamation, that the laws of the United States are opposed, and the execution thereof obstructed, by combinations too powerful to be suppressed by the ordinary course of judicial proceedings, or by the power vested in the marshals by law, any person or persons, his, her, or their agent, attorney, or employé, shall purchase or acquire, sell or give, any property of whatsoever kind or description, with intent to use or employ the same, or suffer the same to be used or employed, in aiding, abetting, or promoting such insurrection or resistance to the laws, or any person or persons engaged therein; or if any person or persons, being the owner or owners of any such property, shall knowingly use or employ, or consent to the use or employment of the same as aforesaid, all such property is hereby declared to be lawful subject of prize and capture wherever found; and it shall be the duty of the President of the United States to cause the same to be seized, confiscated, and condemned.

Sec. 2. *And be it further enacted,* That such prizes and capture shall be condemned in the district or circuit court of the United States having jurisdiction of the amount, or in admiralty in any district in which the same may be seized, or in to which they may be taken and proceedings first instituted.

Sec. 3. *And be it further enacted,* That the Attorney General, or any district attorney of the United States in which said property may at the time be, may institute the proceedings of condemnation, and in such case they shall be wholly for the benefit of the United States; or any person may file an information with such attorney, in which case the proceedings shall be for the use of such informer and the United States in equal parts.

Sec. 4. *And be it further enacted,* That whenever hereafter, during the present insurrection against the Government of the United States, any person claimed to be held in labor or service under the law of any State, shall be required or permitted by the person to whom such labor or service is claimed to be due, or by the lawful agent of such person, to take up arms against the United States, or shall be required or permitted by the person to whom such labor or service is claimed to be due, or his lawful agent, to work or to be employed in or upon any fort, navy-yard, dock, armory, ship, intrenchment, or in any military or naval service whatsoever, against the Government and lawful authority of the United States, then, and in every such case,

the person to whom such labor or service is claimed to be due shall forfeit his claim to such labor, any law of the State or of the United States to the contrary notwithstanding. And whenever thereafter the person claiming such labor or service shall seek to enforce his claim, it shall be a full and sufficient answer to such claim that the person whose service or labor is claimed had been employed in hostile service against the Government of the United States, contrary to the provisions of this act.

APPROVED, August 6, 1861.

Proclamation of August 16, 1861

WHEREAS, on the fifteenth day of April, eighteen hundred and sixty-one, the President of the United States, in view of an insurrection against the Laws, Constitution, and Government of the United States, which had broken out within the States of South Carolina, Georgia, Alabama, Florida, Mississippi, Louisiana, and Texas, and in pursuance of the provisions of the act, entitled "An Act to provide for calling forth the militia to execute the laws of the Union, suppress insurrection, and repel invasions, and to repeal the act now in force for that purpose," approved February twenty-eight, seventeen hundred and ninety-five, did call forth the militia to suppress said insurrection, and to cause the laws of the Union to be duly executed, and the insurgents have failed to disperse by the time directed by the President; and, whereas, such insurrection has since broken out, and yet exists within the States of Virginia, North Carolina, Tennessee, and Arkansas; and, whereas, the insurgents in all the said States claim to act under of the authority thereof, and such claim is not disclaimed or repudiated by the persons exercising the functions of government in such State or States, or in the part or parts thereof in which such combinations exist, nor has such insurrection been suppressed by said States:

Now, therefore, I, ABRAHAM LINCOLN, President of the United States, in pursuance of an act of Congress, approved July thirteen, eighteen hundred and sixty-one, do hereby declare that the inhabitants of the said States of Georgia, South Carolina, Virginia, North Carolina, Tennessee, Alabama, Louisiana, Texas, Arkansas, Mississippi, and Florida (except the inhabitants of that part of the State of Virginia lying west of the Allegheny mountains, and of such other parts of that State and the other States hereinbefore named as may maintain a loyal adhesion to the Union and the Constitution, or may be, from time to time, occupied and controlled by forces of the United States engaged in the dispersion of said insurgents) are in a state of insurrection against the United States, and that all commercial intercourse between the same and the inhabitants thereof, with the exceptions aforesaid, and the citizens of other States and other parts of the United States is unlawful, and will remain unlawful until such insurrection shall cease or has been suppressed; that all goods and chattels, wares and merchandise, coming from any of said Sates, with the exceptions aforesaid, into other parts of the United States, without the special license and permission of the President, through the Secretary of the Treasury, or proceeding to any of said States, with the exceptions aforesaid, by land or water, together with the vessel or vehicle conveying the same, or conveying persons to or from said States, with said exceptions, will be forfeited to the United States; and that from and after fifteen days from the issuing this proclamation, all ships and vessels belonging in whole or in part to any citizen or inhabitant of any of said States, with said exceptions, found at sea, or in any port of the United States, will be forfeited to the United States; and I hereby enjoin upon all district attorneys, marshals, and officers of the revenue and of the military and naval forces of the United States to be vigilant in the execution of said act, and in the enforcement of the penalties and forfeitures imposed or declared by it; leaving any party who may think himself aggrieved thereby to his application to the Secretary of the Treasury for the remission of any penalty or forfeiture, which the said Secretary is authorized by law to grant, if, in his judgment, the special circumstances of any case shall require such remission.

In witness whereof, I have hereunto set my hand, and caused the seal of the United States to be affixed.

Done at the City of Washington, this sixteenth day of August, in the year of our Lord eighteen hundred and sixty-one, and of the Independence of the United States of America the eighty-sixth.

[One assistant U.S. attorney argued, "That from and after the 16th day of August, 1861, the citizens resident within the limits of the States embraced in the President's proclamation of that date became public enemies, and that this condition attached to the loyal as well as disloyal."]

January 29, 1862

[Edwin M. Stanton, the new Secretary of War, prohibited the purchase of any foreign-made items and required anyone claiming to have a War Department contract to provide the particulars within 15 days and submit a written, signed copy of it.]

March 13, 1862

[Secretary of War Stanton appointed Joseph Holt and Robert Dale Owen to form "a special commission to audit and adjust all contracts, orders, and claims on the War Department in respect to ordnance, arms, and ammunition, their decision to be final and conclusive, as respects this department, on all questions touching the validity, execution, and sums due or to become due upon such contracts, and upon all other questions arising between contractors and the government upon such contracts."]

Act of March 19, 1962

An act to provide for the Appointment of Sutlers in the Volunteer Service, and to define their duties.

Be it enacted by the Senate and House of Representatives of the United States of America in Congress assembled, That the inspector-generals of the army shall constitute a board of officers, whose duty it shall be to prepare, immediately after the passage of this act, a list or schedule of the following articles which may be sold by sutlers to the officers and soldiers of the volunteer service, to wit: Apples, dried apples, oranges, figs, lemons, butter, cheese, milk, sirup, molasses, raisins, candles, crackers, wallets, brooms, comforters, boots, pocket looking-glasses, pins, gloves, leather, tin washbasins, shirt buttons, horn and brass buttons, newspapers, books, tobacco, cigars, pipes, matches, blacking, blacking brushes, clothes brushes, tooth brushes, hair brushes, coarse and fine combs, emery, crocus, pocket handkerchiefs, stationery, armor oil, sweet oil, rotten stone, razor strops, razors, shaving soap, soap, suspenders, scissors, shoe-strings, needles, thread, knives, pencils, and Bristol brick. Said list or schedule shall be subject, from time to time, to such revision and change as, in the judgment of the said board, the good of the service may require: *Provided, always,* That no intoxicating liquors shall at any time be contained therein, or the sale of such liquors be in any way authorized by said board. A copy of said list or schedule, and of any subsequent change therein, together with a copy of this act, shall be, without delay, furnished by said board to the commanding officer of such brigade and of each regiment not attached to any brigade in the volunteer service, and also to the adjutant-general of the army.

Sec. 2. *And be it further enacted,* That immediately upon the receipt from said board of said list or schedule and copy of this act by the commanding officer of any such brigade, the acting brigadier-general, surgeon, quartermaster, and commissary of said brigade shall constitute a board of officers whose duty it shall be to affix to each article in said list or schedule a price for said brigade, which shall be by them forthwith reported to the commanding officer of the division, if any, to which said brigade is attached, for his approval, with or without modification, and who shall, after such approval, report the same to the inspector-generals, and the same, if not disapproved by them, shall be the price not exceeding which said articles may be sold to the officers and soldiers in said brigade. Whenever any brigade shall not be attached to a division said prices shall then be reported directly to the inspector-generals, and if approved by them, shall be the price fixed for such brigade as aforesaid; and whenever any regiment shall be unattached to any brigade the acting colonel, lieutenant-colonel, major, and captains thereof shall constitute the board of officers by whom the price of said articles shall be fixed for said regiment in the same manner as is herein provided for an unattached brigade. The prices so fixed may be changed by said boards respectively from time to time, not oftener than once in thirty days, but all changes therein shall be reported in like manner and for the same purpose as when originally fixed.

Sec. 3. *And be it further enacted,* That it shall be the duty of the commanding officer of each brigade, immediately upon receipt of a copy of said list or schedule and copy of this act, as herein provided, to cause one sutler for each regiment in his brigade to be selected by the commissioned officers of such regiment, which selection shall be by him reported to the adjutant-general of the army; the person so selected shall be sole sutler of said regiment. And the commanding officer of each unattached regiment shall, in like manner, cause a selection of a sutler to be made for said regiment, who shall be sole sutler of said regiment. Any vacancy in the office of sutler from any cause shall be filled in the same way as an original appointment.

Sec. 4. *And be it further enacted,* That the sutlers chosen in the manner provided in the preceding section shall be allowed a lien only upon the pay of the officers, non-commissioned officers, and privates of the regiment for which he has been chosen, or those stationed at the post to which he has been appointed, and for no greater sum than one-sixth of the monthly pay of each officer, non-commissioned officer, or private for such articles sold during each month; and the amount of one-sixth or less than one-sixth of the monthly pay of such officer, non-commissioned officer, or private, so sold to him by the sutler, shall be charged on the payrolls of such officer, non-commissioned officer, or private, and deducted from his pay, and paid over by the paymaster to the sutler of the regiment or military post, as the case may be: *Provided,* That if any paymaster in the service of the United States shall allow or pay any greater sum to any sutler than that hereby authorized to be retained from the pay of the officers, non-commissioned officers, musicians, and privates, for articles sold by any sutler during any one month, then the amount so allowed or paid by the paymaster shall be charged against the said paymaster and deducted from his pay and returned to the officer, non-commissioned officer, musician, or private, against whom the amount was originally charged. And any captain or lieutenant commanding a company who may certify any pay-roll bearing a charge in favor of the sutler against any officer, non-commissioned officer, musician, or private, shall be punished at the discretion of a court-martial: *Provided however,* That sutlers shall be allowed to sell only the articles designated in the list or schedule provided in this act, and none others, and at prices not exceeding those affixed to said articles, as herein provided: *And provided further,* That the sutlers shall have no legal claim upon any officer, non-commissioned officer, musician, or private, to an amount exceeding one-sixth of his pay for articles sold during any month. He shall keep said list or list or schedule, together with a copy of this act, fairly written or printed, posted up in some conspicuous part of the place where he makes said sales, and where the same can be easily read by any person to whom he makes said sales.

Sec. 5. *And be it further enacted,* That it shall

be the duty of the inspector-generals to cause the place of sale and articles kept for that purpose, by said sutlers, to be inspected from time to time, once in fifteen days at least, by some competent officer, specially detailed for that duty, and such changes in said place, or in the quality and character of the articles mentioned in said list or schedule, so kept as shall be required by said officer, shall be conformed to by each sutler. And such officer shall report each inspection to the inspector-generals.

Sec. 6. *And be it further enacted,* That no person shall be permitted to act as sutler unless appointed according to the provisions of this act; nor shall any person be sutler for more than one regiment; nor shall any sutler farm out or under-let the business of sutling or the privileges granted to him by his appointment; nor shall any officer of the army receive from any sutler any money or other presents; nor be interested in any way in the stock, trade, or business of any sutler; and any officer receiving such presents, or being thus interested, directly or indirectly, shall be punished at the discretion of a court-martial. No sutler shall sell to an enlisted man on credit to a sum exceeding one fourth of his monthly pay within the same month; nor shall the regimental quartermasters allow the use of army wagons for sutlers' purposes; nor shall the regimental quartermasters' conveyances be used for the transportation of sutlers' supplies.

Sec. 7. *And be it further enacted,* That any sutler who shall violate any of the provisions of this act shall by the colonel, with consent of the council of administration, be dismissed from the service, and be ineligible to a reappointment as sutler in the service of the United States.

APPROVED, March 19, 1862.

[Section 11 of the Act of March 3, 1847 prohibiting sutlers "of their right to a lien upon any part of the pay of the soldiers, or to appear at the pay table to receive the soldiers pay from the paymaster" was repealed by section 5 of the Act of June 15, 1858. Section 25 of the Act of July 28, 1866 abolished the office of sutler as of July 1, 1867 and turned the function over to the subsistence department.]

Act of June 2, 1862

[Required all contracts for military supplies to be in writing.]

Act of June 7, 1862 (in part)

An Act for the collection of Direct Taxes in insurrectionary districts within the United States, and for other purposes.

Be it enacted by the Senate and House of Representatives of the United States of America in Congress assembled, That when in any State or Territory, or portion of any State or Territory, by reason of insurrection or rebellion, the civil authority of the Government of the United States is obstructed so that the provisions of the act entitled 'An act to provide increased revenue from imports, to pay interest on the public debt, and for other purposes,' approved August fifth, eighteen hundred and sixty-one, for assessing, levying, and collecting the direct taxes therein mentioned, cannot be peaceably executed, the said direct taxes, by said act apportioned among the several States and Territories, respectively, shall be apportioned and charged in each State, and Territory, or parts thereof, wherein the civil authority is thus obstructed, upon all the lands and lots of ground situate therein, respectively, except such as are exempt from taxation by the laws of said State or of the United States, as the said lands and lots of ground were enumerated and valued under the last assessment and valuation thereof made under the authority of said State or Territory previous to the first day of January, anno Domini eighteen hundred and sixty-one; and each and every parcel of the said lands, according to said valuation, is hereby declared to be, by virtue of this act, charged with the payment of so much of the whole tax laid and apportioned by said act upon the State or Territory wherein the same is respectively situate, as shall bear the same direct proportion to the whole amount of the direct tax apportioned to said State or Territory as the value of said parcels of land shall respectively bear to the whole valuation of the real estate in said State or Territory according to the said assessment and valuation made under the authority of the same, and in addition thereto a penalty of fifty per centum of said tax shall be charged thereon.

[Section 2 directed the President to declare, on July 1, 1863, which States or parts of States are in insurrection and liable to the tax.]

[Section 3 gave property owners 60 days to pay the tax.]

[Section 4 forfeited all property subject to unpaid taxes to the United States.]

[Section 5 directed the President to appoint

three commissioners for each insurrectionary State to assess valuations, collect the tax, and sell property for a salary of $3,000 per year each.]

[Section 6 directed the board of tax commissioners to keep records.]

[Section 7 required the board to post notices or advertise property for sale for at least four weeks and to sell the property to the highest bidder "for a sum not less than the taxes, penalty, and costs, and ten per centum per annum interest on said tax" or, if another buyer offered cash in gold or silver coin or U.S. Treasury notes at the same or higher price, to conclude the sale to that buyer. The owner or lien holder could appear before the commission within 60 days after the sale, take a loyalty oath, pay the taxes, penalties, and, expenses and reclaim the property. The money paid by the original purchaser was refunded. Minors, nonresident aliens, or loyal citizens overseas had two years to reclaim the property.]

[Section 8 allowed loyal owners one year come forward to prove to the commission that they had not aided the rebellion and were unable to pay the tax because of the war. After that, they had two years to pay the tax and all fees and reclaim the property. The United States could appeal in any district court.]

[Section 9 allowed the United States to make use of any property abandoned by an owner who joined the rebellion.]

[Section 10 required the commission to regulate leases on seized farms "as shall be just and proper to secure proper and reasonable employment and support, at wages or upon shares of the crop of such persons and families as may be residing upon the said parcels or lots of land..."]

[Section 11 allowed the commission to subdivide lands at not more than 320 acres for sale to any one person in lieu of leasing the entire property, advertise the sale for 60 days, and sell it to "any loyal citizen of the United States ... or any person who shall have faithfully served as an officer, musician, or private soldier or sailor in the Army or Navy or marine service of the United States, as a regular or volunteer, for the term of three months..." with a 25 percent down payment and three years to pay it off. A head of a family who owned no other property could do the same.]

Sec. 12. *And be it further enacted,* That the proceeds of said leases and sales shall be paid into the Treasury of the United States, one fourth of which shall be paid over to the Gover-

nor of said State wherein such lands are situated, or his authorized agent, when such insurrection shall be put down, and the people shall elect a Legislature and State officers who shall take an oath to support the Constitution of the United States, and such fact shall be proclaimed by the President for the purpose of reimbursing the loyal citizens of said State, or such other purpose as said State may direct; and one fourth shall also be paid over to said State as a fund to aid in the colonization or emigration from said State of any free person of African descent who may desire to remove therefrom to Hayti, Liberia, or any other tropical state or colony.

[Section 13 authorized the commission to make their own assessment of valuations if original records "shall be destroyed, concealed, or lost..."]

[Section 14 outlined the required record keeping and authorized the hiring of a clerk at $1,200 a year.]

[Sections 15 and 16 dealt with technical and procedural matters.]

[The city of Charleston, South Carolina was occupied on February 17, 1865. The Direct Tax Act commissioners for South Carolina, William Henry Brisbane, W. E. Wording, and D. N. Cooley, set up shop at No. 26 Pitt Street. On March 6 they set about establishing the rule by which property in the State would be assessed using the printed valuations for 1861. There was only one problem as they stated formally:

Resolved, That inasmuch as the records of the last assessment and valuations of the lands and lots of ground under the authority of the State of South Carolina, previous to the 1st day of January, A. D., 1861, are so concealed as not to come within the possession of the commissioners, therefore, upon the evidence taken, and which has come before us, the said commissioners, the said assessment and valuation of the whole real estate in said State, we find to be, and do fix and establish the same at, the sum of $30,833,322.10 and four mills.

Resolved further, That there be assessed upon the lands of the said State the sum of $2 ad velorum for each $100 valuation, and that there be assessed upon the city, town, village, and borough lots the sum of 80 cents ad valorem on each $100 of valuation.

The commissioners used the published records for 1860 and started collecting for the "farming, gardening, or planting lands of St. Phillip's and St. Michael's" by putting up a notice on March 6 on the gate at the commission office, under the porch of St. Michael's church, and at the post office:

> The undersigned, U.S. direct-tax commissioners for South Carolina, having completed the assessment on lots and lands in St. Phillip's and St. Michael's parishes, S.C., are now prepared to receive the taxes on the same at their office, No. 26 Pitt street, Charleston, So. Ca., between the hours of 10 A.M. and 3 P.M. each day, Sundays exempted, for sixty days from this date.

Every unoccupied dwelling in Charleston was regarded as abandoned property and the owners were prohibited from access until the tax was paid.]

Proclamation of July 1, 1862

WHEREAS, in and by the second section of an act of Congress passed on the 7th day of June, A.D. 1862, entitled "An act for the collection of direct taxes in insurrectionary districts within the United States and for other purposes," it is made the duty of the President to declare, on or before the first day of July then next following, by his proclamation, in what States and parts of States insurrection exists:

Now, therefore, I, ABRAHAM LINCOLN, President of the United States of America, do hereby declare and proclaim that the States of South Carolina, Florida, Georgia, Alabama, Louisiana, Texas, Mississippi, Arkansas, Tennessee, North Carolina, and the State of Virginia, except the following counties: Hancock, Brooke, Ohio, Marshall, Wetzel, Marion, Monongalia, Preston, Taylor, Pleasants, Tyler, Ritchie, Doddridge, Harrison, Wood, Jackson, Wirt, Roane, Calhoun, Gilmer, Barbour, Tucker, Lewis, Braxton, Upshur, Randolph, Mason, Putnam, Kanawha, Clay, Nicholas, Cabell, Wayne, Boone, Logan, Wyoming, Webster, Fayette, and Raleigh, are now in insurrection and rebellion, and by reason thereof the civil authority of the United States is obstructed so that the provisions of the "Act to provide increased revenue from imports, to pay the interest on the public debt and for other purposes," approved August fifth, eighteen hundred and sixty-one, cannot be peaceably executed, and that the taxes legally chargeable upon real estate under the act last aforesaid, lying within the States and parts of States as aforesaid, together with a penalty of fifty per centum of said taxes, shall be a lien upon the tracts or lots of the same, severally charged, till paid.

In witness whereof, I have hereunto set my hand and caused the seal of the United States to be affixed.

Done at the City of Washington, this first day of July, in the year of our Lord one thousand eight hundred and sixty-two, and of the Independence of the United States of America the eighty-fifth.

[The 39 counties of western Virginia were admitted as a new state by the West Virginia Admission Act of December 31, 1862 pending certain changes to its constitution. President Lincoln's proclamation of April 20, 1863 declared the Admission Act would take effect 60 days from April 20. Nine other loyal counties of Virginia, and later Berkeley and Jefferson Counties were added to the new State by the Acts of March 10, 1866 and the Joint Resolution of June 18, 1866.]

Act of July 17, 1862

An Act to suppress Insurrection, to punish Treason and Rebellion, to seize and confiscate the Property of Rebels, and for other purposes.

Be it enacted by the Senate and House of Representatives of the United States of America in Congress assembled, That every person who shall hereafter commit the crime of treason against the United States, and shall be adjudged guilty thereof, shall suffer death, and all his slaves, if any, shall be declared and made free; or, at the discretion of the court, he shall be imprisoned for not less than five years and fined not less than ten thousand dollars, and all his slaves, if any, shall be declared and made free; said fine shall be levied and collected on any or all the property, real and personal, excluding slaves, of which the said person so convicted was the owner at the time of committing the said crime, any sale or conveyance to the contrary notwithstanding.

Sec. 2. *And be it further enacted,* That if any person shall hereafter incite, set on foot, assist, or engage in any rebellion or insurrection against the authority of the United States, or the laws thereof, or shall give aid or comfort thereto, or shall engage in, or give aid or comfort to, any such existing rebellion or insurrection, and be convicted thereof, such person shall be punished by imprisonment for a period not exceeding ten years; or by a fine not exceeding ten thousand dollars, and by the liberation of all his slaves, if any he have; or by both of said punishments, at the discretion of the court.

Sec. 3. *And be it further enacted,* That every person guilty of either of the offense described in this act shall be forever incapable and disqualified to hold any office under the United States.

Sec. 4. *And be it further enacted,* That this act shall not be construed in any way to affect or alter the prosecution, conviction, or punishment of any person or persons guilty of treason against the United States before the passage of this act, unless such person is convicted under this act.

Sec. 5. *And be it further enacted,* That to insure the speedy termination of the present rebellion, it shall be the duty of the President of the United States to cause the seizure of all the estate and property, money, stocks, credits, and effects of the persons hereinafter named in this section, and to apply and use the same and the proceeds thereof for the support of the Army of the United States, that is to say:

First, Of any person hereafter acting as an officer of the army or navy of the rebels in arms against the Government of the United States.

Secondly, Of any person hereafter acting as president, vice president, member of congress, judge of any court, cabinet officer, foreign minister, commissioner or consul of the so-called confederate States of America.

Thirdly, Of any person acting as governor of a State, member of a convention or legislature, or judge of any court of any of the so-called confederate States of America.

Fourthly, Of any person who, having held an office of honor, trust, or profit in the United States, shall hereafter hold an office in the so-called confederate States of America.

Fifthly, Of any person hereafter holding any office or agency under the government of the so-called confederate States of America, or any of the several States of the said confederacy, or the laws thereof, whether such office or agency be national, State, or municipal in its name or character: *Provided,* That the persons thirdly, fourthly, and fifthly above described shall have accepted their appointments or election since the date of the pretended ordinance of secession of the State, or shall have taken an oath of allegiance to, or to support the constitution of the so-called confederate States.

Sixthly, Of any person who, owning property in any loyal State or Territory of the United States, or in the District of Columbia, shall here-after assist and give aid and comfort to such rebellion; and all sales, transfers, or conveyances of any such property shall be null and void; and it shall be sufficient bar to any suit brought by such person for the possession or the use of such property, or any of it, to allege and prove that he is one of the persons described in this section.

Sec. 6. *And be it further enacted,* That if any person within any State or Territory of the United States, other than those named as aforesaid, after the passage of this act, being engaged in armed rebellion against the Government of the United States, or aiding or abetting such rebellion, shall not, within sixty days after public warning and proclamation duly given and made by the President of the United States, cease to aid, countenance, and abet such rebellion, and return to his allegiance to the United States, all the estate and property, moneys, stocks, and credits of such person shall be liable to seizure as aforesaid, and it shall be the duty of the President to seize and use them as aforesaid or the proceeds thereof. And all sales, transfers, or conveyances of any such property after the expiration of the said sixty days from the date of such warning and proclamation shall be null and void; and it shall be a sufficient bar to any suit brought by such person for the possession or the use of such property, or any of it, to allege and prove that he is one of the persons described in this section.

Sec. 7. *And be it further enacted,* That to secure the condemnation and sale of any such property, after the same shall have been seized, so that it may be made available for the purpose aforesaid, proceedings in rem shall be instituted in the name of the United States in any district court thereof, or in any territorial court, or in any United States district court for the District of Columbia, within which the property above described, or any part thereof, may be found, or into which the same, if moveable, may first be brought, which proceedings shall conform as nearly as may be to proceedings in admiralty or revenue cases, and if said property, whether real or personal, shall be found to have belonged to a person engaged in rebellion, or who has given aid or comfort thereto, the same shall be condemned as enemies' property and become the property of the United States, and may be disposed of as the court shall decree and the proceeds thereof paid into the Treasury of the United States for the purpose aforesaid.

Sec. 8. *And be it further enacted,* That the

several courts aforesaid shall have power to make such orders, establish such forms of decree and sale, and direct such deeds and conveyances to be executed and delivered by the marshals thereof where real estate shall be the subject of sale, as shall fully and efficiently effect the purposes of this act, and vest in the purchasers of such property good and valid titles thereto. And the said courts shall have the power to allow fees and charges of their officers as shall be reasonable and proper in the premises.

Sec. 9. *And be it further enacted,* That the slaves of persons who shall hereafter be engaged in rebellion against the Government of the United States, or who shall in any way give aid or comfort thereto, escaping from such persons and taking refuge within the lines of the Army; and all slaves captured from such persons or deserted by them and coming into the control of the Government of the United States; and all slaves of such persons found or being within any place occupied by rebel forces and afterwards occupied by the forces of the United States, shall be deemed captives of war, and shall be forever free of their servitude, and not again held as slaves.

Sec. 10. *And be it further enacted,* That no slave escaping into any State, Territory, or the District of Columbia, from any other State, shall be delivered up, or in any way impeded or hindered of his liberty, except for crime, or some offense against the laws, unless the person claiming said fugitive shall first make oath that the person to whom the labor or service of such fugitive is alleged to be due is his lawful owner, and has not borne arms against the United States in the present rebellion, nor in any way given aid and comfort thereto; and no person engaged in the military or naval service of the United States shall, under any pretense whatever, assume to decide on the validity of the claim of any person to the service or labor of any other person, or surrender up any such person to the claimant, on pain of being dismissed from the service.

Sec. 11. *And be it further enacted,* That the President of the United States is authorized to employ as many persons of African descent as he may deem necessary and proper for the suppression of this rebellion, and for this purpose he may organize and use them in such manner as he may judge best for the public welfare.

Sec. 12. *And be it further enacted,* That the President of the United States is hereby author-

ized to make provision for the transportation, colonization, and settlement, in some tropical country beyond the limits of the United States, of such persons of the African race, made free by the provisions of this act, as may be willing to emigrate, having first obtained the consent of the Government of said country to their protection and settlement within the same, with all the rights and privileges of freemen.

Sec. 13. *And be it further enacted,* That the President is hereby authorized, at any time hereafter, by proclamation, to extend to persons who may have participated in the existing rebellion in any State or part thereof, pardon and amnesty, with such exceptions and at such time and on such conditions as he may deem expedient for the public welfare.

Sec. 14. *And be it further enacted,* That the courts of the United States shall have full power to institute proceedings, make orders and decrees, issue process, and do all other things necessary to carry this act into effect.

APPROVED, July 17, 1862.

[President Lincoln's "oath of amnesty" proclamation of December 8, 1863 was pursuant to this Act.]

Act of July 17, 1862 (in part)

An Act for the better Government of the Navy of the United States.

Be it enacted by the Senate and House of Representatives of the United States in Congress assembled, That from and after the first day of September next, the following articles be adopted, and put in force for the government of the navy of the United States:

Sec. 2. That the proceeds of all ships and vessels, and the goods taken on board of them, which shall be adjudged good prize, shall, when of equal or superior force to the vessel or vessels making the capture, be the sole property of the captors; and when of inferior force, shall be divided equally between the United States and the officers and men making the capture.

Sec. 3. *And be it further enacted,* That the prize money belonging to the officers and men shall be distributed in the following manner:

First. To the commanding officer of a fleet or squadron, one twentieth part of all prize money awarded to a vessel or vessels under his immediate command.

Second. To the commander of a single ship,

one tenth part of all prize money awarded to the ship under his command, if such ship, at the time of making the capture, was under the immediate command of the commanding officer of a fleet or squadron, and three-twentieths if his ship was acting independently of such superior officer.

Third. The share of the commanding officer of the fleet or squadron, if any, and the share of the commander of the ship being deducted, the residue shall be distributed and apportioned among all others doing duty on board, and borne upon the books, according to their respective rates of pay in the service.

Fourth. When one or more vessels of the navy shall be within signal distance or another making a prize, all share in the prize, and money awarded shall be apportioned among the officers and men of the several vessels according to the rates of pay of all on board who are borne upon the books, after deducting one-twentieth to the flag officer, if there be any such entitled to share.

Fifth. No commander of a fleet or squadron shall be entitled to receive any share of prizes taken by vessels not under his immediate command; nor of such prizes as may have been taken by ships or vessels intended to be placed under his command before they have acted under his immediate orders; nor shall a commander of a fleet or squadron, leaving the station where he had the command, have any share in the prizes taken by ships left on such station after he has gone out of the limits of his said command, nor after he has transferred his command to a successor.

Sixth. No officer or other person who shall have been temporarily absent on duty from the vessel, on the books of which he continued to be borne while so absent, shall be deprived, in consequence of such absence, of any prize money to which he would otherwise be entitled.

Sec. 4. *And be it further enacted,* That a bounty shall be paid by the United States for each person on board any ship or vessel-of-war belonging to an enemy at the commencement of an engagement which shall be sunk or otherwise destroyed in such engagement, by any ship or vessel belonging to the United States, or which it may be necessary to destroy in consequence of injuries sustained in action, of one hundred dollars, if the enemy's vessel was of inferior force; and of two hundred dollars, if of equal or superior force; to be divided among the officers and crew in the same manner as prize money; and

when the actual number of men on board any such vessel cannot be satisfactorily ascertained, it shall be estimated according to the complement allowed to vessels of their class in the navy of the United States; and there shall be paid as bounty to the captors of any vessel-of-war captured from an enemy, which they may be instructed to destroy, or which shall be immediately destroyed for the public interest but not in consequence of injuries received in action, fifty dollars for every person who shall be on board at the time of such capture.

Sec. 5. *And be it further enacted,* That the commanding officer of every vessel, or the senior officers of all vessels of the navy, which shall capture or seize upon any vessel or vessels as a prize, shall carefully preserve all papers and writings found on board, and transmit the whole of the originals, unmutilated, to the judge of the district to which such prize is ordered to proceed, with the necessary witnesses, and a report of the circumstances attending its capture, stating the names of vessels in the navy entitled to, or claiming an award of prize money shall, as early as practicable after the capture, transmit to the Navy Department a complete list of the officers and men of his vessel, entitled to share, inserting thereon the quality of every person rating, on pain of forfeiting his whole share of the prize money resulting from such capture, and suffering such further punishment as a court-martial shall adjudge.

Sec. 6. *And be it further enacted,* That any armed vessel in the service of the United States which shall make a capture, or assist in a capture, under circumstances which would entitle a vessel of the navy to prize money, shall be entitled to an award of prize money in the same manner as if such vessel belonged to the navy; and such prize money shall be distributed and apportioned in the same manner and under the same rules and regulations as provided for persons in the naval service, and paid under the direction of the Secretary of the Navy.

[The Spanish-American War was the last conflict in which the prize system was used.]

Proclamation of July 25, 1862

In pursuance of the sixth section of the act of Congress entitled "An act to suppress insurrection and to punish treason and rebellion, to seize and confiscate the property of rebels, and for other purposes," approved July 17, 1862, and which act, and the joint resolution explanatory thereof, are herewith published; I, ABRAHAM LINCOLN, President of the United States, do hereby proclaim to and warn all persons within the contemplation of said sixth section to cease participating in, aiding, countenancing, or abetting the existing rebellion, or any rebellion, against the Government of the United States, and to return to their proper allegiance to the United States, on pain of the forfeitures and seizures as within and by said sixth section provided.

In testimony whereof, I have hereunto set my hand and caused the seal of the United States to be affixed.

Done at the City of Washington, this twenty-fifth day of July, in the year of our Lord one thousand eight hundred and sixty-two, and of the Independence of the United States the eighty-seventh.

Proclamation of September 22, 1862 (in part)

I, ABRAHAM LINCOLN, President of the United States of America, and commander-in-chief of the army and navy thereof, do hereby proclaim and declare that hereafter, as heretofore, the war will be prosecuted for the object of restoring the constitutional relation between the United States and each of the states and the people thereof, in which states that relation is or may be suspended or disturbed.

That it is my purpose, upon the next meeting of Congress, to again recommend the adoption of practical measures tendering pecuniary aid to the free acceptance or rejection of all the slave states, so called, the people whereof may not then be in rebellion against the United States, and which states may then have voluntarily adopted, or thereafter may voluntarily adopt, immediate or gradual abolishment of slavery within their respective limits; and that the effort to colonize persons of African descent with their consent upon this continent or elsewhere, with the previously obtained consent of the governments existing there, will be continued.

That on the first day of January, in the year of our Lord one thousand eight hundred and sixty-three, all persons held as slaves within any state or designated part of a state, the people whereof shall then be in rebellion against the United States, shall be then thenceforward, and

forever free; and the Executive Government of the United States, including the military and naval authority thereof, will recognize and maintain the freedom of such persons, and will do no act or acts to repress such persons, or any of them, in any efforts they may make for their actual freedom.

That the Executive will, on the first day of January aforesaid, by proclamation, designate the states and parts of states, if any, in which the people thereof, respectively, shall then be in rebellion against the United States; and the fact that any state, or the people thereof, shall on that day be in good faith represented in Congress of the United States, by members chosen thereto at elections wherein a majority of the qualified voters of such state shall have participated, shall, in the absence of strong countervailing testimony, be deemed conclusive evidence that such state, and the people thereof, are not then in rebellion against the United States.

That attention is hereby called to an act of Congress entitled "An act to make an additional article of war," approved March 13, 1862, and which act is in the words and figure following:

"*Be it enacted by the Senate and House of Representatives of the United States in Congress assembled,* That hereafter the following shall be promulgated as an additional article of war, for the government of the army of the United States, and shall be obeyed and observed as such:

"ARTICLE — All officers or persons in the military or naval service of the United States are prohibited from employing any of the under their respective commands for the purpose of returning fugitives from service or labor who may have escaped from any persons to whom such service or labor is claimed to be due, and any officer who shall be found guilty by a court-martial of violating this article shall be dismissed from the service.

"Sec. 2. *And be it further enacted,* That this act shall take effect from and after its passage."

Also to the ninth and tenth sections of an act entitled "An act to suppress insurrection, to punish treason and rebellion, to seize and confiscate property of rebels, and for other purposes," approved July 17, 1862, and which sections are in the words and figures following:

"Sec. 9. *And be it further enacted,* That the slaves of persons who shall hereafter be engaged in rebellion against the Government of the United States, or who shall in any way give aid or comfort thereto, escaping from such persons and taking refuge within the lines of the Army; and all slaves captured from such persons or deserted by them and coming into the control of the Government of the United States; and all slaves of such persons found or being within any place occupied by rebel forces and afterwards occupied by the forces of the United States, shall be deemed captives of war, and shall be forever free of their servitude, and not again held as slaves.

"Sec. 10. *And be it further enacted,* That no slave escaping into any State, Territory, or the District of Columbia, from any other State, shall be delivered up, or in any way impeded or hindered of his liberty, except for crime, or some offense against the laws, unless the person claiming said fugitive shall first make oath that the person to whom the labor or service of such fugitive is alleged to be due is his lawful owner, and has not borne arms against the United States in the present rebellion, nor in any way given aid and comfort thereto; and no person engaged in the military or naval service of the United States shall, under any pretense whatever, assume to decide on the validity of the claim of any person to the service or labor of any other person, or surrender up any such person to the claimant, on pain of being dismissed from the service."

And I do hereby enjoin upon and order all persons engaged in the military service of the United States to observe, obey, and enforce, within their respective spheres of service, the act and sections above recited.

And the Executive will in due time recommend that all citizens of the United States who shall have remained loyal thereto throughout the rebellion shall (upon the restoration of the constitutional relation between the United States and their respective states and people, if that relation shall have been suspended or disturbed) be compensated for all losses by acts of the United States, including the loss of slaves.

In witness whereof, I have hereunto set my hand, and caused the seal of the United States to be affixed.

Done at the city of Washington this twenty-second day of September, in the year of our Lord eighteen hundred and sixty-two, and of the Independence of the United States of America the eighty-seventh.

Proclamation of January 1, 1863 (Emancipation Proclamation)

WHEREAS, on the twenty-second day of September, in the year of our Lord one thousand eight hundred and sixty-two, a proclamation was issued by the President of the United States, containing, among other things, the following, to wit:

That on the first day of January, in the year of our Lord one thousand eight hundred and sixty-three, all persons held as slaves within any state or designated part of a state, the people whereof shall be in rebellion against the United States, shall be then, thenceforward, and forever free; and the Executive Government of the United States, including the military and naval authority thereof, will recognize and maintain the freedom of such persons, and will do no act or acts to repress such persons, or any of them, in any efforts they may make for their actual freedom.

That the Executive will, on the first day of January aforesaid, by proclamation, designate the states and parts of states, if any, in which the people thereof, respectively, shall then be in rebellion against the United States; and the fact that any state, or the people thereof, shall on that day be in good faith represented in Congress of the United States, by members chosen thereto at elections wherein a majority of the qualified voters of such state shall have participated, shall, in the absence of strong countervailing testimony, be deemed conclusive evidence that such state, and the people thereof, are not then in rebellion against the United States.

Now, therefore, I, ABRAHAM LINCOLN, President of the United States, by virtue of the power in me vested as Commander-in-Chief of the Army and Navy of the United States in time of actual armed rebellion against the authority and government of the United States, and as a fit and necessary war measure for suppressing said rebellion, do, on this 1st day of January, A.D. 1863 and in accordance with my purpose so to do, publicly proclaimed for the full period of one hundred days from the first day above mentioned, order and designate as the States and parts of States wherein the people thereof, respectively, are this day in rebellion against the United States the following, to wit:

Arkansas, Texas, Louisiana (except the parishes of St. Bernard, Plaquemines, Jefferson, St. John, St. Charles, St. James, Ascension,

Assumption, Terrebonne, Lafourche, St. Mary, St. Martin, and Orleans, including the city of New Orleans), Mississippi, Alabama, Florida, Georgia, South Carolina, North Carolina, and Virginia (except the forty-eight counties designated as West Virginia, and also the counties of Berkeley, Accomac, Northampton, Elizabeth City, York, Princess Anne, and Norfolk, including the cities of Norfolk and Portsmouth), and which parts are for the present left precisely as if this proclamation were not issued.

And by virtue of the power and for the purpose aforesaid, I do order and declare that all persons held as slaves within said designated States and parts of States are, and henceforward shall be, free; and that the Executive Government of the United States, including the military and naval authorities thereof, will recognize and maintain the freedom of said persons.

And I hereby enjoin upon the people so declared to be free to abstain from all violence, unless necessary in self-defense; and I recommend to them that, in all cases when allowed, they labor faithfully for reasonable wages.

And I further declare and make known that such persons of suitable condition will be received into the armed service of the United States to garrison forts, positions, stations, and other places, and to man vessels of all sorts in said service.

An upon this act, sincerely believed to be an act of justice, warranted by the Constitution upon military necessity, I invoke the considerate judgment of mankind and the gracious favor of Almighty God.

In witness whereof, I have hereunto set my hand and caused the seal of the United States to be affixed.

Done at the city of Washington this first day of January, in the year of our Lord eighteen hundred and sixty-three, and of the Independence of the United States of America the eighty-seventh.

Act of March 3, 1863 (in part)

An Act for enrolling and calling out the national Forces, and for other Purposes.

WHEREAS there now exist in the United States an insurrection and rebellion against the authority thereof, and it is, under the Constitution of the United States, the duty of the government to suppress insurrection and rebellion, to guarantee to each State a republican form of government, and to preserve the public tranquility; and whereas, for these high purposes, a military force is indispensable, to raise and support which all persons ought willingly to contribute; and whereas no service can be more praiseworthy and honorable than that which is rendered for the maintenance of the Constitution and Union, and the consequent preservation of free government: Therefore —

Be it enacted by the by the Senate and House of Representatives of the United States of America in Congress assembled, That all able-bodied male citizens of the United States, and persons of foreign birth who shall have declared on oath their intention to become citizens under and in pursuance of the laws thereof, between the ages of twenty and forty-five years, except as hereinafter excepted, are hereby declared to constitute the national forces, and shall be liable to perform military duty in the service of the United States when called out by the President for that purpose.

Sec. 13. *And be it further enacted,* That any person drafted and notified to appear as aforesaid, may, on or before the day fixed for his appearance, furnish an acceptable substitute to take his place in the draft; or he may pay to such person as the Secretary of War may authorize to receive it, such sum, not exceeding three hundred dollars, as the Secretary may determine, for the procuration of such substitute; which sum shall be fixed at a uniform rate by a general order made at the time of ordering a draft for any state or territory; and thereupon such person so furnishing the substitute, or paying the money, shall be discharged from further liability under that draft. And any person failing to report after due service of notice, as herein prescribed, without furnishing a substitute, or paying the required sum therefore, shall be deemed a deserter, and shall be arrested by the provost-marshal and sent to the nearest military post for trial by court-martial, unless, upon proper showing that he is not liable to do military duty, the board of enrollment shall relieve him from the draft.

Sec. 18. *And be it further enacted,* That such of the volunteers and militia now in the service of the United States as may reënlist to serve one year, unless sooner discharged, after the expiration of their term of service, shall be entitled to a bounty of fifty dollars, one half of which is to be paid upon such reënlistment, and the balance at the expiration of the term of reënlistment;

and such as may reënlist to serve for two years unless sooner discharged, after the expiration of their present term of enlistment, shall receive, upon such reënlistment, twenty-five dollars of the one hundred dollars bounty for enlistment provided by the fifth section of the act approved twenty-second of July, eighteen hundred and sixty-one, entitled "An act to authorize the employment of volunteers to aid in enforcing the laws and protecting property.

Sec. 20. *And be it further enacted,* That whenever a regiment is reduced below the minimum number allowed by law, no officers shall be appointed in such regiment beyond those necessary for the command of such reduced number.

The Act of March 12, 1863

An Act to provide for the Collection of abandoned Property and for the prevention of Frauds in Insurrectionary Districts within the United States.

Be it enacted by the Senate and House of Representatives of the United States of America in Congress assembled, That it shall be lawful for the Secretary of the Treasury, from and after the passage of this act, as he shall from time to time see fit, to appoint a special agent or agents to receive and collect all abandoned or captured property in any State or Territory, or in any portion of any State or Territory, of the United States, designated as in insurrection against the lawful Government of the United States by the proclamation of the President of July first, eighteen hundred and sixty-two: *Provided,* That such property shall not include any kind or description which has been used , or which was intended to be used, for waging or carrying on war against the United States, such as arms, ordnance, ships, steamboats, or other water craft, and the furniture, forage, military supplies, or munitions of war.

Sec. 2. *And be it further enacted,* That any part of the goods or property received or collected by such agent or agents may be appropriated to public use on due appraisement and certificate thereof, or forwarded to any place of sale within the loyal States, as the public interests may require; and all sales of such property shall be at auction to the highest bidder, and the proceeds thereof shall be paid into the Treasury of the United States.

Sec. 3. *And be it further enacted,* That the

Secretary of the Treasury may require the special agents appointed under this act to give a bond, with such securities and in such amount as he shall deem necessary, and to require the increase of said amounts, and the strengthening of said security, as circumstances may demand, and he shall also cause a book or books of account to be kept, showing from whom such property was received, the cost of transportation, and proceeds of the sale thereof. And any person claiming to have been the owner of any such abandoned or captured property may, at any time within two years after the suppression of the rebellion, prefer his claim to the proceeds thereof in the Court of Claims; and on proof to the satisfaction of said court of his ownership of said property, of his right to the proceeds thereof, and that he has never any aid or comfort to the present rebellion, to receive the residue of such proceeds, after the deduction of any purchase-money which may have been paid, together with the expense of transportation and sale of said property, and any other lawful expenses attending the disposal thereof.

Sec. 4. *And be it further enacted,* That all property coming into any of the United States not declared in insurrection as aforesaid, from within any of the States declared in insurrection, through or by any other person than any agent duly appointed under the provisions of this act, or under a lawful clearance by the proper officer of the Treasury Department, shall be confiscated to the use of the Government of the United States. And the proceedings for the condemnation and sale of any such property shall be instituted and conducted under the direction of the Secretary of the Treasury, in the mode prescribed by the eighty-ninth and ninetieth sections of the act of March second, seventeen-hundred and ninety-nine, entitled "An act to regulate the collection of duties on imports and tonnage." And any agent or agents, person or persons, by or through whom such property shall come within the lines of the United States unlawfully, as aforesaid, shall be judged guilty of a misdemeanor, and on conviction thereof shall be fined in any sum not exceeding one thousand dollars, or imprisoned for any time not exceeding one year, or both, at the discretion of the court. And the fines, penalties, and forfeitures accruing under this act may be mitigated or remitted in the mode prescribed by the act of March three, seventeen hundred and ninety-seven, or in such manner, in special cases, as the Secretary of the Treasury may pre-scribe.

Sec. 5. *And be it further enacted,* That the fifth section of this act to further provide for the collection of the revenue upon the northern, northeastern, and northwestern frontier, and for other purposes, approved July fourteen, eighteen hundred and sixty-two, shall be so construed as to allow the temporary officers which have been or may be appointed at ports which have been or may be opened or established in States declared to be in insurrection by the proclamation of the President on the first of July, eighteen hundred and sixty-two, the same compensation which by law is allowed to permanent officers of the same position, or the ordinary compensation of spe-cial agents, as the Secretary of the Treasury may determine.

Sec. 6. *And be it further enacted,* That it shall be the duty of every officer or private of the reg-ular or volunteer forces of the United States, or any officer, sailor, or marine in the naval serv-ice of the United States upon the inland waters of the United States, who may take or receive any such abandoned property, or cotton, sugar, rice, or tobacco, from persons in such insurrec-tionary districts, or have it under his control, to turn the same over to an agent appointed as aforesaid, who shall give a receipt therefore; and in case he shall refuse or neglect to do so, he shall be tried by a court-martial, and shall be dis-missed from the service, or, if an officer, reduced to the ranks, or suffer such other punishment as said court shall order, with the approval of the President of the United States.

Sec. 7. *And be it further enacted,* That none of the provisions of this act shall apply to any lawful maritime prize by the naval forces of the United States.

APPROVED, March 12, 1863.

Proclamation of April 20, 1863

WHEREAS, by the act of congress approved the 31st day of December, last, the State of West Virginia was declared to be one of the United States of America, and was admitted into the Union on an equal footing with the original states in all respects whatever, upon condition that certain changes should be duly made in the proposed constitution for that state:

And whereas proof of a compliance with that condition, as required by the second section of the act aforesaid, has been submitted to me:

Now, therefore, be it known, that I, ABRA-HAM LINCOLN, President of the United States, do hereby, in pursuance of the act of congress aforesaid, declare and proclaim that the said act shall take effect and be in force from and after sixty days from the date hereof.

In witness whereof, I have hereunto set my hand, and caused the seal of the United States to be affixed.

Done at the city of Washington, this twen-tieth day of April, in the year of our Lord one thousand eight hundred and sixty-three, and of the Independence of the United States the eighty-seventh.

Proclamation of October 17, 1863 (in part)

Now, therefore, I, ABRAHAM LINCOLN, President of the United States and Commander-in-Chief of the Army and Navy thereof and of the militia of the several states when called into actual service, do issue this my proclamation, calling upon the governors of the different states to raise and have enlisted into the United States service, for the various companies and regiments in the field from their respective states, their quotas of three hundred thousand men.

I further proclaim that all volunteers thus called out and duly enlisted shall receive advance pay, premium, and bounty, as therefore com-municated to the governors of states by the War Department, through the provost-marshal gen-eral's office, by special letter.

I further proclaim that if any state shall fail to raise the quota assigned to it by the War De-partment under this call, then a draft for the deficiency in said quota shall be made on said state, or on

the districts of said state, for their due pro-portion of said quota; and the said draft shall commence on the fifth day of January, 1864.

Proclamation of December 8, 1863 (Oath of amnesty pursuant to the Act of July 17, 1863, in part)

I, _____ _____, do solemnly swear, in pres-ence of Almighty God, that I will henceforth faithfully support, protect, and defend the Con-stitution of the United States and the Union of the States thereunder; and that I will, in like manner, abide by and faithfully support all acts of congress passed during the existing rebellion with reference to slaves, so long and, so far as not repealed, modified, or held void by congress, or by decision of the supreme court; and that I will, in like manner, abide by and faithfully support all proclamations of the President made during the existing rebellion having reference to slaves, so long and so far as not modified or declared void by decision of the supreme court. So help me God.

An oath taken under this proclamation:

I, Noble A. Hardee, of the county of Chatham, State of Georgia, do solemnly affirm, in the presence of Almighty God, that I will henceforth faithfully support and defend the Constitution of the United States and the Union of the States thereunder; and that I will, in like manner, abide by and faithfully support all laws and proclamations which have been made during the existing rebellion with reference to the emancipation of slaves: So help me God.

Act of February 24, 1864 (in part)

An Act to amend an Act entitled "An Act for enrolling and calling out the National Forces, and for other Purposes," approved March third, eighteen hundred and sixty-three.

Be it enacted by the Senate and House of Representatives of the United States of America in Congress assembled, That the President of the United States shall be authorized, whenever he shall deem it necessary, during the present war, to call for such number of men for the military service of the United States as the public exigencies may require.

[Section 2 of this Act allowed persons entering the naval service to be reckoned in the draft quotas for each district.]

Sec. 5. *And be it further enacted,* That any person drafted into the military service of the United States may, before the time fixed for his appearance for duty at the draft rendezvous, furnish an acceptable substitute, subject to such rules and regulations as may be prescribed by the Secretary of War. That if such substitute is not liable to draft, the person furnishing him shall be exempt from draft during the time for which such substitute is not liable to draft, not exceeding the term for which he was drafted; and, if such substitute is liable to draft, the name

of the person furnishing him shall again be placed on the roll, and shall be liable to draft on future calls, but not until the present enrolment shall be exhausted; and this exemption shall not exceed the term for which such person shall have been drafted. Any person now in the military or naval service of the United States, not physically disqualified, who has so served more than one year, and whose term of unexpired service shall not at the time of substitution exceed six months, may be employed as a substitute to serve in the troops of the State in which he enlisted; and if any drafted person shall hereafter pay money for the procuration of a substitute, under the provisions of the act to which this is an amendment, such payment of money shall operate only to relieve such person from draft in filling that quota; and his name shall be retained on the roll in filling future quotas; but in no instance shall the exemption of any person, on account of his payment of commutation money for the procuration of a substitute, extend beyond one year; but at the end of one year, in every such case, the name of the person so exempted shall be enrolled again, if not before returned to the enrolment list under the provisions of this section.

Sec. 10. *And be it further enacted,* That the following persons be and they are hereby exempted from enrolment and draft under the provisions of this act and of the act to which this an amendment, to wit: Such as are rejected as physically or mentally unfit for the service, all persons actually in the military or naval service of the United States at the time of the draft, and all persons who have served in the military or naval service two years during the present war and been honorably discharged therefrom; and no persons but such as are herein exempted shall be exempt.

Sec. 24. *And be it further enacted,* That all able-bodied male colored persons, between the ages of twenty and forty-five years, resident in the United States, shall be enrolled according to the provisions of this act, and of the act to which this is an amendment, and form part of the national forces; and when a slave of a loyal master shall be drafted and mustered into the service of the United States, his master shall have a certificate thereof, and thereupon such slave shall be free; and the bounty of one hundred dollars, now payable by law for each drafted man, shall be paid to the person to who such drafted person was owing service or labor at the time of his muster into the service of the United States. The Secretary of War shall appoint a commission in each of the slave States represented in Congress, charged to award to each loyal person to whom a colored volunteer may owe service a just compensation, not exceeding three hundred dollars, for each such colored volunteer, payable out of the fund derived from commutations, and every such colored volunteer on being mustered into the service shall be free. And in all cases where men of color have been hereunto enlisted or have volunteered in the military service of the United States, all provisions of this act, so far as the payment of bounty and compensation are provided, shall be equally applicable as to those who may be hereafter recruited. But men of color, drafted or enlisted, or who may volunteer into the military service, while they shall be credited on the quotas of the several states, or subdivisions of states, wherein they are respectively drafted, enlisted, or shall volunteer, shall not be assigned as state troops, but shall be mustered into regiments or companies as United States colored troops.

[In the Kentucky Draft Cases, the court outlined three ways to avoid the draft pursuant to the Act of March 3, 1863 and the amendment of February 24, 1864: 1) a draftee paid $300 commutation money to release himself from military service; 2) a draftee paid a qualified substitute $300 under a personal contract to serve for him; and 3) if a slave was drafted his master or another person paid $300 to release him.]

Proclamation of March 26, 1864

WHEREAS, it has become necessary to define the case in which insurgent enemies are entitled to the benefits of the proclamation of the President of the United States, which was made on the eighth day of December, 1863, and the manner in which they shall proceed to avail themselves of those benefits;

And whereas the objects of that proclamation were to suppress the insurrection and to restore the authority of the United States; and whereas the amnesty therein proposed by the President was offered with reference to those objects alone:

Now, therefore, I, ABRAHAM LINCOLN, President of the United States of America, do hereby proclaim and declare that the said proclamation does not apply to the cases of persons who, at the time when they seek to obtain the benefits thereof by taking the oath thereby prescribed, are in military, naval, or civil confinement or custody, or under bonds, or in parole of the civil, military, or naval authorities, or agents of the United States, as prisoners of war, or persons detained for offences of any kind, either before or after conviction, and that on the contrary, it does apply only to those persons who, being yet at large, and free from any arrest, confinement, or duress, shall voluntarily come forward and take the said oath, with the purpose of restoring peace and establishing the national authority. Prisoners excluded from the amnesty offered in the said proclamation may apply to the President for clemency, like all other offenders, and their application will receive due consideration.

I do further declare and proclaim that the said oath of the 8th of December, 1863, may be taken and subscribed before any commissioned officer, civil, military, or naval, in the service of the United States, or any civil or military officer of a state or territory not in insurrection, who, by the laws thereof, may be qualified for administering oaths. All officers who receive such oaths are hereby authorized to give certificates thereon to the persons respectively by whom they are made, and such officers are hereby required to transmit the original records of such oaths at as early a day as may be convenient, to the Department of State, where they will be deposited and remain in the archives of the government. The Secretary of State will keep a register thereof, and will, on application, in proper cases, issue certificates of such records in the customary form of official certificates.

In testimony whereof I have hereunto set my hand, and caused the seal of the United States to be affixed.

Done at the city of Washington, the twenty-sixth day of March, in the year of our Lord one thousand eight hundred and sixty-four, and of the Independence of the United States the eighty-eighth.

Act of June 30, 1864 (in part)

An Act to regulate Prize Proceedings and the Distribution of Prize Money, and for other Purposes.

Sec. 32. *And be it further enacted,* That the term "vessels of the navy" shall be included, for the purposes of this act, all armed vessels officered and manned by the United States, and under the control of the Department of the Navy.

Provided for the distribution of prize money in two ways. The first among the capturing vessels' crews or between the crews and the government, the second among fleet officers and individual captors. Allotments in the first category were decreed by a prize court, those in the second by the Treasury and Navy Departments.

A peculiar aspect of this Act decreed that the commander of a single ship making a capture was entitled to one-tenth of the prize money instead of an amount computed from his rate of pay even though his award might be less than his subordinates.

Act of July 2, 1864 (in part)

An Act in addition to the several Acts concerning Commercial Intercourse between loyal and insurrectionary States, and to provide for the Collection of captured and abandoned Property, and the Prevention of Frauds in States declared in Insurrection.

Be it enacted by the Senate and House of Representatives of the United States of America in Congress assembled, That sales of captured and abandoned property under the act approved March twelve, eighteen hundred and sixty-three, may be made at such places, in states declared in insurrection, as may be designated by the Secretary of the Treasury, as well as at other places now authorized by said act.

Sec. 2. *And be it further enacted,* That, in addition to the captured and abandoned property to be received, collected, and disposed of, as provided in said act, the said agents shall take charge of said lease, for periods not exceeding twelve months, the abandoned lands, houses, and tenements within the districts therein named, and shall also provide, in such leases or otherwise, for the employment and general welfare of all persons within the lines of national military occupation within said insurrectionary states formerly held as slaves, who are or shall become free. Property, real or personal, shall be regarded as abandoned when the lawful owner thereof shall be voluntarily absent therefrom, and engaged, either in arms or otherwise, in aiding or encouraging the rebellion.

Sec. 8. *And be it further enacted,* That it shall be lawful for the Secretary of the Treasury, with the approval of the President, to authorize agents to purchase for the United States any products of states declared in insurrection, at such places therein as shall be designated by him, at such prices as shall be agreed on with the seller, not exceeding the market value thereof at the place of delivery, nor exceeding three-fourths of the market-value thereof in the city of New York at the latest quotations known to the agent purchasing: *Provided,* That no part of the purchase-money for any products so purchased shall be paid, or agreed to be paid, out of any other fund than that arising from property sold as captured or abandoned, or purchased and sold under the provisions of this act. All property so purchased shall be forwarded for sale at such place or places as shall be designated by the Secretary of the Treasury, and the moneys arising therefrom, after payment of the purchase-money and the other expenses connected therewith, shall be paid into the treasury of the United States; and the accounts of all moneys so received and paid shall be rendered to, and audited by, the proper accounting officers of the treasury.

Sec. 9. *And be it further enacted,* That so much of section five of the act of thirteenth of July, eighteen hundred and sixty-one, aforesaid, as authorizes the President, in his discretion, to license or permit commercial relations in any state or section the inhabitants of which are declared in a state of insurrection, is hereby repealed, except so far as may be necessary to authorize supplying the necessities of loyal persons residing in insurrectionary states, within the lines of actual occupation by the military forces of the United States, as indicated by published order of the commanding general of the department or district so occupied; and also, except so far as may be necessary to authorize persons residing within such lines to bring or send to market in the loyal states any products which they shall have produced with their own labor or the labor of freedmen, or others employed and paid by them, pursuant to rules relating thereto, which may be established under proper authority. And no goods, wares, or merchandise shall be taken into a state declared in insurrection, or transported therein, except to and from such places and to such monthly amounts as shall have been previously agreed upon in writing by the commanding general of the department in which such places are situated and an officer designated by the Secretary of the Treasury for that purpose.

Act of July 4, 1864 (in part)

An act to restrict the Jurisdiction of the Court of Claims, provide for the payment of certain Demands, Quartermasters' Stores, and Subsistence Supplies, furnished to the Army of the United States.

Be it enacted by the Senate and House of Representatives of the United States of America in Congress assembled,

That the jurisdiction of the court of claims shall not extend to or include any claims against the United States growing out of the destruction or appropriation of, or damage to, property by the army or navy, or any part of the army or navy, engaged in the suppression of the rebellion, from the commencement to the close thereof.

Sec. 2. *And be it further enacted,* That all claims of loyal citizens in states not in rebellion, for quartermasters' stores actually furnished to the army of the United States, and receipted for by the proper officer receiving the same, or which may have been taken by such officers without giving such receipt, may be submitted to the quartermaster-general of the United States, accompanied with such proofs as each claimant can present of the facts in his case; and it shall be the duty of the quartermaster-general to cause such claim to be examined, and, if convinced that it is just, and of the loyalty of the claimant, and that the stores have actually been received or taken for the use of and used by said army, then to report each case to the third auditor of the treasury, with a recommendation for settlement.

[In February 1867 Congress restricted the Quartermaster General from settling any claim "for supplies or stores which originated in a State or part of a State declared in rebellion by the proclamation of July 1, 1862" but there was no mention in the Act of real estate.]

Act of July 4, 1864

[Gave the Third Division of the Quartermaster's Office the authority to commandeer vessels in an emergency.]

Act of March 3, 1865 (in part)

An Act to amend the several Acts heretofore passed to provide for the Enrolling and Calling out the National Forces, and for other Purposes.

Be it enacted by the Senate and House of Representatives of the United States of America in Congress assembled,

That the measure and allowance for pay for an officer's servant is the pay of a private soldier as fixed by law at the time; that no non-commissioned officer shall be detailed or employed to act as a servant, nor shall any private soldier be so detailed or employed except with his own consent; that for each soldier employed as a servant by any officer there shall be deducted from the monthly pay of such officer the full monthly pay and allowances of the soldier so employed; and that, including any soldier or soldiers so employed, no officer shall be allowed for any greater number of servants than is now provided by law, nor be allowed for any servant not actually and in fact in his employ.

Sec. 4. *And be it further enacted,* That every non-commissioned officer, private, or other person, who has been, or shall hereafter be, discharged from the army of the United States by reason of wounds, received in battle, on skirmish, on picket, or in action, or in the line of duty, shall be entitled to receive the same bounty as if he had served out his full term; and all acts and parts of acts inconsistent with this are hereby repealed.

Sec. 8. *And be it further enacted,* That whenever a regiment in the regular army is reduced below the minimum number, no officer shall be appointed in such a regiment beyond those necessary for the command of such reduced number.

Act of March 3, 1865 (in part)

An Act making Appropriations for the Support of the Army for the Year ending thirtieth June, eighteen hundred and sixty-six.

Be it enacted by the Senate and House of Representatives of the United States of America in Congress assembled, That the following sums be, and the same are hereby, appropriated, out of any money in the treasury not otherwise appropriated, for the support of the army for the year ending the thirtieth of June, eighteen hundred and sixty-six:

Sec. 4. *And be it further enacted,* That all officers of volunteers now in commission, below the rank of brigadier-general, who shall continue in the military service to the close of the war, shall be entitled to receive, upon being mustered out of said service, three months' pay proper.

[Congress recognized in early 1865 that the war was all but won and felt it necessary to induce volunteer officers to remain in the service for the final push. If enough left, it might reduce the regular ranks to levels below that necessary to win the war.

Proper pay was subsequently accorded to those "who were in service on the 3d of March, 1865, and whose resignations were presented and accepted, or who were mustered out at their own request, or otherwise honorably discharged from the service after the 9th day of April, 1865."]

Joint Resolution of March 9, 1865

[Addressed the numerous claims from contractors building ships for the Navy: *Resolved*, That the Secretary of the Navy be requested to organize a board of not less than three competent persons whose duty it shall be to inquire into and determine how much the vessel of war and steam machinery contracted for by the Department in the years 1862 and 1863 cost the contractors over and above the contract price, and the allowance for extra work, and report the same to the Senate at its next session, none but those who have given satisfaction to the Department to be considered.]

Proclamation of May 10, 1865

WHEREAS the President of the United States, by his Proclamation of the nineteenth day of April, one thousand eight hundred and sixty-five, did declare certain States therein mentioned in insurrection against the government of the United States;

And whereas armed resistance to the authority of this government in the said insurrectionary states may be regarded as virtually at an end, and the persons by whom that resistance, as well as the operations of insurgent cruisers, was directed, are fugitives or captives;

And whereas it is understood that some of those cruisers are still infesting the high seas, and others are preparing to capture, burn, and destroy vessels of the United States;

Now, therefore, be it known, that I, ANDREW JOHNSON, President of the United States, hereby enjoin all naval, military, and civil officers of the United States, diligently to en-

deavor, by all lawful means, to arrest the said cruisers, and to bring them into a port of the United States, in order that they may be prevented from committing further depredations on commerce, and that the persons on board of them may no longer enjoy impunity for their crimes.

And I do further proclaim and declare, that if, after a reasonable time shall have elapsed for this Proclamation to become known in the ports of nations claiming to have been neutrals, the said insurgent cruisers and the persons on board of them shall continue to receive hospitality in the said ports, this government will deem itself justified in refusing hospitality to the public vessels of such nations in ports of the United States, and in adopting such other measures as may be deemed advisable towards vindicating the national sovereignty.

In witness whereof, I have hereunto set my hand, and caused the seal of the United States to be affixed.

Done at the city of Washington, this tenth day of May, in the year of our Lord one thousand eight hundred and sixty-five, and of the Independence of the United States of America the eighty-ninth.

Proclamation of May 29, 1865

WHEREAS the President of the United States, on the 8th day of December, A. D. eighteen hundred and sixty-three, and on the 26th day of March, A. D. eighteen hundred and sixty-four, did, with the object to suppress the existing rebellion, to induce all persons to return to their loyalty, and to restore the authority of the United States, issue proclamations offering amnesty and pardon to certain persons who had directly or by implication participated in the said rebellion; and whereas many persons who had so engaged in said rebellion have, since the issuance of said proclamations, failed or neglected to take the benefits offered thereby; and whereas many persons who have been justly deprived of all claim to amnesty and pardon thereunder, by reason of their participation, directly or by implication, in said rebellion, and continued hostility to the government of the United States since the date of said proclamations, now desire to apply for and obtain amnesty and pardon:

To the end, therefore, that the authority of the government of the United States may be restored, and that peace, order, and freedom may be established, I, ANDREW JOHNSON, President of the United States, do proclaim and declare that I hereby grant to all persons who have, directly or indirectly, participated in the existing rebellion, except as hereinafter excepted, amnesty and pardon, with restoration of all rights of property, except as to slaves, and except in cases where legal proceedings, under the laws of the United States providing for the confiscation of property of persons engaged in rebellion, have been instituted; but upon the condition, nevertheless, that every such person shall take and subscribe the following oath, (or affirmation,) and thenceforward keep and maintain said oath inviolate; and which oath shall be registered for permanent preservation, and shall be of the tenor and effect following, to wit:

"I, _____ _____, do solemnly swear, (or affirm,) in presence of Almighty God, that I will henceforth faithfully support and defend the Constitution of the United States, and the union of States thereunder; and that I will, in like manner, abide by, and faithfully support all laws, and proclamations which have been made during the existing rebellion with reference to the emancipation of slaves. So help me God."

The following classes of persons are excepted from the benefits of this Proclamation: —

1st. All who are or shall have been pretended civil or diplomatic officers, or otherwise domestic or foreign agents, of the pretended confederate government;

2d. All who left judicial stations under the United States to aid the rebellion;

3d. All who shall have been military or naval officers of said pretended confederate government above the rank of colonel in the army or lieutenant in the navy;

4th. All who left seats in the Congress of the United States to aid the rebellion;

5th. All who resigned or tendered resignations of their commissions in the army or navy of the United States to evade duty in resisting the rebellion;

6th. All who have engaged in any way in treating otherwise than lawfully as prisoners of war persons found in the United States service, as officers, soldiers, seamen, or in other capacities;

7th. All persons who have been, or are, absentees from the United States for the purpose of aiding the rebellion;

8th. All military and naval officers in the rebel service, who were educated by the government in the Military Academy at West Point or the United States Naval Academy;

9th. All persons who held the pretended offices of governors of states in insurrection against the United States;

10th. All persons who left their homes within the jurisdiction and protection of the United States, and passed beyond the federal military lines into the pretended confederate states for the purpose of aiding the rebellion;

11th. All persons who have been engaged in the destruction of the commerce of the United States upon the high seas, and all persons who have made raids into the United States from Canada, or been engaged in destroying the commerce of the United States upon the lakes and rivers that separate the British Provinces from the United States;

12th. All persons who, at the time when they seek to obtain the benefits hereof by taking the oath herein prescribed, are in military, naval, or civil confinement, or custody, or under bonds of the civil, military, or naval authorities, or agents of the United States as prisoners of war, or persons detained for offences of any kind, either before or after conviction;

13th. All persons who have voluntarily participated in said rebellion, and the estimated value of whose taxable property is over twenty thousand dollars;

14th. All persons who have taken the oath of amnesty as prescribed in the President's Proclamation of December 8th, A. D. 1863, or an oath of allegiance to the government of the United States since the date of said Proclamation, and who have not thenceforward kept and maintained the same inviolate.

Provided, That special application may be made to the President for pardon by any person belonging to the excepted classes; and such clemency will be liberally extended as may be consistent with the facts of the case and the peace and dignity of the United States.

The Secretary of State will establish rules and regulations for administering and recording the said amnesty oath, so as to insure its benefit to the people, and guard the government against fraud.

In testimony whereof, I have hereunto set my hand, and caused the seal of the United States to be affixed.

Done at the city of Washington, the twenty-ninth day of May, in the year of our Lord one thousand eight hundred and sixty-five, and of the Independence of the United States the eighty-ninth.

Proclamation of June 24, 1865

WHEREAS it has been the desire of the general government of the United States to re-store unrestricted commercial intercourse be-tween and in the several states, as soon as the same could be safely done in view of resistance to the authority of the United States by combi-nations of armed insurgents;

And whereas that desire has been shown in my proclamations of the twenty-ninth of April, one thousand eight hundred and sixty-five, the thirteenth of June, one thousand eight hundred and sixty-five, and the twentieth of June, one thousand eight hundred and sixty-five;

And whereas it now seems expedient and proper to remove restrictions upon internal, do-mestic, and coastwise trade and commercial in-tercourse between and within the states and ter-ritories west of the Mississippi River:

Now, therefore, be it known, that I, AN-DREW JOHNSON, President of the United States, do hereby declare that all restrictions upon internal, domestic, and coastwise inter-course and trade, and upon the purchase and re-moval of products of states and parts of states and territories heretofore declared in insurrec-tion, lying west of the Mississippi River (except-ing only those relating to property heretofore purchased by the agents, or captured by or sur-rendered to the forces of the United States, and to the transportation thereto or therein, on pri-vate account, of arms, ammunition, all articles from which ammunition is made, gray uniforms and gray cloth), are annulled; and I do hereby direct that they be forthwith removed; and also that the commerce of such states, and parts of states shall be conducted under the supervision of the regularly appointed officers of the cus-toms, who shall receive any captured and aban-doned property that may be turned over to them, under the law, by the military or naval forces of the United States, and dispose of the same in accordance with instructions on the sub-ject, issued by the Secretary of the Treasury.

In testimony whereof, I have hereunto set my hand, and caused the seal of the United States to be affixed.

Done at the city of Washington, this twenty-fourth day of June, in the year of our Lord one thousand eight hundred and sixty-five,

and of the Independence of the United States of America the eighty-ninth.

Act of March 28, 1866

[Extended provisions of the Act of July 4, 1864 to loyal citizens of Tennessee.]

Proclamation of April 2, 1866 (in part)

Now, therefore, I, ANDREW JOHNSON, president of the United States, do hereby pro-claim and declare that the insurrection which heretofore existed in the States of Georgia, South Carolina, Virginia, North Carolina, Tennessee, Alabama, Louisiana, Arkansas, Mississippi, and Florida is at an end and is henceforth to be so re-garded.

In testimony whereof, I have hereunto set my hand and caused the seal of the United States to be affixed.

Done at the city of Washington, this second day of April, in the year of our Lord one thou-sand eight hundred and sixty-six, and of the In-dependence of the United States of America the ninetieth.

Act of May 9, 1866

An Act to extend the Jurisdiction of the Court of Claims.

Be it enacted by the Senate and House of Rep-resentatives of the United States of America in Congress assembled, That the Court of Claims shall have jurisdiction to hear and determine the claim of any paymaster, quartermaster, com-missary of subsistence, or other disbursing officer of the United States, or of his administra-tors or executors, for relief from responsibility on account of losses by capture or otherwise, while in the line of his duty, of government funds, vouchers, records, and papers in his charge, and for which such officer was and is held responsible: *Provided,* That an appeal may be taken to the Supreme Court, as in other cases.

Sec. 2. *And be it further enacted,* That when-ever said court shall have ascertained the facts of any such loss to have been without fault or neg-lect on the part of any such officer, it shall make a decree, setting forth the amount thereof, upon which the proper accounting officers of the treasury shall allow to such officer the amount

so decreed as a credit in the settlement of his account.

APPROVED, May 9, 1866.

Act of July 13, 1866

*An Act to extend the Benefits of Section four of an
Act making Appropriations for the Support of the
Army for the year ending June thirtieth, eighteen
hundred and sixty-six, approved March third,
eighteen hundred and sixty-five.*

*Be it enacted by the Senate and House of Rep-
resentatives of the United States of America in
Congress assembled,* That section four of an act
entitled "Act making Appropriations for the
Support of the Army for the year ending June
thirtieth, eighteen hundred and sixty-six," be so
construed as to entitle the three months' pay
proper, provided for therein, all officers of volunteers below the rank of brigadier-general who
were in service on the third day of March, eighteen hundred and sixty-five, and whose resignations were presented and accepted, or who were
mustered out at their own request, or otherwise
honorably discharged from the service after the
ninth day of April, eighteen hundred and sixty-
five.

APPROVED, July 13, 1866.

Act of July 28, 1866 (in part)

Sec. 12. *And be it further enacted,* That to
each and every soldier who enlisted into the
army of the United States, after the nineteenth
day of April, eighteen hundred and sixty-one,
for a period of not less than three years, and having served the time of his enlistment has been
honorably discharged, and who has received or
who is entitled to receive from the United States
under existing laws, a bounty of one hundred
dollars and no more, and any such soldier enlisted for not less than three years, who has been
honorably discharged, on account of wounds received in the line of duty, and the widow, minor
children, or parents in the order named, of any
such soldier who died in the service of the
United States or of disease or wounds contracted
while in the service, and in the line of duty, shall
be paid the additional bounty of one hundred
dollars hereby authorized.

Sec. 13. *And be it further enacted,* That to
each and every soldier who enlisted into the
army of the United States, after the fourteenth

day of April, eighteen hundred and sixty-one,
for a period of not less than two years and who
is not included in the foregoing section, and has
been honorably discharged after serving two
years, and who has received or is entitled to receive from the United States under existing laws,
a bounty of one hundred dollars and no more,
shall be paid an additional bounty of fifty dollars and no more, and any such soldier enlisted
for not less than two years, who has been honorably discharged, on account of wounds received in the line of duty, and the widow, minor
children, or parents in the order named, of any
such soldier who died in the service of the
United States or of disease or wounds contracted
while in the service, and in the line of duty, shall
be paid the additional bounty of fifty dollars
hereby authorized.

Proclamation of August 20, 1866 (in part)

Now, therefore, I, ANDREW JOHNSON,
President of the United States, do hereby proclaim and declare that the insurrection which
heretofore existed in the State of Texas is at an
end, and is to be henceforth so regarded in that
State, as in the other States before named, in
which the said insurrection was proclaimed to
be at an end, by the aforesaid proclamation of
the second day of April, one thousand eight
hundred and sixty-six.

And I do further proclaim that the said insurrection is at an end, and that peace, order,
tranquility and civil authority now exist in and
throughout the whole of the United States of
America.

In testimony whereof, I have hereunto set
my hand and caused the seal of the United States
to be affixed.

Done at the city of Washington this twentieth day of August, in the year of our Lord one
thousand eight hundred and sixty-six, and of
the Independence of the United States of America the ninety-first.

Joint Resolution of March 2, 1867

*Joint Resolution prohibiting Payment by any
Officer of the Government to any Person not
known to have been opposed to the Rebellion and
in favor of its Suppression.*

*Be it resolved by the Senate and House of
Representatives of the United States of America in*

Congress assembled, That until otherwise or-dered it shall be unlawful for any officer of the United States government to pay any account, claim, or demand against said government which accrued or existed prior to the thirteenth day of April, A. D. eighteen hundred and sixty-one, in favor of any person who promoted, en-couraged, or in any manner sustained the late rebellion; or in favor of any person who, during said rebellion, was not known to be opposed thereto, and distinctly in favor of its suppres-sion; and no pardon heretofore granted, or here-after to be granted, shall authorize the payment of such account, claim, or demand, until this resolution is modified or repealed: *Provided,* That this resolution shall not be construed to prohibit the payment of claims founded upon contracts made by any of the departments, where such claims were assigned or contracted to be assigned prior to April first, eighteen hundred and sixty-one, to creditors of said contractors, loyal citizens of loyal States, in payment of debts incurred prior to March first, eighteen hundred and sixty-one.

APPROVED, March 2, 1867.

Proclamation of July 4, 1868 (in part)

Now, therefore, I, ANDREW JOHNSON, President of the United States, do, by virtue of the Constitution and in the name of the people of the United States, hereby proclaim and de-clare unconditionally and without reservation, to all and to every person who directly or indi-rectly participated in the late insurrection or re-bellion, excepting such person or persons as may be under presentment or indictment in any court of the United States having competent ju-risdiction, upon a charge of treason or other felony, a full pardon and amnesty for the offence of treason against the United States, or of ad-hering to their enemies during the late civil war, with restoration of all rights of property, except as to slaves, and except also as to any property of which any person may have been legally di-vested under the laws of the United States.

In testimony whereof I have signed these presents with my hand, and have caused the seal of the United States to be hereunto affixed.

Done at the city of Washington this fourth day of July, in the year of our Lord one thousand eight hundred and sixty-eight, and of the Inde-pendence of the United States of America, the ninety-third.

Proclamation of December 25, 1868

WHEREAS the President of the United States has heretofore set forth several proclama-tions offering amnesty and pardon to persons who had been or were concerned in the late re-bellion against the lawful authority of the gov-ernment of the United States, which proclama-tions were severally issued on the eighth day of December, 1863, on the twenty-sixth day of March, 1864, on the twenty-ninth day of May, 1865, on the seventh day of September, 1867, and on the fourth day of July, in the present year;

And whereas, the authority of the Federal Government having been re-established in all the States and Territories within the jurisdiction of the United States, it is believed that such pru-dential reservations and exceptions as at the dates of said several proclamations were deemed necessary and proper may now be wisely and justly relinquished, and that a universal amnesty and pardon for participation in said rebellion extended to all who have borne any part therein will tend to secure permanent peace, order, and prosperity throughout the land, and to renew and fully restore confidence and fraternal feeling among the whole people, and their respect for and attachment to the National Government, designed by its patriotic founders for the general good:

Now, therefore, be it known that I, AN-DREW JOHNSON, President of the United States, by virtue of the power and authority in me vested by the Constitution, and in the name of the sovereign people of the United States, do hereby proclaim and declare unconditionally, and without reservation, to all and to every per-son who directly or indirectly participated in the late insurrection or rebellion, a full pardon and amnesty for the offence of treason against the United States, or of adhering to their enemies during the late civil war, with restoration of all rights, privileges, and immunities under the Constitution and the laws which have been made in pursuance thereof.

In testimony whereof, I have signed these presents with my hand, and have caused the seal of the United States to be hereunto affixed.

Done at the city of Washington this twenty-fifth day of December, in the year of our Lord one thousand eight hundred and sixty-eight, and of the Independence of the United States of America, the ninety-third.

Joint Resolution of March 1, 1870

A Resolution to pass to the Credit of the National Asylum for Disabled Volunteer Soldiers the Funds belonging to it for the Relief of sick and wounded Soldiers.

Resolved by the Senate and House of Representatives of the United States of America in Congress assembled, That the unexpended balance of the fund created by the seventeenth section of the act approved February twenty-fourth, eighteen hundred and sixty-four, for the benefit of the sick and wounded soldiers, shall be transferred to the National Asylum for Disabled Volunteer Soldiers, for the support of its beneficiaries.

Sec. 2. *And be it further resolved,* That the moneys withheld because of the desertion of any person from the volunteer forces of the United States, who is borne on the rolls as a deserter, shall not be paid to him except the record of desertion shall have been cancelled on the sole ground that such record had been made erroneously and contrary to the facts, but such moneys shall be and remain the property of the National Asylum for Disabled Volunteer Soldiers for the support of its beneficiaries.

APPROVED, March 1, 1870

Act of June 8, 1872 (in part)

An act to provide for the Redemption and Sale of Lands held by the United States under the several Acts levying direct Taxes, and for other purposes.

Be it enacted by the Senate and House of Representatives of the United States of America in Congress assembled, That all the lands now owned or held by the United States, by virtue of proceedings under the act entitled "An act for the collection of direct taxes in insurrectionary districts within the United States, and for other purposes," approved June seventh, eighteen hundred and sixty-two, and under acts supplementary thereto, or upon the same subject-matter, may be redeemed and restored to such persons as shall make application therefore to the Secretary of the Treasury, through the Commissioner of Internal Revenue, within two years from the passage of this act, and furnish satisfactory evidence to said department that such person or applicant in each case was at the time the United States acquired title thereto, the legal owner of such land, or the heir at law, or devisee (or grantee, in good faith, and for valuable consideration,) of such legal owner; but before such redemption shall be awarded and title restored on any such application and proof, such applicant shall pay into the treasury of the United States the direct tax charged against the lands described in such application, together with the cost of advertising and of the sale of said lands, and all other proper charges against the same, and interest on said tax from the date of its assessment at the rate of ten per centum per annum, and interest on said costs and charges at the same rate, from the time they were accrued and were payable; *Provided however,* That if any other person or persons than such applicant shall in any case make satisfactory evidence to such department that he or they, after the acquisition of the title by the United States, and before the passage of this act, make valuable and permanent improvements on said land in good faith and under color of legal title, it shall then be the additional duty of such applicant for redemption to pay such person or persons the reasonable value of such permanent improvements at the time of actual redemption; and if the applicant and such person or persons fail to agree upon and amicably settle such claim for improvements, then the value thereof shall be assessed and reported to the Secretary of the Treasury, under oath, by three competent and disinterested freeholders, residents of the county or parish in which such land is situate, who shall be appointed for that purpose by the United States district judge of the district where the lands are situate, upon information from the Secretary of the Treasury that a claim for compensation for such permanent improvements is pending in any case, and unadjusted by the parties thereto. It shall also be the duty of said boards of freeholders to state in their report the nature of said improvements, when they were made, by whom and the reasonable value thereof, as aforesaid, and any other facts that may be in their judgment material to a fair and just determination of the rights of the parties. They shall send one copy of such report to the Secretary of the Treasury, and file a duplicate thereof in the office of the clerk of the highest court of record of the State, in the county or parish where such land is situate. The reasonable fees of said board shall be borne and paid equally by the parties to said controversy.

March 3, 1873

[The last day to petition the Southern Claims Commission.]

Act of March 3, 1877

[Congress appropriated $375,000 to reimburse mail contractors for money due in 1859, 1860, and 1861 within Alabama, Arkansas, Florida, Georgia, Kentucky, Louisiana, Mississippi, Missouri, North Carolina, South Carolina, Texas, Tennessee, Virginia, and West Virginia, "*Provided,* that any such claims which have been paid by the Confederate States government shall not again be paid" before the start of the war and no disloyalty could be shown.

In interpreting "the start of the war" the court held that Virginia was engaged in war for the purposes of the Sundry Civil Appropriation Act of March 3, 1877 as of April 17, 1861. Virginia voted to secede on the 17th. The governor of Virginia refused to supply troops from his State in response to President Lincoln's call for soldiers and ordered his military units to stand in readiness to oppose the laws of the United States by military force. The actual shooting began at Fort Sumpter on April 12 with President Lincoln's proclamation and call for troops. The Supreme Court cleared up the issue of dates in a case referred from the U.S. Circuit Court of the Southern District of Alabama.]

January 1, 1880

[The last day to submit claims Quartermaster General's Office.]

Act of June 16, 1880

[Authorized a $100 bounty to the enlisted men of the 15th and 16th Missouri Cavalry Volunteers who served continuously for one year or longer.]

Act of March 3, 1883 (Bowman Act, in part)

An Act to afford assistance and relief to Congress and the executive departments in the investigation of claims and demands against the government.

Be it enacted by the Senate and House of Representatives of the United States of America in

Congress assembled, That whenever a claim or matter is pending before any committee of the Senate or House of Representatives, or before either House of Congress, which involves the investigation and determination of facts, the committee or house may cause the same, with the vouchers, papers, proofs, and documents pertaining thereto, to be transmitted to the court of Claims of the United States, and the same shall there be proceeded in under such rules as the court may adopt. When the facts shall have been found, the court shall not enter judgment thereon, but shall report the same to the committee or to the house by which the case was transmitted for its consideration.

Sec. 3. The jurisdiction of said court shall not extend to or include any claim against the United States growing out of the destruction or damage to property by the Army and Navy during the war for the suppression of the rebellion, or the use and occupation of real estate by any part of the military or naval forces during said war at the seat of war."

Sec. 4. In any case of a claim for supplies or stores taken by or furnished to any part of military or naval forces of the United States for their use during the late war for the suppression of the rebellion, the petition shall aver that the person who furnished such supplies or stores, or from whom such supplies or stores were taken, did not give any aid or comfort to said rebellion, but was throughout that war loyal to the government of the United States, and the fact of such loyalty shall be a jurisdictional fact; and unless said court shall, on a preliminary inquiry, find that the person who furnished such supplies or stores, or from whom the same were taken as aforesaid, was loyal to the Government of the United States throughout said war, the court shall not have jurisdiction of such cause, and the same shall, without further proceedings, be dismissed.

Act of June 3, 1884

An act to provide for the muster and pay of certain officers and enlisted men of the volunteer forces.

Be it enacted by the Senate and House of Representatives of the United States of America in Congress assembled, That the joint resolution approved July eleventh, eighteen hundred and seventy, entitled "Joint resolution amendatory of joint resolution for the relief of certain officers of the Army," approved July twenty-six eighteen hundred and sixty-six, is hereby so amended and shall be so construed that in all cases arising under the same any person who was duly appointed and commissioned, whether his commission was actually received by him or not, shall be considered as commissioned to the grade therein named from the date when his commission was actually issued by competent authority, and shall be entitled to all pay and emoluments as if actually mustered at such date: *Provided,* That at the date of his commission he was actually performing the duties of the grade to which he was so commissioned, or, if not so performing such duties, then from such time after the date of his commission as he may have actually entered upon such duties: *And provided further,* That any person held as a prisoner of war, or who may have been absent by reason of wounds or in hospital by reason of disability received in the service in the line of duty, at the date of his commission, if a vacancy existed for him in the grade to which so commissioned, shall be entitled to the same pay and emoluments as if actually performing the duties of the grade to which he was commissioned and actually mustered at such date: *And provided further,* That this act and the resolution hereby amended shall be construed to apply only in those cases where the commission bears date prior to June twentieth, eighteen hundred and sixty-three, or after that date when their commands were not below the minimum required by existing laws and regulations: *And provided further,* That the pay and allowances actually received shall be deducted from the same to be paid under this act.

Sec. 2. That the heirs or legal representatives of any officer whose muster into the service has been or shall be amended hereby shall be entitled to receive the arrears of pay due such officer, and the pension, if any, authorized by law, for the grade into which such officer is mustered under the provisions of this act.

Sec. 3. That all claims arising under this act shall be presented to and filed in the proper Department within three years from and after the passage hereof, and all such claims not so presented and filed within said three years shall be forever barred, and no allowance ever made thereon.

Sec. 4. That the pay and allowance of a rank or grade paid to and received by any military or naval officer in good faith for service actually performed by such officer in such rank or grade during the war of the rebellion shall not be charged to or recovered back from such officer because of any defect in the title of such officer to the office, rank, or grade to which such services were so actually performed.

APPROVED, June 3, 1884.

Act of March 3, 1887 (Tucker Act, in part)

An act to provide for the bringing of suits against the Government of the United States.

Be it enacted by the Senate and House of Representatives of the United States of America in Congress assembled, That the Court of Claims shall have jurisdiction to hear and determine the following matters:

First. All claims founded upon the Constitution of the United States or any law of Congress, except for pensions, or upon any regulation of an Executive Department, or upon any contract, expressed or implied, with the Government of the United States, or for damages, liquidated or unliquidated, in cases not sounding in tort, in respect of which claims the party would be entitled to redress against the United States either in a court of law, equity, or admiralty if the United States were suable; *Provided however,* That nothing in this section shall be construed as giving to either of the courts herein mentioned, jurisdiction to hear and determine claims growing out of the late civil war, and continually known as "war claims," or to hear and determine the same.

Second. All set-offs, counter-claims, claims for damages, whether liquidated or unliquidated, or other demands whatsoever on the part of the Government of the United States against any claimant against of the Government of the United, shall be allowed under this act unless the same shall have been brought within six years after the right accrued for which the claim is made.

Sec. 13. That in every case which shall come before the Court of Claims, or is now pending therein, under the provisions of an act entitled "An act to afford assistance and relief to Congress and the Executive Departments in the investigation of claims and demands against the Government," approved March third, eighteen hundred and eighty-three, if it shall appear to the satisfaction of the court, upon the facts established, that it has jurisdiction to render judgment or decree thereon under existing laws or under the provisions of this act, it shall proceed to do so, giving to either party such further opportunity for hearing as in its judgment justices shall require, and report its proceedings therein to either House of Congress or to the Department by which the case was referred to said court.

Act of August 14, 1888

An act to relieve certain appointed or enlisted men of the Navy and Marine Corps from the charge of desertion.

Be it enacted by the Senate and House of Representatives of the United States of America in Congress assembled, That the charge of desertion now standing on the rolls and records of the Navy or Marine Corps against any appointed or enlisted man of the Navy or Marine Corps who served in the late war may in the discretion of the Secretary of the Navy be removed in all cases where it shall be made to appear to the satisfaction of the Secretary of the Navy from such rolls and records or from other satisfactory evidence, that any such appointed or enlisted man served faithfully until the expiration of his term of enlistment, or until the first day of May anno Domino eighteen hundred and sixty-five, having previously served six months or more, or was prevented from completing his term of service by reason of wounds received or disease contracted in the line of duty, but who, by reason of absence from his command at the time he became entitled to his discharge, failed to be mustered out and to receive a discharge from the service: *Provided,* That no such appointed or enlisted man shall be relieved under this section who, not being sick or wounded, left his command without proper authority while the same was in presence of the enemy.

Sec. 2. That the Secretary of the Navy is hereby authorized to remove the charge of desertion standing on the rolls or records of the Navy or Marine Corps against any appointed or enlisted man of the Navy or Marine Corps who served in the late war, in all cases where it shall be made to appear, to the satisfaction of the Secretary of the Navy, from such rolls or from other satisfactory evidence, that such appointed or enlisted man charged with desertion or with absence without leave, after such charge of with desertion or absence without leave, and within a reasonable time thereafter, voluntarily returned to and served in the line of duty until he was mustered out of the service, and received a certificate of discharge therefrom, or, while so absent, and before the expiration of his term of enlistment, died from wounds, injury, or disease received or contracted in the service and in the line of duty.

Sec. 3. That the charge of desertion now standing on the rolls or records of the Navy or Marine Corps against any appointed or enlisted man of the Navy or Marine Corps who served in the late war, by reason of his having enlisted at any station or on board of any vessel of the Navy without having first received a discharge from the station or vessel in which he had previously served, shall be removed in all cases wherein it shall be made to appear to the satisfaction of the Secretary of the Navy from such rolls and from other satisfactory testimony, that such reenlistment was not made for the purpose of securing bounty or other gratuity that he would not have been entitled to, had he remained under his original term of enlistment: *Provided,* That no appointed or enlisted man shall be relieved under this act who, not being sick or wounded, left his command without proper authority while the same was in presence of the enemy, or who, at the time of leaving his command, was in arrest, or under charges, or in whose case the period of absence from the service exceeded three months.

Sec. 4. That in all cases where the charge of desertion shall be removed under the provisions of this act from the record of any enlisted man of the Navy or Marine Corps who has not received a certificate of discharge it shall be the duty of the Secretary of the Navy to issue to such appointed or enlisted man, or in case of his death, to his heirs or legal representatives, a certificate of discharge.

Sec. 5. That when the charge of desertion shall be removed under the provisions of this act from the record of any appointed or enlisted man of the Navy or Marine Corps, such man, or, in case of his death, to his heirs or legal representatives of such man, shall receive all pay and bounty which may have been withheld on account of such charge of desertion or absence without leave: *Provided however,* That this act shall not be so construed as to give to any such man as may be entitled to relief under the provisions of this act, or, in case of his death, to his heirs or legal representatives of such man, the right to receive pay and bounty for any period of time during which such man was absent from his command without leave of absence: *And provided further,* That no appointed or enlisted man, nor the heirs or legal representatives of any such man, who served in the Navy or Marine Corps a period of less than six months shall be entitled to the benefit of the provisions of this act: *And provided further,* That all applications for relief under this act shall be made to and filed with the Secretary of the Navy within the period of five years from and after its passage, and all applications not so made and filed within the said term of five years shall be forever barred, and shall not be received or considered.

Sec. 6. That all acts and parts of acts inconsistent with the provisions of this act are hereby repealed.

APPROVED, August 14, 1888.

[As stated by the Court:

"The purpose of the act of August 14, 1888, was to remove from many worthy soldiers the stigma of being deserters and give them all the rights and emoluments to which they would have been entitled had not the charge of desertion been made."]

Act of March 2, 1891

An act to credit and pay to the several States and Territories and the District of Columbia all moneys collected under the direct tax levied by the act of Congress approved August fifth, eighteen hundred and sixty-one.

Be it enacted by the Senate and House of Representatives of the United States of America in Congress assembled, That it shall be the duty of the Secretary of the Treasury to credit to each State and Territory of the United States and the District of Columbia, a sum equal to all collections by set-off or otherwise made from said States and Territories and the District of Columbia or from any of the citizens or inhabitants thereof or other persons under the act of Congress approved August fifth, eighteen hundred and sixty-one, and the amendatory acts thereto.

Sec. 2. That all moneys still due to the United States on the quota of direct tax apportioned by section eight of the act of Congress approved August fifth, eighteen hundred and sixty-one, are hereby remitted and relinquished.

Sec. 3. That there is hereby appropriated, out of any money in the Treasury not otherwise appropriated, such sums as may be necessary to

re-imburse each State, Territory, and the District of Columbia for all money found due to them under the provisions of this act; and the Treasurer of the United States is hereby directed to pay the same to the governors of the States and Territories and to the Commissioners of the District of Columbia, but no money shall be paid to any State or Territory until the Legislature thereof shall have accepted, by resolution, the sum herein appropriated, and the trusts imposed, in full satisfaction of all claims against the United States on account of the levy and collection of said tax, and shall have authorized the Governor to receive said money for the use and purposes aforesaid: *Provided,* That where the sums, or any part thereof, credited to any State or Territory, or the District of Columbia, have been collected by the United States from the citizens or inhabitants thereof, or any other person, either directly or by sale of property, such sums shall be held in trust by such States, Territories, or the District of Columbia for the benefit of those persons or inhabitants from whom they were collected, or their legal representatives: *And provided further,* That no part of the money hereby appropriated shall be paid out by the governor of any State or Territory or any other person to any attorney or agent under any contract for services now existing or heretofore made between the representative of any State or Territory and any attorney or agent. All claims under the trust hereby created shall be filed with the governor of such State or Territory and the Commissioners of the District of Columbia, respectively, within six years next after the passage of this act; and all claims not so filed shall be forever barred, and the money attributable thereto shall belong to such State, Territory, or the District of Columbia, respectively, as the case may be.

Sec. 4. That it shall be the duty of the Secretary of the Treasury to pay to such persons as shall in each case apply therefore, and furnish satisfactory evidence that such applicant was at the time of the sales hereinafter mentioned the legal owner, or is the heir at law or devisee of the legal owner of such lands as were sold in the parishes of Saint Helena and Saint Luke's in the State of South Carolina, under the said acts of Congress, the value of said lands in the manner following, to wit: To the owners of the lots in the town of Beaufort, one-half of the value assessed thereon for taxation by the United States direct-tax commissioners for South Carolina; to the owners of lands which were rated for taxation by the State of South Carolina as being usually cultivated, five dollars per acre for each acre thereof returned on the proper tax-book; to the owners of all other lands, one dollar for each acre thereof returned on said tax-book: *Provided,* That in all cases where such owners, or persons claiming under them, have redeemed or purchased said lands, or any part thereof, from the United States, they shall not receive compensation for such part so redeemed or purchased; and any sum or sums held or to be held by the said State of South Carolina in trust for any such owner under section three of this act shall be deducted from the sum due to such owner under the provisions of this section: *And provided further,* That in all cases where said owners have heretofore received from the United States the surplus proceeds arising from the sale of their lands, such sums shall be deducted from the sum which they are entitled to receive under this act. That in all cases where persons, while serving in the Army or Navy or Marine Corps of the United States, or who had been honorably discharged from said service, purchased any of said lands under section eleven of the act of Congress approved June seventh, eighteen hundred and sixty-two, and such lands afterwards reverted to the United States, it shall be the duty of the Secretary of the Treasury to pay to such persons as shall in each case apply therefore, or to their heirs at law, devisees, or grantees, in good faith and for valuable consideration, whatever sum was so paid to the United States in such case. That before paying any money to such persons the Secretary of the Treasury shall require the person or persons entitled to receive the same to execute a release of all claims and demands of every kind and description whatsoever against the United States arising out of the execution of said acts, and also a release of all right, title, and interest in and to the said lands. That there is hereby appropriated, out of any money in the Treasury not otherwise appropriated, the sum of five hundred thousand dollars, or so much thereof as shall be necessary to pay for said lots and lands, which sum shall include all moneys in the Treasury derived in any manner from the enforcement of said acts in said parishes and not otherwise appropriated. That section one thousand and sixty-three of the Revised Statutes is hereby made applicable to claims arising under this act without limitation as to the amount involved in such claim: *And provided further,* That any sum

or sums of money received into the Treasury of the United States from the sale of lands bid in for taxes in any State under the laws described in the first section of this act in excess of the tax assessed thereon shall be paid to the owners of the land so bid in and resold, or to their legal heirs or representatives.

APPROVED, March 2, 1891.

[A court stated:

"The purpose of this act are beneficent; the intention of Congress was to repair as far as possible any injustice occasioned by the operation of the direct tax laws, which, in South Carolina, fell with peculiar hardship upon the inhabitants of two parishes, and to accomplish this result it divided the sufferers into several classes: First those whose lands had been sold for a sum in excess of the tax, and to these it gives the excess, over the tax, of the value of the lands, at a certain prescribed rate; second, certain third parties who purchased at the sale, made part payment, and failing payment as to the balance due forfeited their rights. These receive the money actually paid by them on account."

In Hogarth v. the United States the court stated:

"In the class of cases to which this suit belongs a right of action is given, in effect, by the Act 2d March, 1891 to owners or heirs of owners who lost their lands in two parishes in the State of South Carolina, St. Helena and St. Lukes, by direct-tax sales during the civil war. The divesture of this property, though by legal proceedings, was exceedingly pitiable, and when the harsher judgments of the war had softened and passed away Congress deemed it an act of justice as well as mercy to award something in the nature of restitution. The amount of restitution in this class of cases was $5 an acre."]

Act of February 24, 1897

An Act To provide for the relief of certain officers and enlisted men of the volunteer forces.

Be it enacted by the Senate and House of Representatives of the United States of America in Congress assembled, That any person who was duly appointed or commissioned to be an officer of the volunteer service during the war of the rebellion, and who was subject to the mustering regulations at the time applied to members of the volunteer service shall be held and considered to have been mustered into the service of the United States in the grade named in his appointment or commission from the date from which he was to take rank under and by the terms of his said appointment or commission, whether the same was actually received by him or not, and shall be entitled to pay, emoluments, and pension as if actually mustered at that date: *Provided,* That at the date from which he was to take rank by the terms of his said appointment or commission there was a vacancy to which he could be so appointed or commissioned, and his command had either been recruited to the minimum number required by law and the regulations of the War Department, or had been assigned to duty in the field, and that he was actually performing the duties of the grade to which he was so appointed or commissioned; or if not so performing such duties, then he shall be held and considered to have been mustered into service and to be entitled to the benefits of such muster from such time after the date of rank given in his commission as he may have actually entered upon such duties: *Provided further,* That any person held as a prisoner of war, or who may have been absent by reason of wounds, or in hospital by reason of disability received in the service in the line of duty, at the date of issue of his appointment or commission, if a vacancy existed for him in the grade to which so appointed or commissioned, shall be entitled to all the benefits to which he would have been entitled under this Act if he had actually been performing the duties of the grade to which he was appointed or commissioned at said date: *Provided further,* That this Act shall be construed to apply only in those cases where the commission bears date prior to June twentieth, eighteen hundred and sixty-three, or after that date when the commands of the persons appointed or commissioned were not below the minimum number required by then existing laws and regulations: *And provided further,* That the pay and allowances actually received for the period covered by the recognition extended under this Act shall be deducted from the sums otherwise to be paid thereunder.

Sec. 2. That the heirs or legal representatives of any person whose muster into service shall be recognized and established under the terms of this Act shall be entitled to receive the arrears of pay and emoluments due, and the pension, if any, authorized by law, for the grade to which recognition shall be so extended.

Sec. 3. That the pay and allowances of any rank or grade paid to and received by any military or naval officer in good faith for services actually performed by such officer in such rank or grade during the war of the rebellion, other than as directed in the fourth provision of the first section of this Act, shall not be charged to or received back from such officer because of any defect in the title of such officer to the office, rank, or grade in which such services were so actually performed.

Sec. 4. That all acts and parts of acts inconsistent with the provisions of this Act be, and the same are hereby repealed.

APPROVED, February 24, 1897.

Act of April 10, 1910

[Set a cutoff date for all pay claims from the Civil War under the Act of February 24, 1897 at January 1, 1911.]

Joint Resolution of May 27, 1910

[Authorized and directed the Secretary of the Treasury to reimburse over 2,000 illegally drafted men identified as having paid $300 commutation of service under the Act of February 24, 1864.]

Act of March 3, 1911

[Allowed the federal Court of Claims to hear petitions for goods seized after June 1, 1865 under the Act of March 12, 1863.]

Act of June 5, 1920 (in part)

"For arrears of pay of two and three years volunteers, for bounty to volunteers, for bounty to volunteers and their widows and legal heirs, for bounty under the Act of July 28, 1866, and for amounts for commutation of rations to prisoners of war in States of the so-called Confederacy, and to soldiers on furlough, that they may be certified to be due by the accounting officers of the Treasury, during fiscal year 1921, $1,000.

"For arrears of pay and allowances on account of service of officers and men of the Army during the War with Spain and in the Philippine Islands that may be certified to be due by the accounting officers of the Treasury during the fiscal year 1921 and that are chargeable to the appropriations that have been carried to the surplus fund, $500."

Appendix IV:
The 1864 Kentucky
Draft Case Claimants

The claimants who paid $300 each as commutation or exemption money for release from military service, or their decedents, and the counties from which drafted and the date of draft in each case in Royse v. the United States.

Adair
Bennett, Benjamin Y., by W. J. Tucker, administrator	May 10
Blair, John	June 18
Royse, Felix G., by G. B. Royse, administrator	May 10

Butler
Neel, Thomas W.	May 16
Phelps, James M.	May 16
Read, J. H	May 16

Casey
Branson, Micajah C.	July 7
Clemens, Richard C., by Martha J. Clemens, widow	May 19
Miller, Samuel L.	July 7

Crittenden
Beard, William C., by Mary A. Beard, administratrix	June 10
Kemp, Dempsey F.	June 10

Grant
Abernathy, Felix B., by Nellie G. White, administratrix.	June 7
Anderson, Thomas J., as Thomas D. Anderson	June 7
Baker, D. N.	June 7
Bromley, James S., (or Brumley) by Mary J. Bromley, widow	June 7
Burch, Ferdinand	June 7
Carlton, William, aka William Colton	July 11
Cheatman (or Chatman), Willis	June 7
Childers, William Harvey, by R. A. Childers, administrator	July 11
Childers, William H., by Brunetta Childers, widow	June 7
Dickerson, James F., by Nellie G. White, administratrix	June 7
Eales, George W.	June 7
Eales, W. R. B., as R. B. Ealo	July 11
Ecler, W. D., by Nellie G. White, administratrix	June 7
Fitch, S. B.	June 7
Forsyth, William	June 7
Gray, Thomas	June 7
Harrison, James F., by Nellie G. White, administratrix	July 11
Hendrix, William, by Nellie G. White, administratrix	June 7
Hicks, Pleasant, by Elizabeth Hicks, widow	July 11
Hogan, Newton, by Nellie G. White, administratrix	June 7
Jemmison, David, (or Jimmison)	June 7
Jump, James V., by Nellie G. White, administratrix	July 11
Lauter, Benjamin	July 11
McGuyer, William	June 7
Mann, Richard, by Dorothy A. Mann, widow	July 11
Osborne, Washington, by Joseph Stone, administrator	June 7
Plunkett, Robert	July 11
Rankin, W. W.	July 11
Stroud, William, by Nellie G. White, administratrix	June 7
Steers, John H., by Nellie G. White, administratrix	June 7
Tucker, Francis M.	July 11
Vaughn, John, by Anerrella Vaughn, widow	June 7
Vaughn, Richard., by Lucy Jane Vaughn, widow	June 7
Waller, William H.	July 11
Williams, William G., by J. H. Williams, administrator	June 7

Wilson, John M., by Nannie Kerr Wilson,
  widow   June 7
Wilson, Joseph, as J. M. Wilson   June 7
Woodyard, James W., by Nellie G. White,
  administratrix   June 7

Grayson
Nelson, Hardin W.   May 16
Railey, James W.   May 16

Jefferson
Allen, Joseph D., by Pamela D.
  Allen, widow   May 11
Bohan, Patrick   May 11
Bohe, Frank   June 4
Briscoe, John W., by N. G. Rogers,
  administrator   May 11
Commerford, Patrick, by Commercial
  Bank & Trust Co., administrator May 11
Coooney, Patrick, by Commercial
  Bank & Trust Co., administrator June 4
Craig, L. Wesley   June 16
Dumeyer, William, by Commercial
  Bank & Trust Co., administrator July 2
Hempel, John W.`   May 11
Klumpp, Jacob   May 11
Krebs, Andrew   June 16
Metzmeir, Xavier F., by Commercial
  Bank & Trust Co., administrator June 4
Mittendorf, Henry, alias Middendorf May 11
Parsons, James   May 11
Rider, John, by Commercial Bank &
  Trust Co., administrator   July 2
Scudder, John B., by Lou E. Scudder,
  widow   May 11
Shake, Adam A., by D. L. Bedinger,
  administrator   May 11
Wier, William   May 11
Woods, Joseph   May 11

Lincoln
Moore, David R.   May 21
Newland, A. Christopher, by H. F.
  Newland, executor   May 21
Shanks, Samuel B.   May 21
Smith, Morgan P.   May 21
Withers, Martin P., by William W.
  Withers, administrator   May 21

Ohio
Austin, John, by Susie B. Austin, sole heir May 14
Ellis, Alexander C., by Mary E.
  Ellis, widow   May 14
Fulkerson, John S. D., by Nancy Jane
  Fulkerson, widow   May 14
McHenry, Henry D., by John J.
  McHenry, executor   May 14
Roswell, Thomas R., by E. L. Roswell,
  administrator   May 14
Shultz, Zebulon W., by J. T. Shultz,
  administrator   May 14
Stewart, Granville T., by O. P. Brunton,
  administrator   May 14

Pendleton
Antrobus, Samuel L., by J. B. Winn,
  administrator   June 6
Arnold, Andrew J.   June 6
Bishop, John P., by Allie Whalen,
  administratrix   June 6
Blackburn, Alanson D.   July 11
Blackburn, James   June 6
Blackburn, John T., by B. K. Wigginton,
  administrator   June 6
Boner, Robert H., by C. W. Carnes,
  administrator   June 6
Brann, Joseph J.   June 6
Browning, Henry, by Susan Browning,
  administratrix   June 6
Bush, Jefferson, by W. S. Clark,
  administrator   June 6
Cahill, John, by Marie J. Cahill, widow June 6
Clayton, Thomas G., by F. C. Clayton,
  administrator   June 6
Colcord, Joseph   July 11
Colcord, Samuel, alias Coleard June 6
Colvin, Augustus R.   June 6
Cushman, Commodore D., by Frank
  A. Cushman, administrator   June 6
Dahlenburg, J. Henry   June 6
Downard, Marion   June 6
Dunn, George W., by James O. Dunn,
  administrator   June 6
Fletcher, Charles   June 6
Fookes, Henry H., by William L. Fookes,
  administrator   June 6
Fookes, William L.   June 6
Gifford, James, by W. C. Carnes,
  administrator   June 6
Highfill, Jacob, by J. L. Highfill,
  administrator   July 11
Hunter, David F., by Lyda Hunter,
  administrator   June 6
Inglis, James, by Martha Inglis, widow June 6
Keith, George T.   July 11
Kennedy, Andrew, by Andrew Kennedy,
  administrator   June 6
Kidwell, John B.   July 11
King, James S., by George King,
  administrator   June 6
Landrum, Richard M., by W. S. Clark,
  administrator   June 6
Leach, John E.   June 6
Light, William S., by Martin Light,
  administrator   June 6
Lovelace, Jefferson   July 11
Lummis, James M.   July 11
McCarty, Nimrod, by C. W. Carnes,
  administrator   July 11
McClanahan, Benjamin P.   June 6
McKee, Thomas J., by Harry M. Wolfe,
  administrator   July 11
McKenney, Alexander I.   June 6
McNay, Richard S.   June 6

Mains, John C., by James M. Mains,
  administrator   June 6
Mills, John W., by A. F. Mills,
  administrator   June 6
Monroe, John W.   June 6
Peters, Hugh M.   June 6
Redman, Edward, by Lewis C. Grimes,
  administrator   July 11
Riggs, Benjamin F.   June 6
Shively, James A.   July 11
Thomas, John W.   June 6
Thornton, William D., by George Hines,
  administrator   June 6
Trowbridge, Jonathan D.   July 11
Vice, James M., by Nellie G. White,
  administratrix   June 6

Woods, James, by Laban Woods,
  administrator   June 6
Wyatt, John, by Mary E. Wyatt,
  administratrix   June 6
Wyatt, John T.   June 6
Yelton, Columbus   June 6

Taylor
Collins, Joseph T., by Mary E. Collins,
  administratrix   May 19
Hubbard, Robert H.   June 18
Peterson, William H.   May 19
Smith, Robert D., by Mary L. Smith,
  widow   May 19

Index